Human Relations
in Business

Fred J. Carvell

CONSULTANT IN
MANPOWER UTILIZATION
AND EDUCATION

HUMAN RELATIONS IN BUSINESS

THE MACMILLAN COMPANY
COLLIER-MACMILLAN LIMITED, LONDON

To
Ed Reighard,
Bob Piersol,
and
Barbara Sherman

First Printing

Library of Congress catalog card number: 70–84435

THE MACMILLAN COMPANY
COLLIER-MACMILLAN CANADA, LTD.,
TORONTO, ONTARIO

PRINTED IN THE UNITED STATES OF AMERICA

Preface

Many of the leading books on human relations, organizational behavior, and interpersonal aspects of management have been based on extensive and original research by authors who have studied management practices in industrial and other types of organizations. Many textbooks also contain new or expanded theories of organization and leadership that are the result of the thoughtful analysis of traditional methods of organizing and managing group activity. Such books frequently suggest new methods for increasing the effectiveness of organizational members in decision making, cooperative action, and interpersonal relations. They are often directed toward upper-division college and graduate students and executives who hold middle-level and top positions in industry.

In contrast, this book is not based on any body of original research by the author. Rather, the underlying concept grew out of my contact with supervisors and students who took courses in human relations in order to help them resolve the demanding day-to-day human problems associated with their responsibility for leadership. In courses and workshops that I have conducted in college and in industry, supervisors consistently inquire about means of improving their interpersonal effectiveness. The skills needed to accomplish this involve contending with others on a face-to-face basis, ability to communicate well, understanding the human needs of others, learning to motivate others to action, and exercising authority in a just and satisfactory manner.

At the same time that supervisors seek to improve their effectiveness, there is a growing number of students who enter college aspiring to become managers. Community and junior colleges have increasingly assumed educational goals aimed at the preparation of middle-level technicians and managers. The primary purpose of this book is to provide both these students and those supervisors who already have taken their places in the world of work with a broad orientation to the human, social, and organizational elements encountered on the job.

Much of the content of this book is a capsulization of existing theories and concepts of human relations. There is no concerted attempt to expound new or unique concepts of management. I admit a degree of presumption in making the choice among a wide array of available material on the subject of human relations, but I remain strong in my belief that such an eclectic approach is valid and useful in assisting the student to draw together and coordinate into a meaningful whole many of the disparate factors found in the work environment. The approach taken in this text is designed for people who will live their productive work lives primarily dealing with other human beings as supervisors responsible for the action and production of others.

The process of leading a group of workers requires certain technical knowledge. Frequently a person is hired or promoted because he has acquired the necessary technical skills in his respective occupational field—accounting, sales, engineering, and so on. However, most employers seem to agree that the vast majority of persons who do not succeed in supervisory positions do not fail through lack of technical competence, but because of poor attitudes and lack of skill in interpersonal relations.

Because many college students are not certain of the occupational enterprise they will enter and because supervisors who are engaged by a given company may be required to change positions, human relations should not be viewed or interpreted too narrowly. In fact, one need not be a supervisor or manager in a private enterprise to profit from an understanding of human relations because such an understanding is paramount to the successful adjustment of nearly all workers in all activities requiring interpersonal contacts. Many elements can affect the attitude and performance of a worker, whether he is employed as a salesman, a secretary, a production worker, or a service worker. The satisfaction a person receives from his work is dependent upon a number of complex elements which operate in an integral and simultaneous fashion. These factors are not only difficult to isolate for thorough investigation, but also their very isolation often distorts their significance and contribution to the whole process of efficient and productive performance as well as job satisfaction received by the worker.

Four general factors are discussed in this text.

1. The individual and his needs and attitudes.
2. Elements of the job environment and the significance of work to the individual.
3. Formal organizations and the systems which are found in the organization.
4. Informal systems and the social environment in work groups which may work both directly and subtly on the worker.

These four factors are neither independent nor static. On the contrary, they interact with each other in varying degrees of force and are all in a constant state of flux. Neither the individual, the job, nor the organization remains constant. The intention of this book is to help the reader develop an awareness of the relationships among these factors. It is hoped that by being more aware of such factors he will be more readily prepared to react to the job responsibilities he will face. Awareness is not an end but rather a starting point from which human relations may be studied, understood, and put into practice.

Acknowledgments

Many of my colleagues and students have assisted in the effort that has gone into the writing of this book. Therefore, it is with great difficulty that I single out a few individuals to thank specifically because of their particular assistance, encouragement, or criticism. Though unmentioned by name, all the others have my sincere gratitude. My particular thanks go to Gervase Eckenrod, Dean of Business at Fresno City College, whose personal encouragement and assistance were most helpful in initiating the development of this text; to Max Tadlock, whose suggestions in the final drafting of the material were invaluable; and to Margaret Mick, who was my tireless typist. A special note of appreciation must be given to John Miner of the University of Maryland for his contribution to the final substance and organization of this manuscript. Ryo Arai and Jack Neifert, editors with The Macmillan Company, were both helpful and patient with me during the arduous preparation and production of this book. Finally, a note of gratitude must go to my wife Joan, who acted in a very real sense as co-author of this book, and to my children Lyn and Randy, who often played in silence while I worked on the manuscript.

I relieve all of the persons who have contributed to this book of responsibility for any errors or omissions in content because I was not wise enough to heed the sound advice they offered.

F. J. C.

Contents

P. 255

1

An Overview of
Human Relations

Having reached young adulthood, most individuals have developed an operating system of "human relations" which works, more or less, in the usual social situations they encounter. However, the same individuals who feel confident in their personal relationships with friends and family often feel uncomfortable about their behavior in a job situation. Whenever one person must interact with others in order to achieve some objective, as he usually must in a business situation, there is always the possibility that he will flounder when various viewpoints and personal goals come into conflict.

Because human relations broadly applies to the interactions and cooperation of people in groups and because these groups can be formed and function in many aspects of life—at home with family; in school with classmates and teachers; in social, religious, military, and governmental endeavors; in neighborhoods and communities facing critical social problems; and in job situations where production depends on group effort—human relations is difficult to define narrowly. For the men and women who have managerial responsibility the concept of human relations has a different dimension than it does in entirely social situations. Managers and supervisors have a role of leadership that requires them to maintain both an acceptable level of sociability with their subordinates and acceptable standards of job performance. This makes it necessary to establish a definition generally accepted by students in order to insure that the remaining discussion in this text is placed in perspective. Therefore, from the viewpoint of a manager or supervisor who has responsibility for leading a work group, *human relations is the integration of people into a work situation that motivates them to work together productively, cooperatively, and with economic, psychological, and social satisfaction* [2, p. 5].* As Davis points out, this approach focuses on positive or

---

* References appear at the end of each chapter.

1

successful human relations, which it is presumed people seek when they interact. Defined in this context, human relations is motivating people in groups to develop teamwork which effectively fulfills their needs and achieves organizational objectives.

When human relations is defined in terms of a work situation, it becomes considerably more complex than the "how do I get along" concept that may suffice in social situations, because the element of achieving both results and personal satisfaction is included. The element of achieving results also opens up avenues of interpretation regarding the most appropriate and effective means of achieving the desired results. This, in turn, leads to the problem of defining human relations in such a way that it includes a value system for guiding behavior as well as an ideal human condition for workers.

The very term *human relations* places emphasis on human beings and their behavior toward others as opposed to man's relationships to economic factors, technology, or organizational structure. However, the practice of human relations is affected by the economic condition of the firm, the degree of automation, and the firm's organizational structure, which define the scope of work and activity in each organizational unit. These, then, affect the way people treat each other and/or react toward the job situation.

Human relations deals with people, and one need not be a psychologist to observe the paradox and contradiction that often accompanies human behavior. A person's perspective of human relations can be influenced greatly by his viewpoint, experience, and position in a group. Each person becomes his own psychologist when analyzing the behavior of others. If a person is successful in his social relations, he tends to believe that his "human relations" practices are effective; therefore, he feels little motivation to change either his behavior or his perspective. On the other hand, if a person has not experienced success or satisfaction in dealing with others, he may believe that the fault lies outside himself. This may be true, but often such an attitude is rationalization. Each person who contributes to a successful group effort must be responsible for his own behavior.

Although some people in a job situation want to be responsible for their own behavior, they are not sure what is expected from them in the way of human relations. Young employees may not understand their newly assigned roles in work groups. They may be inexperienced or uncertain about the actual tasks and responsibilities of their jobs. Young or inexperienced employees are not the only ones who confront problems of adjustment on the job. Any person who changes his role or function in a group is faced with a new set of "human relations problems." Being promoted to a higher position with added authority and responsibility frequently creates a need for changed behavior on the part of that person.

What should that behavior be? How can any desired behavior change best be achieved? These two questions lie at the heart of human relations in any group context. However, human relations in industry is not the study of human behavior for its own sake. The underlying purpose and function of human relations is to help achieve better and more satisfying results from group effort. The accomplishment of this end is no simple matter. Myriad social, psychological, organizational, and physical factors complicate the integration and motivation of persons in groups. This necessarily has required the development of a number of methods and techniques in order to accommodate the integration of workers into an organization.

Human beings are complex and diverse in their talents, goals, ambitions, and values. Each of these characteristics changes with the passage of time and the accumulation of successes and failures encountered. Education can expose a person to new values which conflict with old ones. Experience and accomplishment can alter the ambitions of an individual. These and other elements change a worker's perspective and, consequently, his desire or willingness to cooperate with others.

Organizations vary in size, wealth, profitability, geographic dispersion, economic functions, and technological innovation. A person working in a small retail establishment finds himself confronted by an entirely different set of activities and constraints than one working in an accounting department of a giant corporation. It is true that human beings share certain common needs and drives; however, the means of satisfying these needs on the job are grossly affected by the type of activity and the kind of management leadership found in the firm in which one works. The rules and procedures used to control employees' activities in a large company are usually more formal than those found in small ones; yet they may not be as difficult to cope with as the constant surveillance of a small shop owner.

Work requirements vary greatly in their need for mental and physical abilities. When a person's abilities and ambitions are matched with the demands of the job held, much satisfaction can be derived from the job requirements. If abilities exceed the requirements of the job, boredom may result because of lack of stimulation and challenge. Conversely, if the demands of the job exceed the abilities and/or ambitions of the worker, the job may be frustrating and defeating. Thus, work itself can be a great source of satisfaction to the individual as long as other social and physical conditions found on the job are not major detractors.

These and other factors lead to the conclusion that no single action, program, or approach can adequately facilitate good human relations. The complexity of the job environment does mean that short-term unproven methods, which are more fad than carefully thought-out measures, will not suffice.

Jobs differ in the skills they require, but most jobs require social contact with other persons.

Human relations has been subjected to many practices proffered by experts, some of which have been well intentioned and enthusiastic but not researched well enough to substantiate their long- or short-term results. The procession of management theories began during the early American industrial development.

Once industrialization had reached the stage of mass production and large-scale operations, the era of scientific management emerged. As a result, industrial engineering and time and motion studies dominated the thinking of many managers during the early twentieth century. With the close of World War I, logical organizational structure was the goal of organizational planners who hoped that this would solve problems of worker efficiency.

During the same period paternalistic philosophies dominated the methods used in large companies to integrate workers into the job environment. Paternalistic employers attempted to regulate the lives, both business and social, of their employees, much as fathers would oversee their children. The rise of paternalism during this period stemmed in part from a reaction to the rise of unionism and in part from a genuine concern for the welfare of the employees.

During the late 1920's, the *Hawthorne Studies,* conducted by Elton Mayo, spurred sociologists into the investigation of informal group

4

Some jobs require close personal contact and extraordinary teamwork.

structure, teamwork, and participative leadership methods as means of increasing productivity. After World War II, psychologists contributed the concept of motivation based on human needs. Supposedly, if certain human needs—such as the need for recognition—were satisfied, workers would be happy, cooperative, and highly productive. Post-World War II studies on leadership techniques conducted by staff members of the University of Michigan were a major factor in the human relations movement. Currently, management thinking is directed toward utilization of computers and technology as a means of increasing production and improving efficiency.

In each case where new thinking has been introduced as a possible means of improving efficiency or employee motivation, some managers have been too quick in their attempt to translate theory into practice before the value of the concept has been proved. Such theories cover everything from time and motion studies to piped-in music. Often new management concepts, if they are implemented correctly, are of great value in helping to solve organizational problems. However, it must be recognized that thus far in industrial history the relationship between productivity and morale has not been convincingly proved. In the case of human relations, the concept of providing workers with a sense of dignity and a sense of being appreciated on the job is a positive motivat-

5

ing force, although some methods used by supervisors to achieve such motivation may be questionable.] Flattering a subordinate for trivial accomplishments that are a regular part of his job responsibility is not the same as showing appreciation, and friendly treatment from a superior is not enough to foster a subordinate's sense of dignity. However, many sets of rules recommending these tactics fall under the label of human relations.

A pointed illustration of the questionable practices in human relations is the way the research of Elton Mayo, and other eminent social scientists since him, has often been translated by some managers into simplistic formulas designed to cope with the human problems confronting an organization. The concept of teamwork which Elton Mayo propounded has sometimes been translated into a panacea for lagging employee morale to the point where either the meaning of the original concept has been lost to "group think" or the goal of the concept is being sought by pressuring employees to conform to acceptable modes of behavior. The need to conform to certain socially acceptable behavior while on the job is not detrimental as long as the modes of acceptable behavior do not infringe on the personal values or the freedom of the individual's private life. The lines between a person's personal life and his organizational life are not easily defined; thus, a problem always exists as to how far conformity required on the job is expected to or allowed to impinge upon one's activities outside of the job.

Some industrial critics point out that some firms claim to be tolerant of nonconformity, but that this tolerance seldom runs very deep. What is called tolerance in such circumstances is usually related to the company's desire to hold an exceptional employee who may be high-spirited and independent. In such cases, nonconformity may be indulged, but the individual employee—whether manager or file clerk—had better be an extraordinarily good worker. If not, he might be wise to use moderation in expressing any unorthodox opinions he holds [1, p. 154].

The effort to organize the activities of a firm poses human problems. There are some sound benefits in building logical organizational structures and systems. When an organization is involved in routine production activity, a systems analysis, that is, the careful investigation of the contributing human and technological elements to the production process, can help identify the rational sequence for operations. Controls can be instituted to establish time, quality, and production standards. The contribution of organizational theory is a useful tool for careful definition and alignment of job responsibility and authority. But care should be given to the effect organizational structure has on the individuals who are part of the organizational system. Excessive controls may limit the activity of and the freedom of organizational members, which reduces their incentive to act. Consequently, although the organization chart may end up neat and logical, employee initiative may fall short of its potential.

Since the mid-1950's, computers and technological innovations have contributed substantially to improving management decision-making by providing ready access to important data and rapid communication between organizational units for gathering and analyzing information. However, the use of computers and the application of technology to production processes can reduce the scope of activity on some organizational members, resulting in a reduction of their willingness to go along with the system.

There is a tendency among systems designers to place emphasis on routines and procedures that accommodate the mechanical limitations of equipment rather than the flexibility and adaptiveness of human beings. Inevitably, this leads to restrictions on the alternatives that human beings are allowed to select. The net result of such restrictions to "human intervention" in computerized systems is that employees may devote a great deal of time and energy toward asserting their own importance by devising informal methods of circumventing the formal system.

The point is that new concepts to improve organizational relationships and production processes are necessary to the survival of a profit-making firm, but when the implementation of these concepts affects the lives of employees, the human element needs careful consideration. Human problems require human solutions. Problems of mutual trust and consideration between organizational members, communication, motivation, and leadership require the collaboration of people so that the multiple and open-ended problems confronting the firm can be resolved. As organizational problems become more complex because of increased numbers of workers, greater interdependence occurs between organizational units, and solutions become less apparent. Thus, one man can seldom tackle the whole problem.

The process of finding the solutions for problems having uncertain outcomes is time-consuming and difficult. There are some managers who prefer to circumvent these difficulties by looking for ready-made, easy-to-apply answers. When this occurs, the temptation to use methods in vogue with management is great. But, unless the individual has given careful consideration to the solution he uses, he can fall prey to whatever approach is the fad of the day.

One reason for this breach in sound judgment may stem from the fact that a manager's responsibility is to be alert for new ways to achieve results. This may motivate him to attempt something new even though it may not have been proved valid. Another reason many fads are quickly adopted by managers is that the designers and promoters of certain new, unproved concepts oversell them. In an age of mass communications and mass marketing techniques, it seems that even hard-thinking executives are not going to be totally immune to the convincing promises of some new management ideas that circulate through professional meetings and periodicals.

The end result of the surfeit of fads in management practices has been that some persons reject any new concept or theory because many of the past concepts have proven to be unsuccessful in solving human and organizational equations. The great danger of adopting a closed-mind approach to new theories is that one may reject acceptable and workable solutions along with the fads. The balance of acceptance toward new ideas must be somewhere between the credulous and the cynical. New knowledge should not be denied; yet one must be discerning about accepting singular approaches, untested theories, or rituals as a substitute for answers to complicated human and organizational problems. Organizational members, whether top executive or rank and file, need to be aware of the complexity of the world of work because being unaware does not make organizational life any simpler; it only reduces the effectiveness with which employees can approach their job responsibilities. Thus, a danger associated with any formula approach to management practices and human relations is the assumption that there are prepared solutions for human problems and conflicts. There are no prepared answers to the human problems of management; there are only the answers that evolve through the struggle to be mature, responsible, and open in dealing with other people whether they are peers, superiors, or subordinates.

HOW THE IMPLEMENTATION OF
HUMAN RELATIONS CAN AFFECT THE FIRM

Despite the deluge of distortions that have affected the evolution of human relations since the days of Elton Mayo, there is a body of sound human relations principles which can be used as a guide for personal and organizational behavior. Social science research has added considerably to the knowledge and the understanding of man's behavior in groups and in organizational settings. This information makes possible certain preventative actions on the part of organizational leaders which will help to avert employee unrest and dissatisfaction. The modern trend in human relations is not only to cure but also to prevent organizational disorders.

The extent to which a philosophy of human relations has been translated into practice is reflected in the personnel policies and programs of a firm. Such policies and programs should be formed by taking into consideration both the implication they will have on the working relationships of organizational members and the way they will effect operating efficiency. This consideration will occur before any policy changes are made and not after such changes have been made and put into effect.

Organizational climate will reflect the degree to which employees are encouraged to participate in those affairs which have a direct effect on them. Also, organizational climate is reflected in the methods used to motivate employees, the methods of leadership encouraged in supervisors, and the quality of on-the-job relationships fostered between different echelons of management and rank-and-file employees. Thus, the implementation of human relations is closely related to the way company policies are administered as well as the way they are formulated.

The role of communications is important to the quality of human relations. The methods, content, and network of organizational communications indicate the extent of the effort that has been taken in a firm to develop two-way interchanges. Effective organizational communications encourage upward along with downward and horizontal communications. This means that formal channels of upward communication will operate in a spirit of mutual trust and consideration rather than a superficial avenue for employee complaints with no intention to attempt positive action to accommodate employee requests. The spirit of consideration in organizational communications means that employee attitudes are actively sought by management in order to facilitate greater mutual understanding regarding employee goals and organizational objectives. Furthermore, once employee attitudes are known, management reinforces the bonds of trust between organizational echelons by action which reduces, insofar as is possible, the discrepancy between individual and organizational goals.

Finally, the practice of human relations will be reflected in the quality of the interpersonal relations among organizational members. This is indicated by the willingness of line and staff personnel, superiors and subordinates, and members of different organizational units to collaborate in seeking the solutions to mutual human and operational problems. Conflicts are bound to emerge between organizational members, so the practice of human relations should not be equated with an absence of conflict. On the contrary, the purpose of human relations is not to eliminate difference of opinion between organizational members; it is to help them resolve such differences in a constructive manner which will not discourage individuals from offering their viewpoint on the myriad open-ended questions which must be faced every day in a dynamic industrial world.

A number of tangible results should accrue when human relations is practiced in an organization. The degree to which these results are achieved in any given company might be measured by the honest answers which can be given to the following questions. First, to what extent are organizational members aware of the human and organizational problems which either reduce their effectiveness on the job or threaten to do so? Second, to what extent are they able to solve these problems in a satisfactory and lasting manner, and how well are the problems resolved without deteriorating the problem-solving process? That is, can the human problems of the organization be resolved without causing a gross waste of employee energy? This latter point is important because behavioral scientists have documented the fact that a lot of energy is used by employees in fighting the system. Organizational members may overtly or subtly reject management objectives, strategies, or plans by deliberately reducing output. Apathy or indifference, mistrust, politicking, and conformity may permeate the behavior of organizational members ranging from rank and file to top management as a result of dissatisfaction with the organization.

There are two kinds of costs inherent in a situation where organizational effectiveness is reduced by the behavior described above. One is a financial loss in an accounting sense because of the loss output which directly affects the profit-and-loss position of a firm. The other cost is human and it is just as important in the long-run operations of a company. The lack of flexibility and mutual confidence which results from mistrust and lack of openness among organizational members impedes group cohesiveness. This breakdown between employees can impair their willingness to utilize their talents and energy fully in the resolution of the complex problems which often stand between the organization and the achievement of its goals. Such a reduction of the effectiveness of the human resources in an organization is not easy to measure in absolute costs—at least not in the same sense as the cost of a piece of equipment—but these human costs may be as high in the long run as material costs, or higher.

OBJECTIVES OF HUMAN RELATIONS
FOR THE INDIVIDUAL

The desired and tangible value of human relations to an organization is often expressed as the achievement of a more efficient organizational environment. There has been much misunderstanding on the part of some theorists and practitioners about how the practice of human relations is supposed to create a more efficient organizational climate. Some critics, for example, claim that a human relations approach is designed to make employees happy. This view of human relations is based on the concept that high productivity and employee happiness are two separate and somewhat unrelated responsibilities of management, the former being far more important. Thus, when a supervisor must choose between fostering favorable employee attitudes and high production, emphasis must always be placed on elements of production. If turnover rates, absenteeism, or employee grievances rise to a dangerous level, then apply a little human relations until the situation is resolved. If one stops at making or keeping employees "happy," it could happen that management would have a group of happy employees who are not necessarily productive. Although happy employees may not create many problems, they also may not be particularly adroit at solving the real problems found in a competitive business world. Consequently, a "happiness cult" is not the objective of human relations when one of the primary aims in industry is to maintain high levels of productivity because such an objective fails to deal with the fundamental human problems of the organization.

Many managers believe that human relations means "being nice to people." Few persons object to working with or for genuinely compatible fellow employees. However, the thrust of many "personality development" courses for supervisors is directed toward improving one's ability to get along with others. The result of such training does not insure that the supervisor will be more effective in his interactions with others. Often supervisors feel as uncomfortable in dealing with subordinates after training as they did before. They are people who not only have difficulty leveling with other people but also find it just as difficult to face a decision-making situation. Part of the deficiency of the personality approach to human relations to help a supervisor become a more effective leader is the concentration often placed on changing his behavior, rather than on developing his perception in understanding people and situations so that he can behave more wisely in making decisions and taking action.

Modern human relations does not consist of a set of techniques for handling people, but of an analytic approach to understanding people. Most of the behavior of employees is understandable once the physical, social, and psychological elements affecting them are recognized. This recognition does not require that a supervisor be a psychologist or even a human relations expert. For this reason, it is a basic premise that human relations can be managed and ultimately conveyed to individuals who must interact with others on the job.

What can a supervisor who is studying human relations use as a guide in establishing a framework of reference for his human relations practices? What should he keep in mind while attempting to develop an analytic approach to solving human relations problems?

A supervisor has a responsibility to get a job done. This is a primary responsibility for each person who is hired by the firm—production worker, file clerk, supervisor, or top executive. If each person could accomplish this in isolation, relying only on his own skills and limitations, perhaps his job would be much simpler. Such is not often the case. Most employees work with and for others; consequently, the task of doing a job is complicated immeasurably. This is particularly true of anyone who has managerial responsibility in the United States where his work involves others who have grown up in a democratic society where individual rights pervade the political, social, and moral climate.

A supervisor has a responsibility to respect the rights of others. This does not mean total surrender of his will to others. It does mean that workers have the right to be treated with dignity and respect in daily contacts with other people. It also means that people in positions of authority must keep in mind that even though subordinates may not have the right or power to make decisions, they do have the right to think.

A supervisor has a responsibility to develop in others an awareness of their responsibility and a willingness to accept this responsibility. This is particularly significant for supervisors and managers. In fulfilling this aspect of human relations the manager will find it essential to learn something about the basic factors of human behavior. He will have to develop skill in assessing the needs, goals, and ambitions of his subordinates. In this regard, he will find that the research of the behavioral sciences will be particularly useful in helping him understand the people with whom he must deal. Two characteristics are essential in order to carry out this responsibility: learning to accept people as individuals and learning to understand behavior without making moral judgments.

The first of these characteristics is not as easy to develop as it may seem. Each person has his own attitudes, opinions, and prejudices that can subtly work against it. But other people also have a wide range of attitudes, opinions, and prejudices, and one needs to learn not to expect these to be identical to his own. Some supervisors may find it difficult to accept the cultural and social aspirations of workers from disadvantaged and/or minority groups who are entering industrial jobs in larger numbers. Many of the hard-core unemployed with whom supervisors will have to deal are bound to create new and difficult motivational problems.

Learning to understand behavior without making moral judgments does not mean that a supervisor never judges behavior as good or bad. On the contrary, there are times when one must do just that. For example, a supervisor sees that some action of a subordinate, such as not doing his share of the work load, threatens the cohesiveness or effectiveness of his work group. The supervisor must judge this action and take action of his own to alleviate the situation. If he is then to prevent a recurrence of the situation, he must be able to divorce himself from moral judgments and to understand such behavior in terms of underlying causes. This dispassionate position is an extremely difficult one to assume, but it is especially important to effective supervision.

The task of developing in others an awareness of their responsibility and a willingness to accept this responsibility creates a set of definite responsibilities for the supervisor. First, it is necessary that the supervisor communicate clearly and definitely what is expected of the employees. This aspect of human relations involves not only a realistic training program for workers, but also an objective and periodic evaluation of employee performance where helpful criticism is abetted by constructive suggestions on how to improve performance. To expect workers to perform effectively and productively without adequate training or development not only is a serious breach of sound human relations principles, but also is an unrealistic assumption on the part of management.

The second aspect of developing a sense of responsibility in others involves providing motivation to perform well. Numerous incentives have been developed in industry to accomplish this end. Some involve financial benefits such as periodic wage increases or sharing of profits. Other incentive systems, such as letters of recognition or pictures in company newspapers or magazines (house organs), are also used. These methods of motivation, when properly used, may have merit and contribute not only to higher efficiency for the firm employing these techniques, but also to the satisfaction of individual workers sharing in them. However, the number of employees who see their picture in a company newspaper necessarily is somewhat limited and generally a short-lived satisfaction when it does occur. Thus, it is more than gimmick-ridden programs that constitute long-lived and sound human relations practices. The actions of a firm or any of its management personnel have always spoken louder than its words to employees. Often supervisors make the serious mistake of ignoring the good performance of workers. They believe that being silent or not correcting workers is a reward. Such an assumption on the part of a supervisor is seriously short-sighted in light of modern knowledge about human needs. On the opposite end of the scale, and similarly ineffective, is the supervisor who compliments every little action taken by an employee. Such a course can lead to a situation where even genuine compliments become meaningless.

A supervisor needs to develop the ability to assess in others the results of his own actions. This involves learning to know himself and developing sensitivity or empathy with others. It is important that a supervisor develop perception for the reaction of others and that he see more clearly each situation for what it is rather than for an answer to what he should do now. He should strive to be able to answer the question: If I take this action or give this instruction, what will be the result? To be truly effective, a supervisor must be able to assess how his behavior, opinions, and emotions affect other workers and the whole structure of the organization.

A supervisor needs to be able to place human relations in its proper perspective. In spite of evidence that some firms have used a facade of human relations either as a means of placating employees or because it is fashionable, a supervisor should develop a realistic and honest view of the meaning and use of human relations.

It must be recognized that human relations is not a panacea for all organization ills. Moreover, injecting human relations into the organizational bloodstream will not work miracles overnight. Conflicts between individuals or departments will not cease and operational problems will not disappear because the company hires a human relations director or a group of human relations consultants. The practice of human relations requires constant and conscientious effort. This effort is required not in place of, but in addition to the other responsibilities of the supervisor.

Finally, a supervisor must be able to adjust swiftly to changing conditions. Sometimes this is stated as the ability to tolerate chaos. This does not mean, however, that a supervisor needs to be placid; rather, he must develop a sensitivity to a constantly changing environment and realize that a standard or singular mode of behavior cannot be applied to every situation. Learning to adapt to change is one of the most important aspects of interpersonal and organizational effectiveness.

Change has become a major factor operating in all business and industries. No single individual knows as much about a specific company as is known by the total membership of that organization. The supervisor must learn how to identify, develop, and bring to bear the human resources of his work group on the problems facing both his group and the organization. To do this he must learn to cultivate and utilize the ideas and abilities possessed by his subordinates. In short, he must learn to cope with change through the participation of all members of his work group. Such participation should not be for its own sake, but because such collaboration results in better solutions to organizational problems.

The foregoing list of objectives does not separately mention such specific topics as leadership, communications, or decision-making because these principles or objectives are the foundation of good supervision, communications, and decision-making. Such topics are discussed more specifically in later chapters, but the reader should bear in mind the essence of the principles of human relations rather than any specific list of steps or rules to follow; otherwise he may fall into the trap of merely parroting a programmed method of getting along with others, which is not necessarily being effective with others or understanding the processes in which he is involved.

An individual's attitude toward his work, employer, company policies, objectives, supervisors, and fellow employees is affected by his ongoing experience with the people, the nature of his work, and the organizational climate he finds on the job. The purpose of human relations is to help make these encounters a positive experience. The dynamic nature of human beings and the rapidity of change that are concomitant parts of organizational life should make it obvious that human relations cannot be offered as a formula for solving all the problems associated with employee motivation, leadership, communication, and decision-making. One must admit that despite the contribution of scientific research to the practice of human relations, such practices still remain largely an art. As such, they are imperfect. Therefore, the practice of human relations should be viewed as much as a means of looking at human and organizational problems as a means for solving them.

SUMMARY

1. Human relations in industry involves motivating people to work together productively and cooperatively while they are receiving economic psychological, and social rewards.

2. The study of human relations as a tool of management involves an understanding of several complex and interrelated factors. The individual, the job, the impact of both the formal and the informal organization, and the social environment of the work place interact and affect the individual's perspective and behavior.

3. To a large extent, human relations utilizes the research findings of the behavioral sciences as the foundation of its principles and practices. Happiness, success, and various other personal satisfactions are not dependent solely on the job; however, it is necessary to understand how the individual reacts to many of the conditions found in his work situation if one is to practice human relations soundly.

4. Although human relations occurs in many social, church, military, and business endeavors, the responsibility for its practices cannot be pigeonholed or placed on any single individual's shoulders. Ideally, the principles of human relations act as guides in every activity and aspect of the organization—communications, leadership, and organizational structure.

5. The objectives of studying human relations should be to help each individual understand the actions of others in the organization and to aid individuals to carry out their duties and responsibilities effectively instead of merely reacting to people and situations in a mechanical manner.

DISCUSSION QUESTIONS

1. How does the practice of human relations differ from coercing people to do what you want them to do?
2. Define in your own words the term *human relations*.
3. Who in an organization is responsible for the practice of human relations?
4. What are the principal objectives in studying human relations?

BIBLIOGRAPHY AND
SELECTED COLLATERAL READINGS

1. CARR, ALBERT Z., *Business as a Game*. New York: The New American Library, Inc., 1968.
2. DAVIS, KEITH, *Human Relations at Work*, 3rd ed. New York: McGraw-Hill Book Company, 1967.
3. DUBIN, ROBERT, *Human Relations in Administration*, 3rd ed. Englewood Cliffs, N.J.: Prentice-Hall, Inc., 1968.
4. GARDNER, BURLEIGH B., and DAVID G. MOORE, *Human Relations in Industry*, 4th ed. Homewood, Ill.: Richard D. Irwin, Inc., 1964.
5. HUNERYAGER, S. G., and I. L. HECKMAN, JR., *Human Relations in Management*, 2nd ed. Cincinnati: South-Western Publishing Co., 1967.
6. KNUDSON, HARRY R., *Human Elements of Administration*. New York: Holt, Rinehart and Winston, 1963.
7. LOVE, ALBERT, and JAMES SAXON CHILDERS, *Listen to Leaders in Business*. Atlanta: Tupper and Love, Inc., 1963.
8. MAIER, NORMAN R. F., *Principles of Human Relations*. New York: John Wiley and Sons, Inc., 1952.
9. OGBURN, W. F., *Social Change with Respect to Culture and Original Nature*. Gloucester, Mass.: Peter Smith, 1964.
10. SCOTT, WILLIAM G., *Organizational Theory: A Behavioral Analysis of Management*. Homewood, Ill.: Richard D. Irwin, Inc., 1967.
11. WHYTE, WILLIAM FOOTE, *Men at Work*. Homewood, Ill.: Richard D. Irwin, Inc., and The Dorsey Press, Inc., 1961.
12. ZALEZNIK, A., and D. MOMENT, *The Dynamics of Interpersonal Behavior*. New York: John Wiley and Sons, Inc., 1964.

The Scope of
Human Relations

One way to study a subject is to examine its accompanying definitions, governing laws, and interrelationships with other disciplines. Human relations is dependent upon many other sciences and disciplines. At best, the primary aim of human relations in industry can be said to be directed toward the adaptation of the individual to the job situation.

Another method of approaching the study of a subject is to review its origins and developmental history. In the first chapter definitions and objectives of human relations were presented. This chapter will examine some of the cultural, social, and economic developments which led to modern human relations and some of the major human problems created by modern industrialization. Human relations has a certain scope today, but its scope was different 150 years ago or even 50 years ago. In order to obtain a better perspective of human relations, it is useful to know some of the forces that helped to establish the framework of today's employee-employer relations.

Although *human relations* is a relatively recent term describing the process of adjustment between men and work situations, as long as man has been civilized enough to work with others in groups, problems of leadership have existed. These were just as true in ancient times as they are today although the moral, economic, social, and political forces which govern the relationship between employers and employees have changed substantially.

Generally, until relatively recent times arbitrary and authoritarian methods dominated the relationship between owners of capital resources and the working class. The handcraft or domestic system of production which preceded the industrial revolution was conducted primarily in the small shops of master craftsmen or in the homes of the workers themselves. At best, physical working conditions were not good, hours were long, wages were low, and technology was at a minimum.

During the medieval period several factors began to change the relationship between employers and employees. One of these was the beginning of the migration of labor from the farm to urban centers. This social force is still operating today in most advanced nations of the world. The growth of cities created the large pools of labor that became a necessary commodity when the factory system evolved as a result of the industrial revolution.

Another important element that occurred during the later stages of the medieval period was a significant philosophical shift in emphasis in the cultural and religious viewpoint of art, literature, and government. It was an age of exploration, intellectually and geographically. In the process, the center of reference became man instead of God. This attitude placing man at the center of the universe is frequently defined as humanism. Humanism placed emphasis on the importance and dignity of man himself rather than on the supernatural. This period saw the beginning of the transfer of power and wealth from the medieval church to civil authority and secular interests.

There were considerably more social forces at work during the long period prior to the industrial revolution but these two elements helped establish a broad framework for the practice of human relations in the periods that followed. The development of urban centers, first promoted by the growth of commerce and later by production, created an environment in which large masses of people had to live and work together. This environment also was accompanied by the increased dependence of one person upon others for his survival. Food, shelter, health services, education, protection, and employment had to be provided by someone or something outside the individual's own capability to provide them. This dependency also created or accentuated the need for continuous personal contact between people. Thus, human relations problems became an integral part of urban life in a way they had not been in a rural society.

Humanism, the second element mentioned, changed man's perception of himself. Man began to question the physical and social forces around him. The belief that man as an individual has worth and is deserving of consideration and dignity gradually displaced the acceptance of man being a commodity which could be manipulated or used as a tool without concern for his personal well-being.

The industrial revolution caused some drastic changes in the living conditions of city dwellers. Housing for many was often dismal if not squalid. Many factories employed women and children who had to work long hours for low pay in unsafe conditions. In spite of the excesses, living standards gradually began to rise for many as incomes increased. Working conditions in factories also improved slowly as laborers united in unions in order to demand the material gains and benefits of increased productivity.* Not all gains had to be forced out of management. As technology increased rapidly, many managers gradually became enlightened about the need for improved relationships with employees. One such factory owner was Robert Owen. Though he ended his career labeled a Utopian Socialist, his efforts to improve the physical and social conditions of employment in his own textile mills in England were a marked departure from the raw capitalism practiced in nineteenth-century Europe. Owen's basic philosophy that man is a creature of circumstances led him to try to improve circumstances in his factory which were detrimental to the physical and social welfare of his employees. His efforts ultimately failed when he attempted to extend his concepts of social well-being to an entire community. Despite the political ramifications of his beliefs, he was one of the first factory owners to show that industrialism need not be based on underpaid or physically abused labor. In essence, Owen was one of the first employers during the early industrial period to attempt to implement human relations.

The early nineteenth century saw other attempts by various factory owners to alleviate the plight of the working class. Unfortunately, many of these attempts encroached upon the personal lives of the workers. Many employers believed that if they could improve the health and morals of employees, they would produce more. Accordingly, some employers built company towns and stores, supported recreation halls and libraries, held picnics, and encouraged the education of workers' children, but not of the workers themselves, as is done today [3, p. 91].

One example of such paternalism was the Lowell System, named after a New England textile mill owner who developed the idea of providing dormitories for his employees. As a result of living in accommodations provided by Lowell, many aspects of the workers' private lives became subject to his review. Church attendance, personal conduct, and training in domestic duties for young women were given careful scrutiny [8, p. 6].

The Lowell system was not the only example of paternalism found in early industrial history. Many employer concepts of fair treatment of employees as individuals generated practices which today seem comical. For example, the list of rules once posted by a manufacturer covered many aspects of a worker's private life that would not only be rejected by today's workers, but also resented. (See Figure 2–1.)

Unfortunately, before factory owners implemented major changes that offered more humane treatment of workers and improved working conditions, several important consequences emerged which are still present

---

* Generally, productivity is defined as the number of units produced, divided by the man hours it takes to produce them. The formula: Number of units produced ÷ Total man hours of production.

today. One was the rise of Communist ideology, which considered the exploitation of labor a necessary outcome of the private ownership of capital. If changes had not occurred in the treatment of many factory workers by the early industrialists, Karl Marx's predictions of an increasing class conflict and revolution might have been more accurate.

A second consequence of the early industrial revolution was the confirmation of the old manorial class relationship in a slightly different form. Although the serf had been subordinate and dependent on the nobility, the factory workers became even more dependent on the factory owners in the new industrial order. With class consciousness came a profound difference of viewpoint between wage earners and wage payers. In Europe, where the class relationship was superimposed on the old manorial relationships class-consciousness has persisted more strongly than in the United States, where manorial relationships never actually existed. However, the early immigrants from Europe to the United States brought with them many of their attitudes concerning mill and factory owners.

Rigid class differences have not been a dominant factor in the American culture where class mobility has been a vital part of a dynamic society; nonetheless, a carryover of attitudes similar to those held during the early industrial period manifests itself in the thinking of some employers who regard workers in terms of the employer's responsibility to meet the payroll—that is, as a burden. This opinion is often accompanied by the view that the average worker is dull and lazy and must be prodded and disciplined and even protected against his own foolishness. At the same time some employees tend to think of employers in terms of their own security; that is, as a benefactor who is profiteering at the expense of labor. Although such extremes in employee-employer thinking are not frequently found, a great deal of interpersonal conflict still results from this difference in perspective.

Few, if any, personnel practices of modern firms are as overtly paternalistic as the examples cited; however, the subtle pressure exerted by the work group and the formal and informal employee behavior sanctioned by an organization often impose limits on the individual and create problems of *indirect paternalism*. Styles of acceptable dress for work, location of residence, and membership in social clubs considered appropriate for an employee's position in the company may be strongly influenced by indirect paternalism. Many employees may concede willingly to these subtle pressures. However if an individual senses a limitation, real or imagined, on his personal freedom, it is not unusual for him to resist (or at least resent) the organizational forces or persons responsible for the creation of those limitations. An employee's perceived lack of freedom usually results in conflict between himself and other organizational members. The resolution of such interpersonal conflict is the primary focus for the practice of human relations.

How to Begin the New Year Right!

How would you like to start the year with a nice new set of do's and don'ts for your office?

Try these on for size. They were posted in 1872 by the proprietor of a carriage and wagon works.

1. Office employes will daily sweep the floors, dust the furniture, shelves and showcases.

2. Each clerk will bring in a bucket of water and a scuttle of coal for the day's business.

3. Clerk's will each day fill lamps, clean chimneys, trim wicks. Wash the windows once a week.

4. Make your pens carefully. You may whittle nibs to your individual taste.

5. This office will open at 7 a. m. and close at 8 p. m. daily, except on the Sabbath, on which day it will remain closed.

6. Men employes will be given an evening off each week for courting purposes, or two evenings a week, if they go regularly to church.

7. Every employe should lay aside from each pay a goodly sum of his earnings for his benefits during his declining years, so that he will not become a burden upon the charity of his betters.

8. Any employe who smokes Spanish cigars, uses liquor in any form, gets shaved at a barber shop, or frequents pool or public halls, will give me good reason to suspect his worth, intention, integrity, and honesty.

9. The employe who has performed his labors faithfully and without fault for a period of 5 years in my service, who has been thrifty and attentive to his religious duties, and is looked upon by his fellowmen as a substantial and law-abiding citizen, will be given an increase of 5 cents per day in his pay, providing a just return in profits from the business permits it.

FIGURE 2-1.

ERA OF SOCIAL RESPONSIBILITY

A number of complex cultural and social factors that operate simultaneously have their roots in our own industrial development. Today's firms are part of a larger social order; consequently, human relations practices in any given organization are affected by the actions and attitudes of such outside institutions and groups as labor unions, government, customers, stockholders, and public opinion. Although it is difficult to isolate and measure the exact degree of pressure some of these outside factions have on the human relations practices of a particular firm, most business managers can attest to their presence and force. Aside from the real or potential influence of social institutions, modern management methods have progressed to a point where there is reflected in the internal and external actions of industrial firms something generally termed *social responsibility*. There is room for debate on the extent to which a firm should go and the methods it should use to meet its responsibility to the community, its employees, and its stockholders; however, many of the activities undertaken by the management of modern firms do not reflect the drive for immediate profits that once was exhibited by the raw capitalists that Marx attacked so vehemently. Yet, despite the philanthropic activity of many modern firms, industry has been operating at relatively high profit margins for the past several decades.

Enlightened management has discovered that social consciousness not only creates a good business atmosphere, but also is sound business in itself. When genuine interest for the employees, stockholders, and community well-being is the basis for the practice of human relations, human relations is not used as a device to make workers respond to a particular method of management control; rather, it becomes a tool to be used by management to determine leadership methods which are appropriate to human and social values.

With the growth of social consciousness as a factor in industrial democracy in Western Europe and the United States, a change in attitude toward minority races has occurred. During the decade of the 1960's, there has been a growing awareness of the inequities in employment opportunities for minority groups. According to the *Report of the National Advisory Commission on Civil Disorders*, in riot-torn cities where employment opportunities for Negro men were heavily concentrated in menial jobs, fewer Negro men sought gainful employment. When given similar employment, Negro workers with the same education as white workers were paid less. The Commission concluded that the differential between white and nonwhite employment patterns is so large and so universal at all educational levels that it clearly reflects patterns of discrimination in hiring and promoting practices in many segments of the economy [14, p. 126].

There is still much progress to be made, but equal employment opportunities in many public and private organizations are more of a reality than ever before. Through both concerted efforts of massive training programs sponsored by the federal government and the initiative of private employers, large numbers of Negro workers are entering the mainstream of industrial employment for the first time. A related change is taking place in opportunities for women. Although equal pay laws and fair employment practices certainly have established the framework for many employee-employer relationships, many firms have foregone their passive attitudes regarding the employment and treatment of minority groups and of women. In many cases, firms have voluntarily sought to create employment conditions reflecting fair and equitable treatment of all workers regardless of race, creed, or sex.

The rise of industrial democracy has fostered the emergence of an egalitarian attitude which prevails in a large segment of the work force. This is the philosophy by which one person resists the right of another to tell him what to do, regardless of that person's position—policeman, teacher, clergyman, or supervisor. During the decade of the 1960's there has been an increasing manifestation of such resistance to authority on college campuses, in religious, military, and public organizations, and in industry. Because of this attitude which teaches one to cherish independence, a typical reaction to industrial life includes a certain amount of irritation and a certain unwillingness to cooperate with supervisors carried to a greater extent than is necessary [4, p. 9].

The growing belief in the value of personal independence may not be universal; however, it is a potent enough force to be a good reason to understand human behavior and practice human relations. This importance is compounded in light of social and human values that no longer tolerate arbitrary leadership methods which demean or attack the dignity of the individual.

ORGANIZED LABOR AND HUMAN RELATIONS

As the United States became more industrial and urbanized, the workers found that uniting in labor unions provided a means of furthering their social, political, and economic interests.

The unionization of industrial workers often caused violent anti-union activity on the part of employers. Despite this resistance by many employers, the great impetus to the labor movement in this country came as a result of the passage of the *National Labor Relations Act* in 1935. This act, often referred to as the Wagner Act, affirmed the right of labor to bargain collectively on matters of wages, hours, and conditions of employment while prohibiting coercive action against union members by employers. During the two decades that followed, unions gained in economic, political, and financial strength. Peak membership in unions reached over 18 million by the end of the 1950's and often the union's position was militant and aggressive because of its strength. Since the early 1960's unions have met some difficulty in organizing nonindustrial segments of the labor force in white collar and agricultural fields. At the same time, organized labor has been faced by waning numbers in their industrial ranks. A number of reasons have contributed to the decline in the number of union members in industrial fields: Inroads of automation, reduction in the number of industrial jobs, increased job security, relatively high standards of living, and an increasing apathy on the part of workers toward union activities have made the job of union leaders no easy task.

Despite some of the problems they face internally, unions are definitely a real and vital force in industrial society, and debate regarding the strength of unions is academic from the standpoint of human relations. What is important is the fact that the presence of a labor union in a firm presents a whole set of real and potential human problems.

The reasons why workers choose either to join voluntarily or to abstain from labor union activities stem from many social and personal motives, both rational and emotional, and before any concrete conclusions can be reached regarding the workers' motives far more research will have to be conducted. However, where unions are present in the work situation, knowledge of the problems unions have faced in the past and are presently confronting helps one to understand their position on many factors concerning the work place. Knowing some of the basic reasons why people join and actively support unions helps management and supervisors confront the presence of the union with keener insight into the problems which may arise. For those who equate human relations with peace and tranquility in affairs between the workers and the employer, an abrupt and rude awakening is in store. The presence of a union can complicate employee relations under the best conditions and cause drastic conflict under poorer conditions. Conflicting, not static, relations lie at the very root of human behavior in social living. This should not dismay the employer or the worker. Industrial conflict is a characteristic, rather than a catastrophic, aspect of human relations [15, p. 216].

The Place of Human Relations in Unionized Firms.   When a firm finds that it is confronted with a union representing its employees, it must realize that the relations between all of the members in the organization are affected. Supervisors may find their authority challenged, some rank-and-file employees may find new responsibilities suddenly thrust upon them if they assume the role of shop steward,* and management may find the union a factor in decisions that previously had been their sole responsibility. The new situation demands that adjustments be made. The resumption of activity after a union agreement is entered into requires the patience and cooperation of both management and the union. This is no easy matter when there may have been a great deal of emotionalism and open conflict before an agreement was reached. Any animosity that may have existed before and during negotiations does not die automatically because a contract has been signed.

The place of human relations in such a situation cannot be underestimated. Changing the attitude of the foremen, shop stewards, employees, and executives requires that positive steps be taken to relieve undue tension and to engender a spirit of cooperation in the organization. This places a responsibility both on the firm and on the union to insure that supervisors and shop stewards are well informed on the provisions of the new agreement so that there will be a minimum of confusion in the work group of each department. This principle holds true whether it is a new agreement establishing the place of the union in the organization for the first time or a revision of an agreement that has been in existence.

Often, the stress of union relations is greatest immediately before and immediately after contract negotiations; therefore, training in human relations for foremen and supervisors well in advance of any industrial crisis is a valuable tool in the organization.

The attitude of a union toward a company's human relations practices is largely based on past experience in negotiating with that employer. Obviously, where the union senses that the firm has used human relations to drive a wedge between itself and the workers, it rejects the practice as manipulation. Good working conditions and good relations between the firm and its employees will normally curb the sense of necessity and allegiance held by workers toward unions. This seldom encourages feelings of good will in union officials.

Even when labor representatives are included in the planning and implementation stages of new or changed personnel programs, it must be understood that strained interpersonal relations can still occur between

---

* In industrial firms each department usually has one or more members of the work group act as union stewards. Their responsibilities entail seeing that provisions of the collective bargaining agreement are adhered to by management. They are also the advisers of the union members in their departments in matters concerning their grievances, and present the grievances to the supervisors for action. Shop stewards are usually elected to the post by the workers and although they act as the union spokesmen in their departments, they are still employees of the firm and the supervisors retain authority over them in all matters except union business.

union and company officials. Labor leaders must feel and demonstrate their value to union members and, therefore, for the sake of proving their worth, react strongly to slight changes suggested by management. Company officials, claiming that management prerogatives are being challenged, may also overreact to union suggestions.

Negotiations between labor and management can be particularly explosive when major contract issues must be settled by a given deadline. In such circumstances both sides need to put aside rivalries and jealousies. This requires maturity and good faith and such qualities are difficult to maintain under stress. Labor peace is possible when both union and company officials exercise prudent judgment and establish reasonable requests. An example of such bargaining occurred in the meat-packing industry during contract negotiations in 1967 between Armour and Company and two unions representing company employees. The spirit of the negotiations was pervaded by good faith and amity as a result of continuing dialogue between the unions and Armour through an automation committee established in 1959 to work out the vexing problems arising from the automation of production and the resulting displacement of thousands of workers. This dialogue contributed to the signing of a new union contract six months before the existing one was due to expire, thus avoiding the excessive stress of meeting a last minute deadline on contract negotiations. When human relations practices by the employer include union participation in the development and administration of employee services and benefits instead of a charitable passing down of such benefits to employees, then unions generally agree that human relations is something that furthers the interests of the workers, which is, after all, one of the union's own primary functions.

The Implication of Collective Group Action

An indirect effect of labor unions lies outside the unions themselves. The pattern of collective action established by labor unions has been one adopted by other employee and professional groups who are not in themselves organized. The medical profession in Canada and Great Britain has witnessed concerted group action by doctors to bring pressure on other agencies, such as hospital administrations and the government, to improve employment conditions relating to hours and wages. The same action has occurred in the ranks of professional nursing in the United States. Professional teacher organizations, including some affiliates of unions, have brought pressure to bear on school boards and administrators through collective action or the threat of such action. Engineers and workers in other technical occupations have increasingly shown an interest in organizing into unions or other professional organizations to help protect their interests. Generally, white-collar employees in both public and private organizations have shown a growing propensity to join labor unions in order to protect their job interests.

On a broader scale related to many social and political issues, concerted group action has reflected a changing public attitude toward traditional concepts of power and authority. During the past several decades there is a well-documented history of the reaction of certain segments of the general public toward such pressing public issues as civil rights and the country's foreign policy. All such concerted group action has not proved constructive, but it has made persons in leadership positions aware of the possible repercussions of their actions. As increased education and rapid and widespread communications media help create a better-informed general public, any action taken by a person in power is likely to bring about immediate social response. This reality of modern society is just as applicable to the owner or manager of a business enterprise as it is to political figures. Thus, even in companies or in professions where employees are not formally organized into labor unions, management practices must be prepared to contend with the latent power of collective employee action.

IMPACT OF MODERN INDUSTRIALIZATION ON HUMAN RELATIONS

The human problems that develop for a firm in its relationships conducted with unions, employees, customers, and stockholders take place within the context of a larger framework of social and cultural conditions created by modern industrialization.

The varied social forces which operate in a free industrial society are difficult to isolate and describe. It is even more difficult to determine accurately their effect on any single management practice. There are a number of characteristics which are identified with modern industrialization which have a direct effect on the human beings who are involved in the production of goods and services. Among the chief characteristics identified with such technologically advanced nations as the United States are

1. The development of large-scale enterprise.
2. The advances in technology and automation in production.
3. Mass production, specialization, and standardization.
4. Application of science and research to problems of production, distribution, and manpower utilization.

Each of these characteristics contributes to a set of human problems which should be examined in order to determine the need for and the implications of human relations.

Development of Large-Scale Enterprise

A few generations ago we were a nation of small businesses. Shops, farms, and even manufacturing units were relatively small and often owned and operated by a few individuals. Today our economy appears to be dominated to a large extent by giant organizations which operate internationally, require large-scale financing, produce annual sales which surpass a billion dollars, and employ a multitude of men and women who possess a wide range of skills and aptitudes. Based on the history of the last three decades, indications are that the trend toward largeness will continue.

Accompanying the economies of large-scale operations are exceedingly complex problems of staffing and maintaining and developing personnel. Often, the development of rules and procedures for handling and controlling manpower efficiently leads to what some employees consider to be impersonalization. Most employees of very large firms find that they are assigned to relatively small work groups from which certain social and psychological satisfactions can be derived; however, when the number of workers hired by the company is in the thousands, such practices as assigning employee numbers are inevitable. Such action can contribute to the individual's sense of impersonal treatment and loss of identity. Few people appreciate the anonymity of isolated digits; hence, when an employee feels that he is regarded as a number rather than as an individual, it is difficult to engender his loyalty or best efforts.

Problems of Organization. The vast number of employees working for a large corporation creates other problems affecting human relations. First, the problem of controlling the activities and personnel of a large enterprise requires that careful consideration be given to the organizational structure. Because of the growth in size and diversification of industrial firms during the past three decades, considerable time and effort have gone into the development of organizational theory. It is no simple matter to determine the most appropriate and efficient organization pattern for such giant firms as General Motors, General Electric, Standard Oil of New Jersey, or DuPont, because they no longer can be clearly categorized as part of any single industry. As a consequence, organizational theory and practices are constantly evolving to meet industry's changing demands. Some firms follow principles of centralized control where decisions are made by relatively few high-ranking officials. Other companies have found success in permitting a large degree of decentralization where decision-making is allowed to filter down into the lower ranks of the organization's hierarchy. A number of industrial firms determine the organization of personnel and activities by geographic areas, while others have chosen an organization pattern determined by the type of products manufactured or sold.

There is no one ideal organizational pattern and each firm must try to select those patterns which best suit its circumstances and needs. A fuller discussion of organizational theory will appear later in the text; however, it is important to realize early in the study of human relations that no matter which organizational pattern is adapted to the firm's needs, it affects human relationships as well as operations and functions. Therefore, fatal flaws may turn up in any operation that does not give adequate consideration to the impact of those plans on the people who must function within the organization.

Separation of Ownership and Management. A significant characteristic of large-scale operations, most particularly enterprises that are corporations, is the separation of ownership and management. Often the effect of this separation plays a role both in the way managers exercise their authority and in the attitude workers have toward their supervisors. In small owner-managed businesses and during earlier periods in our industrial history when even large firms were owned and controlled by a few individuals, orders of the owner carried the ultimate authority— ownership of the property and equipment being used by the employee. Today's industrial situation is somewhat more complicated by the fact that managers as well as workers are *employees* of the firm, and it is not uncommon for a worker to own shares of stock in the same company in which he works. Even when the worker does not own stock, his perception of his supervisor's authority may well be influenced by the knowledge that the supervisor is just another employee of the organization. Certainly, the supervisor holds a higher position in the organization's hierarchy, but often the results he obtains and respect he receives are dependent upon the techniques of leadership and motivation he employs rather than on his position.

One of the direct results of the separation of ownership and management has been the development of "professional management." The professionalization of those persons who are responsible for turning the men, money, materials, and machines into productive units has created a new climate and new need for human relations. It has already been mentioned that realization of the fact that men tend to resist being told what to do has brought about an emphasis in management to provide a reason or incentive for doing what is necessary in order to get a job done. In order to know and understand what reasons people have for behaving the way they do on the job and which incentives bring results and which ones fail, a manager must both acquire skill in dealing with people and develop sensitivity to the people upon whom he depends in order to get results.

There is no denying that the professional manager must possess other technical skills in order to be proficient, but without skill in developing sound human relations much of his technical proficiency is lost.

Communications. Concomitant with large operations is the problem of communications. Perhaps the single most important aspect of designing a sound organization is the plan that links together all of the departments, functions, and organizational level with channels of communications. Good communications also could be cited as the most important aspect of sound human relations; yet, in spite of all that has been written about the art and science of communications, it remains one of the most perplexing of human and organizational problems.

In any enterprise involving more than a single person, sending and receiving information is essential if duplication of effort and needless mistakes and misunderstandings are to be avoided. Despite careful planning systems, procedures and channels of organizational communications often break down, leaving important departments of personnel in the organization without vital information necessary for their efficient functioning. To overcome the gap in communications, elaborate inter-office and department communication systems have been employed, classes on communications techniques have been offered in supervisory training programs, and organizational communications networks have been designed in order to insure that information from the top of the organization is passed to employee groups at lower-level positions. Often these formal communication systems emphasize downward communications. Downward communications refers to information that originates at the top levels of the organization and is passed downward to departments and personnel occupying lower positions in the firm's hierarchy. From a standpoint of human relations upward communications channels are equally important, but it is not unusual for management to spend much more effort and money trying to convey their messages downward through such formal media as company magazines or house organs, bulletin boards and posters, and company manuals and directives, while devoting little effort to such formal upward communications channels as suggestion systems or grievance systems. When there is no means of learning what suggestions, complaints, or other information subordinates have relating to their work and other organizational matters, supervisors and managers necessarily must operate without the benefit of the feedback so vital to appraisal and revision of their own ideas, plans, and directives.

Yet, the failure of upward communications is not just a matter of effort and money. There are inherent blocks in a hierarchic system which cause subordinates to hesitate before conveying information which they do not think their bosses want to hear. Even when formal upward channels

A breakdown in communications can contribute to a breakdown of operations.

31

of communication are available to employees there is no guarantee that they will be used. Frequently, upward communications lapse either into a dismal array of employee complaints or, in some instances, a total silence. Both reactions serve to reinforce one of two beliefs shared by some managers: either that workers do not care enough about their work to make constructive criticism or suggestions or that workers are a lot of chronic gripers. Certainly there will be some legitimate grievances voiced by employees who are permitted to do so along with the normal amount of griping which may or may not have sound foundation, and management must learn to live with the latter and face up to the former. But often the silence of employees is interpreted by many managers to mean that conditions are satisfactory. The supervisor who possesses this "let sleeping dogs lie" mentality is usually the first to be shocked when his employees' long-silenced complaints manifest themselves in some type of concerted action such as a strike.

The reasons for the breakdown of organizational and individual communications will be examined in more detail later in the text. However, at this juncture in the discussion of the effects of largeness on the communications process, it is important to realize that even under ideal conditions where only a few people are involved, sound communications are not always easy to establish. When an organization expands in numbers, as well as diversity among its members, it becomes all the more difficult to facilitate adequate transfer of information and understanding, whether the direction be upward, downward or across organizational levels; therefore, one of the primary missions of human relations is to help understand the potential barriers to understanding between organizational members so that both the message and the media of communication are appropriate to the audience. Only in this way can the process of communications be substantially improved, whether through face-to-face human contact or broad-scale organizational communications.

Expansion of Large-Scale Operations into Foreign Countries. Since World War II the United States has found itself economically and politically committed to many foreign countries; businesses also have found themselves expanding into an ever-widening range of foreign operations. The diversity of social and cultural customers found in many of these lands creates human relations problems never encountered before. As a consequence of this industrial expansion, the demand is increasing for personnel who possess both tolerance and willingness to adapt to cultural patterns different from their own. In a broad sense, company management, technicians, and advisory personnel who are sent abroad act as diplomats not only for the company for which they work, but also for the economic system existing in the United States. At a time when our country finds itself in direct competition with other socialistically oriented political and economic systems, this becomes a crucial mission which no company can afford to treat passively.

Foreign operations add another dimension to the human relations problems of the organization and also provides a new vista for innovation and challenging work. As the world shrinks in size due to advances in technology, communication systems, and decreased travel time, this aspect of human relations will grow in importance.

ADVANCES IN TECHNOLOGY AND AUTOMATION IN PRODUCTION

The development of the factory system and its complementary machinery has had its impact not only on the working conditions of employees, but also on the nature and types of jobs available. The early effect of mechanization was to reduce the physical effort necessary on the part of the machine operator. This is still true today. The problem of mechanization arose from the fact that it also reduced the unit of work to be performed to a few simple repetitive tasks requiring little of the skill of the craftsman. As an example of this latter point, the task of making a pair of shoes has about a hundred subdivisions of labor. Each worker becomes proficient in the performance of a few repetitive operations, but none can make a complete pair of shoes. The outcome in terms of productivity and unit costs is beneficial to the employer, but frequently boring and frustrating to the employee. The end result of this situation can be that the total gain made possible through the use of machinery is reduced by the operator's inefficiency, generated by repetitive monotony. Another factor believed to be important to employee satisfaction is also lost in the process: The worker who does not see the end result of his efforts seldom feels the pride of workmanship that the craftsman who completed a whole unit from beginning to end felt.

Whereas early equipment could usually be operated by unskilled or uneducated workers, as evidenced by the large portion of women and children employed in the early factories, today's equipment frequently requires that the operator be highly skilled or at least well trained. This difference between early and modern industrialization has been accelerated by the introduction of automated equipment on the production line and in offices.

There is a question in the minds of some industrialists and economists about automation displacing workers. Whether or not in the long run automation creates as many or more jobs than it eliminates may be debatable, but from a human relations viewpoint several immediate problems arise. First is the problem of what to do with the employees who are displaced by advances in technology and automation. This problem is not confined only to the production line, but also to the offices and warehouses. Second, how or from where should the operators for the more complex machines be obtained? In general, evidence indicates that the operators of the new automated equipment require higher and, in many cases, different skills than the operators of the old; however, the extent to which this occurs depends on the type and degree of automation.

Another major human relations problem created by the introduction of automated equipment into a plant or office is the accompanying change in the social relations of the work group caused by changes in work procedures, routines, and scheduling. Often the workers appear to resist the equipment being introduced, much to the dismay of managers who know that such equipment may actually reduce the workers' physical effort. The point that has been overlooked in such cases is that the workers' real resistance is to the disruption of the social relationships in a group that the new equipment created.

Aside from the change in social relations caused by mechanization or automation, a worker often finds that the work pace of the job is set by the speed of the machinery, leaving little room for changes in routine. Some equipment can be operated only in one way, and once it is placed in operation a worker has no choice but to follow a prescribed routine. This lack of discretion can apply to clerical jobs as well as to the production line. Thus, as certain jobs become more routinized, the intrinsic satisfaction of work can diminish. As this occurs, supervisors may face increasing problems both in motivating employees and in selecting the most appropriate ways of interacting with their subordinates. Thus, executives and labor leaders find that technology has affected many of the relationships between the firm and its workers. Recruiting, selection, training, and union relations have all been touched directly or indirectly as a result of the technological advances of the past decade. Indications are that this trend will continue and expand.

THE USE OF MASS PRODUCTION METHODS

Beginning with the principle of *division of labor* expounded by Adam Smith (*Wealth of Nations*) in the eighteenth century, specialization in the use of men and machines has grown into a hallmark of twentieth-century industrial life. In the fields of medicine and law specialization has permitted individuals to develop expertise that could not otherwise be accomplished. In industry, the growth of engineering and technical specialties has made possible efficiencies in operations that have contributed to increases in productivity and volume of goods produced.

The economic gains to be made through specialization are generally well known and accepted by management and, to some degree, by labor

leaders. What both often forget is the human and organizational consequences of specialization. Specialization means that individuals, departments, and even companies or nations become highly dependent upon
each other. This interdependency makes clear the necessity of sound
human relations, because a breakdown in one part of the system, whether
on the production line of a factory or in the development of long-range
plans by top-level management, means that people in other parts of the
system are affected. Dependency can also be detrimental. In essence,
it means placing oneself at someone else's mercy, because each specialist
must depend on another specialist to provide him with the materials or
information necessary to perform his own specialized set of activities.
When delivery is not forthcoming, the activity of each specialist dependent on another is delayed or even halted. This aspect of interdependency has created a demand for a new type of professional manager
who is familiar with many specialized activities, but who is not necessarily
expert in them. His function is primarily to coordinate the activities of
many separate specialized functions and personnel. In essence, the
division of labor concept has necessitated the emergence of the *generalist*
in management. With the development of the management generalist has
grown the importance of human relations because as the number of
specialized activities and personnel have increased complex problems
have been created, such as the problems of communicating with and
obtaining cooperation between members of diverse disciplines. This cooperation is necessary for concerted group action.

The result of mass production not only affects conditions of employment for workers, it also influences many other aspects of their lives.
Many goods and services are created at a price that they can afford and
that would not be possible otherwise. The end result is a higher standard
of living for more people than has ever been achieved before. The price
of this achievement, made possible through job specialization, is often the
frustration of the individual worker because of the reduction of his
opportunity for self-expression and meaningful participation in organizational activities. To this end human relations faces its greatest challenge in helping to resolve the difficulties of finding satisfactory and
productive places in the industrial community not only for the millions
of persons currently in the work force but also for the millions who will
be taking their places in the coming generations.

THE APPLICATION OF SCIENCE AND RESEARCH TO PROBLEMS OF PRODUCTION, DISTRIBUTION, AND MANPOWER UTILIZATION

The application of the scientific method to the investigation of human
problems has been slower than it has been in the physical sciences. This

gap in the speed and efficiency of compiling information along with the rapidity of technological changes as compared to the relative slowness of social change of the past half century, has given rise to what W. F. Ogburn calls the "cultural lag" [12]. However, since the turn of the century, increasing effort has been made by the behavioral scientists to discover the basis for the actions people take. This is true not only regarding employee motivation, but also regarding consumer habits. Marketing research has turned an increasing eye on why people buy the products they do. The answers the researchers have compiled have affected product designs, colors, packaging, and advertising promotions. The research findings of the behavioral sciences also have had their effect on management philosophy in the treatment of employees. Many incentive systems and participative methods used by management have grown out of an increased awareness of workers as individuals rather than classes or groups that need prodding. More recently, the attention of the behavioral scientists has turned to the social environment of the job and work groups. Some of the research findings of the behavioral scientists will be examined more specifically in the following chapters; however, now the purpose is to discuss some of the broader implications of the research revolution taking place today.

Although scientific investigation is not a new process for man, it is certainly a phenomenon which has been accelerated during the past half century, and even more spectacularly since the news of "Sputnik" splashed across world headlines in the late 1950's. An important consequence of the space age was the immediate and overwhelming emphasis placed on the physical and quantitative disciplines by scientists. In the process, physics, mathematics, and systems analysis were catapulted to the attention of both government and industry. A secondary outcome of this quantitative dominance was that less attention was given to the scientific study of human behavior. In a real sense, the "human relations movement" which began in the 1920's suffered from antithetical trends that placed emphasis on the study and rationalization of organizational systems, production systems, and other nonhuman aspects of industrial operations.

This emphasis toward operations research is why many of the topics discussed in this chapter mention both the implications and the importance of human relations. The practice of human relations involves understanding the realities of both the industrial society and the job environment. If a conscientious effort is to be made by management to integrate employees into the work situation and to provide certain economic, social, and psychological satisfactions for workers in the process, it is necessary that the picture of the work situation be accurate. A supervisor should realize that the pendulum of interest by management is often heavily weighted toward the nonhuman systems of operation. The fact that some management theorists and practitioners do not place emphasis on human relations in either their thinking or actions does not diminish its importance as long as their objective is to achieve results through the efforts of other human beings.

The major characteristics of modern industrialization are highly inter-related, and changes in one sector affect changes in the others. For this reason it is difficult to make many pertinent generalizations about the dynamic industrial society; however, certain trends begin to appear which are important from a human relations viewpoint. One of these trends is the increasing demand for educated personnel in nearly every type of industry. Some industries, such as the semiconductor industry, are heavily dependent on brainpower, if one thinks of brainpower as scientists, engineers, or other college-degree-holding specialists. In the aerospace industry of the scientists and engineers hired between 1935 and 1939, 70 per cent had no degrees and about 4 per cent had advanced degrees, but of those hired from 1960 to 1964, only 18 per cent had no degrees and over 19 per cent had advanced degrees, including 4 per cent having doctorates [16]. Even those industries that may not rely so heavily on technical skills are experiencing a massive upgrading of both the skills and the training required for jobs.

Another trend is the shift away from jobs directly involved in the productive process to other types of jobs. Job opportunities in so-called white-collar groups—those including supervisors, technicians, clerical workers, and marketing and professional people—have been growing much faster than have jobs in the blue-collar, production-worker groups. In 1957, a historic turning point was reached in the United States when the white-collar group became the largest single segment of the labor force, outnumbering the blue-collar workers for the first time. Indications are that this trend will be accelerated during the decades to come [17, pp. 108–9].

The impact of technology and research on the working lives of people is yet to be fully measured. Technology has relieved man of many burden-some tasks, contributed to increased productivity, and emphasized new and higher skills, and it has also brought other major changes to industry. Traditional concepts of organization structure and control have been affected by the swelling ranks of technicians and other administrative personnel. The use of computers has changed communication and in-formation systems in many organizations. The decision-making process in many firms has been altered through the use of electronic brains and new staff positions have been created. The end result has been the creation of new exciting and dynamic organizational environments.

The challenge for human relations, therefore, is to develop practices whereby the people who find themselves a part of an organization, large or small, can adapt rapidly to the environment and, at the same time, glean personal satisfaction from the work they do.

Not all jobs are exciting or permit adequate outlets for creative energy. The practice, therefore, of human relations must begin before an individual is actually placed on the job to insure the chances of his satisfactory adaptation to it. This inevitably means understanding something about the cultural and social environment from which the worker is selected, as well as the internal climate of the organization in which he will be expected to produce. There are individuals who, for their own reasons, value dull or routine work. If such a person is placed in a job with limited responsibilities, he may be satisfied and committed to his employer.

All routine jobs are not without demand for skills, education, or specialized training, but the number of low-skill-level jobs is gradually being reduced. Technology is creating more and more job opportunities that require high levels of education and mental activity. This should not be construed to mean that technology will eliminate dull or routine jobs. Thus, as long as dull jobs are a part of the industrial scene there is always the danger that managers will attempt to motivate workers by trying to sell routine jobs as being more creative than they actually are. All work is not personally fulfilling to the worker. Instead of telling employees that their jobs are meaningful, the supervisor's task should be directed toward helping his subordinates devise ways of minimizing the boring and repetitive aspects of their work and face up to the realities of the job as it exists. This goal implies that knowledge about the nature of the individual is a prerequisite for careful selection, motivation, and development of an employee. The manager or supervisor who is unaware of the human element in the productive process for which he is responsible is only operating at partial effectiveness, regardless of his technological knowledge. As long as a manager must obtain results through other people, he will ultimately have to rely on interpersonal relations with his subordinates, and if he fails in his human relations he may find he has failed in the management function.

SUMMARY

1. The practice of human relations is affected by the moral, economic, social, and political forces of the times. For this reason it is not surprising that the human relations principles of modern industry are different from what they were 150, or even 50 years ago.

2. The early medieval period saw the lot of workers improve only in small ways. The culture and technology was primarily geared to an agrarian society. As increased trade occurred, cities grew in size and importance. Urbanization was accompanied by a growing demand for skilled craftsmen. The guild system emerged in which young men were

given training through an extensive apprenticeship period. The latter stage of the medieval period, known as the Renaissance, was characterized by an exploration of both geographic and intellectual universes, during which increasing emphasis was placed on the importance and dignity of the individual. This attitude is frequently defined as humanism.

3. The industrial revolution brought about many changes in the use of technology and methods in production. The domestic system gave way to the factory system where workers went to work in a centralized location rather than in scattered small workshops. Hours were long, wages low, safety precautions few, and treatment of factory workers was not always humane. An important consequence of the excesses of many early industrialists was the violent reaction of some idealists. Karl Marx preached communism as a defense against capitalism. Labor unions emerged to protect mill workers against arbitrary management actions. Some reformers inspired by the desire to improve the working man's plight experimented with ways and means to cope with the human and social problems of industrialization.

4. Many of the actions and reactions of the workers and employers during the nineteenth century fostered lasting differences in perspective between the two groups. Many of these differences in attitudes have persevered and lie at the base of many management and worker practices today even though social and cultural situations have vastly improved.

5. Modern industry is characterized by the interdependency of many social institutions. Specialization of skills and knowledge has made necessary the cooperation of individuals engaged in pursuit of common goals and objectives. The interaction of industrial organizations with other institutions, such as labor unions, government, and community, has led to an increasing awareness of the responsibility each agency has to the others. This awareness is termed social consciousness, and many modern human relations practices are derived from and affected by the general social and human values affecting the cultural climate of the times.

6. Modern industrialization has been accompanied by certain characteristics that are not entirely analogous with current human values. The large size of some organizations often has led to the implementation of impersonal means of control. Technology also often has increased the degree of task specialization, thus contributing to the insulation of one group of specialists from another. Often automation has displaced workers or reduced the apparent importance of the contribution of the individual worker. All of these factors have created a new and different set of human problems that demand innovations and changes in traditional concepts and methods of leadership and manpower utilization. Human relations plays an important role in the development and implementation of new ways of viewing and dealing with the problems that arise in the

work environment. Human relations need not be contrary to production goals as many managers suspect; rather, human relations is aimed at utilizing the maximum capabilities of all the personnel engaged in the production process, thus affecting high production levels while bringing human values and material values into an equitable balance.

DISCUSSION QUESTIONS

1. How did the guild system change the lot of workers?
2. What impact did *humanism* have on the development of human relations?
3. How did the industrial revolution change the conditions of employment of workers?
4. What impact did Robert Owen have on the practice of human relations?
5. In what ways can the largeness of a firm lead to impersonal treatment of employees? Can this be overcome?
6. What is *paternalism?* Does it exist today in industry? In what ways, if any?
7. What human relations problems are posed by the use of automation in business and industry?
8. What implications do the major characteristics of modern industrialization have on the practice of human relations?

BIBLIOGRAPHY AND
SELECTED COLLATERAL READINGS

1. BURCK, GILBERT, and the Editors of *Fortune, The Computer Revolution.* New York: Harper & Row, 1965.
2. CLOUGH, SHEPARD B., *The Economic Development of Western Civilization.* New York: McGraw-Hill Book Company, 1959.
3. DAVIS, KEITH, and ROBERT L. BLOMSTROM, *Business and Its Environment.* New York: McGraw-Hill Book Company, 1966.
4. GELLERMAN, SAUL W., *The Management of Human Relations.* New York: Holt, Rinehart and Winston, Inc., 1966.
5. GINZBERG, E., and I. E. BERG, *Democratic Values and the Rights of Management.* New York: Columbia University Press, 1963.
6. HAIRE, M., and others, *Managerial Thinking: An International Study.* New York: John Wiley and Sons, 1966.
7. HEILBRONER, ROBERT L., *The Worldly Philosophers,* rev. ed. New York: Simon and Schuster, 1961.
8. HOLZMANN, ROBERT S., *Stormy Ben Butler.* New York: The Macmillan Company, 1954.

9. Honigmann, John J., *Understanding Culture*. New York: Harper & Row, 1963.

10. Kornhauser, A., *Mental Health of the Industrial Worker*. New York: John Wiley and Sons, 1965.

11. Litwack, Leon, *The American Labor Movement*. Englewood Cliffs, N.J.: Prentice-Hall, Inc., 1962.

12. Ogburn, W. F., *Social Change with Respect to Culture and Original Nature*. Gloucester, Mass.: Peter Smith, 1964.

13. Pelz, D. C., and F. M. Andrews, *Scientists in Organizations: Productive Climates for Research and Development*. New York: John Wiley and Sons, 1968.

14. *Report of The National Advisory Commission on Civil Disorders*. Washington, D.C.: U.S. Government Printing Office, Superintendent of Documents, March 1, 1968.

15. Selekman, Benjamin M., *Labor Relations and Human Relations*. New York: McGraw-Hill Book Company, Inc., 1947.

16. Shapero, Albert, and others, *The Structure and Dynamics of the Defense R & D Industry*. Menlo Park, Calif.: Stanford Research Institute, 1965.

17. Silk, Leonard S., *The Research Revolution*. New York: McGraw-Hill Book Company, 1960.

18. Synder, John I., "Automation and Unemployment: Management's Quiet Crisis," *Management Review*, LII, No. 11 (November, 1963), 4–18.

19. Somers, Gerald G., and others, *Adjusting to Technological Change*. New York: Harper & Row, 1963.

20. Stagner, Ross, and H. Rosen, *Psychology of Union-Management Relations*. Belmont, Calif.: Wadsworth Publishing Co., 1965.

21. Veblen, Thorstein, *The Instinct of Workmanship*. New York: W. W. Norton, 1964.

22. Vroom, Victor H., *Work and Motivation*. New York: John Wiley and Sons, 1964.

Human Relations and the Social Sciences

The development of human relations as a discipline has depended to a large extent upon the research and findings of both the social sciences and, most particularly, the behavioral sciences. The term *social science* usually is understood to refer to six disciplines: economics, history, political science, anthropology, psychology, and sociology. The behavioral sciences, more specifically, refer to the latter three or four disciplines.

In addition to the social sciences, other disciplines have contributed to the study of human relations. Philosophy, statistics, law, and organizational theory have had their effect on the development and application of human relations. Branches of the behavioral sciences have crossed disciplinary lines and combined to form such sciences as social-psychology, political-economics, and industrial-psychology. In short, the social sciences, particularly the behavioral sciences, are concerned with the scientific research that deals directly with human behavior.

Because one of the characteristics of modern industrialization is the application of science to business problems, it is extremely useful to be familiar with the scientific method of investigation and how this method has been applied to the human and social problems of the work place. It is wise, also, to know what criteria can be used to measure the validity of inquiry into human problems in addition to the limitations and dangers that science encounters in seeking solutions to such problems.

Although there is a long history of thought and study about man in philosophy, literature, history, political theory, religion, law, and medicine, it was not until late in the nineteenth century that empirical, experimental, and systematic investigation of human behavior really began.

Despite the growth and expansion of the behavioral sciences in recent years there still remain gaps in the knowledge about human behavior, and the dynamic nature of the behavioral sciences has made them subject both to skepticism and rejection by some critics outside of the field and to dissatisfaction and concern from some within. However, the growing body of knowledge about human behavior has contributed significantly to off-setting the impressionistic and unfounded beliefs that have guided many practices of management in the past.

THE SCIENTIFIC METHOD

The scientific method of problem-solving and investigation of human behavior has drawn heavily from the procedures long utilized by the physical scientists. Generally, the scientific method, as opposed to non-scientific or subjective methods, is marked by three distinct characteristics.

First, the scientific method uses precise and accurate measuring devices. Second, scientific investigation is objective; that is, there is no bias or preconceived answer in mind before the investigation takes place. Finally, the extent to which the scientist conducts his research is exhaustive, controlled, systematic, and continuing. When any of these characteristics is absent, the validity of the research findings is significantly impaired.

It should be obvious that where human behavior is the subject of scientific research a number of difficulties arise. People are not chemical elements which remain stable and unchanged by time or manipulation. Thus, the behavioral scientist is at a greater disadvantage than his fellow physical scientist because it is difficult to conduct experiments with people which enable the action and reaction of the subjects to be accurately controlled and measured. For the most part, the behavioral scientist must investigate people as he finds them and must abide by the ethical and moral considerations involved when experimenting with human beings.

Another difficulty confronting the behavioral scientist has to do with the accuracy of the measuring devices he employs in his investigation. Where attitudes, motives, and reasons for human behavior are the subject of study, the methods of collecting data for interpretation are largely dependent upon (1) methods and techniques of inquiry, such as surveys, direct observation, and case studies; (2) methods of interviewing, such as depth or structured interviews; or (3) other methods, such as tests and questionnaires. Few of these methods are recognized as being as accurate as the laboratory devices which can be employed by the physical scientist.

A factor that adds to the complexity of research about human beings is that being highly complex the subjects studied can change behavior as a result of investigation; that is, a person's opinions, attitudes, or reactions are likely to be altered or become biased when subjected to either the questions or the observation of the social scientist.

Added to the difficulties already mentioned is the fact that the behavioral scientists themselves are human. Thus, they cannot, in the same sense as the physical scientists, place themselves as impartial observers outside of society and get a view of the social processes as a connected whole. Their interests, values, and ends lie *within* that connected whole [20, pp. 53–54]. They are subject to human errors in judgment or subjectivity. Because of the awareness of these and other problems, the behavioral scientists have given a great deal of attention to the methods of inquiry appropriate to the field [2].

Normally, the steps taken in the scientific study of human behavior can be classified in the following categories:

1. *Definition of the Problem.* This begins with being aware that a problem exists and may include both a statement of a hypothesis and a statement of the limitation or scope of the study.

2. *Collection of Data.* This step includes determining the research design appropriate to the problem being stated. The collection of data may involve conducting an experiment, surveying individuals through written questionnaires or personal interviews, or simply observing and recording the behavior of individuals in a given set of circumstances. For practical purposes, the researcher must decide which method or combination of methods will render the most valid information. Often limitations on the amount of time and money available to the researcher prohibit his using as many methods as he might like, or other restrictions may limit the number of persons (the size of the sample) from which he may gather information.

3. *Analysis of Data.* This phase of the research involves the breaking down and comparison of the information that has been collected in order to discover the relationships, similarities, gaps, or conflicting elements in the information gathered.

4. *Interpretation of Data.* This step involves the synthesis or bringing together of the information at hand so as either to develop a tentative solution or test the hypothesis.

5. *Draw Conclusions.* In order to be valid the conclusions must be based only on the *findings* of the research. In this step, as in the analysis and interpretation of data, it is important that the conclusions and generalizations drawn by the researcher be free from his own bias or perceptions.

There are dangers in the use of the scientific method: Gaps in information may go undetected, incorrect data may be used or mistakes in judgment may be made during the analysis and interpretation of data. However, no method of investigation known to man can entirely eliminate human uncertainty. The scientific method, more than any other procedure, minimizes the elements of uncertainty which can result from lack of data.

Even though the social and behavioral scientists have taken great care in the collection and interpretation of their research, it appears as if the practitioners in business who draw upon their findings distort, misuse, or overgeneralize the information from the research available to them. James V. Clark, a behavioral scientist himself, has compiled a number of distortions practitioners make in the findings of social science research. Examples of such distortions appear in Table 3–1.

During the recent decade there has been an increasing trend for management and social scientists to work more closely in the amelioration of the work environment. But in light of the many human and organizational problems that remain to be resolved, one might ask why so many distortions occur when practitioners (managers) interpret the findings of social scientists; and why haven't managers themselves applied more vigorously the scientific method when seeking solutions to human problems which confront them. There is no single answer to these questions. However, several factors are recognized as being major contributors to misunderstandings about human behavior or to the rejection of known facts by certain individuals. First, much of the research is conducted by highly trained and educated people who write their findings in a language that is often too technical for the laymen who are the ones who have to put it into practice. Second, because many times the people who do the research do not have to implement the conclusions they draw or the recommendations they make, much of what they reveal in their writing appears vague or too theoretical to the practitioner.

A major reason why the application of the scientific method of collecting information regarding human behavior has had limited application in the work place is that often many motives behind employee behavior are hidden from the obvious view of the supervisor. The supervisor, being untrained in the behavioral sciences, cannot detect the underlying reason for the employee's action and, therefore, he may write off any nonconforming worker as being a troublemaker to be watched closely. Even in cases where a supervisor is knowledgeable in the behavioral sciences, he seldom has the time to delve far beneath the surface of the worker's actions to discover the causes of his behavior. In most cases, the supervisor can only observe the actions of his subordinates and evaluate them in terms of whether or not they contribute to the objective or goals he is responsible for reaching. He cannot always tell whether the workers are gleaning personal satisfaction from their activity.

Another reason why many people either minimize or ignore the behavioral scientists' findings in the practice of human relations is that each person evaluates his effectiveness or success with others based on a set of

TABLE 3–1. Misinterpretations of Behavioral Science Research

Statements Based on Research of Behavioral Scientists	Distortions Made by Nonscientists
1. Knowledge exists about organizational behavior.	If you know enough, you can solve any organization problem.
2. There are nonlogical aspects to people's behavior.	People's behavior is not logical.
3. Group pressure is an important determinant of an individual's behavior.	One's behavior is determined by his membership in social groups.
4. People have many aspirations; they seek membership and acceptance, self-esteem, security, prestige, etc.	Wages—even incentive pay—is not of much importance any more.
5. Informal organizational groups exert much influence on their members; consequently a manager's control is somewhat limited.	A manager cannot really be a leader because of informal groups.
6. It is helpful if a manager understands the reason for conflict between groups.	A manager should get along with everybody and not have conflicts.
7. Shared goals are important for collaboration between groups.	All group members should think alike so they can work together cooperatively.
8. A leader should be able to respond flexibly to different situations.	Consistency of values is neither desirable nor useful.
9. It is important for a leader to pay attention to the internal processes of his group.	If a leader pays attention to human relations, he does not need to know anything else.
10. Some methods in psychotherapy have relevance to a leader's skill in communications.	A leader practically has to be a psychiatrist in order to communicate effectively.
11. A leader should know his own limits.	Leaders should put others ahead of themselves.
12. Leaders should be able to accept feelings of inadequacy.	A leader should be introspective at all times.

Adapted from James V. Clark, "Distortions of Behavioral Science," *California Management Review*, Winter, 1963.

values that have been established over a long period of time. During that time any personal methods or techniques relating to interpersonal relationships that have proven satisfactory or rewarding have been adopted and used again and again until they have become a part of his personality. Once such practices have been internalized by a person, they are not easily abandoned, regardless of how unsound they may be from a behavioral scientist's viewpoint.

Thus, the social sciences must play a vital role in uncovering the basis for human behavior, minimizing much of the impressionism and subjectivity that has been used by many supervisors and managers in establishing human relations practices. Admittedly, there often has been a time lag between the findings of the researchers and the acceptance and implementation of such findings by the practitioners in the industrial community; however, as communications between the two groups improve the time gap will shorten and, hopefully, the distortions will be minimized.

TAYLOR AND SCIENTIFIC MANAGEMENT

Before the social scientists really turned their attention to problems of the job environment, a number of individuals were concerned with the problem of increasing production and efficiency in our factories and mills. Ultimately, the investigation of machines, methods, and processes led to the individuals who operated the machines and equipment. The beginning of a change in emphasis in management thinking came with the investigations conducted by Frederick W. Taylor.

Except for a few efforts made by factory owners and managers, the hundred years preceding the twentieth century was devoted to the invention and refinement of the machines that produced goods. Until the turn of the century economic conditions for workers had been close to subsistence, and employers afforded little time or effort to the priority of human relations. Human interests had been subordinate to material interests. Then management discovered the people who operated the machines. Concern with the discovery of principles bearing on the conduct of business enterprise began during the final decades of the nineteenth century. The management of men, money, materials, and machines had been rather loosely conducted in many respects. However, a group of Americans began an intensive investigation of methods and techniques that would improve the process of management. Henry Gantt, Carl Barth, Harrington Emerson, Frank and Lillian Gilbreth (the parents in the novel *Cheaper by the Dozen*), and Frederick W. Taylor are credited with laying the foundation of a movement generally referred to as *scientific management*.

Taylor, an industrial engineer, was trained in the basic physical sciences and was used to applying the mental tools of a scientist to problems of all kinds. He was the first to apply scientific methods to the problems of the manager and, thus, is credited as being "the father of scientific management." His time-and-motion studies led to a number of techniques directed at more efficient operations. Functional foremanship, standardized tools, differential piece-rates, job training for workers, and cost controls were among the major innovations he believed improved operations. Taylor believed, basically, in the economic man theory propagated by Adam Smith; that is, that each individual is most interested in and directed by his own economic well-being. This theory minimizes the social and psychological drives of man. Taylor departed from the beliefs of Adam Smith when it came to the role of management. Smith believed that the market forces which controlled the external activities of the firm also operated inside the organization. Where Smith saw little importance in the role of the manager, Taylor believed he was very important in obtaining labor productivity. In order to illustrate how Taylor combined this theory with those principles which he believed would improve production methods, several experiments were conducted involving workers and work methods.

Two of the most publicized experiments conducted by Taylor occurred while he worked for Midvale Steel Company. In the first experiment, Taylor observed that each worker in a yard crew used his own shovel even though they sometimes shoveled ashes, sometimes iron ore, and other times coal. This meant that the weight lifted per shovel load varied, depending on the particular material being moved. By experimenting, Taylor found that the most material was moved in a given period when the payload of the shovel was about 21.5 pounds. He had the company buy an assortment of shovels so that the most appropriate size and shaped shovel could be used for the material being moved. In each case he made sure that the larger shovels used for ashes carried about 21.5 pounds and that the smaller ones used for iron ore did the same. The immediate outcome of this simple change was increased output per worker.

The second experiment involved the workers who handled pig iron ingots in the same steel mill. After observing the workers, he became convinced that output could be increased by improved handling methods. He believed the handlers were making the wrong movements, working too hard and too long, and resting too frequently. Taylor offered one of the workers a bonus if he would cooperate by following his directions on handling the pig iron and taking rest breaks. After following Taylor's directions the worker was able to increase his average daily movement of pig iron from 12.5 tons to 47 tons, an increase of nearly 300 per cent. At the same time, the pig iron carrier who participated in the experiment earned about 60 per cent more pay. The result was lower labor cost per ton carried even though the carrier earned more money per day.

In essence, Taylor denied the effectiveness of the division of labor *unaided* by management. He found that workers were inclined to restrict, not increase, output when left to their own devices. In other words, the workers were not as productive alone as they could have been. Productivity really rested with the manager who determined how work should be done, assigned qualified workers, and motivated them. Taylor's methods of motivating employees could be challenged by later research conducted by the human relations school because he paid little attention to the social aspects of work groups. An example of how Taylor solved production problems can be sighted in the case where the job of a large group of women was to inspect ball bearings at a bicycle wheel factory. The girls were paid by the day, worked more than ten hours a day, five days a week, and worked half a day on Saturday. Time studies made by Taylor indicated that the girls were working at a leisurely pace. Taylor instigated a change in procedures. The workers were placed farther apart so they could not talk with each other, hours of work were reduced to eight and one half hours per day, several rest periods were given, and a differential piece rate was paid.

The changes brought about by Taylor resulted in higher earnings for the workers, shorter working hours per week, and a reduction in the number of inspectors necessary because of improved workmanship. Taylor concluded from this that management must take the initiative in determining the best way to do work and then must induce employees to perform in the prescribed manner.

Taylor's methods for improving productivity had several distinguishing features (which shall be compared later in the chapter with the research of Elton Mayo in the Hawthorne Studies). First, Taylor believed in using the scientific method to discover the best method for performing work and establishing physical conditions. Second, providing the proper conditions, tools, and methods should be accompanied by employee training. Finally, financial incentives for the individual worker could induce him to perform at his highest level of efficiency. Before continuing the discussion of later developments in human relations, it might be beneficial to view the attitude of the workers in regard to scientific management as conceived by Taylor and his colleagues.

At the same time that Taylor and his associates were developing and testing their theories of management, organized labor was gaining a foothold in the American industrial scene. The general attitude of labor was that scientific management was just another tool of management to "speed up" the workers. This, plus the fact that scientific methods sometimes reduced the number of workers necessary to perform certain jobs, led to a general resistance to Taylor's methods. Taylor's views did not openly oppose unions; however, he did not see the necessity of unions if his procedures were followed. The initial rejection of scientific methods was largely overcome by the 1920's, as many unions came to realize that there was little reason for hostility to scientific management as long as unions had a voice in the conditions of employment for their members [9]. However, the union's position, even today, is one which openly questions the application of work rules or procedures that endanger the job security of its members, regardless of whether or not such rules are derived through scientific methods.

ELTON MAYO AND THE
HAWTHORNE STUDIES

The research work done at the turn of the twentieth century concentrated on the workers as individuals. This development grew, in part, out of the classical concept of the economic man. The incentives and job methods that had been developed to utilize the workers effectively failed to recognize the social organization within which the workers operated. The research conducted by Elton Mayo, F. J. Roethlisberger, and William Dickson at the Western Electric Company Hawthorne Works, in Chicago, during the late 1920's, brought to light the importance of the informal organization of the work group.

Mayo and his colleagues had tried to find the relationships between the lighting of the work area and the productivity of workers who assembled telephone equipment. An experimental room and a control room were set up. Changes were made in the degree of illumination in the experimental room. When lighting was increased, production rose. When it was decreased, production also increased. Production even increased in the control room when the lighting was held constant. No correlation could be established between lighting and worker productivity. More extensive research followed involving working conditions, length of the working day, number and length of rest periods, and other nonhuman factors of environment. In each case where some factor of working condition was adjusted, output rose. The experimenters then returned the workers to their poorly lighted work benches for a long working day without rest periods and other amenities. The results of this switch astonished the researchers. Output rose to a higher level than it had been under the best of the experimental conditions. The changes in production were not necessarily related to improvements in physical conditions and methods.

The researchers were unable to explain the changes in productivity and were forced to look for factors other than those which had been deliberately manipulated in the experiment. In order to uncover the hidden factors, a long series of interviews was conducted with each of the workers that had been involved in the experiment. It had been evident that employee morale was high during the experiment. The interviews revealed several reasons for the high morale and the motivation to work hard and well. First, the workers felt special because they were singled out to participate in the experiment. They believed that this showed management thought them to be important. Second, the workers developed satisfying relationships with each other and their supervisors because they were given considerable freedom to work at their own pace and to divide work in a manner most suitable to them. Third, the social contact and pleasant relations among the workers made the work more agreeable and enjoyable.

Even though the workers could not always describe what was influencing their attitude, informal groups had been formed, teamwork was practiced, and they sensed a feeling of recognition, participation, and increased self-regard. All were beneficial in raising morale and bringing about increased productivity. A new hypothesis was formulated by Mayo and his fellow researchers as a result of this primary research. The hypothesis was that motivation to work, productivity, and quality of work all are related to the nature of the social relations both among the workers and between the workers and their supervisor.

The early experiments at Hawthorne involved women workers. In order to investigate more systematically the behavior of groups, another experiment was set up involving workmen representing three occupational groups. This experiment became known as the "Bank Wiring Observation Room." The experimental group consisted of fourteen men; some wired banks of equipment (wiremen), others then soldered the wires in place (soldermen), and, finally, two men examined the work before labeling the equipment "finished" (inspectors).

The men worked on a group piecework basis so that the more they turned out, the more they earned. In such a situation one might expect the faster workers to exert pressure on the slower workers to increase their speed and efficiency. But this was not the case. A number of group norms operated within the group and, in order to be accepted as a member of the group, a man had to act in accordance with them.

The norms operating within the group were (1) you should not turn out too much work—if you do, you are a rate buster; (2) you should not turn out too little work—if you do, you are a chiseler; (3) you should not say anything to a supervisor that would get a fellow worker into trouble—if you do, you are a squealer; and (4) you should not act too officious—that is, if you are a boss you should not act like one. In addition to the norms mentioned, the members of the group belonged to cliques within the total group. Each clique indulged in its own special games and habits, and there was a good deal of competition and ribbing among the members of each clique. The importance of this aspect of informal group organization was that output rates for each individual were more closely associated with the social membership in the cliques than with other factors, such as dexterity or intelligence.

The Hawthorne Studies as a whole made clear the importance of the social factor. The degree to which work was performed depended not on the individual alone, but on the network of social relationships within which he operated. The Hawthorne Studies became the basis for much research, and emphasis on informal organization and a change in management's viewpoint about workers' motivation resulted. The concept of team spirit had finally made inroads into industrial thinking, and a new school of management known as human relations was officially formulated.

COMPARISON OF TAYLOR AND MAYO

The research findings of Elton Mayo and his associates at Hawthorne were in some cases diametrically opposed to some of the principles established by Frederick Taylor. There were, however, some noteworthy similarities. Both were concerned with methods of increasing productivity. Their attention was directed toward the worker and his immediate supervisor, and both found the manager's role to be important.

The differences between the two may lie, in part, in the difference of approach the two men used in attempting to increase productivity. Taylor preferred to work with the individual worker, and he offered higher wages as an inducement to use the best work methods. Mayo, working with more than one worker, concluded that membership in a group must be provided for the worker and that the worker should be allowed to communicate with his fellow workers.

Taylor found that physical conditions, tools, and work methods could be improved to increase productivity. Mayo found that changes in physical conditions and methods did not correlate with production changes. Taylor tried to minimize the informal social contacts at work because he believed they interfered with production. In order to accomplish this, he attempted to control social contacts of the worker by isolating his work station. Taylor sought to improve a formal organizational arrangement for the benefit of management rather than for the social needs of the workers.

Mayo attempted to control informal contacts on the job so that they could be channeled to increase production, and he recommended the use of informal organization of workers. He saw that division of labor could have adverse psychological effects on workers. He found that it was not so much the repetitiveness of industrial jobs, but rather the social isolation fostered by division of labor that caused the greater loss of efficiency and output. He believed that management had a responsibility for aiding the worker to achieve social satisfaction at work. If management did this, then productivity would be increased [5, p. 43]. However, the relationship between social satisfaction at work and productivity has not always turned out to be a positive one; therefore, to equate higher production with higher employee morale without qualification is an error.

Beginning with Taylor's concept of functional management, the concern of management with the proper selection, placement, and training of personnel got under way. Prior to Taylor, the foreman or supervisor of a work crew had been responsible for the hiring, firing, discipline, and other personnel matters in his department. Some managers already believed that the foreman's job was too big for a single individual to handle. It was not unnatural, therefore, that the "jack of all trades" concept of management was altered by Taylor's ideas of management specialization. As a result, the responsibility for handling the manpower of a firm grew into a specialty known as employment management, which subsequently became known as personnel management.

THE NEW ERA OF HUMAN RELATIONS

Taylor published his major work called *The Principles of Scientific Management* in 1911. The interest in human relations that followed was accelerated by World War I. A number of professional organizations emerged, and the first Silver Bay Conference on Human Relations in Industry was held in New York. An increasing number of books and articles reflected the new concern of management for the workers as individuals. Oliver Sheldon pointed out in his book *The Philosophy of Management,* published in 1923, that industry could not be rendered efficient as long as the basic fact that it was primarily human remained unrecognized. He stated that industry was not a mass of machines and technical processes. It was a body of men [14, pp. 27–30].

The Hawthorne Studies produced Elton Mayo as the "Father of Employee Human Relations." He and his associates at Harvard University gave academic weight to human relations by offering a course in it in 1936. At the same time, the depression of the 1930's emphasized the importance of the need for industry to assume certain social responsibilities for the people who operated the machines. Social responsibility required that management become more aware of the needs and aspirations of the workers and provide emotional as well as economic securities.

The concept of modern human relations grew from the realization by management that humane treatment of employees, increased safety and health precautions, rest periods, and security benefits did not disrupt production. Human relations, when properly practiced, was not inconsistent with high production and efficiency. The impact of World War II, with its immediate demand for high production and its labor shortage, brought home to many firms the benefits to be obtained from human relations. It is interesting to note that while Taylor himself was no human relationist, his recognition of the fact that human variability in performance could be the basis for developing better methods opened the way for the social scientists who followed him. The capacity of the social scientists to observe objectively and measure both human and organizational variables makes possible the development of sound principles that can guide management in overcoming the problem of building the most productive and satisfying form of human organization.

Since World War II much research has been conducted by the social scientists regarding some specific aspects of human relations. Measurement and identification of many aspects of work which employees find satisfying or discouraging has been intensively pursued by industrial psychologists and sociologists. Effective methods of supervision have been developed through the careful and extensive research conducted by the staff of the Institute for Social Research at the University of Michigan and by other teams of researchers who have actively conducted their studies in the actual work environment of many large organizations. For example, in the early 1950's the contribution of good supervisory leadership to production was examined (in a major life insurance company) by Daniel Katz, Nathan Maccoby, and Nancy Morse of the University of Michigan. In this study twelve work sections with high productivity and twelve with low productivity were selected for investigation. The behavior of supervisors in these two sets of work sections was assessed through interviews with both supervisors and their subordinates. The results indicated a substantial difference in the amount of consideration the low- and high-productivity supervisors showed their subordinates. Supervisors of highly productive work groups were typically characterized as *employee-centered,* for they tended to describe as most important the human relations aspects of their jobs. On the other hand, the supervisors of low-productivity work groups were generally characterized as *production-centered,* for they tended to consider their subordinates primarily as "people to get the work done" [8].

A second study by Katz, Maccoby, Gerald Gurin, and L. G. Floor conducted among railroad maintenance-of-way workers generally corroborated their earlier findings. Despite differences in the nature of the work and the structure of the work group, supervisors in the most productive groups were more frequently described as taking a personal interest in their subordinates, being helpful in training subordinates for better jobs, and being less punitive than supervisors of low-productivity groups [9].

The post-World War II University of Michigan studies and subsequent research on leadership thrust the role of supervision into the mainstream of human relations. As a result, styles of leadership and their impact on production and group cohesiveness have become a central theme for the practice of human relations.

The decade of the 1960's has seen researchers and theorists place increasing emphasis on the impact of group processes on decision-making and supervisory methods. Leading proponents of the use of group process methods are emphatic that such an approach to leadership should not be confused with the use of committees that never reach decisions and that, thereby, allow supervisors to make excuses for inaction because the group could not agree on what should be done. Rensis Likert states that the group method of supervision holds the group leader (supervisor) fully responsible both for the quality of all decisions and for their implementation. The supervisor is responsible for building his subordinates into a cohesive group that makes the best decisions and carries them out well. Therefore, the superior is accountable for all decisions, for their execution, and for the results [10, p. 51].

During the latter years of the 1950's and continuing through the present, communications methods and theory have been explored and new organizational theory has emerged from the social scientists' investigations. Group processes and organizational effectiveness have been critically analyzed, and methods have been developed for integrating the individual into an organizational environment where he can produce at maximum levels while satisfying his own needs. The effect of this massive research effort, which in some degree has been overshadowed by the thrust of the space race, has been the increasing acceptance by management of some of the theories put forth by such men as McGregor, Likert, and Leavitt, who have usurped some traditional management concepts. These theories regarding the efficient utilization of men within an organizational context are the basis of material discussed later in this textbook. In some cases the ideas put forth follow closely what common sense would seem to dictate; in others, old concepts are met with opposing views and opinions. The result has been that the present state of human relations has been the outcome of a long trend toward democratic processes and scientific research which have brought human values more into balance with material values. The development of human relations is not yet complete. As technology advances, as industrial concerns become more complex and widespread, and as the behavioral sciences uncover more valid information about human behavior, the role and importance of human relations should become more prevalent in management practices. Now one of the most difficult problems is to get into practice what is already known. This task will require monumental effort on the part of theorists, educators, management, and rank-and-file employees.

SUMMARY

1. A major characteristic of modern industry is the application of science and research to problems of production, distribution, and manpower utilization. The scientific method has been and will continue to be an important element in the development of human relations, if subjective or impressionistic management methods are to be improved.

2. The scientific method of investigation is characterized by precise and accurate measuring devices, objectivity in the collection and analysis of

data, and exhaustive and systematic study of materials gained through research. When any of these characteristics is absent, the validity of the research is significantly reduced. However, where human behavior is the object of study, a number of problems arise because people are neither stable nor unchanged by time or manipulation.

3. Social scientists recognize the difficulty of accurately depicting human motives and behavior and, therefore, usually carefully define the limits of the conclusions which can be drawn from their investigation. Despite the care taken by the social scientists, often their findings are either rejected by managers or distorted in such a way as to belie the findings of the scientists.

4. Frederick W. Taylor and a group of his associates were among the first theorists to apply the scientific method of investigation to the job environment. Taylor's work laid the groundwork for a movement to improve management methods not only through careful selection and training of workers, but also through the development of the most efficient methods of performing job tasks. Taylor's experiments were widely read by management and led to the recognition of workers as a vital element in the production process. Although not a human relations expert himself, Taylor opened the door for later investigation which led to the development of human relations.

5. Following the era of scientific management launched by Taylor, a study of the effects of lighting on productivity at Western Electric's plant at Hawthorne was conducted by Elton Mayo and his associates. The early results of this investigation led to an extensive study which became known as the Hawthorne Studies. The findings of the Hawthorne Studies pointed to the importance of the social environment of the work place and the existence of an informal social structure which normally was beyond the absolute control of the organization. The Hawthorne Studies established the importance of the social environment of the work place and opened the way for further investigation of the industrial setting by social scientists. Elton Mayo became the father of employee human relations.

6. Frederick Taylor and Elton Mayo approached the problems of increasing worker productivity in different ways. Scientific management was primarily an effort of carefully determining the most efficient methods of performing the job, then making sure that proper tools, training, and worker incentives were provided by management for the worker in order to reach optimum production level. Elton Mayo delved into the human and social factors of the work environment in order to determine how the informal group structure could be incorporated to raise production through teamwork and mutually acceptable norms of performance by members of the group.

7. The University of Michigan Studies conducted after World War II

placed leadership and supervisory styles in the mainstream of human relations. The modern era of human relations has developed as research findings of the social scientists have shed more light on the nature of group processes and human motives. Enlightened management practices have grown as the realization has grown that safety programs, security benefits, and humane employee treatment were not inconsistent with the objectives of high production levels and efficient operations. The development of human relations is not yet complete, but the trend toward democratic methods and increasing awareness of scientific research are of major importance in bringing into balance the human values and material values which necessarily must meet in the process of production.

DISCUSSION QUESTIONS

1. In what ways is the scientific method of problem solving different from using subjective judgment?
2. What are the five steps in the scientific method?
3. Why is it so difficult to apply the scientific method to the solution of human problems?
4. What changes in the treatment of workers were a result of the experiments of Frederick Taylor? Was Frederick Taylor the father of human relations?
5. In what ways did the research findings in the Hawthorne Studies differ from the principles established during the early era of scientific management?
6. What norms of group behavior were developed by the men in the Bank Wiring Observation Room? Do any or all of these norms exist in work groups today?
7. What was the impact on human relations as a result of the University of Michigan Studies?

BIBLIOGRAPHY AND SELECTED COLLATERAL READINGS

1. ARGYRIS, CHRIS, and others, *Social Science Approaches to Business Behavior*. Homewood, Ill.: The Dorsey Press, Inc., and Richard D. Irwin, Inc., 1962.
2. BERELSON, BERNARD, *Human Behavior: An Inventory of Scientific Findings*, shorter ed. New York: Harcourt, Brace and World, Inc., 1967.
3. BROWN, J. A. C., *The Social Psychology of Industry*. Baltimore: Penguin Books, Inc., 1954.

4. CLARK, JAMES V., "Distortions of Behavioral Science," *California Management Review* (Winter, 1963), pp. 55–60.

5. DAIUTE, ROBERT JAMES, *Scientific Management and Human Relations.* New York: Holt, Rinehart and Winston, 1964.

6. DICKSON, W. J., and F. J. ROETHLISBERGER, *Counseling in an Organization: A Sequel to the Hawthorne Researches.* Boston: Harvard Business School, 1966.

7. HYMAN, R., *The Nature of Psychological Inquiry.* Englewood Cliffs, N.J.: Prentice-Hall, Inc., 1964.

8. KATZ, DANIEL, and others, *Productivity, Supervision and Morale in an Office Situation.* Ann Arbor, Mich.: University of Michigan, Institute for Social Research, 1950.

9. KATZ, DANIEL, and others, *Productivity, Supervision and Morale Among Railroad Workers.* Ann Arbor, Mich.: University of Michigan, Institute for Social Research, 1951.

10. LIKERT, RENSIS, *The Human Organization.* New York: McGraw-Hill Book Company, 1967.

11. LIKERT, RENSIS, *New Patterns of Management.* New York: McGraw-Hill Book Company, 1961.

12. NADWORTHY, MILTON J., *Scientific Management and the Unions, 1900–1932.* Cambridge, Mass.: Harvard University Press, 1955.

13. ROETHLISBERGER, FRITZ J., and W. J. DICKSON, *Management and the Worker.* Cambridge, Mass.: Harvard University Press, 1939.

14. SHELDON, OLIVER, *The Philosophy of Management.* Englewood Cliffs, N.J.: Prentice-Hall, Inc., 1923.

15. SIEGEL, LAURENCE, *Industrial Psychology.* Homewood, Ill.: Richard D. Irwin, Inc., 1962.

16. TANNENBAUM, A. S., *Control in Organizations.* New York: McGraw-Hill Book Company, 1968.

17. TANNENBAUM, ROBERT, and others, *Leadership and Organization: A Behavioral Science Approach.* New York: McGraw-Hill Book Company, 1961.

18. TAYLOR, FREDERICK W., *Scientific Management.* New York: Harper & Row, Publishers, 1947.

19. TIFFIN, JOSEPH, and ERNEST J. McCORMICK, *Industrial Psychology,* 5th ed. Englewood Cliffs, N.J.: Prentice-Hall, Inc., 1965.

20. WILSON, GEE (ed.), "Economics," by Allyn A. Young. *Research in the Social Sciences.* New York: The Macmillan Company, 1929.

Human Needs
and Behavior

In previous chapters the discussion included a review of some of the problems, men, and forces that have helped shape human relations into a modern tool of management. Although, as has been stated, human relations is not the study of human behavior for its own sake, this does not preclude acquiring a familiarity with certain general principles of psychology so that one's actions can be more effectively directed.

Usually, the work situation is a social one; that is, one in which people work together in a group. The nature and extent of the social contacts made on the job will vary with the particular occupations or positions involved. A salesman may deal primarily with customers; production-line or office workers may have little or no contact with customers, but will experience the continuous relations between the members of the work group and the superiors.

No matter how large an organization may be, inevitably a person will find himself working in a relatively small group. Groups are made up of individuals, each with a unique personality. In the course of group dynamics each individual is affected by the norms of behavior sanctioned by the others, as was illustrated by the Bank Wiring Observation Room in the Hawthorne Studies. In turn, each individual either has an effect on the group or, at least, has the potential to affect the course of group action. Because of this phenomenon, one must not forget that each group member is an individual with a personality that in as unique as his physical appearance. This is true whether the social contacts made in a group remain constant or frequently change.

Each person tends to observe the actions of others and to evaluate these actions so that he can more appropriately make his own behavior meet the situation. Students try to "psych out" the teacher; workers do the same with supervisors, and vice versa. The problem with the process of playing amateur psychologist is that the interpretations people make regarding human behavior are frequently colored by their personal philosophies or bias. For example, here are a few generalizations that people make in respect to human nature: People are basically good— people are basically bad; people are lazy—people are energetic; people are responsible—people are irresponsible; give a person an inch and he will take a mile—treat a person nicely and he will treat others nicely. The purpose of human relations is not to verify which statements are true or which are false; it is, rather, to develop a reliable guide for determining what individual behavior is appropriate in a work situation. There are no quick and simple means of diagnosing and understanding the actions of human beings. Anyone who studies human nature can verify that people are too complex to be superficially categorized.

Increasingly, scientists are beginning to realize that thinking that the rational, logical approach of science is the only approach to understanding people can inhibit the study of the nonrational, the illogical, and the value aspects of human behavior [4, pp. 201–4].

This realization should act as a reminder that the known elements of human behavior thus far understood may be only a small portion of what is yet to be learned. Furthermore, it should be remembered that a course in human relations is adjunct to the study of the behavioral sciences and not a substitute for such study.

A WORKING CONCEPT OF HUMAN BEHAVIOR AND MOTIVATION

If people are so diverse, are there any assumptions about human nature which can be used in explaining human behavior? If so, what are they? The answers to such questions will vary, depending on who answers— for example, "people are creatures of habit"; "people seek variety in life"; "people are selfish"; "people seek security"; "people do only what they have to do"; "people are the product of heredity"; "people are molded by their environment." These generalizations, like the ones mentioned earlier, seem to contradict each other in some ways. Yet if they are organized and analyzed, a pattern of ideas begins to appear. First, there is the idea that behavior is caused, just as the behavior of objects in the physical world is caused by forces which act upon them. *Causality* is implicit in the beliefs that heredity and environment affect behavior, and that a stimulus from the outside influences what occurs inside a person. The second idea is that behavior is directed or goal oriented rather than random and illogical. In other words, a person acts in a way that makes sense to him, even though others do not understand why he behaves the way he does. The third concept is that motivation* or "push" underlies human behavior [2, p. 8].

The theory of cause, directedness, and motivation leaves room for certain controversy in regard to such concepts as *habitual* or *insane* behavior; however, the theory provides a working concept which can be useful in understanding the actions of people. How the three concepts operate in a behavior pattern can be illustrated in the case of a man who has not eaten for a long period. The man's empty stomach creates a feeling of tension or discomfort which stimulates impulses, interpreted as "feeling hungry." The hunger pangs cause the man to seek food and, finding it, he eats. The food enters his stomach, relieving the discomfort, which in turn eliminates the behavior of searching for food. This elementary example might be diagrammed in the following manner:

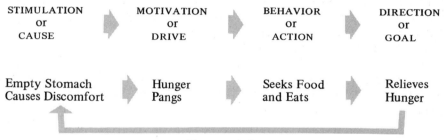

FIGURE 4–1.

It will be noted that the arrows point in the direction of the goal (relieves hunger) from the beginning or cause of the behavior cycle. Once the goal is obtained through the appropriate behavior, the cycle or circuit is completed and the cause for the behavior is reduced or eliminated. Physical drives, such as hunger, can be more simply explained by this theory of cause, directedness, and motivation than other less-definable drives that are psychological and social in nature because the physical causes of behavior are more easily traced than the psychological ones. A number of obvious reasons for this exist. The primary reason, however, is that the physical needs usually have a definite point at which they can be satisfied, while the psychological drives are less easy to identify and to satisfy. There may be no limit to one's psychological need for recognition or power, but a person can eat only so much, sleep so long, or drink a given amount before his primary physical needs are satisfied. A person's

* The term *motivation* is used in this discussion synonymously with such other terms as *reason*, *drive*, *needs*, or *disequilibrium*, which describe roughly the same phenomenon.

drive for power may never be totally satisfied, even after a long series of accomplishments, such as being promoted to higher positions. Thus, we see that the cycle of cause, directedness, and motivation is not completed even though a pattern of behavior may be developed by the individual in his psychological drive for power. The same is true in the case of many psychologically oriented needs. In spite of its limitations, the model of cause and effect in the behavior cycle developed by Leavitt is useful in human relations because it serves as a guide in helping to understand that man's behavior is not irrational to him even though it may appear irrational to anyone who does not recognize that such behavior is caused by and directed toward some goal. Simply stated, the individual behaves the way he does because he believes that he will be better off because of the behavior.

IMPORTANCE OF PERCEPTION

Several points should be made about the foregoing concept of behavior because the cause or stimulation-producing behavior may be either real or imagined. The way that a person *sees* or interprets the situation is as important as what the situation *really* is in the motivation of his behavior. Each person's perception of what goes on around him is colored either by his former experiences in the same or similar circumstances, by what he has been taught to expect, or by a host of environmental factors of which he may or may not be aware. Because of these differences in perception, the same motivation for a group of individuals does not always produce the same individual reactions; nor is the same behavior on the part of several individuals necessarily caused by the same motivation. For example, in an office staff of a large public utility company, several young women were being considered for promotion to office supervisor. When the appointment was finally announced, not only the young lady who received the promotion, but also one of the other contenders, burst into tears. While each may have reacted in order to release tension, the motivation to cry was probably not the same.

A person's perception is often subject to the accepted patterns established by the group or the cultural environment in which he finds himself. This cultural influence affects human behavior in things as simple as satisfying hunger. For example, in the United States a hungry person might satisfy his need with a roast beef sandwich and a glass of milk; in culturally different countries beef may be forbidden and, therefore, some other food would be taken to satisfy hunger.

Within the United States, persons who have grown up in suburban middle-income environments develop a set of values, ambitions, and modes of behavior that may vary widely from the values, ambitions, and behavior of persons raised in urban slums. Yet, often persons from both environments find themselves working in the same work groups. Some major cultural elements that contribute to the development of a person's perception are his religious beliefs, nationality, race, educational level, economic and social status, and the environment in which he was raised. The implications are too complex to be explained simply. It is important to recognize that differences of opinions which threaten cohesiveness among group members may be deeply rooted in vastly differing perceptions resulting from the inculcation of different cultural influences in each individual.

In industrial organizations as well as in military, governmental, or religious organizations, a person's perception can be affected by the position he holds. A man at the top level of an organization is very likely to react differently from those persons below him. His view about the adequacy of the decision-making process in the company, the firm's competitive position in the market, and the feasibility of automating production process are influenced by his perception of himself and his role in company affairs. This perception often differs from those at the rank-and-file level. This results in difficult communications, even when all parties—top management, supervisory or midmanagement, and rank and file—are quite willing to keep an open mind.

One need not illustrate differences in perception merely by using examples of persons holding positions at vastly different levels in the organization. Newly promoted supervisors often find it difficult to maintain the same social relations they have enjoyed with members of their old work groups. Once a supervisor assumes his new role he may find that his view of company affairs is no longer the same as that of his former colleagues. Also, he may find that his decisions call for a broad perspective of company operations that may not necessarily be true of his subordinates. The supervisor may see the importance of maintaining an uninterrupted flow of production when he refuses to let an employee take a day off to celebrate a wedding anniversary. The supervisor may not be able to find a replacement for the man on that day; the subordinate may see the supervisor as a man without a heart who would have to make other arrangements anyway if he, the subordinate, were absent because of illness.

The differences in perception often add to the complexity or interpersonal reactions. Frequently, these differences do not have to be great to cause human relations problems. The following example indicates how a human relations problem can develop when even a minor difference in perception occurs between a supervisor and his subordinate.

A Case in Different Perceptions. In most cases when supervisors refer to human relations problems they are speaking of situations where work-

ers display emotion. Anger, frustration, fear, and aggression are negative
emotions which can interfere with a person's effectiveness on the job;
therefore, supervisors tend to regard them as "human relations problems." Other emotions reflecting joy, contentment, and satisfaction normally
are not viewed with alarm because they do not appear to restrict the
worker's performance except in cases where individuals "skylark" or
"goof off." The problem faced by supervisors is to create an atmosphere
which sustains the worker's emotions somewhere between the extremes
of depression and exaltation, between heated anger and blurry-eyed light-
headedness. Reaching this objective is complicated because different
individuals may both view and react to the same social, physical, and
psychological environment in different ways. To complicate the matter further, not only may different individuals view an identical situation differently, but the same individual may react differently to a seemingly
identical situation at different times. The reasons for this difference in
the worker's reaction to what appears to be an identical situation often,
but not always, lie beyond the control of the supervisor.

A young man who was well liked by all members of the work group,
including the supervisor, was also the most conscientious lens grinder in
an opitcal laboratory. He appeared to enjoy his work and to take pride
in the high quality of the work he did. On one occasion when a particular
rush job required special care, the laboratory supervisor sought him out
and assigned the job to him, stating, "Frank, I'm assigning this work order to you. Take special care to turn out a good job on this one, will you?"
In an instant, Frank retorted, "Why me? Try giving it to one of the other
guys for a change." The supervisor was somewhat surprised by his young
subordinate's reaction since it seemed so out of character.

The question posed by this situation is twofold. What action should
the supervisor have taken when making the assignment? Why did Frank's
reaction vary so from his "normal" one? To answer the first question, the
supervisor's course of action could have followed several directions. He
could have pleaded with Frank to do the job, but this would perhaps
have undermined his authority in the eyes of Frank and the other laboratory workers. The supervisor could have asserted his authority and
demanded that Frank do the job *or else*. This alternative might have compounded a human relations problem, not only with Frank but with the
other workers. Resorting to ultimatums seldom accomplishes sound results,
particularly in situations where it is difficult to carry out the "or else." Or
else, what? If the laboratory supervisor resorted to dismissing Frank, he,
the supervisor, would lose a normally reliable worker and possibly undermine the morale of the work group. This would not seem to solve either
the immediate problem of getting the special job done or the long range
responsibility of maintaining a cohesive and productive work group. A
third possible solution is to have done nothing. This alternative carries

certain obvious dangers also. If a worker can refuse to follow orders, whether they are couched in terms of a simple request or not and nothing is done about it, then what is to prohibit workers from refusing to abide by other rules and orders of the supervisor?

On the surface it might appear that the supervisor's position was futile. Such was not the case. The problem was to get the lenses ground to specification and to complete the job with the least interruption of the regular work schedule. The supervisor had selected Frank to do the job because, in his judgment, Frank could do the best job. When the supervisor's order was met by unexpected resistance, he then was faced by a complex situation: He did not want to lose face, but, at the same time, he wanted to reach his objective of getting the job completed satisfactorily. It might appear that in order not to lose face himself, the supervisor must place the worker in the position of losing his dignity, and this could easily occur if the supervisor asserts his authority, forcing the subordinate to retreat from his position. The ideal solution in this case is for Frank to do the job and, at the same time, not lose his dignity. Is this possible?

The answer to the above question requires that the supervisor have some knowledge of human behavior in order for him to understand why Frank resisted his order. For instance, had the supervisor fallen into the habit of assigning the difficult jobs to Frank so that Frank really was getting a disproportionate share of the harder work? If so, then Frank's protest may have been justified though tactless. Even if Frank had not been assigned more than his share of tough assignments, what reasons did he have for believing he had? Was his protest merely an excuse of the moment even when he knew it was without basis?

When the sequence of events in this case is traced, it seems that a conscientious worker who took pride in his work would have little real reason to react the way Frank did. However, when the supervisor's request is carefully analyzed, we may find an interpretation which might be construed by Frank as criticism. Such may not have been the intention of the supervisor, but as we have mentioned, the way a person perceives a situation is as important to the determination of his behavior as is the reality of the situation. In this case, the final statement of the supervisor, ". . . take special care to turn out a good job on this one, will you?" was interpreted by Frank as an insinuation that he normally did not take "special care" to turn out good work. Another seemingly minor point but nonetheless critical in this situation was the fact that Frank was not told *why* he had been selected to do this particular assignment. Every man has his ego or sense of self-importance, and, in this situation, the supervisor had neglected to utilize this basic fact in appealing to Frank's demonstrated pride of workmanship. This latter point deserves special comment regarding the marked danger of using false flattery to motivate workers to perform. Where honest and deserving compliments on an individual's performance are due, they are appreciated by both the individual who has performed well and by other members of the work group who come to realize that outstanding performance is recognized and appreciated by the boss, just as flattery of mediocre work is soon regarded by workers as superficial and manipulative. It might also be added that a compliment from a supervisor who is held in low esteem by the work group usually does not have much positive impact either on the individual receiving the compliment or on the group.

In the situation described, the supervisor did not weigh thoughtfully what the impact of his request was going to have on Frank. Even in social circumstances few people do weigh this impact; therefore, most of us find ourselves involved, at one time or another, in a chain reaction of emotions which apparently occurred without rhyme or reason. We make an innocent statement or request which affronts the sensitivity of another person, who in turn reacts in such a way as to offend us. We respond defensively and often further aggravate the situation, thus involving ourselves in an emotional turmoil which may block reasonable and rewarding relationships with others. In most social situations this is not serious and is soon relieved by good humor or a change in conversation. In the industrial situation the time that can be afforded to ironing out personal differences is usually more limited because of the pressures to accomplish results and reach group objectives. Yet, compatible interpersonal relations are important on the job because of the long-term nature of the personal contacts usually maintained by the work group. The underlying principles of human behavior, however, are the same in both situations; hence, aside from the fact that learning why people react the way they do helps an individual reach a fuller and more rewarding role in social interaction, it is vital for the effective role the supervisor must play in the work group. Ability to comprehend the needs and wants which underlie human behavior becomes as necessary to the supervisor as his technical skill and knowledge. The example of the supervisor's human relations problem with Frank is illustrative of the consequences of a single oversight in recognizing a human need. Knowledge of human needs does not imply that there is a singular ideal solution to human relations problems; however, such knowledge does help an individual to look beyond the actions of others and seek solutions which are compatible to human values.

HUMAN NEEDS

As a human being our survival and satisfaction in life depends largely upon the attention we give to certain physiological and psychological drives within us. The biological sciences are concerned primarily with examining the physical needs of the individual and only secondarily with the effects of behavior due to certain drives. The behavioral sciences attempt both to define and to explain the behavior of people as individuals and in groups. Members of both sciences recognize the high degree of interdependency of the two fields in explaining human behavior.

The classification of human needs is broken into five categories as an academic means of investigating each one separately and conveniently. Discussion of these human needs and their relationships is beneficial in understanding some aspects of man's behavior. It should be noted that these needs often run concurrently and, in actuality, are difficult to separate.

A. H. Maslow has categorized the needs of man into five primary classifications and much of the following discussion on human needs is adapted from his book, *Motivation and Personality* [3]. Human needs have certain priorities and each level must be satisfied to some extent before the next becomes dominant. The basic needs and their priority as established by Maslow are

1. Physiological: basic physical and biological needs.
2. Safety: physical and psychological security.
3. Social: love, affection, and social intercourse.
4. Esteem: self-respect, independence, and prestige.
5. Self-realization: self-fulfillment, accomplishment, and personal identity.

Physiological Needs. The physical needs are fundamental to man's existence. Survival depends upon the satisfaction of certain physical needs. Frequently the physical needs are attended with little conscious thought until something jeopardizes the process. A person breathes with little effort until a blow to the midsection inhibits the normal process or until he swallows a food particle the wrong way. Then his entire physical organism devotes its energy toward the immediate danger to survival, and during the period of gasping or choking little attention is given to other less urgent needs.

After the need for air, the need for water and food take their place in the hierarchy of physical needs. The need for rest or sleep, excretion, physical activity, and freedom from excessive temperatures all demand attention when they make themselves felt. As each biological drive rises in urgency, it takes precedence over the others and continues to grow in force until it is relieved.

Where physical needs are concerned, a firm cannot afford to overlook the dire needs of employees as human beings; at any rate, not without paying a high cost in efficiency and productivity. Adequate ventilation, lighting, heating and cooling systems, restrooms, drinking fountains, and other physical facilities need to be provided in order to alleviate primary physical drives. Work routines, rest periods, and vacations should be planned and scheduled with not only physical but also psychological needs in mind.

Safety Needs.   Whereas the physiological drives have certain limits to their demand for satisfaction, the other needs seem to be infinite in nature. Excessive indulgence in meeting the physical needs can be harmful, if not fatal to the individual. Once the physical needs are attended even to a minimum degree of satisfaction, other needs begin to increase in their effect on human behavior.

The drive for safety is twofold. First, there is a physical need to survive. This drive is such a powerful one that even in civilized societies laws are designed to protect the individual in this drive. Self-defense may be a justifiable reason to take another man's life. But the physical drive seldom encounters such a primary course of action. The individual, although rarely faced with the alternative of kill or be killed, consciously avoids pain or any deliberate action which he knows will harm him. It should be remembered that individual reaction to pain may vary with the culture, but there are instances where people risk their lives for a cause or in an emergency. To seek pain deliberately appears to be exceptional behavior, especially in our society. The drive for physical safety extends beyond the realm of mere survival or even the avoidance of pain. It frequently can carry a person to extremes in seeking comfort. A man usually is not content to be suspended in the limbo of nonpain; he wants to exist in some state of comfort. A bench will provide a means for sitting, but an overstuffed lounge chair may make the same act more enjoyable. A glass of water relieves thirst on a hot day, but a man might choose a cold soft drink if a choice between the two were offered. So it goes until the range of behavior falling within the drive for physical safety reaches from primitive survival to a quest for absolute comfort.

Secondly, the need for safety extends into psychological dimensions as well as physical. The drive for security can force enemies to unite in order to resist a third enemy stronger than either of them individually. The need for security, physical and psychological, is one which has certain dangers attached if carried to extremes. A man can feel so safe that he becomes careless. Thus, even in relatively dangerous jobs, it has been recognized that workers often need constant safety training that reminds them of the care they need to exercise in the performance of their jobs.

In extreme cases a person can feel so secure that his drives for independence and self-respect fade. In short, an individual can atrophy in the warmth of security until he no longer can endure the severity of tough times. He can become too dependent upon others for his existence and, consequently, lose his effectiveness as an autonomous human being. Often supervisors accuse subordinates of lacking initiative because they will do only what they are told and little more. Whether this is true in any given case depends on a number of circumstances; however, it is true that some workers do little more than they are told to do because they fear the consequences of doing something on their own initiative and failing. Such individuals find security in the fact that someone else makes the decisions and carries the responsibility for them.

The problem that arises from the issue of man's need for security is how much should be provided for him by his supervisor or employer. If too much is provided, he may become overly dependent upon his providers. If too little is given, his energy can be consumed trying to satisfy his drive for security, leaving little energy to spend on reaching the higher order of human needs.

Social Needs.   If the physiological and safety needs are adequately met, the social needs of an individual will emerge in dominance. The drive to belong and to be with other people seems to be universal among men. Some men, of course, control or suppress this particular drive very well. Hermits are an example of individuals who have curbed the more ordinary trend toward gregariousness. The need to be accepted by others takes on tremendous importance to some individuals.

The drive to be with others and to communicate with them has long been recognized. In fact, in many societies isolation of an individual, solitary confinement, is considered one of the worst punishments. Making a recalcitrant child stand in a corner by himself stems from the knowledge that isolation from the group is a form of punishment even though no physical contact was made. Thus, Frederick Taylor's attempt to improve efficiency by isolating workers was in direct contradiction to the normal drive in most people to relate socially to other human beings. Later experiments by Elton Mayo during the Hawthorne Studies showed that the social needs of individuals could be satisfied in the work place without sacrificing production.

An important aspect of this social need lies in the recognition and understanding of the fact that a person seeks harmonious and friendly relationships with others. He is not content to just wait for them to come along. A person may put up with a quarrelsome companion, wife, boss, or fellow worker if no other alternative is open to him, but he usually will seek to sever the relationship as soon as a more enjoyable and congenial association presents itself.

There are dangers connected with the drive for social contact just as there are dangers involved with the excessive drive for security. A person can become preoccupied with social intercourse at the cost of becoming ineffective in his work. A salesman who enjoys "shooting the bull" with customers at the price of not getting orders soon finds himself in jeopardy as a salesman. A supervisor primarily concerned with being a "nice guy," although the result may be a loss of effectiveness at getting the work done, may find the price high when his own performance is evaluated by his superiors.

The drive for belonging, for affection and social activity, is considered by some people as lying essentially outside the concern of the business enterprise. It is argued that social needs should be met outside the job situation. However, a large portion of a man's life is spent in the social environment of his work, and in an affluent society where the standard of living has relieved most people of their primary concern for the first two levels of human needs, social needs are pursued with more energy than at any other time in history. Therefore, some, if not all, of man's social needs must be met on the job. If working conditions inhibit or prevent some degree of social satisfaction, a person will seek to meet this social need elsewhere. In so doing, he may divert energy which he might have been willing to spend on the job.

Esteem Needs. A man needs to feel that he is important. He seeks recognition as a person. Self-respect and dignity are essential to the psychological well-being of the individual who has reached some degree of satisfaction in the first three levels of human needs. Not only is it necessary for a person to feel he has the respect of his fellow man, but he also wishes to give respect to certain people with whom he comes into contact.

The personal philosophy, religious belief, the moral and ethical values of the individual all are factors which affect the manner in which he will try to satisfy the need for esteem. The drive for recognition frequently motivates a person to do things which have an adverse effect on the respect others have for him. This dilemma between the drive for respect and the need for recognition often gives rise to dire conflict within the individual. Thus, some behavior which is designed to bring recognition to the individual may not be considered by others as worthy of respect. Public drunkeness, boisterousness, or obscenity may be an effort to attract attention and recognition, but seldom incurs the real respect of others.

The need for esteem also includes man's desire for prestige and status. On occasion, the efforts made by an individual to obtain status may produce undesirable reactions from others. Vance Packard describes what he believes to be some of the absurdities of the drive for status in his book entitled *The Status Seekers* [7].

While the desire for status and prestige can have its negative aspects when founded on either superficial or inflated accomplishments of the individual, it can also be a powerful positive force in motivating a person to reach great heights of accomplishment. When the desire for prestige and self-respect are coordinated by the individual he may exert great effort and energy to earn the respect of his associates by his outstanding performance on the job or in some endeavor he undertakes.

Self-realization Needs. The final step in Maslow's hierarchy of human needs is self-realization, or *self-actualization.* This is the highest order of man's needs and is as totally psychological in nature as the need for air is physical. It is a strong drive in some men and in others is nearly nonexistent.

The drive for self-realization refers basically to man's desire for self-fulfillment—to be what he must; to try to be what he thinks he can be. It is a complex drive and takes different forms in every individual. It is the thing which drives men to accomplish things even when others may never know about their success. The intelligence and creativity of people with this drive need latitude for exercise and expression. It is also the drive which may express itself in the individuality and independence of the man. The importance of the drive for self-realization is that there needs to be an acceptance of self before a person can gain satisfaction from group participation.

The need for self-realization can impose upon the individual stronger bonds of self-discipline than could be enforced by someone else. It can make a person dissatisfied with his own performance when others praise it. Like other human needs of more basic priority, the drive for self-realization can have pitfalls for the individual. In the extreme, it can become an obsession resulting in psychological or even physical self-destruction. At lesser levels of determination, it can make an individual difficult to work with for any prolonged interval. Frequently, it may lead to eccentric behavior which others find alarming or annoying. Self-realization as a drive can manifest itself in modes of behavior which range from being a perfectionist to being power-hungry.

Though the need for self-realization may not be a dominant drive in all men, it influences nearly everyone. It influences the choice of occupations a person pursues and the degree of satisfaction he receives from his work.

Maslow lists a number of the characteristics which he believes a person would possess if self-realization were attained. A person with a well-developed sense of self-realization would have:

1. A clearer, more efficient perception of reality.
2. More openness to experience.
3. An increased integration, wholeness, and unity as a person.

4. An increased spontaneity, expressiveness, and aliveness.

5. A real self, firm identity, autonomy, and uniqueness.

6. An increased objectivity, detachment, and transcendence of self.

7. A recovery of creativeness.

8. An ability to fuse concreteness and abstractness.

9. A more democratic character structure.

10. An increased ability to love others [4, p. 148].

Maslow points out that the possession of these qualities in a person who has achieved a degree of self-realization needs confirmation through further research. However, the ideals which he has outlined give an indication of the nature of the highest level of human needs.

When analyzing the motivation and behavior of the individual, attention cannot be placed on any single need to the exclusion of the others because, in reality, their separation within the whole man is impossible. People are driven by many needs simultaneously and usually satisfaction must occur concurrently. Human existence does not consist merely of a process of satisfying a complex succession of needs, but of satisfying a complex interaction of simultaneous needs. The division between the needs is not sharp, but is, rather, characterized by a shading and blending of drives which motivate the behavior of the individual on or off the job.

The physical needs may be said to be primary in that they dominate behavior first and foremost when they become strong enough. But even this assertion is a difficult one from which to generalize because of the way some individuals learn to dominate the priority of their needs. One individual may steal food even when he is not hungry, while another would have to be starving before he would accept a charitable apple. However, in most cases, an individual who is hungry enough will steal food even though it is against his personal values and morals. There have been enough martyrs to religious and political beliefs to state that there are exceptions even to the universal rule of self-preservation.

The physical drives and the need for safety can be rebuked in some cases where the individual feels a strong enough psychological motive. Even where the drives are primarily psychological in nature, one drive may dominate others until it is relieved by some action. The psychological needs which deal with security and safety can be said to cause dependence in the individual, whereas the higher-level needs of esteem and self-realization are more ego-oriented in nature and frequently express themselves in highly independent behavior.

Though exceptions exist, Maslow's classification and priority of human needs are generally agreed upon, with certain variations and modifications, by other writers. Douglas McGregor's theory of motivation is similar to Maslow's except that he places ego-needs and self-fulfillment in the two highest positions on the scale of human needs. The difference between the two theories is mainly semantic, each using different terms to describe much the same thing [5, pp. 36–39].

Ross Stagner has another closely related viewpoint: He points out that the importance of a particular need is relative, depending upon the circumstances of the moment. He also states that goals differ to some extent within each group, especially as conditions change over time. The groups to which Stagner directed his attention were executives, workers, and unions [9, p. 117].

Although there is some discussion as to whether the hierarchy of human needs is unique to each individual as a result of his cultural background and personal experience or whether such a hierarchy is universal among all human beings, most theories on human needs are related to the extent that there is general agreement about the existence of an order or hierarchy of needs. The problem posed to management by this hierarchy is what to do about it in its efforts to motivate the workers. According to the needs concept, typified by Maslow and McGregor, management has the task of arranging organizational conditions and methods of operation so that people can achieve their own goals best by directing their own efforts toward the objectives of the organization. This becomes a process primarily of creating opportunities wherein the individual not only satisfies his basic needs through adequate economic rewards, but also by providing the conditions in which the individual can grow, release and exercise his potential, and find satisfaction through the recognition of his accomplishments and the guidance to overcome his occupational weaknesses. This then becomes the ground upon which human relations is to be practiced. It does not mean the abdication of management, the lowering of standards, a weakening of leadership or any of the characteristics associated with the "soft" approach.

MODES OF BEHAVIOR WHEN SATISFACTION OF INDIVIDUAL NEEDS IS BLOCKED

The human needs act to motivate behavior which is directed toward some goal or satisfaction. It would appear that if all needs could be met as they arose, life would be tranquil; such is not the case because needs do not necessarily act one at a time, but may act simultaneously. Some goals are short term and easily satisfied; others are long range, and satisfaction is never total. As one need is satiated, tensions created by another need arise to take its place so that behavior is motivated toward it; thus the process of satisfying needs is continuous.

Frustration and Conflict

In light of current knowledge about human needs and motivation, one might ask what happens to the individual whose needs are blocked? It is not uncommon to have satisfaction of human wants and needs blocked by practical exigencies. A worker may want higher wages, but finds that his employer is unable or unwilling to increase his pay. Another employee may work diligently for a promotion only to find that a fellow employee with longer tenure on the job receives one before him. The social, political, and psychological realm of the work place often confront the individual with situations which place barriers between himself and the satisfaction of his needs.

Such satisfaction may not be possible for a number of real or imagined reasons; however, frustration and conflict occur whether the barriers are real or not. A hungry person who cannot find food may face a real barrier to the satisfaction of a basic human need. A young man who hesitates to ask his boss for a raise because he fears that he will not receive it is coping with a barrier which is either real or imagined. The only way he will resolve his problem is to ask when the circumstances are most appropriate.

The diagram given earlier in the chapter illustrated the relationship between cause and actual goal-directed behavior. The same diagram can be used to illustrate what happens if need satisfaction is blocked.

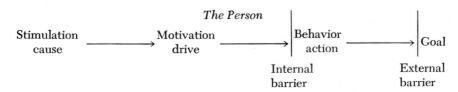

When a goal is not reached or goes unsatisfied, tension or motivation will persist or increase until the block is overcome and the goal is reached or until a substitute goal can be found to reduce or eliminate the tension. Barriers to goal satisfaction may be *internal*, within the psychological make-up of the person himself, or *external*, imposed by the social or physical environment of the person. As long as either the original goal or a substitute goal is not reached because of some barrier, the tension created is *frustration* or *conflict*. When the motivation to reach a goal is a strong one and the barrier happens to be a person, the frustrated individual will often engage in some type of aggressive behavior. The manner in which the frustrated person reacts can range from a scowl to an outright physical attack, and this reaction will be influenced by his personality. The psychological response or mode of behavior may not be chosen consciously by an individual, but is, rather, the product of unconscious learning.

A number of unconscious reactions to the tension created by frustration or conflict are called *defense mechanisms*. These reactions can be classified into three broad types, but a degree of overlap occurs between each of the classifications: (1) aggressive reactions, (2) substitution reactions, and (3) escape or avoidance reactions.

Aggressive Reactions. Aggressive reactions are characterized by some direct or indirect action against the source of frustration. Often such emotional behavior can cause further frustration, making alternative, constructive behavior more difficult to see and follow.

Substitutional Reactions. Substitutional reactions are reactions where substituted or lowered goals replace the thwarted original goals. Generally they provide a more satisfactory adjustment for both the individual and society than the other types of defense mechanisms.

Overcompensation occurs when an exaggerated attempt is made to overcome some real or imagined shortcoming. The methods used to do this are numerous and can be observed in varied types of affected behavior. Classic examples are given of short men who try to make up their imagined deficiency by acting tough, or of uneducated people who use big words. These are only examples. Positive aspects of this behavior occur when an individual overcomes some weakness by trying harder. A boxer who wins over a superior opponent and an underdog football team that plays extra hard are illustrations of how this mechanism can be useful in generating positive action.

Identification is another example of substitution where an individual obtains vicarious pleasure from the success of another person when his own success is blocked. As with the other defense mechanisms, identification has both its positive and its negative aspects. To the extent that identification provides opportunity to exercise constructive and creative responses, it is beneficial; however, when it becomes an excessive mental crutch, it becomes an inadequate mode of adjustment.

Rationalization is basically illogical thinking or blindness to the facts at hand, and it causes an individual to reach conclusions he wants to believe and hopes others will believe. A worker who makes such statements as, "I've been working too hard lately, so I'm entitled to knock off a day from work," is probably rationalizing. Likewise, when an employee who was passed over for promotion says that he did not want a promotion because it would have been too much trouble may be rationalizing.

Escape or Avoidance.   *Regression* is another way of dealing with frustration. This behavior pattern is characterized by a return to immature or childish behavior: sullenness or negativeness; frequent reference to "the good old days."

Repression is the excluding of thoughts associated with the unpleasantness of shame, guilt, or anxiety. The repression or exclusion from the consciousness is often a reaction to some idea or feeling that endangers one's emotional comfort. Forgetting and repression are similar in that recall is impeded; however, repression is normally associated with painful or distressing experiences. *Repression,* however, is usually an unconscious action, whereas *suppression* is a conscious one.

Other modes of behavior characteristic of escape reactions are excessive daydreaming or avoidance. In either case, by withdrawing from reality a person does not have to cope with his problems.

Conflict is a source of tension in a person and often creates indecision or confusion. Conflict results when two or more mutually exclusive goals are sought and cannot be obtained at the same time. In general, there are three types of conflict: (1) a situation that presents two equally desirable goals which motivate the individual in two different directions, as when a person receives a job offer from two companies for which he wants to work; (2) a situation that provides two equally undesirable goals, as illustrated when a worker is transferred to a job he does not like at a reduced pay rate because of a new equipment change which was approved by his union. His choice is to keep a job he does not care for or to quit and take the risk of prolonged unemployment if he cannot find another job; (3) a situation where two goals are provided, one of which is good; the other undesirable. A man is offered a promotion with a substantial increase in pay, but he would also have to move from a community in which he and his family enjoyed living.

The solution to these problems illustrating the three general types of conflict would depend on more factors than are given, plus the multitude of personal traits possessed by the individual who has to make the decision. The dilemma presented in each case can certainly cause conflict and frustration, and a person facing such a decision may well not act in his usual manner during the period of stress.

Human behavior that is directed toward reducing the tension created by the drive to obtain goals or satisfy needs is called *adaptive* or *adjustive behavior.* Good mental health is associated with individuals who meet the conflicts and frustrations in their lives with both a high degree of effectiveness and certain satisfaction. Life presents situations which appear to be more trying at some times than others. A person who makes satisfactory adjustments to the emotional stresses of his social, business, and personal worlds might be called well adjusted. Adjustment, however, is not a matter of absolutes. As with other human characteristics, it is measured by degree. It must be remembered that adjustment is not necessarily synonymous, without qualification, to good mental health. Mental health, for most persons, implies coming to acceptable terms with their physical, social, and psychological environment; however, one must keep in mind the way and kind of adjustment made to these environmental elements.

Usually, well-adjusted people do possess several characteristics which can be used as guides for evaluating or interpreting their actions and behavior.

1. They feel comfortable about themselves. Their own emotions—fear, love, jealousy, guilt, worry—do not overwhelm them. They retain their sense of humor about themselves and others, and they feel able to deal with most situations that come to them in life.

2. They can accept other people. They can be a part of a group, have a sense of responsibility about others, and can love and respect the feelings and ideas of others. They usually trust others and expect others to trust them. They enjoy relationships with other people.

3. They are able to meet the demands of life. They set realistic goals for themselves and plan for the future without fearing it. They meet their problems and take action to solve them. They put their best efforts into their activities and derive satisfaction from them. They make use of their capacities.

There are many other characteristics which could be added, but these features characterize mature, relatively well-adjusted people. They do not try to eliminate their feelings and emotions; they try to control them, within limits, and make them appropriate to the situation.

Understanding the individual as a person, knowing his goals and ambitions, becomes primary if incentive and motivation are to be provided by management. This involves knowing both the ways people are alike and the ways they are unique.

A job adds another dimension to the life of a worker, one which presents its own sources of social and psychological satisfactions and frustrations. The pattern of adjustment that a worker has developed to meet life outside the work place also carries over into the job. Learning to understand the unique modes of adjustment of each worker is an important factor in coordinating the efforts of that worker with the objectives of the group of which he is a member. In the following chapters a closer look will be taken at the nature of work—of employee attitudes and the things that workers want and expect to gain from their employment.

SUMMARY

1. The work situation is normally a social situation where we work with other people. Each person with whom we come into contact is unique in personality and physical appearance. We are affected both by what is real in other people and situations and by what we perceive, and this perception is largely colored by our experience, personal philosophies, and bias. Because of individual perception, there is a danger that the generalizations that are made regarding other people's behavior are based on myths rather than on known facts.

2. A working concept of behavior involves a theory of cause, directedness, and motivation. Although one must recognize the limitations of any model of human behavior, such a model does provide a concept which helps to understand the rationale of people's actions. The same motivation for a group of people does not always solicit the same reaction from each individual. Nor will the same individual always react identically to the same motivation. Thus, the cause for the behavior becomes a crucial point for understanding the behavior, rather than the reactions, of people, which are more readily observed.

3. The human needs are a continuously acting group of forces which create tension in the individual which he seeks to relieve. While classification of human needs is somewhat artificial because they are interdependent in nature, their separation for purposes of analysis is useful. The separation of human needs by Maslow indicates a priority of needs which evolve from the purely physiological to the highest order of psychological needs, known as self-realization.

4. Although it might be argued that the work place is not the appropriate place to be concerned with satisfying certain kinds of human needs, the fact remains that at present so much of a person's adult life is normally spent in a work situation that it is an unavoidable reality of industrial society that more and more human needs must be met on the job. The question is how much and what kinds of human needs should employers try to satisfy.

5. The total satisfaction of human needs cannot be met on the job, even when employers are willing to try to do so. Certain goals are blocked from satisfaction by the constraints and realities imposed by the job. When need-satisfaction or desire is not obtained, the result is frustration or conflict. In the case of frustration or conflict, behavior may manifest itself either in aggression or in other defense mechanisms, such as day dreaming or rationalization.

6. Human behavior is directed toward reducing the tension created by the drive to obtain goals or satisfy needs. This is called adaptive or adjustive behavior. Normally, such behavior is healthy, both physically

and mentally, for the individual; however, being "well adjusted" is a matter of degree and not a matter of absolutes. Therefore, one must also view what is being *adjusted to* and what kinds of adjustment are made.

7. In the context of modern industrial society there are some characteristics of well-adjusted individuals that help evaluate and interpret their actions and behavior. Essentially, they are a feeling of comfort about themselves, an acceptance of other people, and an ability to meet the normal demands of life.

DISCUSSION QUESTIONS

1. What is meant by the statement, "behavior is caused"?
2. What are the human needs? Is there a hierarchy to these needs?
3. How do you explain the behavior of a man who would rather suffer pain than divulge a secret? Is he satisfying a *need?*
4. Of what use can the knowledge of human needs be to supervisors or leaders of a group?
5. What are some of the causes of frustration or conflict that are found on the job?
6. In what ways can a person react in order to escape frustration or conflict on the job?
7. What are some of the characteristics of well-adjusted persons?

BIBLIOGRAPHY AND SELECTED COLLATERAL READINGS

1. KATZ, DANIEL, and ROBERT LESTER KAHN, *The Social Psychology of Organization.* New York: John Wiley and Sons, 1966.
2. LEAVITT, HAROLD J., *Managerial Psychology,* 2nd ed. Chicago: University of Chicago Press, 1964.
3. MASLOW, A. H., *Motivation and Personality.* New York: Harper & Row, 1954.
4. MASLOW, A. H., *Toward a Psychology of Being.* Princeton, N.J.: D. Van Nostrand Company, 1962.
5. McGREGOR, DOUGLAS, *The Human Side of Enterprise.* New York: McGraw-Hill Book Company, 1960.
6. McGREGOR, DOUGLAS, *The Professional Manager.* New York: McGraw-Hill Book Company, 1967.
7. PACKARD, VANCE, *The Status Seekers.* New York: David McKay, 1959.
8. STAGNER, ROSS, "Psychological Aspects of Industrial Conflict: Motivation," *Personal Psychology,* III, No. 1 (Spring, 1950), 1–15.
9. STAGNER, ROSS, *Psychology of Industrial Conflict.* New York: John Wiley and Sons, 1956.

The Nature of Work

In the last chapter the individual's needs and the motivation that affect his behavior were discussed. Much of what can be said about the successful adaptation of the individual to life is also applicable to the integration of the individual into the work situation. The adjustment of the individual to his job is dependent upon many factors which operate simultaneously: the work he performs, the group of which he is a member, the treatment he receives from peers and superiors, and many other facets of the work environment. The meaning of work to the individual is important to the overall view of human relations, not because it is the only factor contributing to his satisfactory adjustment, but because it is germane to the adjustment which transpires in the work place.

The individual can change his attitude about the job he does, the firm he works for, and the people with whom he works, but the disposition he has toward the work environment is one that has its roots in the values and experiences that the worker brings to the job. The attitude that a worker has toward work itself can influence how quickly and willingly he will adapt to his job.

Any supervisor or employer who attempts to practice human relations needs to have a working understanding of the role work plays in the lives of people, if he is going to be effective in assisting the worker adjust to this role.

In a very broad sense, rational, productive people fall into two categories—one to whom work is work and fun is fun; another group to whom work and fun are much the same. The reasons for this phenomenon are buried deep within the psychological recesses of each individual, as well as in the social environment of the work place.

Normally, work is considered an activity for which a person receives pay, whereas the hobbies or sports in which one participates are done for fun and pleasure. This differentiation might suffice in some cases, but several factors should be kept in mind. First, there is not necessarily a direct relationship between remuneration and work. For example, an artist may work hard on a painting only to find that he cannot sell it. He has worked nonetheless. In the opposite vein, a hobbyist might get a great deal of pleasure from making a ceramic ashtray that a neighbor admires so much that he buys it. However, while the hobbyist was making the ashtray he had no intention of selling it. Another reason why work cannot be equated solely in terms of money is that much of the activity of the housewife would have to be excluded—something which would be a major oversight in the minds of many wives and mothers.

The amount of effort put forth by an individual is an equally deceiving criterion for differentiation between work and recreation. The activities considered as work have a very broad range—from purely physical labor to extreme mental effort. Digging ditches with pick and shovel is hard physical work, but not considered taxing mentally. Solving mathematical equations requires little physical exertion, but it demands concentration and mental activity. The men engaged in either activity can feel exhausted at the end of the day, yet one has not had to think a great deal and the other has not had to exert much physical effort.

As a final point of discussion of work as an activity, one needs to remember that every man approaches his "work" with a different attitude about it and with different expectations toward it. Studies suggest that there is a correlation between the prestige people place on a given occupation and the satisfaction workers receive from performing it. If a job holds high prestige in the public's view (or at least in the mind of the worker), even if there are undesirable elements associated with the actual work involved, workers will tend to value the status of the job [16]. Perhaps this explains the appeal of so-called white-collar jobs to many persons when blue-collar jobs may offer higher financial returns but lack status appeal.

A man who does not like or who lacks the ability required for a particular job may find that he has to work hard, whereas another person possessing both the interest and aptitude finds the same work stimulating and enjoyable. For this reason, it is helpful to realize that a difference exists between "hard work" and "working hard." In either case the person doing the work can perform the task involved with exuberance and diligence, or he can goldbrick on the job; however, other factors, such as group pressure, can influence the degree to which this occurs.

THE MEANING OF WORK

For the purposes connected with the study of human relations, it is a futile task to try to define *work* in terms of pay or pleasure; however, it might be more profitable to explore what work means to an individual than it would be to attempt to define *work* as a word. Man needs to occupy his life with some array of mental and physical activity and, certainly, work is not the only means of satisfying this need; yet many men spend nearly half of their waking hours working. The nature and significance of work would be important as an area for study, if only on the basis that it occupies so much of a man's life span. Still, few people consciously think about it.

In the advanced Western nations, technology has brought forth revolutionary changes in work methods and the productivity of the individual worker. Homes are equipped with automatic washing machines and toasters, offices with typewriters and posting machines, factories with moving assembly lines and automated milling machines, all of which were designed to remove from man the arduous and taxing aspects of physical labor. Today the growth of the use of computers in applications of business and industry is even relieving man of many aspects of mental retention and activity. But it was man who invented the machines and found practical applications for them in industrial and domestic life in his long drive to make work easier. Why is it then that some men have always looked for a way to relieve themselves of work and yet dreaded the thought of inactivity and retirement?

John Diebold, who has been a leader in the development of automated equipment in business and industry, has said that one of the leading social problems in the future will be learning how to occupy the leisure time created for the worker by the increased application of automated machines in industry. Although there is the growing problem of leisure time for many people, there always have been and probably always will be some individuals who find work repugnant. An extreme aversion to work has been termed *ergophobia* by the psychologists. Such cases do exist, but are rare. What is equally interesting is that some men who, through the grace of good fortune or large inheritances, have not needed to work have done so anyway.

There are men who work whether or not they are pressed by economic needs. It would appear that for most men the need to work is deep rooted in their psychological make-up and that the meaning of work takes on a significance beyond mere material well-being and economic satisfaction. Work is and has been a major theme in our culture. Western industrialized culture tends to teach us that things have to be useful, practical, and have a purpose. Thus, work is viewed not only as a means to an end, but as an end in itself.

In the United States, there seems to be a stigma attached to prolonged unemployment. Of course, this state of affairs may be involuntary on the part of the individual, but that makes little difference in the general attitude toward the unemployed individual. On the federal and state level elaborate programs are designed to help keep employment high and unemployment low. The logic behind these programs is too involved in economic, political, and social philosophy to be explained easily, and it is outside the purpose of this book. The point is that there is a keen awareness of the unemployed, both in the national consciousness and in the consciousness of the individual. Unavoidable idleness and leisure seem to be frowned upon. This general attitude in the United States may stem from what scholars term "the Puritan ethic."

The ties between diligence, hard work, resolution, frugality, and industry are strongly presented in the text of the Puritan essayist Cotton Mather and are further expressed in Benjamin Franklin's *Autobiography*. According to our Puritan forefathers, the fruits of hard work and industry almost always bear profit and honor [13, p. 7]. Furthermore, work was regarded as necessarily hard and disagreeable. Today some people have the same sentiment even though they may not realize that the source originally was Puritan. Wealth and success is the goal of many a modern worker, and an absence of this ambition is generally mistrusted.

Although we have departed in many ways from the Puritan ethic in our beliefs about the soul-saving value of work, it is agreed in many quarters that work is the psychological glue that holds the entire man together. Some men make work out of play and others make play out of work, yet few people really think about what work means to them. A man's work can be a major social device for his identification as a person. Much of his identity, to himself as well as to others, is interwoven with how he earns his livelihood [9, p. 8].

In our society work enables a man to fulfill another definition of manliness: being the head of the family. Most men take this role for granted, and can do so until they have no work. Then the significance of work becomes painfully clear. During the extended Depression of the 1930's, a study of the unemployed conducted by the economist Eli Ginzberg disclosed that when a man lost his job and was placed on relief, frequently his whole family's attitude toward him changed. He was often considered less of a man than he had been while employed. Often his children declined to accept his discipline or advice. By his unemployment he demonstrated that he was neither successful nor powerful. After all, it was relief, not his fruitful employment which supported them [5].

Other extensive studies of the effect of unemployment on workers tend to support the findings of Ginzberg. A study of unemployment in a New England community during the period between 1932 and 1939, conducted by Wight Bakke, revealed that unemployment not only altered the worker's economic status, it also affected his social status and friendships, family affairs, and recreational activities [2]. In the study made by Mirra Komarovsky, it was found that relationships were altered when the head of the household was out of work, and, in some cases, the fathers lost the respect of their children [8].

More recent studies of family life-cycles and values among the poor and unemployed in the urban ghettos across the United States appear to substantiate the findings that Ginzberg and other researchers made during the years of the Great Depression.

It might be noted that much of the current research devoted to unemployment and the other social problems found in urban ghettos has indicated that the attitudes of many socially and economically disadvantaged persons do not reflect the same values regarding work that are normally attributed to the majority of the aspiring middle-class population. Often, the youngsters living in such depressed neighborhoods do not find adult models to emulate in developing either good work habits or positive attitudes toward the prestige and value of holding a job. Their parents, older siblings, and neighbors are frequently unemployed, or the jobs available to them fall into the unskilled or, at best, semiskilled category, offering little opportunity for advancement, high income, or status. It is little wonder that such conditions foster attitudes of suspicion and hostility toward the world of work.

Even though exceptions occur, it appears that work lends status to a man's existence. It can give him the feeling of independence, power, dignity, and purpose. Without work, particularly when he wants it, he may feel dependent, superfluous, or even socially dead. However, not all men feel so strongly about the importance of work. The degree of skill involved, the prestige of the job, and the creativity exercised while working all contribute to the meaning and significance of work to the individual.

THE LIFE CYCLE AND WORK

It is easy and possibly misleading to generalize about the value of work for every person who holds a job, but some gauge of its meaning can be helpful in understanding the attitude people hold toward their job. As an aid in reviewing this complex problem, a number of studies have tried to illustrate the changing role of work in a person's life by tracing the work-experience pattern for workers [11, Chapter 3].

The hypothetical work experience and life cycle outlined on Table 5–1 may aid in tracing a general pattern of the significance of work in a male worker's life. The life cycle is divided into decades merely for the convenience of analysis and, obviously, might vary for each person who works.

The significance of work during the first decade of a person's life is relatively small in terms of actual time and effort spent. Household chores may be introduced during this period, but dependency upon the family for the majority of one's physical, economic, and social wants and needs is dominant. However, even though the individual may not be directly involved in work himself, it is a period in which attitudes regarding work

TABLE 5–1. Work Experience and Life Cycle for Males

Birth

	Usually very little work experience.
	Attitudes toward work can be learned from parents and other social contacts.
10	Work contact increases. Casual jobs and chores are introduced.
	Part-time jobs taken.
	Formal education is primary occupation of most. Decision about continuing higher education must be made. First full-time job may be taken. Occupational choice grows in importance.
20	For many, military service must be completed. Formal education completed. First full-time job undertaken. Starting wages are relatively low. Job changes occur more frequently and easily. Learning the ropes and gaining technological knowledge of job is primary.
30	Occupational field is chosen. Firm may be chosen for occupational career. Job changes grow more difficult and less frequent toward end of this period.
	Drive for advancement increases. Economic returns and status of work increase. Accumulation of job experience grows.
40	Income increases until peak years are attained sometime during the next two decades.
	Production increases until peak is reached.
	Promotion pattern indicates whether top positions will be attained or whether height of career has been reached.
50	Usually top positions to be attained during work careers are achieved. Personal goals have or have not been achieved for most men. Readjustment must be made by those whose goals were unattained. Frequently (but not always) the struggle to advance gives way to the struggle to retain what has been acquired.
60	Retirement becomes prevalent. Drive for security may grow in importance. Active participation slows down.
	Role of adviser grows.
70	Retirement becomes a reality. Income regresses. One may act the role of adviser as active participation declines. Adjustment to less participative role necessary.

are gleaned from members of the family and other social contacts. Older siblings and parents can contribute strongly to the child's outlook on work as being a curse or blessing.

In many respects, the period between the ages of ten and twenty is turbulent for most individuals. Physical and emotional development is usually rapid and complex. Generally work begins to play an increasingly significant role in life. First, casual labor such as occasionally mowing neighborhood lawns gives way to part-time employment, such as a newspaper route. This may be necessitated by the economic needs of the family, but often it is a means whereby the individual can exercise some independent action and help defray the cost of his increasing propensity to spend.

Most young people have the primary task of obtaining the formal education that they will need later in life. In school, courses directed toward occupational preparation are often included in the educational pattern of a student. From the exposure received in school and actual job experience, the individual develops an attitude toward work. The favorable or unfavorable impression of work developed at this time may stay long into his adult life.

Where the opportunity exists, the individual must decide whether or not to continue his education in college or another post-secondary training institution. For many, the opportunity for higher education does exist, and it is pursued. Those students who either enter and complete college or take additional occupational training beyond the high school level appear to have a decided advantage, both in terms of economic returns and in employment opportunities. Part-time jobs may be held in college, after school hours or during vacations, but school occupies the primary interest of the student. This does not mean that it is his total concern, but those who permit extracurricular activities to dominate their time may find that staying in school is difficult. As the end of formal education nears, either through graduation or from other reasons prior to graduation, the pressure to think about full-time employment increases. Some know what they want to do when they leave school, but many are uncertain. For many men, military service must be completed and, thus, occupational pursuits are delayed for a time. Inevitably, some time during the second or third decade of life, full-time employment becomes a reality.

ADJUSTMENT TO THE WORK SITUATION
FOR BEGINNING WORKERS

The transition from career training in school to early establishment in a job poses its own set of problems for an individual. In the choice of an occupation or career he needs to assure prospective employers that he is both technically competent and personally acceptable. Once a decision has been reached by a student and an actual job offer is accepted, the task of making personal and interpersonal adjustments begins.

Some of these tasks are outlined below as they were developed by Robert and Rhona Rapoport in their study of work and family in contemporary society.

Establishment of Early Career

Personal Tasks:

1. Developing a rhythm of life geared to the world of work.

2. Adapting one's performance to the multiple criteria for good job performance, to which the skills learned in the training phase must be accommodated.

3. Broadening the range of tasks dealt with in the course of one's work to suit the expectations of the work role.

4. Developing gratifying leisure activities.

5. Developing a self-image consistent with the new status.

Interpersonal Tasks:

1. Accommodating oneself to relations with peers on the job.

2. Accommodating oneself to the authority structure of the job.

3. Developing commitment to work and loyalty to the organization and to one's professional reference groups [15, p. 390].

For some of the more fortunate young entering workers, the correct occupational field is chosen; for others, mistakes may be realized and more time spent searching for the right position. In either case, the period of first entrance in the working world is one of experimentation, trial and error, and development, often accompanied by a number of job changes. Even for most college graduates this period is usually a time of relatively low income and little responsibility.

The degree of satisfaction that young workers derive from their jobs depends largely on how well they adjust to the factors they encounter on the job. Generally, research indicates that their morale is high during the early years of employment; however, this period of high morale often is followed by diminishing job satisfaction. The low point is reached between the mid-twenties and the early thirties. After this period, job satisfaction appears to climb steadily with age [6, p. 6].

The pattern of job satisfaction in workers is characterized by the diagram shown in Figure 5–1.

It is difficult to predict accurately at what age the highs and lows of job morale begin and end. The ages for those who began their work after high school would probably be different from the ages of those who started after college. Other factors which might affect these cycles would be the type of work, the length of time spent in preparation for an occupation, or the length of time one works for the same company.

MIDCAREER ADJUSTMENTS

The decade between thirty and forty is one in which the search for an occupational field is usually resolved. After a number of job changes, a worker may find himself employed by a firm in the industry he wants, and the drive for advancement may become more intense. He is still learning and gaining experience, but if he has chosen his field correctly, success may come either in the form of pay raises or promotions and increased responsibility.

Although among very creative individuals significant contributions are

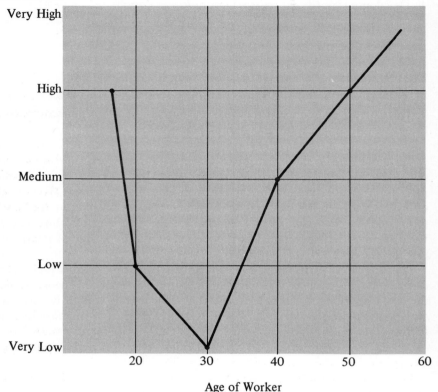

Degree of Satisfaction

Age of Worker

FIGURE 5–1. Change in Employee Job Satisfaction.

often made early in their professional career, the two decades between forty and sixty are usually the most productive in a man's career. The education, experience, and skill gained and developed during the prior twenty years can now be exercised, weighed by mature insights and judgment. Peak years are usually reached in earning power, responsibility, and production, regardless of the individual occupational field. Assuming that health remains, this can be the period during which the man's mark and contribution to his profession and/or employer is the greatest. It is also the period when a man realizes that the occupational goals dreamed about may not be possible and that adjustments must be made.

The years after sixty can be when experience and mature judgment make a man extremely valuable as an adviser to the operations of the firm and the activities of younger men. It may be the time of declining physical activity and active participation in business affairs. It can be a period of great satisfaction and relaxation if adjustment has been made to the thought of retirement.

Retirement Years.   When retirement does arrive, the adjustment to inactivity in business must be made by the individual if depression is to be avoided. Hobbies and recreational pursuits need to absorb the energy and drive previously spent on the job.

Life and occupational progress do not always come in as neat a package as the cycle just described. The transition from one stage to another may not be so smooth. At any age, failures or setbacks, real or imagined, can frustrate and confuse the individual. Some men choose unrealistic goals; for others, personal tragedies may interfere with occupational progress. When an individual becomes aware that personal or occupational goals may not be realized, his psychological reactions may be disturbing. Rebellion may take the form of various physical or social excesses. For other individuals, attitudes may become bitter, hostile, or apathetic. Some men may never find a satisfying occupational career and, therefore, may spend years that are clouded by frustration, despair, or unfulfilled ambition.

For a few rare individuals, new endeavors and careers begin when other people are preparing for retirement. Not all men age at the same rate. For example, Konrad Adenauer was a world leader until his eighties; Albert Schweitzer remained active and vigorous as a medical missionary in Africa at ninety; Winston Churchill took charge of the British war effort at sixty-six, a year past the mandatory retirement age in many firms. Benjamin Franklin, Bernard Baruch, Supreme Court Justice Oliver Wendell Holmes, and Andrew Carnegie each made overwhelming contributions to their respective professions long after the normal retirement age had been passed. On the other hand, some men begin to decline mentally and physically by the age of forty.

A NONCOLLEGE CAREER PATTERN

The pattern of occupational success for those who do not obtain any college education may be slightly different from the one just described. The belief in the widespread availability of opportunities for fame and fortune has perhaps found its most popular expression in the stories that relate the careers of prominent American industrialists: Henry Ford, John D. Rockefeller, Andrew Carnegie. These men within their lifetimes climbed the ladder of financial success [10, p. 82]. Also, popular novels have publicized the careers of fictional characters who reached the heights of power and fame in typical Horatio Alger fashion. However, the belief that the common worker, through his own efforts, can rise to the position of chairman of the board is dying fast. In spite of the evidence that the stock-clerk-to-president career pattern has been greatly magnified, many young men start an unskilled job thinking it is only a stop-gap endeavor. The job they take is only temporary; they expect to earn enough money to buy a car or save enough to go to school or buy a business. However, they get caught up in marriage, family, mortgages, and other expenses and this causes their dreams to diminish. Gradually they come to realize their limitations, and they need to re-evaluate their personal and occupational goals [18, p. 37]. As time and seniority add up, it becomes increasingly difficult to quit a job and attempt to change occupations, even if the work is not satisfying.

The foregoing description is not meant to insinuate that all college-trained men are happy or successful and that all noncollege job holders are not. Certainly this is not the case. In the first place, happiness is a most elusive thing, and work, although important, is not the only factor involved. Many men who do not attend college obtain sound occupational preparation through apprenticeship or other on-the-job experience, vocational training, or individual study and effort. The men who possess the skills and ambition often rise within their chosen field to positions of responsibility, and they may achieve great personal satisfaction. However, in the light of the increasing technological knowledge and skill required by the majority of jobs in industry, it is wise to view occupational opportunities realistically and to realize that a formal education has become increasingly important in both blue-collar and white-collar jobs.

CHANGING ATTITUDES TOWARD WORK AND EMPLOYERS

By 1980, nearly 45 per cent of the labor force in the United States will be younger than thirty-five years old. The implications of this phenomenon are far-reaching when one considers that the coming generation of workers will be more highly educated, better informed, very mobile, and more affluent than any preceding group of workers. The aspirations and expectations of these workers may differ considerably from those of either present or past work forces. Their outlooks and ambitions will depend on their abilities, education, and training, but almost certainly the coming generation will be more demanding to employers.

Because the majority of young workers are far removed from the impact of the economic depression of the 1930's, they will probably be more willing to take risks in changing jobs. Job motivation will become increasingly difficult for employers and supervisors. Entering workers, particularly among the better trained and educated, will want greater responsibility and challenge and more rapid avenues of advancement in their early jobs. They will probably want more interesting and less routine work, and it can be expected that the young work force will be more concerned with the social value of its work. To a much larger extent than in previous generations, entering workers will be attuned to participative and demo-cratic management methods as opposed to traditional or authoritarian techniques of leadership. This seems to dictate the need for placing in-creasing emphasis on the human aspects of jobs rather than on the tech-nical elements of work.

Increasingly, young workers are more aware of the employment alter-natives and opportunities available to them. This, combined with gen-erally higher levels of education and a more open attitude toward change, means that changing jobs or even changing professions will become even more common than at present. Concepts of company loyalty will depart from those expected by employers during the first half of the twentieth century. Emphasis will shift toward greater individual concern over per-sonal and professional growth. In short, job mobility will probably con-tinue and expand as more employees seek to improve their economic and occupational status through job switching.

According to several surveys, job mobility among corporate managers showed a definite upward trend during the early 1960's. This trend is expected to continue unless some catastrophic depression or other calam-ity revives the inhibiting fears and anxieties that still haunt so many man-agers who entered business in the 1930's [1, p. 139].

While the dimensions of the value systems of the new generation of workers are still unknown, supervisors can expect that the emerging psy-chological, social, and economic attitudes of young workers will confront them with baffling new problems and challenges. An aggressive array of youthful ambition and ideas will add to the dynamics of work groups in every occupation and industry. This vital resource, properly channeled by thoughtful and conscientious leadership, can be deployed in the solu-tion of complex operational problems confronting the organization; if thwarted, it can turn against employers and create additional human and social problems for the organization.

The direction that the energy of the coming generation of workers will take appears to hinge on two key factors: First is the ability of employers to provide work that is challenging, relevant, and rewarding for new employees. The second is the style of leadership used by employers. In most cases, leadership will have to provide opportunities for meaningful participation in affairs affecting the lives of workers and must consider the intelligence, pride, and dignity of these workers.

CHANGING WORLD OF WORK AND LEISURE

The impact of technology on production, clerical, and distribution meth-ods is changing the skill requirements of the jobholders in such fields. With these changing requirements a major change is being brought about by the increased amount of leisure time being afforded by automation. The length of the work week has constantly declined in most industries since the period prior to the beginning of the twentieth century. Many authorities believe the downward trend will extend long into the future, although in most occupational fields the work week has remained close to forty hours. However, the number of paid holidays and vacation periods has shown an upward trend over the past several decades.

The increase of leisure time already accrued during the past decade has had a marked effect on the increase in company-sponsored recreational programs which permit the individual worker and his family to participate in sports, hobbies, and educational activities. As leisure time increases, each worker will find more freedom to pursue areas of his own interest. Such freedom is going to necessitate a revision in the traditional concepts of the Puritan values of hard work and self-denial for self-esteem. Man will have to learn to cope with his leisure if he is to avoid ennui and lost sense of dignity. In the highly automated world of tomorrow, new avenues for personal fulfillment, creativity, and usefulness will have to be sought in activities outside of work in addition to the satisfactions found in the social relations, physical and mental activity, and challenges of the job.

SUMMARY

1. We find that work is mental or physical activity directed toward some end rather than being an end in itself. The manner in which a man approaches work is influenced by a great number of interacting factors. The work itself may be difficult or simple, strenuous or easy. The tasks involved in the job can directly influence the attitude of the person performing them; however, the social environment and physical setting of the job can do much to affect a person, too. If the worker feels that the work he does has no status or prestige, he may quit it as soon as he finds some occupation he believes is more suitable. The attitude a person possesses in regard to work is affected by the people with whom he works: his superiors, peers, or subordinates. How hard he works depends on what he gets out of working in the way of economic, social, and psychological satisfaction. The worker's view of work may change as his age, skills, experience, and home and job responsibilities change. The person's values and philosophy of life have a significant bearing on whether he "works to live," or "lives to work."

2. Although little conscious thought is given to the meaning of work, it is something that a supervisor should understand if it is his responsibility to get work done through the motivation of his subordinates. The work a man does cannot be separated from the man, and the meaning of work to a man is, therefore, part of him. Understanding that meaning

can be a key to understanding the man and a guide to improving his performance.

3. When the meaning of work is viewed as being an integral part of a man's existence, we find that several generalizations can be made which can be useful as a guide in the motivation of employees: (1) Work is an essential part of a man's life since it gives him status and, in a broad sense, binds him to society. Ordinarily, people like to work as long as the physical conditions, social environment, and job activities meet their needs. (2) The morale of the worker is not *directly* related to only the material conditions of the job, but these conditions can be a significant factor to his physical health and comfort. However, an employer needs to be concerned with job factors other than the physical ones of lighting, noise, time and motion, and temperature. (3) There are many incentives, of which money is not usually most important, which the employer can provide in order to motivate the worker: training, opportunity to advance, recognition, security, and other job factors which must be recognized. (4) Unemployment becomes a powerful negative incentive because it deprives a person of his normal relationship to society.

4. The leisure time that has developed during the past half century because of automation and changing social conditions is not only affecting the skill and educational requirements of many workers, it is also going to call for a reassessment of the Puritan values of hard work and self-denial. Many companies sponsor recreational programs which permit a man and his family to expand and explore their interests in sports, hobbies, and education in order to provide creative outlets for employee leisure time. As leisure time increases, human relations practices should include provisions to assist workers make the transition from traditional concepts of the meaning of work with long hours to the world of leisure time. Such assistance is not necessarily altruistic, but is designed to deter the possible apathy that workers developed during their leisure from lapping over into their jobs.

DISCUSSION QUESTIONS

1. How does the meaning of work differ with different individuals?
2. Would the meaning of work be the same for a young college student as it is for a man who is working for a large corporation? Working for himself? Working for a small store? If not, why might it differ?
3. What factors might explain why employee satisfaction or morale may drop in the early years of his occupational career?
4. What role of importance does work play in a man's life?
5. How does the threat of unemployment affect a person's feelings toward his job? His social status? His role in the family?

BIBLIOGRAPHY AND
SELECTED COLLATERAL READINGS

1. ALBROOK, ROBERT C., "Why It's Harder to Keep Good Executives," *Fortune,* **78**, 6 (November, 1968), 136.
2. BAKKE, E. WIGHT, *Citizens Without Work.* New Haven, Conn.: Yale University Press, 1947.
3. BOROW, H., *Man in a World at Work.* Boston: Houghton Mifflin, 1964.
4. CHILMAN, CATHERINE S., *Growing Up Poor.* U.S. Department of Health, Education, and Welfare. Welfare Administration, Division of Research, Washington: U.S. Government Printing Office, 1966.
5. GINZBERG, ELI, *The Unemployed.* New York: Harper & Row, 1943.
6. HERZBERG, FREDERICK, and others, *Job Attitudes: Review of Research and Opinion.* Pittsburgh: Psychological Service of Pittsburgh, 1957.
7. IRELAN, LOLA M. (ed.), *Low Income Life Styles.* U.S. Department of Health, Education, and Welfare. Welfare Administration, Division of Research, Washington: U.S. Government Printing Office, 1966.
8. KOMAROVSKY, MIRRA, *The Unemployed Man and His Family.* New York: Dryden Press, 1940.
9. LEVINSON, HARRY, "What Work Means to a Man," *Think* (January, 1964), pp. 7–11.
10. LIPSET, SEYMOUR MARTIN, and REINHARD BENDIX, *Social Mobility in Industrial Society.* Berkeley, Calif.: University of California Press, 1962.
11. MILLER, DELBERT C., and WILLIAM H. FORM, *Industrial Sociology,* 2nd ed. New York: Harper & Row, 1964.
12. MORSE, NANCY C., and ROBERT S. WEISS, "The Function and Meaning of Work and the Job," *American Sociological Review,* **XX** (April, 1955), 191–98.
13. NASH, GERALD D. (ed.), *Issues in American Economic History.* Boston: D. C. Heath and Company, 1964.
14. OSIPOW, S. H., *Theories of Career Development.* New York: Appleton-Century-Crofts, 1968.
15. RAPOPORT, ROBERT, and RHONA RAPOPORT, "Work and Family in Contemporary Society," *American Sociological Review,* **XXX**, 3 (June, 1965), 381–94.
16. SAYLES, LEONARD R., and GEORGE STRAUSS, *Human Behavior in Organizations.* Englewood Cliffs, N.J.: Prentice-Hall, Inc., 1966.
17. SHOSTAK, A. B., and W. GOMBERG, *Blue-Collar World.* Englewood Cliffs, N.J.: Prentice-Hall, Inc., 1964.
18. STRAUSS, GEORGE, and LEONARD R. SAYLES, *Personnel: The Human Problems of Management,* 2nd ed. Englewood Cliffs, N.J.: Prentice-Hall, Inc., 1967.
19. WARNER, W. LLOYD, and NORMAN H. MARTIN, *Industrial Man.* New York: Harper & Row, 1959.

Employee Attitudes and
Management Philosophy

Aside from a few early attempts at improving the general welfare of workers similar to the efforts of Robert Owen, there is little evidence that prior to the twentieth century employers were particularly concerned with worker *morale*. The concern displayed for employee welfare during the stress of the early industrial era was more frequently rooted in altruistic motives rather than in the belief that it was related to worker productivity. Frederick Taylor and others did much to direct management's attention toward the relationship between the individual worker and productivity. Later, the studies made by Elton Mayo and his associates turned direct attention to the importance of employee attitudes.

Today the evidence indicates that employers are greatly concerned with attitudes in the general belief that if morale is high employees are satisfied and happy about their conditions of employment. It is further generalized that when employee morale is high, they produce more and/or more efficiently, and when morale is low both the quantity and quality of production suffer accordingly.

In response to this general belief it must be pointed out that a clear relationship between employee morale and production is unproved. In fact, Brayfield and Crockett conclude that there is little convincing evidence that individuals in any group who have more favorable attitudes toward the company do a better job [2]. This generalization applies to a wide variety of occupational groups, including insurance agents, employees paid by the hour, office workers, plumber's apprentices, supervisors, and other employee categories in various business and industrial companies [17, p. 185]. Studies by other researchers indicate that the relationship that may exist between morale and productivity is at best a slight one [6, p. 113].

While differences may exist in the methods used to determine the relationship, thus far research does not conclusively support any correlation between employee morale and attitudes and productivity. The difficulty in soundly establishing a relationship between the two stems from many factors, but two of the most prevalent are the difficulty of defining morale and, once it is satisfactorily defined, the difficulty of accurately measuring it. Because of these and other problems, management had traditionally based the conditions of employment and the type of control it utilized over workers on certain assumptions about the nature of worker mentality and needs. Therefore, it is important that the assumptions supervisors and managers make about workers are accurate, or, at least, carefully substantiated, before any programs or action is taken based on such assumptions. If a supervisor attempts to motivate his subordinates without regard for their goals and objectives, he may well find that his actions meet with open hostility or, at best, passive resistance.

The task of determining employee attitudes or morale is complicated further by the difference in perceptions between many employees and their superiors. Each individual may look for different need-satisfactions from his work, and often the emphasis placed on such needs changes with the nature of the job, the individual's place in the organizational hierarchy, and the individual's changing aspirations. The inaccuracies that can accompany differences in perspective of people in the same organization were well illustrated by the results of a survey shown in Table 6–1.

A list of ten items was provided to nearly 2,500 workers from which they ranked their preferences when asked, "What are the things you yourself feel are most *important* in a job?" The data in Column I of the table show the frequency of choice when each worker's first three preferences are used. The foremen in the same plant were asked to indicate how they thought their subordinates would rank the ten items, and then what they themselves felt were the most important things in a job. Column II shows how the foremen believed the workers would rate the items; Column III indicates the importance the foremen themselves placed on the same ten items.

The items indicated on Table 6–1 are grouped according to economic, human satisfaction, and other job factors; not in the order in which they were asked. As may be noted, the foremen consistently overestimated the importance their subordinates placed on the economic factors and underestimated the importance to the workers of the human factors. The foremen would have been more accurate in their estimates of what workers wanted if they had attached roughly the same value to each of the factors for their subordinates as they did for themselves. Although the table does not show the results of the data collected when the general foremen (the superiors of the foremen responding to the survey) were

TABLE 6–1. What Subordinates Want in a Job Compared with Their Superior's Estimates

Job Factors	Column I Workers Rated Themselves	Column II Foremen Estimated Workers Would Rate	Column III Foremen Rated Themselves
Economic Factors			
1. Steady work and steady wages	61%*	79%*	62%*
2. High wages	28	61	17
3. Pensions and other old-age security benefits	13	17	12
Human Factors			
4. Not having to work too hard	13	30	4
5. Getting along with fellow workers	36	17	39
6. Getting along with my supervisor	28	14	28
7. Good chance to turn out good-quality work	16	11	18
8. Good chance to do interesting work	22	12	38
Other Factors			
9. Good chance for promotion	25	23	42
10. Good physical working conditions	21	19	18

Total Number of Cases
Workers   2,499
Foremen   196

Compiled from Robert L. Kahn, "Human Relations on the Shop Floor," *Human Relations and Modern Management*, E. M. Hugh-Jones, ed. (Amsterdam: North-Holland Publishing Co., 1958).
* Per cent of individuals rating this job factor as one of the top three most important.

asked to rate the same ten factors for themselves and as they believed their subordinates (the foremen) would rate the factors, the same general pattern of overestimation and underestimation occurred. The general foremen believed that the foremen placed much higher value on the economic variables than the foremen actually did; also, they underestimated the importance the foremen actually placed on the human and other job factors.

The point that emerges from this survey is that often supervisors and managers base their actions and treatment on unfounded assumptions about the attitudes and values of their subordinates. The difference in perception indicated by the data shown in Table 6–1 is not simply explained; however, the tendency of superiors to believe their subordinates attach a higher priority on the economic aspects of the job than they actually do stems in part from the "economic man" theory that molded many traditional management concepts of worker treatment and motivation.

TRADITIONAL MANAGEMENT CONCEPTS OF WORKER ATTITUDES

THEORY X

Douglas McGregor summarizes a few of the typical traditional management beliefs and calls them "Theory X."

> 1. The average human being has an inherent dislike of work and will avoid it if he can.
>
> 2. Because of this human characteristic of dislike of work most people must be coerced, controlled, directed, threatened with punishment to get them to put forth adequate effort toward the achievement of organizational objectives.
>
> 3. The average human being prefers to be directed, wishes to avoid responsibility, has relatively little ambition, wants security above all [10, pp. 33–34].

These assumptions have not been substantiated by careful research by the social sciences; however, a number of modern management practices still appear to follow the thinking that is supported by the premises of Theory X. As might be suspected, the morale of the workers is a difficult thing to control directly for many reasons. The traditional view of direction and control would eliminate the necessity of determining worker attitudes. Thus, it is accepted by some supervisors or managers because it circumvents many problems associated with attempts to obtain such information.

The major objections often raised about trying to determine employee attitudes can be placed into several categories.

1. There is the belief that attempting to find out what employees are thinking is a sign of weakness and something with which the competent manager who has adequate control over his workers will not need to concern himself. Part of the reason for this viewpoint is the misunderstanding that determining employee attitudes means management will subsequently have to spoonfeed the employees or give in to all they desire and that hence, it will be undermining management's authority.

2. Another objection is that determining employee attitudes is unnecessary because employers know already what the workers think and feel; that is, they think and feel in a way that Theory X says they do. This

belief is so common and so rarely justified that it might well be placed in the category of "famous last words." Too often, managers have drawn the conclusion that all was well only to find some crisis arise reflecting employee discontent.

3. The next objection is a more scientific one based on the belief that the results of any attempt at determining employee attitudes are likely to be inaccurate. The reasons for this may be either because the employee, expecting later repercussions, fears to reveal his true attitudes, or because employee attitudes may not be closely related with their actions. (Each of these will be discussed more fully later in this chapter.)

4. A final objection, although less rational than the others and often unspoken, is management's fear of workers. This may be expressed in such sayings as, "Let sleeping dogs lie." Some managers seem to feel that they are sitting on top of a smoldering volcano which may erupt at any moment, and instead of solving the problem by attempting to release the tension, they try to suppress it still further [3, pp. 168–72].

WHAT IS MORALE?

Although there are a variety of objections to determining employee needs, an increasing amount of attention has been devoted to the topic. Realizing the limitations and complexity of terminology relating to attitudes, Heckman and Huneryager offer the following guideline. *Morale is loosely defined as a combination of employee attitudes toward employment.* It is a synthesis, or bringing together, of how workers think and feel about their jobs, working conditions, supervisors, company, wages, and other aspects of employment. Defined in this way, the term includes individual and group morale; *individual morale* being the structure of a single employee's attitudes toward employment; whereas *group morale* reflects the general tone or esprit de corps of employee attitudes in a firm, a particular office, or department [5, p. 120].

The very nature of morale creates its own set of problems when an attempt is made to measure it. Morale involves *attitudes* which are a response or feeling that a person has for objects, people, situations or ideas. It is usually conceded that attitudes are learned and can be modified or lost. Attitudes are, in part, based on emotions and can change although they are considered to be more stable than mere emotional outbursts. An individual has an attitude about myriad factors he encounters both on and off the job.

The following four attitudinal areas which contribute to the degree of employee satisfaction are based on those developed by Nancy Morse in her study of clerical workers in a large company:

1. The particular work that he performs—the variety of tasks, the skill and training required, and the relative freedom of action allowed on the job.

2. The group in which the worker is a member.

3. The company or organization for which an individual works.

4. The community and social groups of which the worker is a member [11, p. 12].

The diversity of attitudes that a person can have complicates the problem of measuring them accurately. Our feelings about many things can range from strong to neutral, for or against; and thus, they fall within a broad range which is not always easy to define. If a relatively large number of employees has only a slightly unfavorable attitude about some aspect of the job, it may not pose as urgent a problem to management as when a small group of workers has strong feelings about the same subject. Therefore, the difficulty of uncovering employee attitudes is compounded by the problem of determining the intensity of their feeling.

METHODS USED
TO MEASURE EMPLOYEE ATTITUDES

Although the nature of morale is complex, an indication of employee attitudes toward various factors of employment can be accomplished in a number of ways. A company can ask employees what they think through the use of techniques of attitude or opinion polls. This method is most direct and can serve several functions within the firm. First, a survey can be used as a means of discovering specific sources of employee irritation at an early stage of its development. Second, the survey itself may act as a safety valve where pent-up employee resentment can be let off. However, it should be kept in mind that unless management intends to do something about such sources of irritation, the conducting of an opinion poll can in itself become a source of irritation and resentment. Finally, the opinions revealed can be utilized by management in the formation of its own policies and practices when changes in programs or systems are being undertaken. Many firms spend hundreds or even thousands of dollars on items which employees neither want nor use, yet ignore quite simple matters which would cost little or no money because these employee needs remain unknown.

The success of any attempt by management to gain insight into employee morale through survey methods depends on several important factors, not the least of which are management's own attitudes and past action in regard to such matters. Earlier it was mentioned that one of the objections to attempts to determine employee attitudes was that no accurate measure was possible. The scientific validity of many psychological measuring devices leaves much to be desired, but the most important consideration from the workers' viewpoint is the spirit in which such attempts are made. If filling out opinion polls has become a routine part of the job, and no tangible results have been achieved through improved conditions and no management communications have been issued to explain why the changes have not been made, workers may justifiably revolt against them.

The degree of accuracy that can be achieved on attitude surveys also depends to a large extent upon their proper administration. Both the type of questionnaire and the language used should be carefully chosen. Words that are not understood or that have a different meaning to workers and management need careful explanations. For example, the word *profit* may have one meaning to management, another meaning to the rank-and-file employee.

Semantic differences are not the only barrier to more accurate results of employee opinion polls. The actual method of filling out the questionnaire is likely to affect how honestly the worker is going to answer the questions. Some surveys are designed so that the worker chooses from a list of multiple-choice questions, others require a check mark next to the answer selected by the worker, others require that employees write a comment or two about the way they feel on certain topics ("What do you think about your chances for advancement with this firm?"), and still other surveys employ a more projective technique in which employees complete unfinished sentences or phrases ("My boss is . . ."). Whatever type of question is asked, the honesty of the worker's response may be influenced by his feeling that management is going to be able to identify him. Therefore, efforts to keep the worker anonymous will aid in getting more accurate opinions. Willard Kerr has developed a questionnaire which utilizes perforated tabs which the worker tears off to indicate his answers. This insures that even his handwriting cannot be identified [7, pp. 275–81].

Another device that not only helps insure the anonymity of employees but also facilitates rapid tabulation of employee responses to morale surveys is the use of data processing. In this method questionnaires are designed and printed on IBM tab cards. Employees mark their response to questions directly on the tab cards, which are then tabulated automatically and rapidly on electronic data-processing equipment. See an example of IBM-type questionnaire in Figure 6–1.

Regardless of the type of questionnaire or method used to collect employee responses, one administrative detail needing careful planning is the timing of the survey. If the survey is conducted right after Christmas bonuses have been passed out, the validity of the responses is highly suspect because the holiday spirit might distort real employee sentiments. A final detail involves the time allotted for employees to complete the

Employee Opinion Survey

Directions: Indicate Your Answer by Filling in Oval

(Fill in Only One)

	Yes	No	Statement
1.	O	O	Male
2.	Ø	O	I am twenty-five years of age or over.
3.	Ø	O	I have worked for this firm less than a year.
4.	O	O	I have worked for this firm for more than five years.
5.	O	O	On the whole, working conditions are good.
6.	O	O	More staff meetings are needed.
7.	O	O	My performance reports are usually discussed with me.
8.	O	O	There is too much favoritism in this office.
9.	O	O	For the most part, my co-workers are friendly and easy to get along with.
10.	O	O	Morale in this office is poor.
11.	O	O	On the whole, I would say that the firm is a leader in most respects.
12.	O	O	My training in this firm (or department) has not been adequate.
13.	O	O	My supervisor is friendly and easy to get along with.
14.	O	O	Advancement depends more upon whom you know than individual merit.
15.	O	O	All the employees work well together.
16.	O	O	Information about our benefit program is inadequate.
17.	O	O	Work is distributed evenly.
18.	O	O	My supervisor does not show enough interest in the people he works with.
19.	O	O	I feel free to express my own ideas and suggestions.
20.	O	O	My supervisor changes his decisions a lot.
21.	O	O	Career opportunities for women are good in this company.
22.	O	O	I don't like to tell people I work for this company.

FIGURE 6–1.

survey. The length of time required will vary with the type and number of questions asked. Regardless of how long or short the survey might be, it is usually a sound practice to have it done on company time.

Surveys may be one of the most direct and, within limits, most accurate methods of uncovering employee attitudes, but they are not the only means. Some companies have sponsored essay contests and given awards for the best answer to questions such as, "Things I would do to improve our company." The results of such contests can lend insight to employee thinking, but they have the serious handicap of identifying the authors. Frequently, the employee who enters the contest will be more concerned with winning than with making known any real criticism he may have, and his entry will reflect what he thinks management wants to hear. Other methods of uncovering employee attitudes are interviews of employees who are leaving the firm (exit interviews), suggestion systems, or other channels of communication which allow workers to voice their opinions.

Exit interviews, if skillfully conducted, can be useful in discovering why a particular employee is leaving the firm. If the interviews are not conducted well, many employees are likely to give neutral answers, like, "I've always wanted to open my own hobby shop and now that my wife's uncle died I have enough money to do it." They seem reluctant to give the real reason for leaving the firm and, unless the person interviewing them is extremely perceptive and skilled, a possible source of dissatisfaction in the company will remain undiscovered.

In one study of suggestion systems used in small manufacturing firms, the majority of managers in the companies surveyed stated that one of the primary purposes of their suggestion systems was to increase employee morale and to take the pulse of employee attitudes. While it may not be a primary function in all firms, a suggestion system certainly has usefulness as an indication of what is on the employee's mind.

Whatever means are developed by a firm to keep tabs on employee morale, it is important that these means be conducted in a spirit of good faith rather than in one of spying on the employees. One way to indicate that management has honest intentions is to make known to employees the results of any morale surveys it conducts. This can present a painful situation to management when areas of strong employee dissatisfaction occur, but to disguise or gloss over such items would only confirm any employee suspicion that the survey was a fake. This means that management must act upon those things that are sources of irritation to employees as quickly as possible or explain why such action is not feasible. The ultimate sign of good will on the part of management is the action it takes.

The type and frequency of morale surveys used by any particular firm depend on the firm's size and budget, but usually it is not feasible to conduct such surveys very often because of the limitations on time, man-power, and money. The day-to-day contacts with employees can reveal much about the general state of their attitudes when records are main-tained in the following areas: labor turnover, absenteeism, tardiness, and employee production costs [9, pp. 89–108]. Most of the data pertaining to these indicators are already available to management. The relationship of these factors to morale when taken singularly, is difficult to establish; when considered as a whole, these factors can give a good indication when something may be amiss and closer investigation should be made. The factors listed above are symptomatic of possible low morale, just as high fever in a patient is a symptom that he is ill. The fever of a patient or the measuring of poor (low) morale in workers *does not indicate what is wrong*. A judicious doctor does not prescribe medicine before knowing the reason for the high temperature in his patient because he knows that drugs he might administer indiscriminately could aggravate rather than cure the condition of the patient. Managers who frantically dole out "medicine" to cure low employee morale may find that they have done precisely the opposite of what was needed.

A CASE OF EMPLOYEE ATTITUDES
AND JOB SATISFACTION

The following brief case serves to illustrate how careful analysis of the cause of employee discontent is vital to the satisfactory implementation of corrective measures by management.

In a family-owned paint manufacturing plant the owners decided to modernize the offices when sales reached a volume high enough to warrant the use of electronic data-processing equipment. A new, sound-proof, air-conditioned room was added to the administrative wing of the plant. The older offices were painted and office equipment was either painted to match or replaced with new models. The floor was carpeted and new conveniences, such as coffee urn and soft drink dispenser, were added to the employee lounge. Upon completion of the remodeling the owner gave a little "housewarming" for all of the employees in the new offices. A number of production employees were invited for "refreshments" on a prescribed morning. The owner gave a little speech thanking everyone for the effort they had been making which had contributed to increased sales and profits. In a spirit of good fellowship he handed everyone an envelope with a small bonus check enclosed. Everyone appeared happy.

During the following week four of the production men known as loaders, because they carried boxes, each weighing about 40 pounds, from a storage area to the mixing vats and then opened them and poured the contents into a bin that automatically fed into the mixing vats, com-plained of strained back muscles; and two took a half day off in order to recover. Two of the other loaders claimed they were going to see a doctor for treatment. The owner checked the group hospital plan in force for employees and explained to each of the men how much it paid for therapeutic treatment.

The men went to the doctor to obtain heat treatments and for several weeks were placed in other production jobs which did not require any lifting. Two other men were transferred into their place from the packing department. Efficiency was lost because of their inexperience and a strain was placed on the two remaining experienced loaders. After a week one of the experienced loaders went to see the owner and said he was sorry, but he was going to have to quit. When asked why, he stated that the load had become too much for him and that he could no longer carry the heavy boxes without straining his back. The owner asked the man to stay until things were settled and the two loaders who were temporarily transferred to another department could return. The plant was behind in filling its orders and the man agreed to stay, but only until the regular loaders returned and his replacement could be found and trained.

The weekend following the loader's conversation with the owner, the owner went back to the loading department and looked around. He moved and loaded a few boxes of pigment himself to see how heavy the work really was. After going through the movements, he concluded that the weight was not the real problem and that the pace of the job was not overly taxing. Upon returning to his own office to think about the problem the solution dawned on him and he corrected the situation that weekend.

The solution may appear obvious to the reader, but the answer to many human relations problems is relatively simple once all of the elements of the problems are uncovered. This does not mean that all human relations problems are simple or easily solved. In this case the owner painted the mixing room a new color, placed rubber mats on the floor, and provided a small cart at the disposal of each loader. The loader who thought he was going to quit did not, and the two who had been placed in another department soon recovered and returned. Productivity was soon regained and the problem seemed to iron itself out.

Several points in this case bear reviewing. The paint in the mixing room was not drab or dirty before the new paint job. The new paint job may or may not have been an improvement from an interior decorator's point of view. The rubber mats which were placed on the floor may have added to the comfort of the workers, but they apparently did not raise the productivity of the loaders because productivity only regained the standard that it had been before the backaches began. The carts were seldom used in the actual loading operations because the men returned to their old practice of hand-carrying the boxes, and then only used the carts to sit on during rest periods or lulls in production. If none of these things did contribute (mechanically) to production, what purpose did they serve?

The answer in this case was that it served to show that the owner was concerned about them as people. One might comment that the loaders' behavior was childish or even irrational. The answer here is a matter of interpretation. The point is that it was caused, no matter how irrational one might consider it. The owner was astute enough to realize it and took the appropriate action necessary to resolve it. How about the cost involved? One cannot paint everyone's department every time they threaten to quit. True. In the circumstances of this case, painting the mixing room was a relatively inexpensive operation and proved the simplest solution when compared with the cost of lost efficiency and the possible loss of a good experienced loader. In other situations the solution might have to be different, but the *cause* would have remained the same. Any solution which was attempted would have to be directed at the need for recognition and importance of the workers.

MANAGEMENT PHILOSOPHY AFFECTING EMPLOYEE ATTITUDES AND THEIR MEASUREMENT

The preceding discussion addressed some of the human and mechanical difficulties a company may encounter in obtaining an accurate picture of its employees' attitudes and motives. Aside from workers' problems, the actual capacity of management to obtain accurate data from workers is greatly influenced by the manner in which such information is put to use. This is particularly true over a long period of time.

Nearly all members of an organization will resist measurements which they feel will be used against them in the form of disciplinary action or increased restrictions. In order to protect themselves, employees with such fears will subtly or overtly distort their answers in an attempt to show themselves in a favorable light; that is, they may convey what they think management wants to hear. Regardless of how slight this "fudge factor" may be, it can easily lead managers to incorrect conclusions about their subordinates' attitudes and performances.

When day-to-day management behavior does little to cultivate employee trust and endorsement, any attempt (even an honest one) to gain insight into employee opinions and attitudes is probably going to be met with distrust. Despite this, many such companies unfortunately devote time, energy, and money to conducting employee surveys. Often the results are either useless or of small value in making necessary operational changes. The reason for this waste of resources frequently lies in a basic lack of understanding of human needs and an over-reliance upon traditional management concepts (Theory X). In such cases, supervisors seldom trust the integrity, intelligence, or competence of their subordinates and rely, instead, upon close methods of supervision to oversee workers so that they will do what they are told, the way they are told to do it. The result of such an approach often leads to distrust not only of supervisors but also of the company. Solutions to this mutual distrust cannot be found in increasingly sophisticated and elaborate data collection instruments and methods. Employees will meet these attempts with equally innovative means of circumventing and distorting the data collection and measurement.

The importance of the management philosophy and concomitant management practices in a company become paramount, not only to the collection process used to gauge employee attitudes, but also to the actual formation of favorable attitudes among organizational members. In a company where the motives of management appear nebulous or even antihumanitarian, workers find little motivation to divulge their honest attitudes. When overall company policies and management practices appear generally constructive and supportive of workers' needs, both nonsupervisory and supervisory personnel recognize the importance of accurate information in helping them make decisions and improve performance. This latter approach clearly calls for a departure from the traditional management concepts that may dominate management philosophy and practices.

MODERN CONCEPTS OF MANAGEMENT'S ATTITUDE TOWARD THE WORKER

In addition to McGregor's interpretation and analysis of management's traditional assumptions of worker values and attitudes, Argyris also has analyzed many management practices and concluded that many organizations appear to be designed to cope with men who are dependent, passive, and use few of their abilities. The assumption that workers are, as a whole, immature ignores the fact that most people, but not all, develop into capable and effective adults who find the lack of recognition of their adulthood demeaning. The reactions of individuals treated as if they were immature are frustration, failure, short time perspective, and conflict. The formal organization principles cause the subordinate to experience competition and rivalry and to develop a focus on the parts rather than on the whole of the organization's activities. This part-orientation increases the amount of time a leader must spend to coordinate the activity, resulting in a much greater input of organizational resources to obtain the same constant output. Of course, the trend may be reversed by decreasing the basic antagonism by using new employees who do not aspire to be mature adults.

A second way suggests that greater organizational flexibility be built into its structure and modes of leadership and control so that greater individual freedom and imagination can be exercised by workers [1, pp. 232–37]. Such flexibility may be easier to suggest than implement in large formal organizations, but another suggestion of Argyris pertaining to the interpersonal dynamics of the firm may be more feasible. He recommends T-Group or sensitivity training for managers in order to increase their ability to make their purposes more intelligible to subordinates, peers, and superiors. Sensitivity training is a process in which an individual learns to understand his impact on others and to assist him in eliminating unintentional barriers to effective communication. Such training methods will be discussed further in a later chapter.

THEORY Y

What do employees want from their work and what should management's attitude be toward trying to satisfy employee desires? Earlier in this chapter Theory X outlined the traditional assumptions about the nature of workers. McGregor also has outlined some assumptions which are in diametric opposition to those. The newer assumptions are more closely aligned with what the social scientists have developed and provide a basis for a practice of management called Theory Y. These assumptions are quoted from McGregor as follows:

1. The expenditure of physical and mental effort in work is as natural as play or rest.
2. External control and the threat of punishment are not the only means for bringing about effort toward organizational objectives. Man will exercise self-direction and self-control in the service of objectives to which he is committed.
3. Commitment to objectives is a function of the rewards associated with their achievement.
4. The average human being learns, under proper conditions, not only to accept but to seek responsibility.
5. The capacity to exercise a relatively high degree of imagination, ingenuity, and creativity in the solution of organizational problems is widely, not narrowly, distributed in the population.
6. Under the conditions of modern industrial life, the intellectual potentialities of the average human being are only partially utilized [10, pp. 47–48].

The assumptions of Theory Y involve a set of managerial attitudes and values different from the ones used to support Theory X. Those of Theory Y are dynamic, and they stress the growth and development of the worker as opposed to those assumptions that stress absolute control and place the worker in a static position of limited growth as a person. The assumptions of Theory Y not only place the onus on management to seek the collaboration of the workers, but they also encourage creativity and the sharing of responsibility for planning and obtaining the objectives of the organization. However, despite its seeming advantages, McGregor's Theory Y has not been accepted uncritically by many practitioners and some human relations theorists. The reasons for this lie in the difficulty of implementing the principles expounded by the theory. It is difficult, if not impossible, to get some managers to relinquish some of the authority that Theory Y would have them share with subordinates.

Gellerman points out another major drawback to the ideas proposed by McGregor:

> Another difficulty with theory Y is that it demands innovation. There is no simple formula whereby it can be applied. (Given our experience with human relations fads, however, this may be a blessing in disguise.) Theory Y requires a continuing dialogue between a manager and his men in which their capacity for controlling their own work is continuously stimulated, tested and enlarged. More than mere delegation is involved. The manager must first develop a realistic appreciation of what each man can do and of how he would prefer to be treated and then convey his willingness to deal with the man on his own terms (or at least to meet him halfway). What is required is more of an exchange of attitudes and of confidence than of promises or instructions. In other words, theory Y places a heavy burden on the manager's interpersonal competence. It does not permit him to be aloof or indifferent or defensive [4, p. 51].

Although McGregor's modern theory of management may not be the total answer to resolving employee difficulties, it does lead the way to a different perspective from which to investigate and evaluate employee motivation. The analysis and theories promulgated by such scholars and critics as Argyris [1], Likert [8], and McGregor [10] indicate that the most powerful incentives for employees usually must involve both financial rewards and a work environment that encourages creative and individual avenues of action. High wages in an unstimulating job environment usually will not satisfy the higher psychological and social needs of the worker; nor will inadequate financial rewards for responsible and demanding jobs enhance the degree of care and effort an individual is willing to exercise in his work. In either situation—poor pay for fascinating work or high remuneration for a dull job—the result is likely to be disillusionment for the individual worker; and this may manifest itself in high turnover rates, poor quality work, or other organizational inefficiencies.

The research evidence revealed by the behavioral scientists thus far generally supports the concepts advocated in Theory Y, and it seems that the use of such precepts by managers and supervisors in formulating their treatment of subordinates would contribute to more positive results than would reliance on the assumptions underlying the traditional theory of management. It should be recognized, however, that satisfactory implementation of management practices based on the concepts of Theory Y depends on the maturity of both supervisors and subordinates. Some arguments might be raised regarding the distribution of "maturity" among both workers and supervisors. Often the superiors are inclined not to relinquish tight controls over the activity of their subordinates because of their belief that workers lack the maturity for self-control. Essentially, this position defines maturity in mutually exclusive terms as a state of existence which an employee either does or does not possess. Actually, maturity is more accurately defined as a goal rather than as something static. Maturity is developed, and the rate at which it develops depends, in a large degree, on the environmental factors which allow and encourage it to grow in the individual. Argyris concedes that some employees are less mature than might be desired, but he also believes that there are enormous reserves of untapped maturity in the labor force that would respond to more realistic methods of supervision based on what is known about human needs and psychological development and that the recognition of this maturity would result in a significant increase in worker effort.

Another assumption which underlies modern concepts of management is that when the goals of the worker are the same as the goals of the organization, he will work harder to attain them. It is doubtful whether organizational goals can always be identical to those of the individual; however, the number of goals the two have in common is often greater than some managers assume. Even when the worker's goals are not identical to the organization's, it does not mean that the two have to lie in diametric opposition. When the worker does find that his personal ambitions are thwarted by organizational restrictions, he may find that the best way to resolve the conflict is to resign from the company. Such a course of action may well be a high price for both the firm and the individual to pay; therefore, the organizational flexibility and freedom suggested by Argyris may be the best defense against either loss in worker efficiency or actual loss of the worker to another organization.

Another step that management can take to insure that their actions and the employee personnel programs they establish are not in absolute conflict with the majority of the needs of the workers is to find out what aspects of the job the workers find satisfying and what aspects they find discouraging.

JOB FACTORS AFFECTING WORKER MORALE

The satisfactions a person seeks in his work are as diverse and complex as the number of individuals who are employed. Each person has his own physical, mental, and emotional structure, but he also shares certain needs common to all human beings. Because of this last factor, workers have some commonality in the needs they seek to satisfy at work. A number of studies of employee attitudes in different occupations and industries have begun to show a pattern of the most prevalent of these needs.

The number of studies published relating to job factors and employee job attitudes has steadily increased every decade since 1920. The results of each study vary depending on the method used to collect the data, the number of workers included in any particular survey, and other variations of research design and analysis. However, when the results of the studies are viewed as a whole, a relatively clear picture begins to emerge regarding what workers want from their work and which factors of employment contribute to job satisfaction. It will be noted that the relationship between job satisfaction and morale is assumed to exist, although the precise relationship between the two is somewhat uncertain and requires more research. It also must be remembered that the same job factor can be the source of dissatisfaction to one employee and the source of satisfaction to another. As an illustration of this point, two employees were working in a department doing similar jobs and each was earning a salary of $8,000 yearly. In this case, the salary factor is the same, but one of the workers was a man who had established a goal for himself to earn $15,000 yearly; the other had regarded $6,000 as the annual income to which he aspired. We can see how one might be very satisfied with the salary he was earning, while the other might be extremely discontented. The same divergence of opinion could exist about many job factors.

The number of job factors affecting worker attitudes are many. In an analysis of the job factors occurring most frequently in about 150 surveys and studies of job attitudes, ten major factors were identified and each major factor had a number of specific aspects which related to it. Frederick Herzberg and his associates list and define these major job factors and the aspects relating to them in their extensive report on job attitudes. Table 6–2 is adapted from their report. The list of major job factors and the specific aspects of each factor is not exhaustive nor complete, and it does not place the factors in their relative importance to workers. The list does not contain a number of off-the-job factors which can also have a significant bearing on job attitudes. Aspects of the individual's life away from the job that could also influence his attitudes would be his marital status, education, socio-economic status, intelligence, and outside interests.

TABLE 6–2.   Specific Job Aspects of Ten Major Job Factors

Major Job Factor	Specific Aspects
Intrinsic value of the job	Prestige, status, dignity, importance, respect, power, recognition, public service, self-respect, creativity, self-expression, interest in work, appropriateness to training, abilities, aspirations, plans, initiative, challenge, opportunity for travel and mobility.
Supervision	Consideration, fairness, courtesy, tact, sincerity, permissiveness, keeping promises, sociability, loyalty to workers, personal counsel, giving information on status and progress, appreciation, encouragement, empathy, understanding, closeness, consistency of orders, discipline, technical competence and aptitude, delegation of authority, opportunity for employee decision-making.
Working conditions	Clean, orderly, safe, attractive surroundings; adequacy and condition of equipment, tools, supplies, temperature, ventilation, music, lighting, recreational facilities, food, medical care, parking facilities; hours; shifts; location; and community.
Wages	Pay, profit-sharing, economic incentives, frequency of raises, fairness of compensation.
Opportunity for advancement	Merit, seniority, economic advancement, promotion from within, promotion policies, ambition in relation to advancement.
Security	Steadiness of employment, continuous work prospects, seniority, feeling of being valued by the firm, having a trade, opportunity to learn a trade or skill.
Company and management	Company attitude toward cooperation with union, sponsorship of athletic teams, employee housing developments, pride in company and product, training program, size of organization, organizational structure, company reputation and public relations, interpretation of fairness, intentions, good sense of management, foresight, planning.
Social environment of job	Congenial coworkers on or off the job, competent coworkers, pride in belonging to a team, social approval, cooperation and group effort, group dynamics, size and function of work groups, interpersonal relationships.
Communications	Information on new developments, what

TABLE 6–2. Specific Job Aspects of Ten Major Job Factors (*continued*)

Major Job Factor	Specific Aspects
Employee benefits	company is doing or plans to do, employee status, personnel policies and procedures, lines of company authority, suggestion systems, annual reports, company magazines and newspapers. Retirement, leave, vacations, holidays, provisions for emergencies: illness or accidents, insurance programs.

Adapted from Frederick Herzberg and others, *Job Attitudes: Review of Research and Opinion* (Pittsburgh: Psychological Service of Pittsburgh, 1957), pp. 39–40.

In a compilation of about twenty studies covering over 11,000 employees, the general pattern of relative importance of job factors and their specific aspects began to emerge [6, pp. 43–47]. However, there are some serious limitations to be placed on any interpretations to be made from such data. Some of the studies from which the information was taken did not make any systematic attempt to determine how stable or reliable employee attitudes were. The ranking of the ten most important job factors was based on the average rank of each factor as they appeared in the studies from which they were derived; *Wages* may have been ranked anywhere from first to tenth in importance by the workers surveyed. From its placement in the compiled data of the studies it ranks about midway. Table 6–3 shows the relative ranking of the ten, as well as the rank of six of the most important aspects of certain job factors. It should be noted that the major job factor of *supervision* ranked ninth out of a total of sixteen, while a specific aspect of supervision, *appreciation from supervisor,* ranked fourth. The same pattern occurred with *intrinsic value of the job,* which ranked eighth, whereas a more specific aspect of this factor, *interest in work,* ranked second.

The ranking of job factors into a hierarchy of importance presents several significant problems. The terminology used in attitude surveys can have various meanings to different workers. The meaning of *security* to a young man may be different from that to a man who is ready to retire; likewise, *supervision* has so many aspects to it that perhaps no two workers are rating the same thing when they answer a question pertaining to it on a questionnaire. Because of the many different connotations for each job factor checked in the studies, ranking them precisely is most difficult. Another problem inherent in the rankings is that the difference between the first-ranked factor and the tenth-ranked factor may not be very large to the worker. This may account for the difference in the order of job factors in various studies of employee attitudes.

Attitude studies reported by Ross Stagner reveal a slightly different

TABLE 6–3.

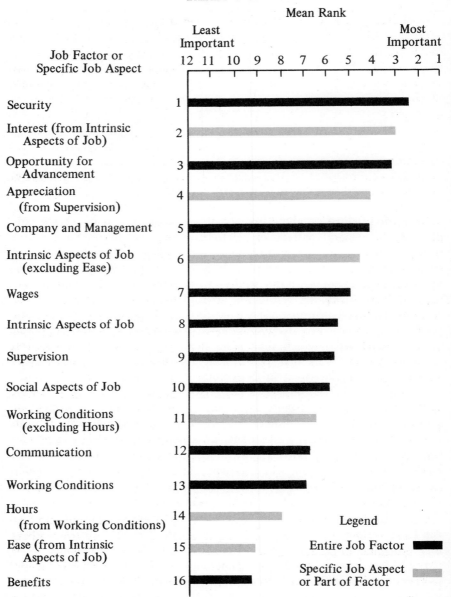

Job Factor or Specific Job Aspect		

Mean Rank

Source: Frederick Herzberg and others, *Job Attitudes: Review of Research and Opinion* (Pittsburgh: Psychological Service of Pittsburgh, 1957), p. 44.

order than the one shown in Table 6–3 [16, p. 122]. Results of another job factor study mentioned by Robert Peterson differs from Stagner's list [13, p. 3]; and a survey reported by the National Industrial Conference

Board differs from the others [12]. The relevancy of a comparison of these studies is that many of the job factors are similar even though they are not ranked in the same order. Other surveys indicate differences in importance of job factors when variables such as clerical or factory worker, male or female worker are compared [6, pp. 52–53]. As a point of interest, it should be noted that in the majority of attitude surveys money or wages does not rank at the top. This fact differs considerably from the stereotyped picture that many managers (employers) have regarding employees' needs. Ross Stagner reports that in one survey of fifty top executives, twenty-two believed that money alone motivated workers, fourteen believed that additional reasons may also motivate workers but money was the most important reason, and the remaining fourteen executives said that money was an important reason but not necessarily the most important [16, p. 128]. It is apparent that the evidence does not support the convictions of many managers regarding wages.

Earlier it was stated that job factors that contribute to employee satisfaction are assumed to have a relationship to morale. It is also feasible that the relationship is two-way. Morale has an influence on the degree of satisfaction an employee has with the factors he encounters on the job. The interrelationship between the two is complex and not yet fully understood, and perhaps it explains the discrepancy that often appears between what the worker expresses and what his actual performance is —hence, the difficulty in establishing the correlation between employee morale and productivity.

If one analyzes the various factors and aspects of the job to which workers react, it becomes readily apparent that they tend to follow the pattern of human needs outlined by Maslow and McGregor (see Chapter 4). The physical and safety needs are sought in the conditions of employment which pertain to creature comfort, health, and safety of the individual. In an industrialized society which fosters such a high degree of dependency between people, the economic needs of the worker are met by the wages he earns on the job. Because he ordinarily does not grow his own food supply, build his own shelter, or make his own clothes, the worker needs the money he earns to obtain these things from others who specialize in producing them. Economic factors of employment meet not only the primary human needs but also the higher order of needs, prestige and status, which money can help provide. This may explain why inadequate wages received so much attention by organized labor during the early period of its activity. However, once an adequate wage is attained by the worker, other factors of employment serving his social and ego needs receive much more attention.

Thus far in this chapter, employee attitudes and their relationship to production, job satisfaction, and morale have been discussed. Companies face a problem in translating what is known and reasonably well verified about these relationships into personnel programs and other conditions of employment that are conducive to high levels of production and employee satisfaction. The programs and employment conditions established in a company to accomplish this objective must be tailored to the human and financial resources of that company. However, the company philosophy that determines *what* programs and conditions are to be attained, as well as *how* they are to be implemented, is as important as the programs themselves.

Some companies hold the philosophy that good wages and good treatment will automatically motivate employees to work harder. It has already been stated in this chapter that this concept is an oversimplification of human behavior. This does not mean that properly presented personnel programs, fringe benefits, or employee services are a waste of time and money. On the contrary, if such company efforts may help attract and hold good workers by reducing employee turnover and adding to employee security, some contribution to higher productivity has been made. However, factors such as good wages do not contribute directly to the individual worker's desire to be a better employee nor to his desire to improve his performance. The motivation to do a better job, or at least to turn in a good day's work, is tied to a combination of factors including the employee's own set of goals, values, ambitions, and the intrinsic satisfaction found in the actual job. Other motivating elements are found in how well matched an employee is to the demands of his work, the systems and procedures used by the firm to place, train, advance, and reward employees, the adequacy of company personnel programs to meet employee's human needs, and the interpersonal relationships that are developed between the employee, his fellow workers, and his supervisors.

These latter topics are the subject of the remainder of this book. The focus of most of the discussion is on the relationship of the foregoing elements to employee performance and satisfaction. To the degree that it is possible, emphasis is placed on improving the supervisor's effectiveness through an awareness of the impact of these elements on the members of his work group.

SUMMARY

1. Many managers assume that if employee morale is high, their subordinates must be satisfied and, therefore, will produce more. Actually, the relationship between morale and productivity is not easy to measure scientifically. Part of the difficulty lies in satisfactorily defining *morale* and then measuring it once it has been defined. Generally, *morale* is defined as a combination of employee attitudes toward their jobs, working conditions, supervisors, wages, and other aspects of employment. There

are two aspects involved in morale. One is individual morale and the other is esprit de corps or group morale.

2. Despite the problems inherent in measuring employee morale, the use of morale surveys has grown widespread since the early 1920's. Four attitudinal areas frequently covered in morale surveys are satisfaction with the particular aspects and conditions of: the job itself, the group in which the employee is a member, the company, and the community and social groups of which the worker is a member. The various methods of collecting information regarding employee attitudes include the use of questionnaires or interviews. Regardless of the method used, management should be sure that no retaliation is taken against employees who voice dissatisfaction with some aspect of employment and that the survey is conducted in good faith. Many firms use morale questionnaires which allow the worker to remain anonymous in an effort to obtain a more honest picture of employee attitudes.

3. Although many firms utilize some method of obtaining feedback from employees, a large number of managers operate with little knowledge about the way their workers really feel or what needs employees seek to satisfy on the job. The traditional assumptions upon which some supervisors base their treatment of subordinates have been categorized and labeled "Theory X" by Douglas McGregor. Essentially, the traditional concept of management emphasizes threats and coercion as a primary means of directing and controlling employee behavior. The antithesis of the assumptions found in Theory X are outlined by McGregor in Theory Y. Although neither theory may be correct in its entirety, the assumptions made in Theory Y regarding human nature are more analogous with the research findings of the social scientists. The difficulty in applying the managerial concepts of Theory Y lies in the requirement that managers relinquish some of their authority to subordinates and places a heavy burden on the manager's interpersonal competence.

4. Research indicates that the satisfactions a person seeks in his work are as diverse and complex as the number of persons who are employed; however, both the general and the specific aspects of employment have been categorized so that some patterns can be observed. Although there are dangers in placing too much reliance on the way employees rank their job-related needs, at least the knowledge of such worker attitudes by management can help close the gap between the preconceptions of management and the actual desires of the workers.

DISCUSSION QUESTIONS

1. What are some of the reasons why employers resist trying to determine employee attitudes?

2. What methods can be used to find out worker attitudes? Which methods are most reliable? Why?

3. In the case of the paint loaders' dissatisfaction, what other courses of action might have been taken if it had not been possible to repaint the mixing room?

4. What is morale? How do worker attitudes affect individual or group morale?

5. What are some of the assumptions regarding human nature which underlie the traditional view of management control over workers?

6. Is money a major concern of workers today?

7. What conditions of employment can an employer create that are conducive to employee satisfaction?

BIBLIOGRAPHY AND SELECTED COLLATERAL READINGS

1. ARGYRIS, CHRIS, *Personality and Organization.* New York: Harper & Row, 1957.

2. BRAYFIELD, ARTHUR H., and WALTER H. CROCKETT, "Employee Attitudes and Employee Performance," *Psychological Bulletin,* Vol. 52 (September, 1955), 396–424.

3. BROWN, J. A. C., *The Social Psychology of Industry.* Baltimore, Maryland: Penguin Books, 1954.

4. GELLERMAN, SAUL W., *The Management of Human Relations.* New York: Holt, Rinehart and Winston, 1966.

5. HECKMANN, I. L., and S. G. HUNERYAGER, *Human Relations in Management.* Cincinnati: South-Western Publishing Company, 1960.

6. HERZBERG, FREDERICK, and others, *Job Attitudes: Review of Research and Opinion.* Pittsburgh: Psychological Service of Pittsburgh, 1957.

7. KERR, WILLARD A., "On the Validity and Reliability of the Job Satisfaction Tear Ballot," *Journal of Applied Psychology* (June 1948), 275–81.

8. Likert, Rensis, *New Patterns of Management.* New York: McGraw-Hill Book Company, 1961.

9. LUCK, THOMAS J., *Personnel Audit and Appraisal.* New York: McGraw-Hill Book Company, 1955.

10. McGREGOR, DOUGLAS, *The Human Side of Enterprise.* New York: McGraw-Hill Book Company, 1960.

11. MORSE, NANCY C., *Satisfactions in the White-Collar Job.* Ann Arbor, Mich.: University of Michigan, 1953.

12. NATIONAL INDUSTRIAL CONFERENCE BOARD, INC., "Factors Affecting Employee Morale," *Studies in Personnel Policy,* 85, 1947.

13. PETERSON, ROBERT L., *Work Incentives for Your Personnel.* University of Illinois Bulletin, Vol. 49, No. 46 (February, 1952). Urbana, Ill.: University of Illinois, 1952.

14. PORTER, L. W., and E. E. LAWLER, *Managerial Attitudes and Performance.* Homewood, Ill.: Richard D. Irwin, Inc., 1968.
15. SHAW, M. E., and J. M. WRIGHT, *Scales for the Measurement of Attitudes.* New York: McGraw-Hill Book Company, 1967.
16. STAGNER, ROSS, *Psychology of Industrial Conflict.* New York: John Wiley and Sons, 1964.
17. VROOM, VICTOR H., *Work and Motivation.* New York: John Wiley and Sons, 1964.

7

Human Problems
Encountered in the
Work Enviroment

A number of the physical and social conditions an employee finds on the job create problems which must be resolved if he is to obtain personal satisfaction and worth from this work. Such problems also can create barriers in reaching maximum levels in production. Since the advent of time and motion studies, many jobs have been engineered to emphasize the speed and efficiency of the worker and little room has been left for variation in activity or the pace of the job. This is particularly true on the assembly line jobs where the pace of the job is set by the machinery. When the conditions of the job limit the freedom of the individual to work at his own pace or to vary his activity, fatigue, monotony, or boredom may occur. The result of these factors is often reflected in both the quantity and the quality of the work produced.

Some of the specific problems which a worker encounters on the job could be termed *nonhuman* because they are not directly connected with the social relationships which are usually encountered in the work situation. They are, rather, a part of the work environment or are related to the nature of the job, i.e., repetitiveness of work. Such problems do require human adjustments; therefore, they are considered in this chapter on human problems encountered in the work environment.

FATIGUE AND MONOTONY

Elements such as fatigue and monotony are a part of many occupations, but are more prevalent in some jobs than others, particularly those jobs which require minimal skills or training. Many of these factors impose severe restrictions on the freedom of action of the worker and can be-

120

come a source of dissatisfaction to him. Other factors are more directly related to the social contacts made on the job and also can become a source of irritation.

A number of studies have shown that workers want to have a voice in setting the pace of their work activities and arranging the pattern of their work to suit their levels of skills or aspirations. This is not always possible in many work situations, particularly in jobs on assembly-line operations where mechanization determines the speed with which work must be performed and may reduce the number of tasks a worker performs to a few simple operations.

Time and motion studies, which grew out of the scientific management era of the early twentieth century, are concerned with the efficiency with which motor tasks can be performed. Some critics of such studies point out that the aim of obtaining greatest output for a minimal expenditure of time is not always concomitant with the physiological nature of man. It frequently emphasizes the speed of movements, rather than the rhythm of motion which is most favorable for the least expenditure of energy in work [6, pp. 56–57]. Frequently, the most efficient methods developed leave little latitude for the worker to vary the pattern of his activity. The monotony of such repetitive mass production work can have psychological and physical effects on the worker. Complaints of fatigue and boredom are sometimes voiced by workers as a result of performing short, repetitive tasks requiring little mental effort. The outgrowth of this situation can often leave the worker with an inadequate sense of accomplishment and progress and little opportunity to exercise his skill or *autonomy* (independence).

Fatigue. The physical sensation of fatigue is produced by an accumulation of waste products in the tissues of muscles and nerves in the body. Localized fatigue results from constant use of particular parts of the body; fingers, hands, arms, legs, eyes, and so on. Fatigue of such a nature can readily be demonstrated by rapidly and constantly flexing the index finger. After a period the finger seems to stiffen and motion becomes jerky and difficult to control. The sensation which is felt is called muscular fatigue. Normally, muscular fatigue can be overcome by proper rest and is not a major problem in industry where machines now do most of the lifting, pushing, or pulling of heavy materials. However, muscular fatigue is not the only kind of fatigue; nervous fatigue is also a cause of tiredness and, in some cases, fatigue may often be caused by a lack of interest. On a production line job, too heavy a tool or a too rapidly moving assembly line can become a source of fatigue. For this reason, careful planning is necessary to insure that proper types and sizes of tools be provided for

Courtesy of the U.S. Forest Service.

Reproduced by permission of Monkmeyer Photo Service.

Photo by Roche. Reproduced by permission of Monkmeyer Photo Service.

Each job has certain aspects which can create boredom, monotony, or fatigue.

the worker and that machinery speed be geared to standards which fall within human capacity. Norman Maier is adverse to any practice which speeds up the running of machinery during the early part of the day and then slows it down later; such a practice is based on the mistaken belief that men should spend their energy when they have it available. In actuality, men would spend their full day working in a state of fatigue [10].

Regardless of the causes of fatigue—lack of interest, nervousness, or muscular activity—its results are normally believed to be reflected in a diminished capacity for work in the worker. Although such a definition does not adequately explain the physical condition of the employee, it is adequate for a preliminary description of the condition and the problems which arise from it. Generally, it is understood that fatigue builds up gradually and manifests itself in rates of output, errors, accidents, and other actions of workers. Furthermore, it is believed that fatigue is cumulative in that it becomes more noticeable with the passage of time and

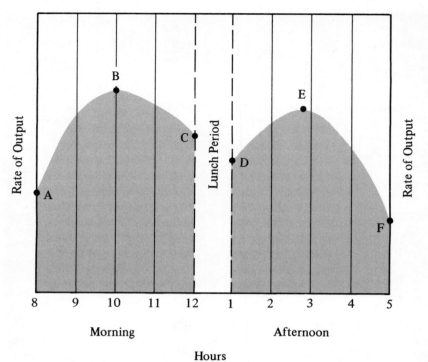

FIGURE 7–1. Typical Fatigue Curve for a Work Day.

reduced output. When the output rate for a worker is graphically plotted, a curve similar to the one in Figure 7–1 is recorded.

When one analyzes a hypothetical fatigue curve it is wise to remember that the shape of any such curve will vary, depending on the activity of the worker or individuality of the worker performing the task. For instance, the curve depicting the output of a ditch digger might decline more rapidly than one depicting a secretary typing form letters. At the same time, the shape of the curve can vary depending on the training or practice the individual might have received or the attitude he possesesed on a particular day. In any case, the relatively low rate of output at the beginning of the work day (point A) is attributed to the fact that the worker has not warmed up to his job. As he warms up to it, his output increases until the cumulative effects of fatigue begin to affect the rate of speed at which he can work (point B), and then it tends to drop progressively until the end of the morning work period (point C). The lunch period allows the worker partially to recover from his morning fatigue, but he also "cools off," thus, he begins the afternoon (point D) at a point somewhat lower in output than he ended his morning period. From this point it proceeds upward to the highest level of afternoon production (point E) in a shorter time than it took in the morning. It should be noted, however, that the rate of output in the afternoon usually does not

124

attain the morning output peak. After reaching this afternoon peak, output steadily declines until quitting time (point F). This point is lower than the beginning morning one.

Monotony.   Whereas fatigue may result from either strenuous physical activity or lack of interest, *boredom* usually grows out of the monotonous routine of the job. The effects of boredom on a worker who wants more variety and challenge from his work can be continuous irritation and listlessness. Frequently the worker will indulge in daydreaming as he allows his mind to wander in an attempt to break the monotony. His attention shifts to and from his work; as a result, his output rate may fluctuate widely. A graphic illustration of employee output in monotonous work is typified in Figure 7–2. It contrasts the fatigue curve in that it is not really a smooth one. Output rates can rise and fall as the worker's attention leaves and returns to work. Usually a monotony curve shows a tendency for the rate of output to drop during the middle of the total working period and to rise toward the end of the day. The final rise in output near the end of the day is apparently an expression of relief at the prospect of being released from the boredom of the job. This "end spurt" is a distinct characteristic of the monotony curve.

When the relationship between fatigue and monotony is considered,

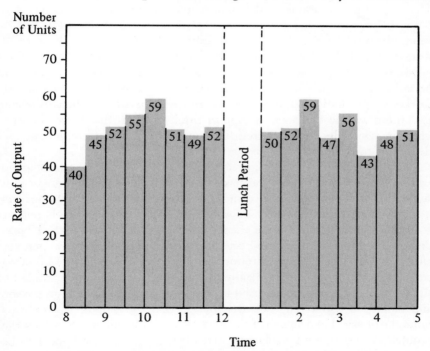

FIGURE 7–2.   Hypothetical Monotony Curve of Output.

several factors should be kept in mind. First, the curves represent the rate of output or number of units produced within a given time span and are not really absolute indications of the fatigue or boredom the worker senses. They merely reflect the overt manifestations of these sensations in worker output. Another important factor to remember is that although monotony may produce a feeling of tiredness in the worker, a fatiguing job may not be caused by monotony. A lumberjack may work hard physically and get tired, but his work is not necessarily boring. An added consideration is that not all people find monotonous work offensive. Some people have little desire for creative exercise on the job; they are content to work where little mental effort is required. However, when one analyzes the hypothetical fatigue and monotony curves, it is apparent that when both fatigue and boredom are real factors of the job, some problems are going to arise; for example, the results of fatigue generally are reflected by a steadily declining rate of output toward the end of the work period, where the monotony curve usually reflects a final spurt of output. It would appear that some modification in the shapes of the curves would occur when both fatigue and monotony are present.

ATTEMPTS TO RELIEVE FATIGUE AND MONOTONY

The working conditions under which the fatigue and monotony hypotheses were assumed to operate were ones in which no work breaks were given and no changes are introduced to try to alter the rate of worker output. The Hawthorne Study researchers tried to test the changes in worker output when working conditions were altered. When rest periods, shorter working days, and a five-day work week were introduced, worker output increased; however, the researchers reached the conclusion that there was no evidence to support the hypothesis that increased output rates were due to relief from fatigue. With respect to monotony, no definite conclusion could be drawn [14, p. 127].

The researchers did remark that boredom is primarily a state of mind and cannot be assessed on the basis of output alone. Furthermore, it is subject to such a wide variety of interpretations that almost any improvement in mental attitudes may be said to be due to relief from boredom.

In order to help the worker escape the throes of fatigue and/or boredom, many firms have initiated practices of rest periods, exercise periods, and piped-in music. Some production jobs are rotated, thus allowing workers to change jobs periodically to break the monotony of a single assignment. Another approach used in industry has been to enlarge the job and include a wider range of activities so that the worker can exercise different physical and mental functions. Some employers try to attack the problem of monotony by selecting and placing people who appear to be the least likely to be irritated by routine work in these positions.

An example of the steps that a firm can take in expanding the scope of the job has been demonstrated by IBM in enlarging the jobs of the maintenance men working in their plants. The job responsibilities of men holding such jobs were expanded and each man was given the title of "general maintenance man." In the change, job duties were expanded to include a variety of activities: plumbing, carpentry, electrical skills, and general repairs. Such an expansion of job responsibilities permitted the individual to draw on a wide variety of skills and to receive satisfaction from solving new and different problems as they arose. Many industrial firms have followed the same pattern of expanding job responsibilities in boring or monotonous work created through specialization or mechanization.

It should be noted that, in unionized companies, any efforts to expand or enlarge the activities connected with any given job should be cleared with union representatives. Problems with changed wage rates or job classifications resulting from job enlargement should be ironed out prior to the initiation of efforts to enlarge the scope of jobs, so that labor is not led to believe that such changes are intended to "speed up" the workers without compensatory changes in wages.

Even in nonunion companies or jobs, plans for job enlargement should include the participation of the work group. The reasons for this are simple and obvious though often overlooked. First, the employees closest to the job being enlarged probably know a great deal about ways to achieve the task by including related activities which might make the job more interesting and more efficient. Second, through their participation in designing the job enlargement, employees are often more prepared to accept the changes in work procedures that result from job enlargement. To this end, a supervisor plays an important role in the encouragement of the work group to offer their suggestions for ways to enlarge the scope of their jobs.

Even though employers may make efforts to reduce monotony in the work place, employee satisfaction or dissatisfaction with the situation is often reflected in labor turnover, absenteeism, accident rates, disciplinary problems, grievances, work stoppages, or restriction of output. This latter practice is one in which employees purposely produce less than they can. The limits on output or "bogeys" are usually accompanied by group pressure to adhere to them and reflect the group norms that were noted in the bank wiring observation room of the Hawthorne Studies.

As a final point, a trend toward reducing the scope of work, particularly in industrial plants, has been encouraged as a result of the Federal Government's efforts to find jobs for larger numbers of low-skilled workers from the ranks of the hard-core unemployed. While the task of finding more jobs in industry for unskilled and disadvantaged persons is an urgent one, it would seem that efforts to simplify production jobs by "breaking them down" into smaller task units is at best a short-term and inadequate solution to creating employment. Job simplification may be justified in some industrial plants; however, as an overall effort it would appear that such efforts are generally contrary to the known human needs for variety and relief from monotonous routine. Thus, job simplification is antithetical to the objectives of job enlargement not only in terms of reducing rather than expanding the scope of activity connected with work, but also in terms of creating work which provides little opportunity for full use of human potential. Alternative solutions to finding jobs for the hard-core unemployed might lie in the area of better pre-employment conditioning and orientation and more effective training in order to raise the skill levels of the hard-core unemployed to a point where they can meet typical performance requirements.

JOB PRESSURE

Although it is most difficult to capsulize the problems of stress and tension created by job pressures, the fact that some jobs are bound, by the nature of their activity, to create pressure on the individual employee is a reality. Many jobs in clerical, sales, and production categories find occasions when peak activity or rush periods create chaos for the employee. Deadlines or tight time schedules can also add pressure to many jobs. Each individual may react differently to unexpected rushes or havoc in the job situation. Seldom can such situations be completely eliminated from the job, but they can be planned for before they occur. Careful orientation and training of workers can warn employees and prepare them to meet some of the pressures they will encounter.

A Case Study in Job Pressure. An example of the way tight scheduling, fatigue, and pressure to meet standards of performance resulted in an emotional outburst is illustrated by the following case which occurred in a small data processing service bureau.

The firm was a small one started by a man who had been the manager of the data processing center for a large corporation. When he started his own enterprise he hired a man to run the tab equipment and a girl to operate the key-punch machine. He acted as the sales representative for his small company and spent most of the day contacting customers, soliciting new business, and picking up customer invoices and other data from which his firm received the information to process customer reports. Because the capital he had to invest in the company was limited, he tried not to hire more than the two people already mentioned, and he worked at nights himself whenever it was necessary to catch up on accumulated work so that customers could receive their reports on time. The two employees often had to work overtime, but the owner had explained when he hired them that this would be the case. On such occasions they were given an allowance to buy dinner and were paid double time, based on a rate they earned in their regular monthly salaries.

The business had grown and overtime periods became more frequent. The owner decided to look for another employee. Several girls had applied but were not hired, either because he did not feel they were qualified or because they did not want to be subject to overtime as a requirement for employment. Before an additional girl could be hired, the end of the year arrived and the majority of the firm's customers wanted year-end reports with which to close their books. The week before the deadline to get all of the year-end reports back to customers the owner and his two employees began to put in a full day, plus an additional four to five hours at night. As the week passed each person's patience grew more strained whenever an error was made. On several occasions the two men argued loudly, with little restraint to their language. The last night of the critical work found all three people tired and nervous. The key-punch operator had worked continuously during the evening in silence, only answering questions that were asked her.

About two hours before the last reports were completed, the tab operator angrily commented to the owner that one of the reports did not balance because several IBM cards had been punched incorrectly by the key-punch operator. When the owner approached the girl to inquire into the matter, she bolted out of her seat and threw a stack of invoices she had been working on at him and announced that she had "had it," and if he didn't like it he could find another operator. She then put on her coat and left in tears.

Later in an interview with the key-punch operator, she revealed several factors which helped explain her actions. The girl had been married only a few months. She and her husband had purchased some furniture and they needed extra income to make the payments. She was an efficient key-punch operator and had taken the job primarily because the salary was attractive. She usually liked her work. Her relationships with both the owner and the tab operator had been congenial. At first, the overtime had been welcomed because it brought needed additional income; however, she had not expected the overtime to be as extensive as it had become. She had expected some relief from the situation when girls started applying for a job, but was disappointed when none had been hired.

Most of the time when the owner was not in the office she could handle the volume of work with little trouble and could work as fast or as slowly as she liked and would take "breathers" whenever she felt like it. Normally, the repetitive nature of the job was not bothersome because much of it could be done without much concentration. However, when the stress of meeting deadlines occurred on the job she felt a great deal of pressure to complete the work, and when the owner was present did not feel free to work at her normal pace or to take breaks.

On the night when she "exploded," she said she felt that every time an error was discovered she was being blamed for it, even though neither the owner nor the tab operator had said so directly. The reason for this feeling was that every time a mistake was found, the first thing the owner said was, "Did the tab cards have any mistakes punched into them?" To her knowledge only one such mistake had been related to an incorrectly punched card, but the inference was made every time something went wrong, and this placed added pressure on her. The comment by the tab operator that the report which was being processed was incorrect because she had not punched some cards correctly was the final straw. She commented, "I had worked hard all week long and didn't have time to verify every card the way I ordinarily do. They would pick up a stack of cards as soon as I was through punching them without checking on them. I felt that was placing too much responsibility on me. After all, I was tired and could have made a lot more mistakes than I did."

The point illustrated by the foregoing case is that the tension created on the job can build to the point where relief must be found. In this case, an emotional outburst was the reaction. Other people may have reacted differently under the same situation. However, stress is a part of nearly every type of job found in business and industry. Accountants find periods of strenuous activity increase as the income tax deadline nears. Sales clerks, waiters, or service industry personnel find periods of peak activity when tension and physical exertion is more demanding than at other times. Firemen, forest rangers, or policemen may find that their jobs are relatively tranquil until an emergency arises—then sometimes a great amount of chaos ensues with which they must cope if the situation is to be handled effectively.

The job situation has numerous occasions when pressure will build. Knowing beforehand that such pressure may exist can help a supervisor plan more carefully what his course of action is going to be in making work assignments and in scheduling the work of his department. Some employees enjoy the stress found in their work and it acts as a stimulus for them. One highly successful insurance executive related during an interview that when he was a salesman he made the Million Dollar Round Table several years by selling nearly a quarter of a million dollars worth of business in the last few months of the sales year. He would "slack-off" for several months until he knew the pressure was on to go out and sell some insurance, then he worked feverishly until he had made his quota. In this instance, the individual imposed pressure on himself as an incentive to work harder. Other people might find such artificial stimulation unnecessary or even ineffectual.

Executives often find that the stress of making decisions is a source of both strain and of great personal satisfaction. Supervisors may discover that dealing with the human problems of their subordinates, in addition to the technical aspects of their jobs, can be both frustrating and satisfying. However, the pressures created by these activities are an integral part of the manager's and the supervisor's job.

COMPETITION

Not all job pressure stems from time schedules and rush periods or from problems of meeting the standards of performance placed on the employee by the job. Often there is a type of job pressure that arises from the inherent structure of an organization—competition for advancement, better jobs, better working conditions, and improved job status. Each individual reacts differently to the organizational factors which place stress on them. Some weather the pressure of tight time schedules with little difficulty, whereas others are little affected by organizational competition. However, many new and uninitiated workers are surprised when they do encounter the degree of competition they find in an organization; they are not necessarily alone, as many veteran employees suffer pangs of frustration as they see other workers advance or obtain rewards they were seeking to acquire. The pace and stress of modern industrial life is often cited as a prime contributor to the ulcers that attack some businessmen. Yet, competition and stress will appear in some form in all but a very few jobs in most organizations.

Competition is a natural part of life and the methods used in competition are frequently established by the standards of the society in which an individual is a member. At one time dueling was an accepted method of dealing with an opponent. Today, civilized nations have outlawed such modes of behavior. Small children learn to vie with their siblings for the attention of parents. As a child grows and enters school, wider areas of competition open. A student soon learns that all the pupils do not make A's. There must be competition for these. Boys, in particular, may channel their competitive urge in athletic activity. Track, tennis, swimming, boxing, and wrestling are sports in which an individual can compete against others openly and exercise his skills in an accepted manner. Other sports involve a combination of competition and teamwork. Several players may try out for a single position on a football, baseball, or basketball team. Only one person may play on each of the first team positions at a time, so competition between members of the team for first string positions is an essential part of selecting the best players. However, the competition between the players of a team should not overshadow the fact that the team as a whole must compete against other teams on the playing field. If intrateam competition becomes too

Competition is the essence of some professional activity.

vicious and disrupts the team spirit, winning games against other teams can be jeopardized.

On the job, competition for promotion, recognition, or more power can and does take place between members of the organization. The firm may attempt to improve the performance of its employees by having contests in areas of sales, production, or safety. Departments within the firm may vie with one another for performance records in these and other areas, or individuals may compete for awards which may be given for top performance.

The competition which is openly fostered by the firm can be a healthy means for allowing workers to emerge in competitive activity. Supervisors should recognize the motivational value of "friendly" competition and its role in satisfying a variety of human needs. However, excessive emphasis on competition can be extraordinarily frustrating to those who do not receive rewards for their endeavor. Not all competition carried on within a firm is known or sanctioned by it. The firm is much like an athletic team in respect to the number of positions open for authority and responsibility. Seldom is the number of positions of authority exactly equal to the number of people who want to be in such positions. It would not be a healthy thing for a firm to have more positions of leadership open than there were people who wanted (and were capable enough) to fill them.

When a position in the firm is vacated, the men who compete to fill the vacancy can use either ethical or unethical methods to achieve that position. The saying, "All's fair in love and war," is an easy rationalization for some men to use in their ascent up the ladder of power in an organization. Not all men are ruthless or unethical in their methods to achieve advancement, but every organization has its share of individuals who are hard-driving, ambitious, and aggressive in their efforts to attain organizational success. And the organizational climate can have a bearing on the methods which are tolerated or encouraged to promote competition within its ranks.

Men generally are stimulated by friendly competition, and most firms have formal programs for training and developing the people within them so that as positions open up in the higher levels of the hierarchy people will be prepared to move into them. Modern industrial organizations have learned that relying on the "natural rise of superior individuals" is neither the most efficient nor effective method of obtaining their leaders. For this reason, rank-and-file workers who show signs of wanting to advance within the firm are often encouraged to do so, and training programs are designed to prepare them for such advancement. The same thing is usually true all the way up the line so far as management training and development programs go. Ultimately, the reality must be faced by members of an organization that advancements may not be as fast nor as far up the line as might have been hoped.

Some Negro employees become frustrated by the slow progress they think they are making in obtaining positions of responsibility, authority, and salary. Often members of minority groups suspect that their slow progress is due to hidden and unspoken prejudices (although sometimes little attempt is made to disguise such prejudices) which inhibit their advancement even when they have demonstrated their skills. The validity of this suspicion varies in each individual case; however, the fact is generally recognized that minority groups face particular difficulties when competing in a dominantly white-anglo business world.

As an example, a Negro department manager in a large retail store exceeded his sales volume quota by a substantial margin. When he did not receive the same recognition and financial rewards as his successful white counterparts, he brought the issue to the store manager's attention. His superior pointed out that in striving to surpass the department's quota he had been "pushy" with the sales clerks in his department. Other department managers had been appropriately "aggressive"—he had been "pushy." Thus, the definition of aggressiveness was left open to interpretation, and in such circumstances knowing how to compete successfully can be most difficult, as well as frustrating.

Engagement in and reaction to competition, like other aspects encountered on the job, are not the same in all individuals. Many people appear to be overtly competitive in their behavior, while others seem to avoid situations where they are pitted against others in any activity. Some people do not aspire to be president of the firm; others seek the position with vigor. A person's values and his concept of success will have an influence on the importance he places on advancement. The norms of the group of which he is a member and the climate of the organization for which he works also play important roles in the level and degree of an individual's aspirations. Regardless of the aspirations of an individual, it is wise for him to realize that he will meet competition from others who also have similar goals.

Many of the subtle pressures placed on the individual are beyond the direct control of the organization. The type of organizational climate may designate the degree of open competition fostered among employees. Ideally, a firm will discourage the use of ruthless or backbiting methods of competition among its employees, but one must realize that in industry, as in other walks of life, some of the individuals most apt to use unethical methods are also most adroit at disguising the use of them. It is recognized that the nefarious methods of competition practiced by some individuals often cause damage to the morale of the work group. Such methods are not always detected by the supervisor until after some reward or advancement has been received. The supervisor has a responsibility to try and detect employees who compete unfairly for recognition and other organizational rewards and curb such practices by making it clear that he does not sanction such methods. Most companies are opposed to unprincipled competitive behavior because they are aware that it can damage the morale of others, and they attempt to foster conditions where healthy competition is rewarded and each employee is allowed to attain satisfaction in the social relationships found on the job.

FREEDOM AND OPPORTUNITY TO USE SKILLS AND ABILITY

The satisfaction that a person obtains from his job will be molded, in part, by the opportunity he has within the firm to use his abilities, by the scope of freedom he is allowed, and by the fairness with which he believes he has been treated. In a study conducted by Wight Bakke, which included about 1,500 participants who worked for a communications company in New England or were officials in the union representing the employees of that firm, it was revealed that among members of management and union officials satisfaction with the opportunity to use their ability ranked very high, whereas nonmanagement employees ranked satisfaction with this factor relatively low. Fairness of treatment was ranked slightly higher by management than by employees or union officials. An interesting note was that members of management in the particular company studied were less satisfied with the scope of their freedom than either the employees or union officials [1, p. 40]. Bakke points out that such a finding only applies to the particular company investigated and that no generalizations can be drawn for industry at large. This particular finding does give an indication that freedom of action can be a subject of dissatisfaction among executives as well as among production workers.

The finding of Bakke's study is somewhat contrary to the customary conceptions of many people regarding the characteristics of our industrial system. The popular belief is that it is management that experiences freedom of activity and employees who experience a regimentation and restriction of personal activity. A number of studies seem to confirm this. One such study by Porter revealed that higher-level managers received more satisfaction from their work than workers at lower levels of the organizational hierarchy [13]. These results imply that the greater satisfaction of higher-level managers is due, at least in part, to greater opportunities to satisfy esteem, independence, and self-realization needs.

A point of discussion tangent, but related, to the desire for freedom to use one's abilities is the desire of most people to do a good job. Although there is evidence from daily experiences that modern industrial society is plagued by both poor workmanship and poor quality, many people take, or want to take, pride in what they do. Edwin Flippo states that many people disclaim any need or desire for pride of work; yet the need is present, and when there is no constructive outlet for it, the workers' energies are diverted toward other channels which often prove to be undesirable to management [5, p. 4].

A number of students planning their occupational careers in the field of retailing have expressed a desire to work in specialty shops or department stores which handle high quality merchandise rather than low-grade goods. It must be realized that the definition of *high-* or *low-grade goods* lies mainly in the mind of the individual. A number of social values and references to status symbols could be brought into play during any discussion of this topic, but the salient point is that the desire to work with or produce quality products is a real element in the job satisfaction of some people. Craftsmen who still have an opportunity to exercise their skills in our industrialized society usually seek to do a good job. To illustrate this point, recently a carpenter quit his job with a large subdivision contractor and started his own small contracting firm. He explained that he had become tired of doing nothing but hanging doors in houses that were all beginning to look alike. He wanted to be able to take pride in the completion of a whole structure.

Mass production has had the effect of making many goods uniform in quality and design. It also has divided the work of turning out a product into many specialized subtasks, and this does not provide any single employee with an opportunity to say, "I produced that table." The effect can be demoralizing for anyone who has the urge to take pride in his work. Thus, one of the greatest tasks of a superior is to motivate employees while using the available technology in production processes and, at the same time, to create a job environment where workers can fully utilize their human potential. Restrictions placed on the scope of a person's job activities contribute to the feeling of loss of identity in the organization system—the feeling that one is only a cog in the wheel. When such feelings permeate a worker's attitude, he seldom takes pride in his work and may lose interest in it. A loss of interest on the part of the worker may merely be the first step in a chain of events which leads to his departure from the company.

WORKING CONDITIONS AND ENVIRONMENT

The physical conditions found in the work place do not appear to be highly related to production unless they are so poor as to pose a health or safety problem. Even so, many firms attempt to create a physical environment that more than meets minimum physical needs. Plush offices, decorator colors, and adequate physical facilities are frequently taken for granted by workers; thus, companies have found it necessary to provide such accommodations to attract and hold employees. A discussion of working conditions could include such environmental factors as temperature, humidity, ventilation, noise, vibration, lighting, and physical layout of the work station. In a broader view of working conditions, factors such as hours, decor of office, building, or other working areas, availability of drinking fountains, restrooms, cafeteria and other employee creature comforts, and conveniences would have to be included. Research has indicated that little correlation can be drawn between the physical conditions of work and productivity as long as they do not inhibit the work process. This does not indicate, necessarily, that working conditions are unimportant to the worker, but rather the worker accepts them as a standard part of the job with less thought to their importance than to other job factors.

The contribution of working conditions to an individual's job satisfaction varies widely, but, generally, it is considered relatively small. In individual cases, employees have voiced complaints about the height that mirrors are placed on the walls of restrooms, the cooped-up feeling they have if there are no windows in the work area, the distance of parking facilities from work locations, and other annoying aspects of the physical layout of the plant. Generally, many of these sources of irritation can be corrected by minor changes or careful planning in architectural design [6, pp. 93–100].

JOB STATUS

Research has revealed the relative importance of certain specific aspects of working conditions to workers. Taken as a whole, working conditions appear to be more important to women than to men. Working hours, when considered alone, are more important to men than are other aspects of working conditions, but they are of even greater importance to women—especially married women. Working conditions have been found to be of more importance to factory workers than to clerical or sales personnel. Part of the increased importance for factory workers may stem from the necessary attention to safety conditions. With the exception of working hours, working conditions appear to be somewhat more important among employees with higher educations; the single aspect of hours appears less important to the more educated group [7, pp. 74–75].

Normally, higher status is attached to the people having better working conditions; in other words, the higher the status, the better the working conditions. Keith Davis points out that this is why white-collar jobs usually carry more status than blue-collar jobs of equal skill and pay. Most people seem to prefer the white-collar surroundings and the conditions of soft chairs, air conditioning, and clean hands. Because these things are sought and because there is limited supply relative to the demand for them, these things receive higher status. In this respect the status *value* given to different conditions has a supply and demand relationship similar to that in economics. When supply is adequate relative to demand, status value will be less than when demand exceeds the supply [4, p. 50]. For example, when all of the members of an office staff are given desk blotters, the desk blotters may become less important as status symbols than when only a few members are given them. As one status symbol becomes generally available to all members of a group and no longer acts as a mark of distinction, other status symbols will rise to take its place. This appears to be based on the need of people to distinguish between members of a group.

Vance Packard discusses a few of the status symbols used among executives in organizations. They include size and location of office, parking spaces, dining rooms, make and model of automobile, keys to wash rooms, type of desk, and office equipment [12, p. 103]. These and other job factors can and do play a part in the status found on the job. It is wise to remember that not all people seek status or its symbols with equal vigor; nevertheless, status is a part of the world of organizational norms and behavior.

SUPERVISORY RELATIONS

Problems mentioned thus far in this chapter have been general and apply in varying degrees to most of the personnel in a business organization, regardless of the position held. The supervisor, however, is faced by some rather special problems created by the position he occupies in the organization. The importance of the supervisor's behavior cannot be understated because his actions have a direct effect on the attitudes cultivated and displayed by his subordinates. The degree of friendliness and concern the supervisor demonstrates for his subordinates has a large influence over the patterns of behavior conducted within the work group. This particular aspect of the supervisor's influence over group behavior and morale in an organizational unit merits special consideration at this point, even though a discussion of supervisory styles and methods will appear in a later chapter.

The supervisor has often been described as the man in the middle. Many research studies have concentrated on the problems of the supervisor, and any broad generalizations may fall wide of the mark in accurately defining all the problems the supervisor faces in his day-to-day tasks and responsibilities. The crux of many of the supervisor's problems lies in the fact that the supervisor is responsible for getting the production of his department turned out on time, in sufficient quantity and quality to meet the firm's standards. At the same time, he often finds himself embroiled in personal relationships with his subordinates. If he befriends members of the work group, he may find that it is difficult to give orders to or discipline such members. If there are members of the work group who, for real or imagined reasons, do not feel that the supervisor likes them as much as some of the other workers, they may feel that he is playing favorites. Therefore, such members may also subtly or openly resist the supervisor's efforts to sustain the production level of the group.

On the one hand, the supervisor is judged successful by his own superiors if he is able to meet company objectives; on the other hand, he is judged as good or bad by the very subordinates he must depend upon in order to meet company objectives—quite often by an entirely different set of criteria. If the supervisor chooses to ignore the expressed needs of his subordinates, he may find that he loses their real support which he needs in order to reach the objectives set for him by his own superiors. His actions are constantly scrutinized by both sides.

There are several courses of action some supervisors take in order to avert the difficulties created by the middle position they hold. One is to remain aloof from the work group and avoid personal relations with any subordinate. When this course of action is followed, it is usually in the belief that no single member of the group will ever be able to accuse the supervisor of favoritism. Such behavior may also simplify the problem of giving orders and of handling discipline in the group.

An opposite tack can be taken, one in which the supervisor plays buddy to everyone in the group. He may even take sides with the work group he directs against management by pointing out that he thinks the directions he receives are stupid, but that he can do nothing but pass them on.

Neither of these extremes in attitude are commonly found in industry. The extreme courses of action mentioned are an attempt to move away from the middle and to identify more closely with either the work group or with higher management. Such patterns are seldom successful over a long period. Identifying entirely with the men, rather than with management, ultimately creates its own problems when it comes to translating company policies and objectives into concerted group action. Sooner or later the subordinates find that merely expressing disdain by the supervisor over orders passed on from higher up does little to change them, and the supervisor's position and authority in the group can be seriously jeopardized. To ignore totally the needs of subordinates ultimately creates conditions in which group members become demoralized because of lack of recognition. The result can lead to decreased efforts and low production. The trailing off of production may take time, but if and when it does occur, the supervisor may find his own performance no longer satisfactory to his own superiors.

Being caught in the middle position between rank-and-file workers and higher management, a supervisor must decide which set of criteria to use to determine whether he is effective—those of the subordinates or those of his superiors? If both had the same goals and objectives there would be no problem, but the realities of industrial life are such that frequently the rank-and-file workers do not have the same goals as the company, or, at least, they are only the same in a relatively narrow band of interests.

Ideally, the effective supervisor would be one whose department had a high level of production and at the same time was one in which the majority of workers found personal satisfaction in their work and group relations. Actually, much research has been conducted on the relationships between productivity, supervision, and employee morale. One of the major studies which attempted to measure the relationship between these factors was conducted by a group of researchers at the Survey Research Center at the University of Michigan [8]. In this particular study conducted in the clerical offices of a large insurance company, work groups were classified as either high-producing or low-producing. It was then assumed that, other things being equal, differences in the way these groups were supervised might account for the differences in productivity. Findings of the study indicated that the supervisors of high-producing groups were employee-centered, whereas supervisors of low-producing groups more often tended to be production-centered. Also, it was observed that the closer the supervision,* the lower the group productivity. A number of studies conducted by other researchers in other industrial situations generally confirm the findings cited above.

The difference between employee-centered and production-centered supervisors refers to the degree of emphasis placed on each by the supervisor in his own behavior and in his relations with the subordinates in his work group. Employee-centered supervisors do not necessarily forego attention to production. Rather, they translate company objectives into terms acceptable to employees and treat subordinates as an integral part of reaching such objectives. This method of supervision requires that supervisors know their subordinates as individuals, and reinforces the importance of knowing the way employees feel.

Using the employee-centered approach is not without some problems. There are still some questions to be answered regarding what constitutes employee-centered supervisory behavior. How employee-centered or how permissive should the supervisor be? This and other questions related to supervisory styles will be discussed in a later chapter. It can be stated here that whether one considers the objectives of the company as most important—therefore employees must adhere to them—or whether one asserts individual goals as most important, the supervisor must create a working environment in which there is some harmony between the two.

---

* Close supervision refers to the number and type of directions a supervisor continues to give a worker after assigning a task. The more frequent the orders and directions a supervisor gives to a subordinate on a single assignment, the closer is the supervision. Close supervision cannot be judged as good or bad without knowing the circumstances and personnel involved in the situation. If the subordinate is inexperienced, time is short, and there is little margin for error, close supervision may be advisable. With an experienced worker doing a routine job, close supervision may be a hindrance.

The common assumption that rank-and-file employees, given freedom, will goof off and not produce does not seem to be supported by the findings of the study made by Survey Research Center when close supervision is interpreted to mean constant direction-giving and constant checking on the worker. High production depends on the conditions that accompany the freedom that supervisors give their subordinates. In the Survey Research Center study managers achieving high performance from their work groups did so by setting general goals and providing less specific direction than the managers of the low-producing groups. The high-producing supervisors used more participation and achieved higher involvement and greater interest in work, while assigning greater individual responsibility for achieving results to their subordinates.

The evidence collected thus far indicates that high production units are more likely to be managed by supervisors who follow the assumptions stated in McGregor's Theory Y; although Vroom cites a number of examples where there are important individual differences in employees' desire to participate in the decison-making process [15, p. 225]. Employees whose personal contacts with their supervisors on the job are neither frequent nor prolonged apparently preferred that their supervisor behave in a highly directive manner. In contrast, those employees who were placed in continuous and direct contact with their supervisors preferred that they behave more informally and democratically. Therefore, one must allow for the exceptions, but the long-run maintenance of high levels of production seems to favor supervisory methods which emphasize concern for the employee as an individual.

The specific factors mentioned in this chapter are areas which create problems of adjustment for the individual employee. They are, of course, not the only factors of which supervisors should be aware; but they are elements which are common to nearly all occupations in one degree or another. Any or all of them can be a source of dissatisfaction for the worker. However, satisfaction in all of them does not guarantee the worker complete job satisfaction.

SUMMARY

1. A number of the physical and social conditions that an employee finds on the job create problems that he must resolve if he is to obtain personal satisfaction and worth from his work. Such problems also can create barriers in reaching maximum levels in production. Since the advent of time and motion studies, many jobs have been engineered to emphasize the speed and efficiency of the worker, leaving little room for variation in activity or pace of the job. This is particularly true on assembly-line jobs where the pace of the job is set by the machinery. When the conditions of

the job limit the freedom of the individual to work at his own pace or to vary his activity, fatigue, monotony, or boredom may result. The result of these factors is often reflected in the quality and quantity of the work produced. Other human problems can also accrue and be reflected in labor turnover, absenteeism, carelessness that causes accidents, work restriction, or other means which workers can devise to indicate their dissatisfaction.

2. Although it is most difficult to capsulize the problems of stress and tension created by job pressures, the fact that some jobs are bound by the nature of their activity to create pressure on the individual employee is a reality. Many jobs in clerical, sales, and production categories find occasions when peak activity or rush periods create chaos for the employee. Deadlines or tight time schedules can also add pressure to many jobs. Each individual may react differently to unexpected rushes or havoc in the job situation. Seldom can such situations be completely eliminated from the job, but they can be planned for before they occur. Careful orientation and training of workers can warn employees and prepare them to meet some of the pressures they will encounter.

3. Not all job pressure stems from time schedules or rush periods. Often there is a type of job pressure that arises from the inherent structure of an organization: competition for advancement, better jobs, better working conditions, and improved job status. The pressure of time schedules may greatly affect some employees, whereas others may be little affected by the pressure of organizational competition. Many new and uninitiated workers are taken by surprise when they do encounter the degree of competition they find in an organization. They are not necessarily alone because many veteran employees suffer pangs of frustration as they see other workers advance or obtain rewards they were seeking to acquire. The pace and stress of modern industrial life is often cited as a prime contributor to the ulcers that attack some businessmen. Yet competition and stress will appear in some form in all but a very few jobs in the organization.

Most companies are opposed to unprincipled competitive behavior because they are aware that it can damage the morale of others, and they attempt to foster conditions where healthy competition is rewarded and which allow each employee to attain satisfaction in the social relationships found on the job. However, it should be recognized that methods of unprincipled competitive behavior are not always readily detected in the organization; some may be discovered only after some reward or advancement has been received by the individual using such tactics.

4. Freedom and opportunity to use skills and ability are not always found in the work place to the extent that some workers would desire. Jobs in factories and offices may be largely comprised of routine tasks that

do not provide opportunity for a sense of great personal achievement. This is particularly true of low-skilled or semiskilled jobs. Surprisingly, however, managers who occupy higher positions in the organization's hierarchy frequently complain about the limitation that is placed on their freedom to act or do as they please.

5. The physical conditions found in the work place do not appear to be highly related to production unless they are so poor as to pose a health or safety problem. Even so, many firms attempt to create a physical environment that more than meets minimum physical needs. Plush offices, bright colors, and adequate physical facilities are frequently taken for granted by workers; thus, companies have found it necessary to provide such accommodations to attract and hold employees.

The status symbol is a peculiar phenomenon which seems to change as values and modes of living change among the workers. No attempt seems to be successful in eliminating them, and many companies utilize such items as location of offices or permission to use separate lunch rooms as symbols of a person's position in the organization. Some individuals are troubled by the myriad formal and informal indications of status found on the job.

6. Supervisors may find they face a whole set of personal problems in their interpersonal relationships, caused by the particular role they play in the conduct of organizational affairs and by the place they hold in the organization. They are caught between the actual rank-and-file employees and higher management, and this often places the supervisor in the untenable position of serving two masters. Human relations training may have taught the supervisor to be concerned with the human needs of the workers, yet his own superiors may not appear to show this concern when they give him his orders. He is responsible for maintaining production and, at the same time, morale. Frequently he finds the action he must take to accomplish one objective is in conflict with the other. The supervisor must develop a style of leadership which is compatible to his own personality and helps him create an environment in which workers will be motivated to produce at or above the level he must meet. The situation sometimes creates a balancing act that must be resolved by the type of supervision he gives. Studies indicate that employee-centered supervision may produce higher results than production-centered supervision. Depending on the particular circumstances of the job to be done, close supervision may be a hindrance to production. Although there is no answer to supervision that will serve in all instances, research has indicated directions that supervisors can follow effectively to reach company objectives while maintaining sound group cohesiveness and human relations.

DISCUSSION QUESTIONS

1. What are some of the specific problems connected with the application of time and motion studies to industrial jobs?
2. What effects does fatigue have on the individual?
3. In what ways does boredom differ from fatigue? How does the production rate of a worker who is fatigued differ, usually, from the production rate of the bored one? What can management do to relieve the worker from fatigue? From boredom?
4. How can a person react to the pressure of the job? In what ways can such pressure be destructive? In what ways is it helpful?
5. Does competition between individuals conflict with team spirit? If so, how? If not, why? In what ways is there competition on the job?
6. In what ways does a person exercise freedom on the job? How can the firm curb or encourage the use of this freedom?
7. How can working conditions become "status" symbols on the job? Why do they become status symbols?

BIBLIOGRAPHY AND SELECTED COLLATERAL READINGS

1. BAKKE, WIGHT E., *Bonds of Organization*. New York: Harper & Row, 1950.
2. BARTLEY, S. H., and F. CHUTE, *Fatigue and Impairment in Man*. New York: McGraw-Hill Book Company, 1947.
3. BRAYFIELD, ARTHUR H., and WALTER H. CROCKETT, "Employee Attitudes and Employee Performance," *Psychological Bulletin*, Vol. 52, No. 5 (September 1955), 396–424.
4. DAVIS, KEITH, *Human Relations at Work*, 3rd ed. New York: McGraw-Hill Book Company, 1967.
5. FLIPPO, EDWIN B., *Principles of Personnel Management*. New York: McGraw-Hill Book Company, 1961.
6. FRIEDMANN, GEORGES, *Industrial Society*. New York: The Free Press, 1955.
7. HERZBERG, FREDERICK, and others, *Job Attitudes: Review of Research and Opinion*. Pittsburgh: Psychological Service of Pittsburgh, 1957.
8. KATZ, DANIEL, and others, *Productivity, Supervision, and Morale in an Office Situation*. Ann Arbor, Mich.: Institute for Social Research, 1950.
9. McFARLAND, D. E., *Personnel Management: Theory and Practice*. New York: The Macmillan Company, 1968.
10. MAIER, NORMAN R. F., *Psychology in Industry*, 3rd ed. Boston: Houghton Mifflin Company, 1965.
11. MINER, J. B., *The Management of Ineffective Performance*, New York: McGraw-Hill Book Company, 1963.

12. PACKARD, VANCE, *The Status Seekers*. New York: David McKay Company, Inc., 1959.

13. PORTER, LYMAN W., "Job Attitudes in Management, I. Perceived Deficiencies in Need Fulfillment as a Function of Job Level," *Journal of Applied Psychology*, Vol. 46 (1962), 375–84.

14. ROETHLISBERGER, F. M., and WILLIAM J. DICKSON, *Management and the Worker*. New York: John Wiley and Sons, 1964.

15. VROOM, VICTOR H., *Work and Motivation*. New York: John Wiley and Sons, 1964.

Organization in the Work Environment

The formation of groups is a common activity in a dynamic society. Nearly everyone participates in a variety of groups from early childhood through adulthood—in the family, church, school, social activities, and occupational life. Not all of these play the same importance in one's life, nor is one's participation in some groups enduring. Because of the vast number and types of groups one encounters, some scholars have tried to categorize groups according to their function and the type of participation called for by group members.

H. H. Jennings distinguishes between the two types of groups, socio-groups and psyche-groups [8]. The socio-group is one in which there is association for purposes of work or for living and it is based on a collective criterion; that is, it exists for the purpose of the organization rather than for the individual needs of its members. The psyche-group is based on association for the private and personal satisfaction of its members. In the latter group the uniqueness of each individual is supposedly appreciated and encouraged, whereas, in the former, individual differences are subordinated to the dominant tasks or goals of the group. The primary distinction between the two groups lies in the degree to which *tasks* are emphasized in the socio-group and the personal satisfaction of group members is emphasized in the psyche-group. Looked at in this way, the two types of groups represent opposite poles. At one end of the spectrum, a group operates with scarcely any recognition of the personalities of its members who are completely preoccupied with a prescribed task or job. On the other end is a group in which members do nothing but enjoy each other's companionship. Between these extremes are the groups and organizations of real life in which modifications of these aspects are interchanged [14, p. 139].

The socio-group versus the psyche-group concept presents an interesting model for the analysis of business organizations. Ordinarily, a

Courtesy of the Educational Affairs Department, Ford Motor Company.

Courtesy of the Union Carbide Corporation.

Most jobs have opportunities of participation in both socio- and psyche-groups.

business firm operates within a concept of making a profit which places emphasis on efficiency of operations. This orientation toward profitability makes organizational structure or design important because it can affect both costs and operational efficiency by either covering up or exposing possible deficiencies. Yet, if one accepts the premise that one of the greatest assets of any industrial organization is the creative power retained within the talents, intellects, and personalities of its employees, then one begins to realize how important the formal organizational structure can be in either emphasizing human creative power or suppressing it. The question that arises from this dual approach (profits versus people) to organization is: Which do you emphasize when organizing a firm—the tasks and functions of the organization or the individuals who must perform those tasks?

TRADITIONAL CONCEPTS OF FORMAL ORGANIZATION

Most people work with and for other persons in a group, and this group context is part of a larger social framework. Usually the social contacts connected with a job are with other organizational members, but many jobs also involve contacts with individuals outside the organization, such as customers and suppliers of the firm. In either case, the social group within which most people work is usually structured. That is, the individuals are placed in some hierarchy of authority and are bound by some set of formal job requirements. Where the relationships between functions and people are prescribed and assigned, the organization is known as *formal. Informal* organizations also exist. They differ in nature from formal organizations in that the authority and the responsibility of an individual are not assigned according to pre-established group objectives. More will be said later in this chapter on informal groups; for now the discussion will concentrate on aspects of formal organization and group structure.

Today a wide range of viewpoints exists pertaining to the most effective methods of organizing and managing the activities and personnel of a business firm. However, few industrial leaders paid much attention to the organization and management of business firms before the industrial revolution. As businesses grew in size and complexity, some business practitioners turned to organizations that had endured for some time to get their clues for organizational structure. For this reason, many organizational principles used in industry were taken from military and church organizations. Theo Haimann believes that, in all probability, managers borrowed more heavily from the military than from the church, because they had greater familiarity with military organization [7, p. 5].

The outcome of the early reliance upon military and church organizations as models for industry was that traditional organization theory emphasized the structure and functions of the organization with only secondary regard for the people who were a part of it. From the traditional viewpoint, organizational structure is determined on the basis of organizational principles and then the people are fitted to it in the best way possible. This approach to building organizational relationships was further emphasized as a result of Frederick Taylor's book published in the early 1900's. In the introduction to *The Principles of Scientific Management,* Taylor wrote:

> In the future it will be appreciated that our leaders must be trained right as well as born right, and that no great man can (with the old system of personnel management) hope to compete with a number of ordinary men who have been properly organized so as efficiently to cooperate.
>
> In the past the man has been first; in the future the system must be first [15, pp. 6–7].

Taylor's approach to management placed more emphasis on training and organization of employees—managers and production workers alike —than had been true in industry prior to the emergence of scientific management. It also emphasized the *one best way of doing things* and, therefore, carried with it the mandate for greater control over the individual activities of each organizational member. Thus, formal organization became an increasingly important element in industrial life.

CHARACTERISTICS OF A FORMAL ORGANIZATION

A formal organization has aspects which are more discernible than an informal or social one. According to traditional organization theory, a number of basic concepts underlie the unification of individuals into an organized endeavor. These basic concepts are

1. A formal organization has *a common set of goals or objectives* that bind its members together.
2. In order to achieve organizational objectives there must be *functionalization or division of labor* among organizational members.
3. Division of labor requires that there be *coordination of activities.*
4. Coordination of activities calls for *a hierarchy of authority* in the organization.

Each of these underlying organizational concepts has implications for the practice of human relations. Some of these implications are discussed in the following section.

Common Organizational Goals.   The first idea of formal organization is the existence of common goals or objectives. There may be a number of objectives for which a group is organized. Some may be short term, others long range. Some goals are formal and publicized in policy statements which indicate the organization's objectives in relation to the community, unions, employees, or customers; other objectives are not so formal or clearly communicated.

Perpetuation of the organization is obviously one basic goal. In a free-enterprise system it is presumed that the profit motive is one of the primary means of achieving this goal of the firm. It is certainly true that profits help insure the existence of a firm; however, many of a firm's actions are deliberate, yet not necessarily profitable. Firms contribute funds and manpower to community projects and community improvements; they donate large sums to scholastic endeavors which may be tax deductible, but do not bring any direct dollar return. Such actions are usually taken to incur the intangible, but important, good will of people outside of the organization. Many company dollars are spent on modernization of offices and displays seen by the public. Often the money so spent is also intended to convey the prestige and status of the firm. All such monetary expenditures may be justified as investments which will pay in long-run profits to the firm. In reality, proving that a long-run profit is directly related to such expenditures is usually difficult.

Whatever the organizational goals may be, the formal ones, at least, need to be communicated to the members of the organization. Generally, the more agreement there is about goals, the stronger will be the unification of the organization's members. Organizational goals which are in part synonymous with individual goals serve as a motivation for concerted group effort. If a member does not believe in the company's objectives, chances are he will not make a maximum effort to attain them. Thus, an organization is faced with the task of either selecting members already attuned to its goals or trying to inculcate its members with the desirability of the goals.

Most companies have policy statements relating their goals. Generally these organizational creeds prepared for their employees and the general public express the company's role in providing social goods or services, its desire to make a reasonable profit, and its obligation to employees, consumers, community, and other elements of the general public. Such policy statements are usually unassailable and there is little problem either in finding people already willing to subscribe to such goals or in inculcating employees with them once employees are hired.

Acceptance of organizational goals, at least the ones that are publicly stated, is not a major problem. There are instances when, for personal reasons, employees may not agree with the nature of the goods or services produced by a given company. For example, certain employees may object to their employer's production of war materials or other products they deem harmful. However, the greatest difficulty encountered in acceptance of organizations has to do with the nature of the organizational systems and procedures necessary to achieve organizational objectives. Human relations problems are likely to emerge whenever there is excessive conflict between the areas of freedom that an employee considers his own and the systems of control the organization inaugurates to achieve its objectives.

Functionalization or Division of Labor. A second manifestation of the organization is the concept of functionalization or division of labor. Organizations develop because a single individual does not possess all of the skills, time, or endurance to achieve all of his own objectives. In order to accomplish organizational objectives, a rational division of activities must occur. There is variance of opinion regarding how the activities should be divided. Most frequently, the functions that are most closely related are grouped together for convenience and ease of control. For example, if a firm has as an objective the production and sale of a particular household item, the total objective is best achieved through some division of effort. It would be impractical for a single person to select and purchase all of the raw materials necessary for the product; to stamp, cut, and assemble it; to package it; to advertise it; and to make the calls on the customers in order to sell it. This procedure may be followed in a very small business operation, but the impracticability would be obvious in a firm of 30 or of 3,000 employees if each went through the entire processing of an article from start to finish.

It is infinitely more efficient if each of the functions—purchasing, production, and marketing—is divided among a few employees who specialize in some particular aspect of the total process. In this way, individuals are given more of an opportunity to work in the particular function which is most suited to their skills, needs, and interests. A man who wants to sell does not have to be involved in the other functions, and a man who is most interested in production does not have to sell. It would be ideal if both the goals of the organization would be accomplished more efficiently by a division of labor and individual satisfaction would be more likely to be served in the process. Unfortunately, such is not always the case. The human problems associated with job specialization that create monotonous dull jobs were discussed in Chapter 7.

Further human relations problems occur because there are differences in the perspectives of organizational members assigned to different organizational units. Those individuals in one department with special technical assignments may not appreciate the general operating problems of people in another department. Thus, organizational members who are supposed to help each other may find that their assistance is rejected or resented. Salesmen may find that their efforts are restricted by people in a far-removed credit department. The production department may find its operations are interrupted because the purchasing department delayed ordering necessary materials. Thus, the very concept of functionalization that was intended to make the organization more efficient may break down because of human failures in communications and unforseen interpersonal conflicts.

Coordination of Activities.   Common goals and functionalization are not enough to insure against havoc and confusion in an organization. A third essential element in organizational theory is the coordination of activities. The gain achieved through proper communication of common objectives and functionalization or division of labor would be jeopardized if the members of the organization proceeded in a helter-skelter fashion with little regard for the activities of others. The concept of *coordination* is concerned with the timing and sequence of the activities in an organization. Often this concept is confused with the much emphasized term *cooperation,* which is concerned with the willingness of individuals to work voluntarily with others. Cooperation is needed in a group effort, but so is coordination. A simple illustration will help clarify the difference between the terms and, at the same time, show their relationship. A small boy is helping his dad water the lawn by turning on the faucet when his dad sets the sprinkler where he wants it (cooperation). Unless the boy waits until his dad has moved a sufficient distance from the sprinkler before turning on the water, he will have a wet dad (coordination).

When the concept of coordination is applied to an organization producing consumer goods, the purchasing function would be in tune with the production function in terms of the quantity and quality of raw materials and the delivery schedule. The production function would be properly attuned to the efforts of the sales force in terms of the number and type of units produced and in having production scheduled in time for delivery according to the provisions of customers' sales contracts.

Here, again, the success of the coordination of activities depends on the degree of success organizational members have in communicating with each other. The degree to which organizational members are willing to coordinate their activities with other organizational units and personnel is largely dependent upon the quality of the continuous and ongoing relationships between them. In this the supervisor plays an essential role. Coordination over short periods of time may be obtained by coercion through the use of authority; however, over the long run, such methods are generally unsatisfactory because, in the absence of authoritative pressure, coordination may deteriorate. Thus, even from the viewpoint of traditional organization theory, human relations principles would be a positive force in improving the quality of teamwork necessary to coordinate organizational activities.

Hierarchy of Authority. The concept of authority is germane to traditional organization theory—authority being the power to make decisions, to select courses of action, and to enforce decisions. The existence of authority in an organization creates a hierarchy of power so that control over every unit (and, consequently, every individual) can be exercised. In the previous discussion of coordination it was made apparent that coordination of the various functions in an organization will not necessarily emerge automatically. The idea of coordination implies that some means of controlling, guiding, or limiting the activities of many diverse individuals or departments is carried on by some authority. It was illustrated that even the willing efforts of a father and son when watering a lawn may break down if one individual disregards the activities of the other. According to traditional concepts of organization, the use of authority rather than the use of individual initiative is the best way to insure coordination.

Usually the authority in an organization is distributed in a complex hierarchy of ranks and positions. Each position, generally, has a defined area of responsibility and, theoretically, is accompanied by enough authority to insure that its part of the job will be accomplished according to the plan conceived by some higher authority. Thus, positions of authority are linked from the top of the organization (the president) to the lowest level of authority in the organization (first-line supervisors). Theoretically, each *layer* of authority in the organization is accountable (responsible) to the next higher one; consequently, positions closer to the top of the organization are vested with more power than those in the middle or those closest to the rank-and-file workers. Thus, a chain of authority or command is created. This chain-of-command concept is usually illustrated in an organization chart showing the relationship between each unit in an organization (see Figure 8–1).

These concepts—common goals, functionalization or division of labor, coordination of activities, and hierarchy of authority—underlie the existence of a formal organization. It should be noted that, according to traditional concepts, emphasis is placed on the coordination of *activities,* not on the people themselves. This means that in an organization the concept of a division of labor does not in itself specify what person is to perform it; thus, a corporate organization as large as General Motors has a position known as the *president,* but there is no provision specifying who the specific person should be who occupies that position. The same is true of most other corporations. If the president should retire from office, the position remains, and the vacancy is filled by another person. There may be rules regarding the procedures to be followed in filling a vacant president's position in a given organization, but they are incidental to the autonomy of the position. Thus, a business firm may be divided into departments, each with a position of authority at the head of it. Should a man who is a department head die or retire, the position normally is not eliminated.*

USE OF ORGANIZATION CHARTS

The relationship between the areas of responsibility and the functions in an organization are often graphically diagrammed. Such a diagram or blueprint is referred to as a formal organizational chart. Some organizational planners and theorists have indicated disenchantment with the use of organization charts because many aspects of informal organization cannot be shown. Nevertheless, the use of such charts remains both a useful tool for analyzing formal organizational structure and a device for graphically showing the arrangement of functions within the firm. Henri Fayol, a French industrial organizational planner during the early twentieth century, indicated that organization charts enable one to grasp at a glance the organic whole of a company—its departments, its hierarchy of power, and its lines of formal communications—much more readily than any lengthy verbal or written description [5].

Changes in one part of the organization have a potential effect on other parts or the general operations of a firm as a whole. Therefore, the organization chart is useful in detecting how proposed changes might influence the existing organization before such modifications are actually implemented. Such information is valuable in clarifying reporting relationships in an organization. If these relationships are vague to organizational members, whether they are executives or rank-and-file employees, they may find it difficult to function effectively in their work.

Small groups seldom need much formal organization. As organizations grow in size and complexity the need arises to rationalize more clearly the whole operation, which inevitably becomes segmented and compartmentalized as activities are divided into specialized functions. According to traditional concepts, such organizational planning becomes necessary in large firms as a means of keeping order and unity among organizational members. Furthermore, those individuals responsible for the activities and personnel in the organization need to have information and control so they can keep track of what is going on.

In order to illustrate the use of an organizational chart, a hypothetical

---

* There may be exceptions to this in a case where the organization has changed its structure and eliminated a particular position but did not want to initiate the change until the person holding the position was retired or transferred.

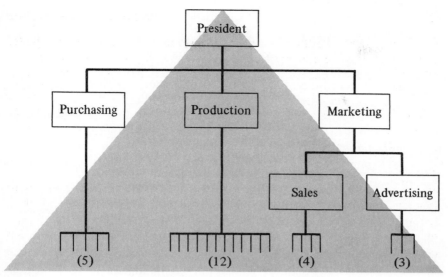

FIGURE 8-1. Organization Chart.

one for a manufacturing firm employing thirty individuals appears in Figure 8–1.

This simple formal organizational chart shows that the functions in the firm were divided into three main categories, each having a position of authority. The lines connecting each of the positions indicate the flow of authority and responsibility. In this case, purchasing, production, and marketing are three functional areas of responsibility that report to and receive orders directly from the position designated as president.

In the functional areas of purchasing and production, the workers are directly responsible to the heads of their respective departments. No positions are below the workers, so they have no authority over anyone else. It will be noted in following the lines connecting each of the positions on this chart that the five workers in purchasing report only to the head of their department; the twelve workers in production report only to their department head. Following the lines of authority, the head of purchasing has no direct authority over any workers other than those directly responsible to him. The same is true in production.

The marketing function is further divided into two subareas of responsibility, sales and advertising. Each of these subareas is directly responsible to the position above it—in this case the director of marketing. There are four salesmen responsible to the sales manager and three positions responsible to advertising.

The formal organization chart shows that one position, the president, is in charge of all functions in the organization. Each of the functions, marketing, production, and purchasing, is responsible for a designated area of the total operations; the head of each function is equal in the hierarchy of authority because each reports directly to the president. Only the marketing function is shown as being divided into further subdivisions of responsibility. If the thirty people in our hypothetical organization were now placed in the organization according to the chart, each person would occupy a position. One would be president, three would be heads of various functions, two would be in charge of more specific functions under marketing (sales and advertising), and the remaining twenty-four people would occupy rank-and-file positions in the various functional departments.

Several factors are shown on an organizational chart, including the lines of authority, which theoretically flow downward from the president to the bottom layer of rank-and-file workers. The lines of responsibility flow upward from the bottom layer of positions to the top position of president. Finally, the lines of formal communications flow upward and downward and horizontally. Horizontal communications occur when members at the same level in the hierarchy of authority communicate with each other.

The sample organizational chart in Figure 8–1 also shows another important characteristic of most organizations. Because it has one top-ranking position and twenty-four rank-and-file positions, with five middle positions, the organization, if one visualizes its outline without the boxes or connecting lines, assumes the shape of a triangle or pyramid. This pyramidal shape will vary depending on the number of layers of management from top to bottom and the number of divisions of labor or functions into which the organization is divided. The nature of the relationships and organizational character caused by this will be more thoroughly discussed in the following chapter.

A final point about organizational charts needs to be emphasized: The chart indicates the official relationships between the positions in an organization, but it does not show the personal and social ones. These latter relationships are termed *informal* and can be as important as the official or formal ones designated on the chart. It should be noted also that many organizations do not have a formal organizational chart, and some other means must be employed to analyze the internal operations of the firm. In cases where no blueprint of the organization exists, something about the hierarchy and structure of the firm can be gleaned by noting the titles of positions held by members of the organizations and by observing who reports to whom in the organization.

ALTERNATIVE APPROACHES TO ORGANIZATION

Traditional organizational concepts have been criticized because they emphasize the structure of functions and interpersonal relationships to achieve organizational goals rather than to satisfy human needs. Using the socio-group versus the psyche-group model mentioned in the beginning of this chapter, one would find that most business organizations lean decidedly toward the socio-group concept.

Traditionally, in industrial organizations emphasis has been placed on fitting the man to the job, because it is more convenient than fitting the job to the diversified capabilities of the man. Orderliness is a principal characteristic of traditional organization theory. Moreover, traditional theory strives to reduce the power of the individual to make him more responsive to formal authority [6, p. 70].

As new industries have emerged since the end of World War II, technological innovation has changed traditional organizational relationships, and new organizational patterns have been sought. Attempts have been made to develop organizational patterns which emphasize the people rather than the functions of a firm. Such attempts are built upon the premise that *people* perform the work to be done. In order to maximize the use of each person's talents and potentialities it is best not to limit the functions of people. Because no two people are alike, no two will do a particular job exactly alike; hence, the jobs in the organization are redesigned to fit the people performing them. In effect, each person creates his own job. This approach appears to work at higher levels in the organization where executives need latitudes and flexibility in order to make decisions and to carry out their responsibility; however, there seem to be limitations to its application in all organizations or to all levels in any given organization.

Another approach which may be used in constructing an organization is one which does not define or assign responsibilities carefully to any particular member of the organization. Such an approach encourages the personal initiative of the members of the organization. This can and does foster competition among members and operates best when the members are highly skilled and highly motivated, but it also presents the danger that the efforts and energy of the people involved will be spent on personal rather than organizational objectives. There is also concern that organizational members will become involved in playing politics and that organizational effectiveness will end up depending on the personalities of individuals rather than the objectivity of an organizational system. It might be noted that such a criticism overlooks the fact that even organizations following the strictest of traditional patterns are made up of human beings who will find ways of beating the so-called objective systems.

Modern attempts to update and revise organizational and management theory have been relatively slow to take effect in many industrial firms that have been in operation for a long period of time. The changes that have occurred often follow patterns which managers of business firms believe best suited to the political or economic considerations of the moment, rather than because of any regard for the long-run social or psychological well-being of organizational members. This is an important consideration, though not surprising, because traditional organizational theory has evolved for centuries, whereas human relations concepts have only developed into an accountable state during the past three or four decades, paralleling the growth of the behavioral sciences.

While older and more established industries have been relatively slow to alter their traditional organizational relationships, newer industries and business activities emerging during the past several decades have been more receptive to innovative organizational patterns. It might be noted that resistance to people-oriented organizational patterns has not been entirely from top-level executives in either the older or newer industries. Resistance has also arisen from the ranks found in the middle and lower echelons of the organization, as well as from labor unions.

ORGANIZATIONAL ROLES

A variety of reasons exist for individual resistance to organizational patterns which depart from traditional concepts. Among these reasons is the fact that in situations where an individual's job is not clearly defined, he may find the ambiguity of his role frustrating. *Role* is social behavior oriented to the general expectation of others and it arises as a result of occupying a position in a social structure. Thus, a supervisor has a role of leadership in a work group; however, he also plays other roles both on and off the job. On the job, he also has a role as a subordinate to his boss. In the work group, he may play the role of adviser and counselor to its members. Outside of the job, he has other roles, such as father, husband, social club officer, and so on. In each of these roles a different pattern of behavior is expected by the persons with whom he must interact.

The existence of role expectations can cause role conflict when a person's own perception of the behavior that is expected of him differs substantially from what others actually expect from him. When this occurs, the individual cannot meet one expectation without rejecting the other.

Workers also have roles on the job. They are subordinate to their supervisor, but they are also possibly lathe operators, union members, and members of the bowling team. The behavior of workers and supervisors alike is directed by their *role perceptions;* that is, how they think they are expected to act in a given situation. Because each individual has many roles, he needs to be highly adaptive in order to change from one role to another. A supervisor who leaves a safety meeting with his work group to attend a production meeting with his department head must be prepared to change his role rapidly and smoothly.

In organizations where areas of job responsibility are not as clearly defined as they might be according to traditional concepts, workers may encounter ambiguity and frustration in the way they are supposed to perform. For example, in one research and consulting firm a young college graduate who was hired as a research assistant constantly complained that he did not know what was expected of him. His assignments involved working on a variety of projects with a variety of senior professional consultants, each with special areas of competence and interests. In some projects the research assistant was required to work independently, conducting interviews with members of client's management staff. Some projects required hours of library research and still other projects required statistical tabulations and interpretation of quantitative data. Although the young man was technically capable of performing each of these activities, he found that the rapid changes in role and the multiple responsibilities were a highly dissatisfying experience.

The traditional organizational pattern provides more security to organizational members who wish to operate within relatively definite areas of responsibility and where role changes may be less abrupt or drastic than those in organizations in which people make their own job by doing whatever needs to be done. Not only does the latter situation create occasion for role ambiguity, it also can be the cause of role conflict.

INFORMAL ORGANIZATION

A business firm has people working for it. The people come from a society into the organization, and they bring with them their varying talents, aptitudes, skills, and the influence of their culture. These individuals not only develop relationships with each other that are officially sanctioned by the firm, but they also develop patterns of behavior among themselves not suggested or sanctioned by the firm. These relationships are called *informal* organization or groups. Such informal social patterns arise spontaneously or implicitly out of the interactions of people without involving a rational coordination for the achievement of explicit common goals. Generally, such associations follow the model of psyche-groups more closely than formal business organization, no matter how innovative it may be.

Because informal groups are dynamic in nature they cannot be so easily diagrammed as the formal relationships that appear on an organization chart. Informal groups are usually unplanned and grow out of the personal needs of the group; as such, they are not accountable to any part of the formal organization.

Some managers and supervisors have expressed a desire to eliminate the informal group, or at least certain aspects of it, such as the *grapevine* —the grapevine being the informal communications system among employees. Needless to say, there is no socially acceptable way to abolish the informal organization, and even if there were, to do so might be to draw the life blood out of a formal organization. Therefore, more constructive use of energy might be spent trying to understand the nature and function of informal groups rather than in trying to eliminate them.

Informal groups arise because they satisfy human needs and perform certain social functions. For one thing, informal groups perpetuate common social and cultural values of employees. Informal meetings and groups occur at all levels in the organization. Top executives share interests and mutual problems over lunch or on the golf course, engineers discuss mutual problems, as do secretaries, supervisors, and maintenance workers. In each case, individuals with common interests and values find a degree of social support for their own feelings and beliefs. For this reason, to ignore or attempt to suppress such group can cause them to coalesce and form a subtle or even open resistance to the formal organization. In many instances, the movement toward unionization grows out of the employer's failure to understand or act upon the individual needs of workers when it might have been a relatively simple matter to discern such needs through the pulse of informal organizations.

Closely related to the first function of informal groups is the social satisfaction that employees derive from memberships in these groups. The friendships that arise on the job provide companionship for workers. Furthermore, membership in informal groups allows some workers recognition and status that they would not receive from the formal organization. These elements add an enjoyable dimension to what might otherwise be a dull and laborious work day.

Informal groups provide a communication system for employees. This is commonly called the grapevine. Such an informal communications link between employees satisfies their need to be kept informed about factors which can and do affect their lives. Rumors and half-truths, as well as truths, pass through the grapevine with surprising rapidity.

The distortions that occur in the informal communications system are even more difficult to control than the distortions found in the official organization's channels of communication because they are uncontrolled by managers or supervisors and there is no guide for receiving and passing on information. The organization itself can contribute to the array of distortions and rumors that are circulated by not providing accurate or adequate information to employees.

Another principal function of informal groups is the provision for norms of behavior among workers. This phenomenon was discovered in the Hawthorne Studies in relation to levels of production. It also applies to other areas of employee behavior and conformity. Many details on expected employee behavior are not explicitly made known by employers. Informal groups provide a frame of reference for workers in ambiguous situations—how long should one really take on coffee breaks; how do you obtain supplies; how do you respond to a supervisor when asked about production schedules; and so on. The informal group provides a standard of conformity within which individual employees find security. This conformity can affect modes of dress, language, other social behavior, and levels of production.

Informal groups can be a constructive element in maintaining group solidarity and performance when members assist one another. Older employees help train newer ones by showing them the tricks of the trade, enabling new employees to adapt more quickly to the work environment, where the restrooms are located, how to fill out a requisition for supplies, who to see about payroll deductions, and so on. In these and myriad other ways the informal group can be a constructive force in maintaining cohesiveness among workers and can directly and indirectly contribute to the productivity of the organization.

Every informal group has its leaders or pace setters. These leaders differ from the organizationally appointed leaders (supervisors, department heads, and so on) in that they do not possess organizational authority. Even though informal leaders may not possess the authority to give orders or to dismiss or transfer fellow employees, they do, in fact, exercise influence over the behavior of other employees. They function as communicators among employees, and often they initiate action. Perhaps this is merely collecting donations for a gift for a member of the group or acting as group spokesman on a grievance which calls for a response from the formal organization.

In the final analysis, in many respects the formal and informal organizations are mutually dependent. A change in one system can produce a change in the other. A new piece of machinery or a different operating procedure initiated by the formal organization will result in a change in the work group social structure. Thus, the process of change may affect not only the formal organizational relationships in a firm, but also the informal ones.

Understanding the interface between the formal and informal social systems of an organization requires a broad comprehension of many psychological, sociological, and business principles beyond the scope of this book. Organizational behavior is a rising discipline concerned with investigating and describing formal and informal aspects of human behavior in an organizational environment. As this investigation progresses, the relationship between the observable formal aspects of organization and the less definable elements of informal and social organization that exists in every business concern becomes clearer. As this occurs, the practice of human relations can continue to advance toward constructive means of making organizational life more productive and satisfying for every organizational member.

SUMMARY

1. Work for most people is carried on within the context of a group, which means that if everyone's efforts are to be utilized most efficiently certain organizational patterns or controls must be developed. The pattern or structure of an organization is designed by its creators either by rationalized planning or by allowing the organization to develop its own shape and structure according to the physical, cultural, and technological environment within which it must operate. If wasted effort and duplication and gaps in activity are to be averted, the creators or managers of the organization must carefully decide what the purpose of the organization is, what the work or functions are to be, and who is responsible for seeing that the functions are executed and making sure that the organizational goals are being met or strived for by the members of the group. This means that a hierarchy or authority of power must be developed.

2. Formal organizations have certain characteristics which distinguish them from informal social organizations. These characteristics are the existence of organizational goals, the division of labor, and an hierarchy of authority. The existence of the preceding characteristics creates the need for coordination and cooperation between the separate departments and personnel found in the organization. Coordination refers to the careful timing and sequence of activities in a group. Cooperation depends on the willingness of group members to abide by the rules of the group and the willingness to carry out their assigned responsibilities.

3. An organization chart is a blueprint of the formal relationship between the functions and personnel in a group. It also shows the relationship of authority or power between members in a group. Because most organizations have fewer people in command at the top of the organization than rank-and-file employees at the bottom, the organization takes on a shape resembling a pyramid.

4. Many traditional organizational concepts evolved from church and military organizations. Many of the principles upon which formal organizations have based their structure and management controls are not entirely compatible with human relations principles which are founded on the research findings of the behavioral sciences. Many theorists have attempted to alter the principles of organization used in industry, but any such changes have been slow to take hold and more often follow patterns which the managers of business firms believe best suited to political or economic considerations of the moment, rather than on the long run social or psychological well-being of the organizational members.

Formal relationships between members of an organization can be diagrammed on an organization chart, but the informal relationships between members are not so easily charted. Informal relationships are usually unplanned by the creators of the organization. Such relationships grow out of the personal needs of the group and are not accountable to any part of the formal organization. Friendships or social gatherings between employees of the same firm are examples of informal relationships. The nature and duration of such relationships may change quickly and radically. The dynamic nature of informal relationships does not diminish their importance to the smooth operations of the group or to the impact on group morale.

DISCUSSION QUESTIONS

1. What is the essential difference between the orientation of socio-groups and psyche-groups? Why would most business firms fit the pattern of a socio-group rather than a psyche-group?
2. Give an example of how a technological change can change the social environment in an organization.
3. What is the purpose of a formal organization chart?
4. What information is not given in an organization chart?
5. What is informal organization? Does informal organization exist within a firm? If so, give an example.
6. What causes role conflict in an organization?
7. In what ways can the formal structure of an organization affect the practice of human relations? Can human relations practices affect the formal organization structure? If so, how?

BIBLIOGRAPHY AND SELECTED COLLATERAL READINGS

1. ALBERS, HENRY H., *Principles of Organization and Management,* 2nd ed. New York: John Wiley and Sons, 1965.
2. BASS, BERNARD M., *Organizational Psychology.* Boston: Allyn and Bacon, Inc., 1965.
3. DAVIS, KEITH, *Human Relations at Work,* 3rd ed. New York: McGraw-Hill Book Company, 1967.
4. DAVIS, KEITH, and ROBERT L. BLOMSTROM, *Business and Its Environment.* New York: McGraw-Hill Book Company, 1966.
5. FAYOL, HENRI, *General and Industrial Management.* Translated by Constance Starrs. London: Sir Isaac Pitman and Sons, Ltd., 1949.
6. GOLEMBIEWSKI, ROBERT T., *Men, Management, and Morality: Toward a New Organizational Ethic.* New York: McGraw-Hill Book Company, 1965.
7. HAIMANN, THEO, *Professional Management.* Boston: Houghton Mifflin Company, 1962.
8. JENNINGS, H. H., *Leadership and Isolation,* 2nd ed. New York: Longmans, Green, 1950.

9. JOHNSON, R. A., and others, *Theory and Management of Systems,* 2nd ed. New York: McGraw-Hill Book Company, 1967.
10. LEVITT, THEODORE, " 'Creativity' Is Not Enough," *Harvard Business Review* (May–June 1963), pp. 72–83.
11. METCALF, HENRY C., and L. URWICK (eds.), *Dynamic Administration, The Collected Papers of Mary Parker Follett.* New York: Harper & Row, 1942.
12. PFIFFNER, JOHN M., and FRANK SHERWOOD, *Administrative Organization.* Englewood Cliffs, N.J.: Prentice-Hall, Inc., 1960.
13. SCHEIN, EDGAR H., *Organizational Psychology.* Englewood Cliffs, N.J.: Prentice-Hall, Inc., 1965.
14. SPROTT, W. J. H., *Human Groups.* Baltimore: Penguin Books, Inc., 1963.
15. TAYLOR, FREDERICK W., *The Principles of Scientific Management.* New York: Harper & Row, 1916.
16. THOMPSON, J. D., *Approaches to Organizational Design.* Pittsburgh: University of Pittsburgh Press, 1966.

Factors Influencing
Organizational Patterns
and Behavior

As discussed in the previous chapter, formal organization is a means of arranging activities and functions, defining areas of responsibility and authority, and establishing organizational relationships in order to accomplish the objectives of a firm. Traditionally, to insure that organizational goals are achieved, the activities of organization members are carefully planned so that no gaps or unnecessary duplication of effort occurs. This responsibility usually is placed in the hands of management. The systems and controls selected and instituted by management have a definite influence on all the members of the firm and often result in actually determining the structure and climate of the organization.

The organization has been designed around the jobs to be done. The total job to be done has been subdivided into smaller tasks and placed into separate little boxes which are then arranged into a pattern which seems rational to the organizational designers. Job descriptions define the activities of each of the people who are placed into each of the boxes on the organization chart. The result is a neat organization chart where a certain amount of authority is put into each box along with certain responsibilities which are expected to balance the package [6, p. 192]. Then, information and control systems are used to tie together all of the boxes and all of the people occupying them.

Today a number of theorists and businessmen are concerned with the problem of organizing business firms in the most effective manner. Thus, a number of carefully conducted studies have been made to determine how effective and responsive organizations are to the real demands of a rapidly changing business environment. The search for more effective ways of organizing a group of people so that their talents can be utilized more readily to solve problems is an endless one. Furthermore, most

165

organizational theorists recognize that no single pattern is ideal for all business operations. The most appropriate organizational pattern for one company may not be effective for another. The principal thrust of investigation among those who study organizational behavior is to discover ways that will help an organization capitalize on its human resources to the same degree that efficient use has been made of technological and material resources. To do this, better understanding about the relationship between functions and people in an organization must occur.

A consideration of at least five elements will help a student appreciate the impact of the relationship between functions and people on organizational behavior and the practice of human relations. These five elements are stated briefly as follows:

1. The overall perspective of the organization, including its size, social environment, utilization of technology, its function and goals, and the human and operational problems that accompany the attainment of its goals.

2. Recognizing the organization as a living or human system to be integrated with physical, financial, technological, communication, and other systems vital to its existence and perpetuation.

3. Understanding the management principles which are used by the leadership of the organization to coordinate the activities of the organization.

4. Understanding the principles of motivation in human behavior which affect the interpersonal relationships among organizational members.

5. Realizing the dynamic nature of an organization which must be flexible and responsive to changing social, political, and economic environmental conditions.

Understanding these five elements requires a broad comprehension of many psychological, sociological, and business principles that are far beyond the scope of this book; however, most of the organizational elements mentioned here have implications that deserve a place in the continuous study of human relations. They should act as a guide for examining the effectiveness of an organization's utilization of its human resources.

THE IMPACT OF CHANGE ON THE ORGANIZATION

A number of factors influence the way a company organizes. If it is to survive and grow, it must be adaptive to the dynamic environment in which it exists. The forces that affect the organizational systems used by a company may come from the external social, political, economic, and cultural environment. For example, labor unions may directly influence the establishment of procedures for handling employees, so may government laws and regulations. Because the organization has no direct control over the nature of such forces, although it may work to change them, they are called *external* systems with which the organization must cope and adapt to if it is to exist successfully. However, an organization develops within it a number of patterns and norms which are not necessarily specified by external influence. These are called the *internal* system and appear to be an outgrowth of the interaction of the social contacts made by members of the organization. The internal system of relationships is made of those that are officially sanctioned and intended by it (formal organization) and those patterns of behavior not even suggested by the firm, which are referred to as the informal organization.

Until recently, most companies have ignored the informal organization; a few have tried to suppress it, but few attempted to make constructive use of it. The reasons for this are rooted in industrial antiquity. Most large organizations have existed long enough to have been created when organizational principles were limited primarily to organizing tasks rather than people. Even some rather large companies which have been organized within the past few decades follow the traditional concepts of organization because their creators emulated traditional models in existence.

The way a large firm is organized often evolves out of its own history. The period in which it was founded, the personality and character of its management, the nature of the industry into which it entered, the number of persons working for it—all have an effect on the size and shape of the formal organization. Changes in the social, economic, and political world occur rapidly, and a firm must be sufficiently flexible to adapt to changes if it is to survive. Consumer demand for new or more products can create the necessity for new manufacturing plants and processes. Determining the best methods of distribution or production creates a demand for new research activities. Complex new tax laws require new accounting systems. Electronic data-processing equipment and computer systems create a demand for new technical skills. Different and more accurate information and communications methods are required as a result of the need for faster, more accurate management decision-making. The list of changes is nearly endless, and each change conceivably can affect the organizational structure of a firm.

New functions can add to the number of departments in an organization. Expansion of business activities into broader geographic territories can add to the number of production plants and sales offices. These are examples of functional or technical changes to which a firm must adapt. There are other changes which are more subtle, but just as important.

A sweeping change in the attitude toward authority has occurred in today's workers. The assignment of X amount of authority to a particular box on an organization chart is not a simple matter in light of the progressive change in the role of the individual. Modern egalitarian attitudes of employees complicate immeasurably the process of using power to coerce individuals to perform their duty. The underlying threat of dismissal which once used to accompany an employer's orders no longer carries the same weight in a corporation where the supervisor is not the owner, but simply another employee of the firm.

The growth in power of labor unions has eroded the absolute power of supervisors to make arbitrary work assignments or dismiss employees. Governmental constraints on employment practices have further reduced the use of discrimination in the hiring and treatment of workers. Thus, organizational authority now has its absolute limits in dealing with organizational members. Such external restraints on the use of power have forced managers of small and large companies to take a look at ways of organizing the company's functions and human resources so that company objectives can be reached without the use of organizational power that once was so prevalent.

GROWTH OF THE ORGANIZATION

Obviously, there are other pressures placed on a business enterprise to seek more effective organizational patterns than externally placed restraints on power. For example, some companies, as they grow in size and diversity, find that internal organizational patterns need to be changed.

As a business grows in size, a change in its organizational structure is inevitable if it is to keep pace with the changes in activites and functions that accompany the growth. In a very small business, one or two people may divide the activities of the business between them. Coordination of their activities may not be too difficult because there is daily contact and closeness in their association. As the business grows in size and more people are required, a greater degree of specialization takes place. For example, in a small firm owned and operated by only a few people, the business activities may be divided and shared between them with minimal problems of coordination.

As a business operation expands to include many products, large geographic areas, and many people, the organizational structure can become complicated by new factors. Labor unions may enter and require the full-time attention of some company official; the number of employees may be great enough to require the attention of a special payroll department; employee benefits and services may demand close control; and widespread business activities of the firm may require legal assistance to interpret myriad federal, state, and local laws regulating business affairs.

In the early stages of the organization's development, business activities may be relatively simple and require only a minimum of specialization. Often the division of labor in small enterprises is made along the lines of the personal talents and interests of the individuals involved rather than because of the logical relationships between tasks. Therefore, it is not uncommon in small firms to have important elements of the business neglected because none of the organizational members possess either knowledge about them or interest in them. As the business grows in size and becomes complex, specialized areas of knowledge and skill increase in importance. As specialization is accompanied by increased numbers of people, organizational planning requires coordination of effort. Thus, organization charts depicting the structure of organizational relationships become an important tool of management in understanding and planning the organization's growth and development.

CENTRALIZED AND DECENTRALIZED ORGANIZATION

An increase in the size and scope of a company's business operation is accompanied by the need to spread decision-making power over a large number of organizational members. The problem of power distribution in an organization gives rise to the concepts of *centralized* and *decentralized* control and authority. Although the implementation of each of these concepts has an impact on the shape and structure of an organization, in reality, they more accurately describe the extent to which decision-making power is given to members in an organization.

CENTRALIZATION

In a centralized company, decision-making power is usually held by members at or close to the top of the organizational hierarchy. Although this may facilitate rapid decisions for a company as a whole, this factor limits the degree of participation that members below this level are permitted to exercise.

The concept of centralization grew out of the early belief in the concentration of power upon which traditional organizational theory was built. In small companies and in organizations where operations have not reached a very high level of diversification, centralization may operate with a high degree of efficiency because of close personal contact between top management and other organizational members. In large, diversified firms, the use of computers and information-retrieval systems makes possible faster, more unified decisions by managers closer to the top of the organization than was possible or practical before. Such technical advances have, in some cases, reduced the necessity for on-the-spot decisions and have reduced the need from a technical standpoint for decentralization. However, a centralized system can contribute to the sense of frustration and loss of significance many middle managers and supervisors feel. They become order takers without real authority and responsibility. While a centralized organization may serve the technical needs of a company in conformance with traditional standards, it may create an organizational climate which employees find stifling and unrewarding.

DECENTRALIZATION

The concept of *decentralization* refers to the wide allocation of decision-making authority and responsibility downward to the smallest unit that is practical throughout the organization. Actually, the concept of *decentralization* is both a philosophy of management and a technique. As a philosophy it refers to top management's belief that all managers and personnel in the organization should have maximum opportunity to develop and utilize their talents as responsible members of the organizational team. As a result, managers and their staff should be given the necessary authority to make decisions in their own areas of responsibility. As a technique, decentralization is a means of organizing which distributes authority to each semi-independent decision-making unit in the organization, but carefully devised communications systems and controls are used to insure that all the separate units in the organization are working toward commonly accepted goals [1, p. 220].

Decentralization may be applied in a number of ways: *geographic dispersion,* allowing decision-making in each plant regardless of geographic location; *federal* decentralization, allowing vast freedom to make decisions regarding nearly all aspects of operations (purchasing, selection of personnel, production, and marketing); and *functional* decentralization, setting up distinct integrated units allowing large areas of freedom in decisions and operations. The key difference between functional and federal decentralization is that, normally, only in the latter situation do the separate organizational units compete with each other as well as with other firms for profits. In both cases managers are given wide latitude for making decisions.

Limits of Decentralization. Decentralization is compatible with the principles of human relations in that it allows greater participation of organizational members in the company affairs calling for more than mechanical responses. Decentralization calls for capable and highly motivated people who *want* to accept the responsibility for decision-making in problem-solving situations. It must be recognized that not all employees wish to accept such responsibility, and those who may want to may not possess the necessary skills to do so effectively. This means that in the latter case, companies wishing a decentralized system must provide adequate opportunities for training and development of both the technical competence and the interpersonal skills of their employees who are deficient in such areas.

It should be remembered that decentralization is not a panacea for all organizational ills or all human relations problems. Many firms that have tried it have had to retract their efforts or modify decentralized practices. One major electric appliance manufacturer found that its decentralized practices led to the purchase of parts produced by a major competitor for use in the appliances assembled in one of its branch plants. The decentralized managers of the assembly plant found that such parts could be obtained less expensively outside the company. When top-level management discovered this fact, changes in purchasing were rapidly ordered.

A decentralized approach requires that all managers and supervisors possess an understanding of the goals and procedures used in a company. The operation of several (or many, depending on the size of the organization) decision-making units may also contribute to intergroup rivalry which may result in inconsistency in the decisions reached. One group may try to outdo the other. This can be a healthy form of competition as long as the quality and nature of decisions are in accordance with the overall objectives of the company. However, should the inconsistencies of decisions create havoc and should intergroup rivalry destroy the overall organizational cohesiveness, the benefits derived from having productive on-the-spot decisions give way to organizational units working at cross purposes, contributing to the confusion of the company's operation and needless waste of effort and materials.

Other limiting factors exist in a decentralized organization. Decisions may take longer because of the time necessary to reach a consensus among decision-making units. Costs may be higher than in a centralized organization because of increased duplication of manpower. Each decision-making unit may need its own technical staff in order to make necessary decisions; thus, instead of one central staff of technicians, several organizational units may have to be staffed. Scarce human resources may be needlessly duplicated. Costs of maintaining communications links between decentralized units may be higher than in a centralized firm. Exchange of information is vital in every organization regardless of the decision-making process; however, in a decentralized firm much of the communication may lapse into social dialogue rather than necessary input for making better-quality decisions.

COMPARISON OF CENTRALIZED AND DECENTRALIZED ORGANIZATION

Absolute centralization and decentralization are opposite poles on the same broad spectrum of delegation of authority. In most cases the absolutes will not be found in industrial practice. Usually, managers attempt to develop an organizational pattern which is optimum to the needs of the firm, thus avoiding the inherent weaknesses of each extreme.

The following table outlines the relative strength and weaknesses of centralization and decentralization:

Strengths	Weaknesses
Centralized Organization	
Assures uniformity of standards and policies among organizational units.	Floods communications lines to a few individuals at the top of organization.
Allows use of outstanding talent in managers by the whole organization rather than a single unit.	Makes great demands on a few managers rather than spreading responsibility.
Decisions are uniform.	Personalizes decisions to the judgments of a few key decision-makers.
Helps eliminate duplication of effort and activity.	Forces top managers to possess a broad view which may be beyond their capacity.
	Gives vast amounts of power to a few individuals.
	Reduces sense of participation for all but a few people.
Decentralized Organization	
Reduces total responsibility to more manageable units.	Lack of uniformity of standards and policies among organizational units.
Helps develop more personnel in decision-making process.	Capable managers are not always available or willing to participate in decision-making.
Shortens lines of communication.	Creates problems of coordination between separate organizational units.
Places decision-making closer to situations affected by decisions.	Interunit rivalry can interfere with the total organization's operations.
Allows more people to use skills and talents in decisions.	Requires training programs which may be time-consuming and costly.
Disperses power among many persons.	

Once the comparative advantages and disadvantages are carefully weighed, the organizational pattern or combination of patterns most appropriate for a particular firm may be selected. Some organizational experts favor an organizational pattern in which organizational planning and controls are centralized and authority and responsibility are decentralized. Such division of planning and doing does not answer the question of what happens when a project fails. Who is to blame—the planners or the people responsible for carrying out the plans?

Auren Uris feels that planning done in one parent organization and execution carried out in a suborganizational unit cannot be called decentralization [16, p. 49]. What is a supposedly decentralized organization results in a pseudo-decentralized organization in which the parent organization forces the divisions that are supposedly doing both the planning and executing to play the game as the top management dictates.

The concepts of centralization and decentralization do more than affect the shape of formal organizational structure. In a real fashion, the philosophy of management underlying either a centralized or decentralized organization permeates the climate within the company. In companies where major decision-making authority is confined to a few members at the top of the management hierarchy, others below them, such as supervisors, tend to restrict rather than encourage the ideas and suggestions of their own subordinates. The reason for this appears to be a matter of emulation of management styles. That is, where a supervisor is not encouraged to participate in problem solutions and decisions by his superior, he finds little incentive to encourage his subordinates to offer suggestions and ideas to the problems facing the work group. From a human relations viewpoint, the undesirable outcome of this chain reaction is that few employees are provided enough individual freedom and autonomy to foster self-development and growth.

PROBLEMS CREATED BY ORGANIZATION

It has been mentioned that changes in attitude in the general population toward authority and the search of theorists and enlightened business managers for more effective organizational patterns have contributed to the assault that has been made on traditional concepts of organization. Yet, in a real sense, organization is unavoidable in any group activity. Before mentioning some new concepts to be used in creating an organization, it might be helpful to review a few of the major problems which exist when people are placed in any organizational situation.

DELEGATION OF AUTHORITY AND RESPONSIBILITY

The traditional concepts of organizational structure present a number of human relations problems that must be faced by managers and rank-and-file employees. The division of labor in an organization means that the total task of meeting organizational objectives is divided into a number of smaller ones and assigned or delegated to members of the organization. Although the concept of delegation is closely related to the concepts of centralization and decentralization, it should be made clear that an organization may prosper without being decentralized—but there can be no organization without delegation, that is, the conferring of certain specific authority and responsibility by a superior to one or more of his subordinates. The amount of authority that any given supervisor delegates to his subordinates depends on a number of factors which will be discussed shortly. The nature of authority has several aspects and can be generated by the use of force or by personal charm; however, in traditional usage it usually refers to the power to act within the scope of a position in the organizational hierarchy. A manager may have the official authority to give orders pertaining to a subordinate's job duties but not the official authority to give him orders in matters regarding his private life. This point is an interesting one which supervisors should keep in mind, because in organizational affairs, as well as in private ones, it is the subordinate who controls the response to authority. The supervisor should remember that the use of delegation allows him to accomplish more by assigning to others part of the authority and responsibility which is assigned to him.

Responsibility is the obligation of an organizational member to do something and to account to a higher authority for its performance. The delegation of responsibility has one important qualification, the delegation of responsibility to others by a supervisor does not relieve him of the ultimate responsibility. Thus, to delegate is not to give away, and a supervisor is ultimately responsible for the actions of his subordinates as well as his own.

Keith Davis lists the degrees of delegation which set the relationship between the person assigning and the person receiving the delegation of duties, responsibility, and authority. Here are five distinctly different degrees or steps in current use:

1. Authority to act with no prior notice, no approval, and no reporting required.

2. Authority to act, with reporting required, but no prior notice or approval.

3. Authority to act with prior notice.

4. Authority to act only after consulting an appropriate staff adviser.

5. Authority to act only with approval [1. p. 185].

The difference in the power to act held by a person with a latitude of freedom is obviously much broader in step 1 than it is in step 5. In the case of a supervisor, it is important that he know precisely what degree of power he has before he takes action—for instance, in the firing of an inefficient employee. In step 1 he could do so without notifying anyone of his action. In step 2 he could do so, but he would have to notify his superior or the personnel department after he had taken his action. From steps 3 through 5 he would have to notify his superior or the personnel department *before* he took any action.

Reasons for Lack of Delegation. Delegation is not without some problems. Some supervisors hesitate to delegate because they believe they can do the job better than any of their subordinates. A few supervisors fear that delegation to subordinates will weaken their own position because they do not understand the nature of the process. Such supervisors may not feel secure in their position of leadership of a work group because so many elements have already undermined their scope of authority. Personnel departments handle many aspects of selection—hiring, promoting, and transferring employees—so that the supervisor may feel his voice in such matters is only an echo. Labor union contracts may lay down work rules and procedures which apparently limit the extent to which a supervisor may direct the activities of his subordinates. Taken together, the gradual usurping of supervisory authority may well lead a supervisor not to "give away" voluntarily any more of his prerogatives.

A general guide followed in delegation is that authority and responsibility should be coequal. In other words, give a man enough authority to carry out what he is asked to do. Some supervisors neglect to utilize delegation effectively because they do not assign enough authority along with the responsibility they delegate. This latter weakness is one which frequently leads to frustration and dissatisfaction among subordinates. Some supervisors feel the identical pangs of frustration because their own superiors violate this concept and assign them a disproportionate share of responsibility without sufficient authority.

SPAN OF CONTROL

Closely related to the problem of delegation is a concept referred to as *span of control* or *span of supervision*. This refers to the number of subordinates a manager or supervisor can directly supervise effectively. There would appear to be some physical limit to this number imposed by both the capacity of the manager and the time he has available. No absolute rule exists in this matter; however, a number of factors exist which must be considered in determining the span of control for any given manager. The capacities of the supervisor must be considered. Men vary in personality and in physical and mental limitations. The skills and ability of those persons being supervised are another determinant of the number a single supervisor can directly control. Unskilled or untrained workers often require closer supervision and, thus, could reduce the span of control of a supervisor.

Regardless of the particular industry or type of organizational structure, the concept of span of control is important to the practice of human relations because it influences the face-to-face contacts between management and workers, which in turn affect the communications, relationship between the supervisor and his subordinates, and the extent to which each employee is directly controlled and developed by his supervisor.

Impact of Span of Control on Organizational Structure. In order to see an example of how the span of control can be reflected in the shape of the organizational structure, note Figure 9–1, where a hypothetical organization with twenty-seven members has a span of control of twelve. Compare this organizational shape with the one shown in Figure 9–2, where the same number of people are employed in an organization in which the span of control is only three. The effects of the difference in the size of

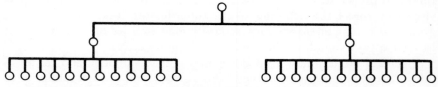

FIGURE 9–1. Flat Organization Developed by Large Span of Control.

control can be seen in the flattened shape of Figure 9–1 (span of control 12) when it is compared with the taller organizational structure of Figure 9–2 (span of control 3). In the flat organization with the larger span of control, it will be noted that fewer supervisory positions are required. Figure 9–1 indicates that only two layers of management are required to control the activities of the twenty-four operational rank-and-file workers. Thus, only one general manager and two supervisors are required.

In the taller organizational structure shown in Figure 9–2, with no

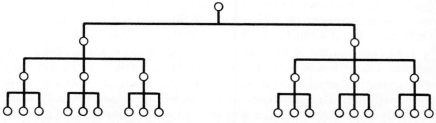

FIGURE 9–2. Tall Organization Developed by Small Span of Control.

more than three persons reporting directly to any supervisor, three layers of management are necessary to control the activities of eighteen rank-and-file employees, one president, two department heads, six supervisors. The larger an organization is and the smaller the span of control, the greater the number of supervisory and management personnel necessary to direct the activities of the firm.

In the taller organizational structure the process of communication is complicated because of the additional layers of management between the top official and operational employees. However, because no more than three persons report to any given superior, opportunity to know each individual person in the work group is greater, and closer control of the performance of the employees is permitted. Ideally, development of employees should be fostered in a situation where the span of control is small; however, another factor enters which might alter this. If the head of the organization is a strong individual who believes in close control, then the tall organization would permit him to make most of the decisions in the organization. When this occurs, the managers who are subordinate to him may not be encouraged to develop decision-making and action-taking abilities because the president reserves the right to do so for himself.

It may be concluded that both the tall and the flat organizational structures have advantages and disadvantages. The flat organization is usually simpler and where managers are well trained, efficient operations occur because of the independence and initiative such an organizational structure provides. This possible advantage may be reduced if the persons holding management positions are inadequately trained or have poor judgment. Tall structures provide the opportunity for closer control and contact with organizational members, but the structure is more complex and may pose problems of coordination between more numerous department heads and supervisors.

The dynamics of the flat organization might be summarized in the following way. Because there are few layers of management, communications both downward and upward might be more rapid and accurate. The relatively large number of employees reporting to a supervisor might cut down on the face-to-face contact between them and there might be less opportunity for building close rapport, but there would be less individual control over activities and less time for the development of subordinates.

The fewer the number of subordinates that report to a supervisor, the greater the opportunity the supervisor has to exercise close control. However, a small span of control does not automatically mean that the supervisor will exercise close supervision. The extent to which a supervisor keeps close control over his subordinates depends also on other factors such as his style of leadership.

LINE AND STAFF RELATIONS

As the complexity of the organization increases, some of the activities are concerned more directly with the production and distribution of products than others. This division of labor within the organization lends itself to an organizational concept adapted from military institutions known as line and staff functions. Much has been written about line and staff, yet much is misunderstood about the relationships between the two. Misconceptions sometimes have led to disunity and conflict among employees of the same company.

Any definition of line and staff has to be tempered by the understanding that a degree of overlap occurs between the two and that the activities of the two functions will be modified by the particular firm or industry in which they occur. Generally, a *line function* is one which is involved in or contributes directly to the main business activity of a firm. It differs with each business organization. In a finance company, taking in and paying out money are line functions, so are making loans and making collections. In a hotel, renting rooms and catering to customers are line functions. An oil company may explore for oil and operate oil wells, pipelines, and oil refineries as line functions. A bus company operates vehicles, sells tickets, and handles luggage as line activities. In each case, the activities constituting the primary business operations of the firm are line functions.

Staff functions are those functions which help or assist line functions accomplish the primary objectives of the enterprise. They are activities which are indirectly related to the major objectives of the firm. Thus, we see that in a finance company an activity such as washing windows is not a part of the primary function of the firm, neither would it be in a hotel; it is, therefore, a staff activity. However, in a janitorial service company it would be a line function. In rendering assistance to the line departments, the staff personnel advise, suggest, assist, or serve the line in some way so that the line may perform its activities more efficiently.

Normally, staff personnel are specialists in some area of business and often are referred to as experts. In modern industry many persons are specialists and this easy classification of staff personnel can lead to confusion and resentment on the part of other company personnel. Labeling staff personnel merely as advisers is also a narrow classification because in some cases staff executives are given the power to act in the scope of some line official's authority and also to have line authority over the personnel within their own departments. It must be remembered that line executives also give advice; for example, when a production manager advises the president of a firm on manufacturing matters. Thus, we see that some overlap occurs between line and staff functions.

Although no particular activity can be labeled as staff until the main line of activity in an organization is designated, a manufacturing firm might have staff functions in the following areas: legal, economic analysis, public relations, labor relations, personnel, and market research. An organization chart which included several such staff departments might look like the one in Figure 9–3.

The placement of staff departments varies with the particular organization, but usually they are shown with some type of broken line connecting them to the main lines of authority and responsibility in order to indicate that they do not have authority over other line departments.

THE HUMAN RELATIONS PROBLEMS OF LINE AND STAFF

The use of staff departments requires that staff personnel devote part of their time and effort to developing sound human relations with others. In most cases their advice and services are rendered without the direct power to enforce their recommendations and, therefore, need to rely on personal influence rather than direct authority. Often, line personnel resent specialists from outside their own departments coming in and trying to change operations. What may begin as advice from a staff member may lead to direct intervention if a line official tells the staff member to "go ahead and take care of the matter." Such a directive can imply that the staff member has direct authority to see that his recommendations are carried out. The result can be that a slice of the line executive's authority has been taken by the staff member.

Another area of sensitivity between line and staff members occurs because staff positions are often placed closer to the top of the organizational hierarchy than are those of the line officials with whom they work. This occurs when such staff departments as personnel are closer to the position of the president or department head than the foreman they may assist in training or personnel selection. Such a situation can cause line supervisors to be cautious about conflict with a staff member because they believe that should a conflict occur, the staff adviser would win because he is closer to top management.

Staff people usually enter the work situation as specialists and often convey an attitude of "I know what's best." Resentment to this type of attitude is easy to understand. Another problem can arise from the methods used by staff people. The line personnel are involved in the integration of materials and machines and human factors which are not always logical. The staff member may enter the picture armed with a narrower view and a more rigid concept of what is rational or logical. Because of this difference in viewpoint, staff members often get impatient with line personnel who do not seem to comprehend or appreciate what they are

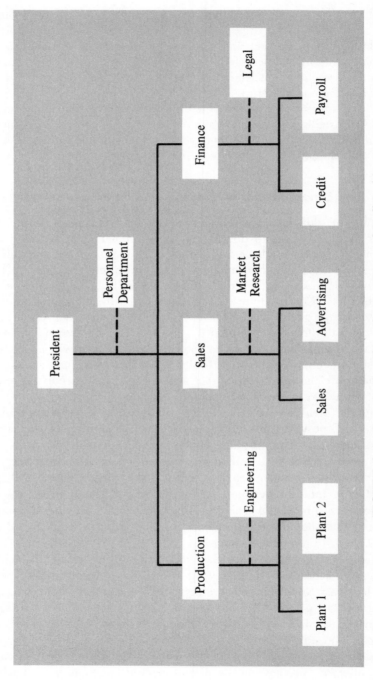

FIGURE 9–3. Organization Chart Showing Line and Staff Positions.

doing. If a line member is slow to accept the offered advice, he may be viewed as being uncooperative by many staff people.

The specialized interest of staff members may lead them to adopt plans or procedures which do not take into consideration many factors of which a line member may well be aware. Occasionally the staff man becomes absorbed in a problem and does not communicate what plans or changes he is going to recommend until he "springs" them on the line member. In his efforts to reduce costs and improve operations, the staff specialist recommends changes in procedures or may even eliminate jobs. The changes that may result lead many workers to fear that their security is endangered. These feelings on the part of line workers do not encourage their cooperation with staff members.

The problems of integrating the activities of staff departments with those of the line are many. As business advances in the wake of technological process, cooperation between the two areas is important. The role of human relations in paving the way for such cooperation is a large one. This role may begin with a clear and concise definition of the staff department's role and function so that both line and staff members have a basis for understanding the other's position. This results in greater empathy, cooperation, and coordination between members of line and staff departments.

Understanding the special problems of each function can be facilitated through training and better communications. It is interesting to note that the problem of integrating line and staff functions is not new; it was recognized early by the military organizations from which business evolved. Early in the nineteenth century, a Prussian general named Scharnhorst was concerned with the possibility that line and staff officers might become segregated. An efficient training program for staff officers was developed in which they were returned periodically to line duty. Some management writers believe this principle of rotation may serve a useful purpose in executive development programs today [4, p. 4].

THE QUESTION OF ORGANIZATION EFFECTIVENESS

Earlier in this chapter a question was posed regarding the problem of choosing an organizational design, and the topics discussed thus far have touched on some of the major difficulties encountered by organizational planners when they attempt to make choices among the alternatives available to them. In this regard, organizational theory is most helpful when the creators of an organization are attempting to rationalize, separate, and organize the functions of a firm. It might be noted that not all organizations are carefully planned; many organizational patterns emerge and change as the growth of a business requires additional manpower and support activities. New departments are added as needed;

other departments are split as the number of workers in a unit grows too large to be handled by a single supervisor. So the process goes in fits and starts until the organization reaches a state where coordinating the activities of various additional departments is cumbersome and ineffectual. Such a state cannot be allowed to last for long in any organization which is engaged in a competitive industry. Organizational inefficiency can contribute to decreased profits which may ultimately force the company either to organize more efficiently or go out of business.

Bureaucracy.   Unfortunately, the term *bureaucracy* has taken on a negative connotation in the minds of some management students and practitioners because the systems and practices in some public and private organizations become inflexible and needlessly complex. The term, coined by the sociologist Max Weber, was intended to denote a type of organizational structure in which impersonal and standardized systems and procedures were designed to regulate the activities of organizational members.

Perhaps the implication of the word *impersonal* has been misinterpreted by some organizational planners and this has, thus, added to the confusion about bureaucracy. Actually, the intent of designing organizational systems to handle routine administrative tasks without the necessity of individual decisions in reoccurring situations has some merit. When a standard procedure is developed and implemented to handle such situations, more equitable treatment may be accorded the individuals involved. The intent of a bureaucratic system was to insure that individuals would be accorded this uniform and equitable treatment in a given similar situation rather than fall prey to the individual whim of minor officials. In this regard, the original intent, uniformity of administrative procedures, was a positive factor. The negative aspects resulted because exceptions to the rule were not taken into consideration. Thus, from a human relations standpoint such a system proves unsatisfactory unless provision is made for the inevitable exceptions that occur in human affairs.

Organizational structure can become unwieldy even when it has been carefully planned. Some deficiencies do not show up on an organization chart. Bureaucracy can complicate the process of communications and decision-making through the growth of protected, self-perpetuating work groups which require reams of paper work, red tape, and audits so their jobs will go on regardless of the need. C. Northcote Parkinson humorously describes the mayhem of organizational bureaucracy in his book *Parkinson's Law*. The tendency of some managers to build up the importance of their department by adding unnecessary personnel, more equipment, or expanded facilities can add to organizational ineffectiveness. Both of these tendencies contribute to an organizational environment which not only is inefficient, but stifling and frustrating to the individuals who must cope with them.

In addition to the problem of selecting an organizational structure or pattern which creates the best environment for accomplishing the firm's goals, there is the perplexing problem of evaluating an organization after it has been established. How does one tell when an organizational structure is effective?

Traditional theories of organization were content to talk of profit maximization, high productivity, or high employee morale as criteria of effectiveness. A number of modern social, technological, and political changes have diminished the sole use of these criteria. Automation may contribute to high productivity without complex changes in organizational structure. The trend toward social responsibility sometimes causes a business to behave in a manner which seems to reduce short-term profits, and long-range profits are difficult to ascribe to any single action taken by a firm. With the increase of leisure time, employee morale is affected by many facets of life beyond the scope of the work environment.

Traditional organizational theory appears to ignore the fact that many large modern organizations have multiple goals, some of which may be in conflict. Edgar Schein cites a number of examples where organizations, such as colleges, teaching hospitals, or prisons, have several goals, all of which are primary and essential. Colleges must perform the teaching function and they must expand knowledge through research. A teaching hospital must attempt to cure and it must provide learning opportunities for interns, nurses, and resident doctors. Prisons must keep criminals out of public circulation and they must provide opportunity for rehabilitation. Is organizational effectiveness to be judged by the performance of one of these functions? Both, but separately? Some basis which integrates them [14, p. 97]?

MODERN CRITERIA FOR JUDGING ORGANIZATIONAL EFFECTIVENESS

Numerous attempts have been made by modern organizational theorists and students to develop criteria for gauging organizational effectiveness at a given point in time without falling into the trap that such effectiveness is dependent on any single factor. Modern criteria tend to relate the organization as a whole, recognizing that many factors must operate simultaneously, in harmony, much the same way a human organism must have all its functions operating satisfactorily if it is to attain a healthy state of existence.

Traditional theories of organization tended to focus on the way work was rationalized and allocated. Modern theories tend to recognize that merely dividing the total task into subtasks does not necessarily insure the attainment of objectives. In short, modern organizational theories recognize workers and work groups as an integral part of any organization. The basic decision is not whether to have them, but how to create conditions under which groups can work toward organizational goals instead of against them. The research of behavioral scientists indicates that if workers feel threatened or unappreciated in the formal organizational environment, they will protect themselves by forming informal groups which can work against organizational goals. In order to counter the formation of informal groups whose purpose is subtly or openly to work against the objectives of the firm, organizational planners or managers must create an environment where workers do not feel physically or psychologically threatened, and where workers are more likely to find their own goals compatible with organizational objectives. This is not to say that the organization must try to prohibit informal groups from operating. No such feat would be possible by any socially accepted means, even if management wanted to do so. Management should avoid creating an organizational environment which provides a reason for the informal groups to work purposely against the firm's objectives.

The criteria by which modern organizational theorists would judge a firm's effectiveness are related to (1) the flexibility and adaptiveness of the organization to changing conditions in its environment; (2) well-conceived and well-stated goals for the organization which are openly communicated to members of the organization; (3) the organization's ability to perceive accurately and interpret correctly the realities of its environment; and (4) the degree of integration of the subparts of the total organization so that the parts are not working at cross-purposes.

A comparison of traditional organizational concepts with those which have been more recently developed reveals that the traditional ones emphasize nonhuman aspects of organization—production rates, costs, profits, labor turnover—in determining effectiveness. Modern theory emphasizes the human aspects—communications, employee training and development, motivation, work groups, leadership. In short, one approach emphasizes work, the other the workers. Thus, organizational patterns may emerge which are based on the relationship of the people who must work together most closely, rather than on the logical relationship of mechanical processes.

It might be argued that modern concepts of organization emphasize aspects which are not easily measured. Leadership is a most difficult thing to quantify. Communications are constantly being studied, but their effectiveness is difficult to measure. Arguments regarding the difficulty of evaluating organizational effectiveness by standards of modern theory have some basis. A broader view of organization which includes an examination of group processes rather than merely concentrating on specific end results does not ignore traditional measurements, such as profits or productivity; rather, the work group and its functions in the process of making profits and raising productivity is included in modern organizational theory. This emphasis stems from the belief that members of the group are capable and willing to improve their performance in reaching the traditional objectives of higher profit margins or lower costs when the organizational environment is conducive to doing so. (See the discussion of McGregor's Theory Y in Chapter 6.)

The transition from traditional concepts of organization to modern ones is not easy for many managers. Most managers have spent their careers in organizations which were built on traditional accounting concepts, and to change over to a viewpoint which does not offer the same tangible guides is a new experience which may not be eagerly sought. Though problems may arise because older organizational concepts emphasize work rather than people, causing some serious conflicts between the workers and the organization, many managers prefer to stick with the old system. They know that any system or organization, including those proposed in modern theories, is not without problems, and they prefer to contend with problems connected with traditional organization rather than cope with new problems which may be even more complex than the old ones. Many managers have little desire to change organizational patterns because they have considered the traditional measures of organizational effectiveness satisfactory.

AN INTEGRATING PRINCIPLE OF ORGANIZATION AND LEADERSHIP

Even the use of traditional measurements of organizational effectiveness shows growing evidence that the managers who achieve the highest levels of productivity, lowest production costs, least turnover, and highest levels of employee morale are the ones who deviate from traditional concepts of organization and leadership.*

A major difficulty in articulating any new theory of organization and leadership is the fact that high-producing managers who have been successful while deviating from traditional concepts have not yet developed a concise statement of principles to follow. The total pattern of deviate methods is not yet clear. In his book *New Patterns of Management* Rensis Likert has attempted to draw such practices into more concrete terms which he calls an integrating principle.

Likert's theory is based on research findings which indicate that

---

* Since the role of leadership is germane to modern theories of organization, some discussion of it appears in this section even though it is the major topic in a later chapter.

management and organizational patterns are most successful when workers are treated as human beings rather than just as persons who are to get work done. This approach recognizes the individual differences in each worker's background, experience, and expectations that can affect the interpretation he makes of all the interactions between himself and the organization. It also recognizes that a worker's perception of his environment is as important as the reality of that environment. Therefore, to have an interaction viewed as *supportive* by the worker, it is necessary that it occur in a light which is viewed by him as one which builds and maintains his sense of personal worth and importance [10, p. 103].

Supportive relationships are viewed by Likert as essential for the success of an organization. To be highly motivated, each member of the organization must feel that the organization's objectives are significant and that his own particular task is important in the attainment of those objectives. The next step in the development of an effective organization is to place each worker in an organizational environment where he can participate in activities which contribute to his own sense of worth. Since satisfaction of the desire to feel important is obtained in a large degree from personal contacts made on the job; work groups become important. A worker spends much of his time with the other people in his work group, and he generally seeks their approval and support. Likert contends that, in order for management to make full use of its potential human resources, each person in the organization should be a member of one or more functioning work groups that have a high degree of group loyalty, effective skills of interaction, and high performance goals.

When conditions are such that an individual is attracted and loyal to a group, he will be more likely to accept the goals and decisions of the group. He will be motivated to communicate more freely and honestly with other group members, attempt to influence the goals of the group so that they are more compatible with his own, and he will more readily help implement the goals and decisions deemed as important to the group.

The role of the supervisor in such a group context is to develop supportive relationships between himself and his subordinates and between members of the work group. To do this the supervisor must emphasize teamwork and group methods of supervision in which members pull together toward commonly accepted goals. Likert concludes that in order to achieve and maintain high levels of performance it is necessary that subordinates as well as supervisors have high performance goals and have their work well organized. He states further that subordinates are unlikely to set high performance goals for themselves and to organize their work well if their supervisors do not have such aspirations for each worker and for the whole work group. Therefore, a supervisor with high performance goals and excellent job organization is much more likely to have subordinates who set high goals for themselves and organize their work well when he uses group methods of supervision and applies the principles of supportive relationships effectively than when he does not [9, p. 63].

From the foregoing principles it could be concluded that an organization will function best when its members operate within a group context rather than as independent agents. Consequently, organization planners should deliberately endeavor to build effective groups, linking each group into an overall organization by means of people who hold overlapping group memberships. Thus, the supervisor of one group is a subordinate in the next group and the process of dual membership continues throughout the organization until each level in the organizational hierarchy is linked together by well-knit groups comprised of members from several levels in the organization. When this linking-pin concept is used to bind an organization together, a model such as the one in Figure 9–4 would emerge over a traditional organizational structure.

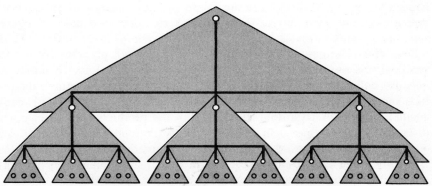

FIGURE 9–4. Likert's Linking-Pin Model.

(From *New Patterns of Management* by Rensis Likert. Copyright 1961 by McGraw-Hill Book Company, Inc. Used by permission of McGraw-Hill Book Company.)

In an organizational model such as the one shown, each person above the rank and file in the organization would be a member of at least two groups. In one group he would be a leader and in the other he would be a subordinate. For example, a foreman would be a leader in the group comprised of himself and his work crew. In a group comprised of other foremen and the department supervisor, he would be a subordinate. In a group comprised of department supervisors and a division manager, the department supervisors are subordinate and the division manager is the leader. Each group comprised of multilevel organizational members would have a leader until the group at the top would be headed by the company president, and the subordinates would be vice presidents.

Members of each group in the overlapping group form of organization would not only be comprised of personnel from different levels in the organizational hierarchy; they could come from different functions or departments in the organization. In addition to the groups mentioned in this organizational system, line and staff personnel would share membership in some of the regular multilevel organizational groups and, in addition, ad hoc committees which would provide multiple overlapping groups through which additional linking functions are performed, thus binding together all members.

In the pattern of organization described greater opportunity would exist for the exchange of vital information between group members during face-to-face meetings which would be regularly scheduled. Company decision would be determined through the joint of personnel representing various viewpoints in the organization. At interdepartmental meetings sales people might learn about the problems of the production staff in meeting deadlines on new products or model changes. Such first-hand information would add to the salesman's appreciation of production difficulties. Salesmen might then attempt to allow for more delivery time when making sales to customers. This act of cooperation could relieve the production department of unwarranted pressure until the problem was resolved and, at the same time, reduce customer complaints because deliveries were not made when promised. At the same face-to-face meeting, sales personnel might provide the production staff with customer feedback regarding the quality of the products. From this open discussion, improvements in product quality or model design might be considered that might otherwise have been overlooked.

Ideally, after face-to-face meetings in which group members participated in decisions and in setting goals at one level in the organization, each group member would return as a leader to his own department and work group at another organizational level and report firsthand the group proceedings in which he had just participated. In the group meeting with the personnel in his own department, he would direct the process of obtaining reactions and suggestions for carrying out the group's assignments and responsibilities.

The process of face-to-face group meetings comprised of members from several organizational levels would continue until the decisions reached by a top-level group finally were carried down to each of the affected rank-and-file work groups. It should be remembered that the decisions reached by the top group should have reflected some of the suggestions and ideas from members lower in the organization and members who represent viewpoints from several different organizational functions. This feat should occur because group meetings which facilitate downward communications also would facilitate upward communications.

The linking-pin concept of organization is not faultless. Likert states that further research and experimental testing of the theory will probably yield evidence pointing to modifications of many aspects of this newer theory as presented [10, p. 97]. Whether the indicated changes are great or small, the new theory as it stands is a dramatic departure from traditional concepts.

Modern theories of organization which give cognizance to the human element appear to be soundly reinforced by research evidence accumulated thus far regarding the performance of high-producing work groups. In the next chapter the problems of implementing such theories will be discussed along with other difficulties related to employee motivation.

SUMMARY

1. Formal organizational structure is influenced by the interaction of both human and institutional forces. Organizational patterns should result from planning which considers the objectives of the firm, the capabilities of its members, and the internal and external environment in which it must operate.

2. The formal structure of an organization must change if it is to keep pace with the changes in activity and functions that accompany growth. When a firm is small, coordinating the functions and personnel may be relatively simple and little formal organization is necessary; but as the firm expands, careful planning becomes necessary if duplication or gaps in activity are to be avoided.

3. The degree of delegation of authority in an organization determines the extent to which it is centralized or decentralized. In a centralized firm major decisions are made by personnel high up the organizational hierarchy. In a decentralized firm decision-making authority is placed as far down the organizational structure as is practical.

4. The shape of the organizational structure, much like the architectural design of a building, may be tall or flat. Factors which influence the shape of the structure are span of control, extent of the delegation of responsibility and authority, and the use of line and staff departments.

5. Line and staff organization concepts were derived from the military. Line functions may differ in each organization, depending on the industry. Generally, line functions are defined as those activities which are directly related to the primary profit-making operations of the firm. Staff functions are those functions which assist line personnel or departments to carry out their mission. Thus, in a manufacturing firm the production department, sales department, and accounting department would usually be

considered line functions, whereas product engineering and marketing research would be staff functions.

Staff personnel are usually experts in some narrow aspects of the total business operations of the firm. Often human relations problems arise between line and staff personnel because staff people may cross over lines of authority, which line managers consider an infringement of their domain. Some resentment may occur because staff personnel try to impose their suggestions on line personnel or because staff positions often occupy a place close to higher executives in the organization.

6. Some organizations are not carefully planned by owners or managers. In such cases the organization may develop in a haphazard fashion until coordination of activities is too difficult for managers. Unless some organizational changes are made when such a state is reached, either the firm will lose its competitive position or it will be forced out of existence. In carefully planned organizations there are some inefficiencies which do not show on an organization chart. Bureaucracy and empire-building can bog down the process of decision-making and communications with needless red tape and procedures. Unless steps are taken to minimize these tendencies, employees may find themselves stifled or frustrated.

7. Traditional theories of organization stress the division of work, assignment of authority and responsibility, and means of controlling activities so that organizational goals can be achieved. Traditional criteria for measuring organizational effectiveness have been profit margins, productivity, and other quantifiable devices. The nonhuman aspects of traditional organization have led to structures which stress conformity to rules, regulations, or procedures which may not be related to the individual needs or goals of the members.

8. Modern concepts of organization emphasize workers and work groups rather than the work itself. This entails a broader view of the organization as an operating social system in which group processes are a vital part. Leadership, training, and communications skills become germane to modern theories of organization where individual participation in group decisions and goal-setting are a part of the motivational forces used to improve organizational effectiveness.

9. The integrating principle is one of the new organizational theories which utilizes groups to strengthen organizational effectiveness. Each person, with the exception of rank-and-file workers, is a member in at least two groups. A foreman would be the leader in the group comprised of his work crew and himself and a subordinate in the group comprised of other foremen and the department head.

Such a theory would bind together each group in the organization with linking-pin members. This system would help facilitate decisions and goal-setting functions which more fully utilized each person's capacities and would provide the opportunity for employees to derive satisfaction from supportive relationships from other group members.

This new theory is not without some weaknesses, but it is an innovative departure from traditional concepts of organization which give scant attention to modern research findings about human nature.

DISCUSSION QUESTIONS

1. What is the meaning of cooperation? How does it differ in meaning from coordination?
2. What is the meaning of *authority* in an organization? What is meant by "the employees control their reaction to authority"? Why is this important to a human relations approach to management?
3. Why do some managers hesitate to delegate responsibility and authority to subordinates?
4. Compare the advantages and disadvantages of a span of control of twenty persons with one of five persons. What is the ideal span of control?
5. What is a staff function? A line function? What are some of the possible reasons for conflict between line and staff members? Can human relations principles be applied to reduce the friction between line and staff members? How?
6. How does Likert's "linking-pin" concept of organization differ from traditional organization concepts?

BIBLIOGRAPHY AND
SELECTED COLLATERAL READINGS

1. DAVIS, KEITH, *Human Relations at Work,* 2nd ed. New York: McGraw-Hill Book Company, 1962.
2. GEORGE, CLAUDE S., JR., *Management in Industry,* 2nd ed. Englewood Cliffs, N.J.: Prentice-Hall, Inc., 1964.
3. GREENWOOD, WILLIAM T., *Management and Organizational Behavior Theories.* Cincinnati: South-Western Publishing Company, 1965.
4. HAIMANN, THEO, *Professional Management.* Boston: Houghton Mifflin Company, 1962.
5. HAIRE, MASON, *Organization Theory in Industrial Practice.* New York: John Wiley and Sons, 1962.
6. HAIRE, MASON, *Psychology in Management,* 2nd ed. New York: McGraw-Hill Book Company, 1964.
7. JURAN, JOSEPH J., "New Life for Staff Departments," *Management of Personnel Quarterly* (Summer, 1962). Ann Arbor: University of Michigan Bureau of Industrial Relations.

8. KOONTZ, H., and C. O'DONNELL, *Principles of Management*, 4th ed. New York: McGraw-Hill Book Company, 1968.

9. LIKERT, RENSIS, *The Human Organization*. New York: McGraw-Hill Book Company, 1967.

10. LIKERT, RENSIS, *New Patterns of Management*. New York: McGraw-Hill Book Company, 1961.

11. MAIER, NORMAN R. F., *Principles of Human Relations*. New York: John Wiley and Sons, 1952.

12. "Manpower Ratios in Manufacturing," *Factory*, Vol. CXXIII, No. 3 (March, 1965).

13. O'CONNELL, J. J., *Managing Organizational Innovation*. Homewood, Ill.: Richard D. Irwin, Inc., 1968.

14. SCHEIN, EDGAR H., *Organizational Psychology*. Englewood Cliffs, N.J.: Prentice-Hall, Inc., 1965.

15. URIS, AUREN, *The Executive Breakthrough: 21 Roads to the Top*. Garden City, N.Y.: Doubleday, 1967.

16. URIS, AUREN, *The Management Makers*. New York: The Macmillan Company, 1962.

10

Group Participation
and Motivation

Modern theories of organization and leadership are intended to do more than merely permit work to be done. They are intended to create an environment which motivates workers to produce at higher levels through greater participation in the affairs and decisions of the organization. If such is the real intent of modern organizational theory, how does the improved organizational effectiveness transpire?

HOW THE NEW THEORY
IMPROVES ORGANIZATIONAL EFFECTIVENESS

Some of the reasons why managers resist a departure from traditional concepts of organization have already been mentioned in Chapter 9. These reasons do not mean that managers will not change to newer concepts if they see a need for change. They do mean that managers must see how modern theories of organization offer some possibility for improved organizational effectiveness before they will adapt them. Such adaptations require more than a rejuggling of the boxes on an organization chart. More often modern organizational concepts affect changes in management philosophy, attitudes, and practices which permeate the firm.

Traditional organization creates a pattern of one-to-one relationships between organization members in which superiors deal with their subordinates individually—obtaining information from single individuals at a time and making assignments to each subordinate apart from the others in the group. This is not to say that individual consultation with employees is not necessary or useful on occasion. Sometimes a one-to-one meeting between a supervisor and subordinate is the only tactful means of handling a situation. Disciplinary action normally is best handled in this manner. In such matters as discipline, discussions between superiors and subordinates are usually best conducted in private, but traditional organization tends to go beyond this measure and separate workers in their relationship with superiors in many aspects besides discipline. Decisions, goal-setting, work standards, information dispersion, and other behavior controls seem to fall exclusively within the realm of the superiors, whereas the subordinate is expected to do what he is told.

Modern concepts emphasize group relationships in which a supervisor holds membership in groups which include his subordinates. This shift in emphasis is a dramatic one because group interactions require greater participation on the part of organizational members, which in turn places more weight on the leadership and communications skills of managers. The development of such skills often requires training and a change in leadership techniques. Thus, a change from traditional concepts to modern ones requires a change in management attitudes—from those attitudes associated with Theory X of McGregor's to those which support Theory Y. Such a change would be difficult for some managers unless overwhelming evidence could support the advantages of making a change. Enough evidence is simply not present yet to convince some managers.

The results which managers typically use to measure organizational success are pretty well locked to information which can be gathered and balanced by accounting procedures. The end results reflected in sales, profits, inventory turnover, or production figures tend to ignore some other human factors which contribute to these end results, such as loyalty of employees, the development of work skills, communications, effectiveness, and decision-making processes. These factors which influence the end results are called intervening variables by Likert [6, p. 61]. He concluded that when emphasis is placed on end results alone in measuring organizational effectiveness, there is the danger of drawing faulty conclusions regarding the state of the internal conditions in an organization, as well as mistakes in determining what kinds of management and leadership yield the best results.

Some high-pressure and threatening leadership methods can achieve impressive short-term results, particularly when coupled with high technical competence. However, when short-term improvements in production are achieved through pressure-oriented means, the gains are obtained at a substantial and serious cost to the organization. The danger of the use of high-pressure leadership methods by managers and supervisors is constant in most organizations because of the thrust of upward mobility which is usually a part of the organizational climate. Men who have the ambition to rise in the organizational hierarchy realize that their chance for promotion depends, to a large degree, upon the results they obtain in the position they currently hold. Since their effectiveness is gauged by traditional end result criteria, they may feel the need to increase the levels of performance in their work group in the most expedient way. They resort to high-pressure leadership methods to achieve the results which they hope will lead to a promotion. The pattern of organizational mobility in most large industrial firms permits a manager to change jobs about every three years, either through a promotion or transfer; thus it is possible that he can move out of a particular department or work group before he has to pay the price for the poor leadership he has exercised with his subordinates. The man who replaces him in his old position may be the one who will have the problem of trying to rebuild group morale and cooperation. If the new man does not succeed quickly, he may be judged a poorer manager than the individual who preceded him. The man who actually created the conditions is now in another position where he may be starting the process of high pressure all over with another group.

The significance of this type of leadership pattern in a business firm is great because of the nature of the continuing relationship between management and employees. Most people are familiar with the high-pressure tactics of some salesmen. They are not concerned whether the product suits the needs of the potential customer. Their primary objective is to make a sale. The success of such sales methods is credited to the fact that after the sale has been made, chances are the salesman will not have to encounter the same customer. Thus, a high-pressure salesman can go through a given territory and compile an impressive sales record. His success on repeat sales might not be so great, or even worse, the company's own reputation may be tarnished in that territory, increasing the job of good customer relations for the salesman who must follow a "hard-sell" salesman.

The manager who employs high-pressure methods on his subordinates can build an impressive short-term record, but even after he is gone, his former subordinates may have been demoralized to a point where for the most part they are no longer willing to cooperate with other superiors in any but a cursory or superficial way. When such an attitude prevails in an organization, it is highly unlikely that the full potential of its members' human energy and resources is going to be applied to solving the problems which lie between the company and the attainment of company objectives.

If high-pressure methods are believed undesirable for long-term results, how do modern concepts of organization and leadership obtain necessary results? Do modern concepts preclude the use of authority? To answer the first question one needs to understand that every business firm, large or small, is faced by certain factors which cannot be ignored if it is to survive. There are production deadlines, financial limitations, and profits to be made. These realities impose limitations on the actions of the organization and the decisions of managers. Every manager or supervisor should be aware of these limiting factors when they apply to the operations of his work group; in making decisions he and his group should not lose sight of them. If the group is divided in the way to approach a situation which meets certain limiting requirements, the superior has the responsibility of making decisions which are appropriate to the situation. Here, in part, is the answer to the second question. Modern concepts do not preclude the use of authority by supervisors. Modern concepts do attempt to establish the guidelines for the use of such authority.

When a supervisor does find that time and circumstances permit the group to offer solutions to the problems confronting them, he may be wise to accept such solutions from the group, particularly when the group has the responsibility for implementing their own suggestions. If he does not feel that the group's decision is compatible with the objectives of the organization or the limitations imposed by the situation, he should present the evidence which supports his viewpoint. If further discussion does not convince the group of the soundness of his own conclusions, the supervisor must make a decision. He can overrule the group or yield to the group's decision. If he chooses the first course of action, he can endanger group cohesiveness and lower group loyalty if the group feels strongly about its viewpoint. The supervisor may decide to follow the dictates of his own judgment if he feels that allowing the group to have its own way would be too costly. If he decides that the group's suggestion is not entirely correct but not so costly that it will cause irreparable damage in meeting deadlines or budget limitations, he may let the group decision stand. A supervisor may know that his solution is better but be willing to permit the group to attempt its solution and possibly learn from the experience. In any event, whichever course of action the supervisor takes, he is responsible and must accept full responsibility for what occurs [6, p. 112].

The decision-making process which has just been described can occur at a meeting between the president of the company and its vice presidents or at the bottom of the hierarchy in a meeting between a foreman and his work crew. The process is the same: Group members participate in the decisions made in this modern concept of leadership.

First, it should be readily apparent that decisions made by groups near the top of the organizational hierarchy have far-reaching implications for many members who hold lower positions in the organization. Decisions made at the top usually involve greater sums of money, major policy changes, and longer-range implications; they require vast stores of information and expertise in order to insure their accuracy. Consequently, one can see that if the group process breaks down in groups near the top of the organization, the results could be catastrophic. One might note that decisions made by a single individual at the top of an organization carry the same kind of risk. The chances for accurate decisions, with fewer exceptions, would seem to increase as more individuals have a voice in the final decision.

Regarding the group process of decision-making one might ask that if a superior allows his subordinates to influence what goes on in the group, does he lose control over the group? Does a supervisor have less influence if he permits the group to exert their influence? In any attempt to answer, one must define what goes on in the group and what decisions are made in the group. Likert defines "what goes on" as pertaining to action, and action involves both decisions and their implementation. If a supervisor is to have influence over what goes on in his group, he must have influence on decisions as well as the motivation and skill with which to carry out these decisions. If his influence ceases once the decisions have been made and the decisions are poorly executed because of a lack of motivation or skill in his subordinates, then his influence over the group is not very great [6, p. 180].

DEMOCRACY IN THE WORK GROUP

Questions regarding supervisor versus subordinate influence over the affairs of the group stem from some misunderstandings about the democratic processes which are appropriate to the work group in an industrial organization. As a political concept democracy elicits a favorable reaction from most persons brought up under the influence of Western civilization. As a political concept, democracy embodies the right to vote, or majority rule. In a broader connotation it is something more. It is a philosophy of life affecting men in all their human relationships. The egalitarian attitude described in Chapter 2 is a hallmark of democracy.

If pure political democracy were carried to its logical extreme in a business organization, every employee would have a right to vote on every major decision. However, such a pure concept is not even followed in political life. Responsibility for making many decisions is delegated to the political representatives who are elected. Managers and supervisors are not usually elected by employees. They are selected and appointed by higher company officials, who in turn are chosen by a board of directors elected by the stockholders.

Only in the broadest sense of the word and only on a very limited scale is a business corporation democratic. In smaller, owner-managed businesses the extent of political democracy is less. Therefore, when we refer to democratic planning or decision-making within an organization we are not referring to the right of every employee to vote on every action and issue affecting the organization. More accurately we are referring to group planning, effective communications, and participation of workers in making decisions which affect the way some things, but not all, are to be done.

Participation is sometimes referred to as human relations. Sometimes it is related to methods of leadership, but in either case the reason for permitting employees to have a voice in what they do and how they do it is to solicit their voluntary effort to get the things done which must be done in order to achieve organizational goals. There is a high degree of mutual dependency between an organization and its members. If the organization is to survive, certain goals must be reached—sales, production, accounting, research, and so on. These goals are achieved through the efforts of people. If the members of an organization do not achieve these goals satisfactorily, the organization will perish. If it perishes, the jobs and the incomes associated with those jobs cease to exist. But the relationship between an organization and its employees is not so simple. Mere survival is seldom the goal of an organization. In a free enterprise system the organization must adapt to changing conditions that require different activities and different talents if it is to prosper and grow. When the employees feel a stake in the goals of the organization, usually they will be more willing to do what is necessary to reach them.

THE ROLE OF PARTICIPATION IN MEETING CHANGE

The rate of change in the social and technical world has increased rapidly during the past two decades. Who should decide what should be changed in an organization's operations? When? How can acceptance of change best be facilitated and how can implementation be made to preserve and enhance human dignity? These are the questions which every organization must resolve in determining if changes are to be made.

Often there are forces, conflicting and simultaneous, which exert pressures for both stability and change—status quo versus the counterforce of change. When change appears to be a threat, the human response is either to escape or to postpone action in the hope that the situation will resolve itself. Others seek some scapegoat rather than cope with the problem. Such people rationalize their actions by blaming incompetent bosses, uncooperative subordinates, poor organizational structure, or big government for not averting the conditions that demand that a change be made.

Rationalizations circumvent the fact that orderly change must have a direction. Leadership must be exerted. To do so, a supervisor must receive more than cursory aid and courtesy from subordinates if that leadership is to be effective. The instigation of change which affects others in the organization is not a one-man operation. The participation of others is invaluable for pinpointing difficulty, collecting information, suggesting improvements, and lending cooperation. A person who helps to plan change is in a better position to understand why it is needed and how such a change can bring about improvement in the organization, the work group, or his job. By participating in the planning of change, an employee has a stake in the success of that change.

There are circumstances when the use of participation in planning for change is complicated by intense pressure for immediate change in a complex situation. When such occasions do arise there is a likelihood that the underlying reason for change will be overlooked or ignored. For example, when workers suddenly complain bitterly that work standards are too high, there may be great pressure placed on the supervisor to lower those standards. Often the things people complain about are not the things that really trouble them; therefore, quick action by the supervisor may only treat the symptoms of discontent for a much deeper and significant cause and not remedy that cause at all. The pressure placed on the supervisor by his subordinates may act as a barrier to an accurate diagnosis of the problem. Under the circumstances, the supervisor might do well to delay his judgment until he has had a chance to hear why the work standards suddenly became unreasonable.

Resistance to Change. In some cases there is a resistance to change on the part of organizational members because an admission that a change is necessary is felt to be an admission that their jobs were not being done satisfactorily in the past. Often suggestions for improved methods are taken to be a criticism of the job being done. In such a case, any change would stand a much better chance for success if the need for the change were seen or suggested by the worker himself rather than being imposed by his superior.

The necessity for change is not always seen by organizational members. Many times monetary or material incentives are offered by management to motivate workers to accept the change with a minimum of resistance. Economic rewards are not without their value, but often human resources are underestimated, neglected, or misused. Frequently, even when workers have not had the opportunity to determine what changes are to be made, they may be able to provide practical information on how to initiate such a change. Some members of the work group may be more alert to the problems of making the change than the higher-placed officials who decided to make it. The work group can act as a valuable sounding board to evaluate planned changes and suggest methods of implementing them.

Open discussion regarding planned changes may help members of the group become aware of their resistance, bring their fears into the open, and identify their anxieties, thereby giving them relief and making them more willing to accept the change.

Organizational Climate and Planning for Change. Organizational climate includes feelings people have about whether management really wants suggestions for improvement, with what degree of frankness, in what areas, under what circumstances, and with what resultant rewards or punishments. An atmosphere conducive to change, without the use of force, would be permissive to the extent that people can say what they feel without the fear of reprisal. Criticism of the way things are done should be encouraged when such criticism is backed with constructive suggestions for improvement. How can such a climate be developed by a supervisor? Goodwin Watson and Edward M. Glaser of the Human Interaction Research Institute have summarized what they have found to be important steps in planning for change and creating a climate where change will be accepted more willingly.

Steps in Planning Change

1. Make clear the needs for change, or provide a climate in which group members feel free to identify such needs.
2. Permit and encourage relevant group participation in clarifying the needed changes.
3. State the objectives to be achieved by the proposed changes.
4. Establish broad guidelines for achieving the objectives.
5. Leave the details for implementing the proposed changes to the group in the organization or personnel who will be affected by the change.
6. Indicate the benefits or rewards to the individuals or groups expected to accrue from the change.
7. Materialize the benefits or rewards; i.e., keep the promises made to those who made the change [12].

During the past two decades behavioral scientists have elaborated on the fact that force in human affairs, as in physics, breeds counter force. The degree of ingenuity that workers can exercise in the restriction of output and the kinds of subtle and overt resistance to change they use have taught most managers to avoid trying to use force to bring about change. If resistance to change is met by stronger mandates from management to make the change, tension is heightened and there is still little assurance that the change will be successfully made. It is often, not always, wise to concentrate on the reasons *why* resistance to change occurs. After the reasons have been discovered, efforts can concentrate on reducing those reasons rather than trying to overwhelm them.

If resistance stems from economic considerations, then evidence of cost or wage improvements would be appropriate. If resistance is based on fear of losing the approval and support of associates, economic evidence is irrelevant. What would be needed is a convincing demonstration that the proposed change will not threaten the respect or regard of associates. If the change does in fact threaten the economic or personal well-being of the workers affected by the change, then compensating factors and offsetting advantages should be sought before the change is initiated.

Resistance may not always be overt and crystallized. It may be latent, lodged in employee resentment because the change was imposed from higher management levels, rather than having evolved from the ranks of the personnel affected. Avoidance of this kind of resentment is one of the strong cases for modern organizational concepts because changes that a group devise for its own unit carry far more appeal than those imported and imposed from outside of the group. Outside changes may receive only partial and half-hearted support.

Where time and circumstances make it possible it might be wise to attempt a test run of the proposed change which permits those persons affected to test the new system and try themselves in their new roles. Such proceedings may banish unfounded fears and restore their confidence and enhance their acceptance of the change.

Change by Mandate. Although it is usually advantageous to get support for a change before it is put into effect, there may be occasions when it is impossible to do so. In some cases the affected personnel may not have the technical competence to measure accurately the impact or necessity of a change. In other cases, it may be more effective to introduce the change without preliminary suggestions of the group affected. Such action runs counter to much that has been stated about enlisting participation in planning for change. In some cases the effects of change cannot be determined until after the change has been introduced [12]. Only after new computers had been placed in operation during the early fifties could the benefits be felt. Only after trade unions had legally gained a collective bargaining position did the vast majority of industrial managers learn to achieve constructive cooperation with them. Only after department stores started to hire Negro sales clerks did management discover that most customers accepted the change as a matter of course.

The success of the changes made by mandate is not sufficient to make them a sound organizational policy. The success of such instances does force managers to consider the circumstances which make a move necessary. Generally, if the consequences of change can be realistically understood by the people affected, their cooperation in designing a change is helpful and the participative method is most effective. In the rare cases when the results are not rationally predictable, experience may be the best teacher.

Change Through Participation.   One classic study of how participation
aided in the acceptance of change was carried out by a garment manufacturer, Harwood Manufacturing Company. A change in garment
design necessitated a change in work assignments, relearning of new
assignments, and a potential reduction in piece-rate earning power until
the operators adapted to their new assignments. For these reasons there
typically was strong employee resistance to change in designs.

Because circumstances made job changes necessary, an opportunity
existed for an experiment in group participation. In this experiment, four
groups of sewing-machine operators were formed. These groups were
matched for the difficulty of new jobs and for the level of productivity
before the experiment. In one group the change to new jobs was made in
the customary manner. They were told why the change was necessary,
what the new jobs would entail and what the new piece rates would be.
In a second group, a moderate degree of participation was allowed. The
group was allowed to choose representatives who, in turn, participated in
designing the new jobs, setting new piece rates, and later, training the
other members of the group.

In the two other groups, members participated directly in designing
the job and setting the new piece rates; in general, all members had a
greater degree of participation in the job change than the two previously
mentioned groups.

After the change was instituted, the differences in production of the
groups was dramatic. The first group, for whom the change was introduced in the usual way, suffered the usual loss in production efficiency,
and many operators in this group quit their jobs. In the second group,
the one that participated in the change through their chosen representatives, production dropped to begin with, but it consistently improved
over time until it reached a level slightly above that maintained prior to
the change. Production levels of the two groups which participated
directly in planning the change only dropped slightly and briefly after
the change, and continued to increase substantially above the prechange
level. Not only was the change in productivity after the change proportional to the degree of participation of the groups, but turnover rates,
and the amounts of aggression expressed against management, were
inversely proportional to the degree of participation [2, pp. 512–32].

PARTICIPATION AND THE QUALITY OF DECISIONS

In general, the available evidence indicates that a solution worked out
by a group is more acceptable to it than one imposed on it by a supervisor. Thus, the relationship between participation and acceptance is

fairly well proved; however, a supervisor needs to be concerned with the quality of group decisions as well as with their acceptance. Acceptance of poor solutions does little to improve the performance or efficiency of the group.

There are a number of indications pointed to by Norman Maier [7, p. 302] that group decisions are superior to the decisions made by a single individual. This does not preclude the possibility that the thinking of certain individuals working alone may be superior to that of a group. It is quite possible that highly creative ideas of an individual may be diminished in luster through group discussion with less creative persons. In the majority of human and technical problems faced by the work group, solutions can be improved through group discussion because the men who actually do the work become aware of facts and conditions pertaining to a solution which neither an outside expert nor someone unfamiliar with the intricacies of the problem would probably be aware.

Because any solution involving cooperation between human beings requires acceptance and because even solutions of lesser quality accompanied by acceptance might be more effective than solutions of higher quality without acceptance, the supervisor might do well to settle for the former. Unless there is a great deal at stake, the supervisor would probably find that going along with the group on some decisions that he would not make himself will gain their support on other decisions he alone must make. This might be called bargaining, but in the realities of the work place such interaction between all levels of organizational members is a common practice.

Does the supervisor have to accept poor decisions from the group? Is it manipulation to get the group to agree to a solution the supervisor has in mind? In answer to the first question, the supervisor's job is not to obtain inferior answers to problems facing the work group or the organization at large. When the supervisor possesses exceptional ability in solving problems, he need not sacrifice such ability in order to maintain the good will of the group. Solutions to most organizational problems are highly subjective; however, this does not make all solutions equally valid. If a supervisor has a substantially better solution to a problem than the group, he should attempt to stimulate the group's thinking to improve his proposed solution, thus sharing in some sense. However, the superiority of his ideas must stand up to the realities of the situation. He must also be prepared to accept modifications to his solution suggested by the group if they are an improvement. The acceptance of *his* ideas will depend on the nature of his relationship with the group and the degree of confidence they hold in him as both a leader and a person.

The answer to the second question depends on one's definition of manipulation. A supervisor who influences members of the group in constructive ways would not be considered a manipulator except by those who hold manipulation and influence to be the same thing. If the supervisor is surreptitious about his motives in wanting a certain solution to a problem, he runs a risk of losing the trust of the group should he be discovered. To the degree that the supervisor levels with his subordinates regarding the solutions he thinks best and why he thinks they are best, his word will be trusted and he will be respected even though all group members may not agree with him.

The circumstances under which a supervisor should encourage the participation of his subordinates is discussed in the following chapter.

ASSUMPTIONS AND EXPECTATIONS IN THE USE OF PARTICIPATION

The modern concept of organization is designed around the use of talents and skills of organizational members who are bound together in cohesive groups. These groups are linked by overlapping memberships which provide communications both upward and downward. Horizontal communications are provided by the groups comprised of members from the same level in the organizational hierarchy and by ad hoc committees in which both line and staff personnel share membership.

This organizational concept is based on certain assumptions and attitudes about human behavior and on certain expectations which are expected to result. The use of participation is essential to modern organizational and leadership concepts. At this point, a model of participative leadership with its underlying assumptions about people and the expectations of participation might be stated in the following way:

I. Assumptions About Human Behavior
   A. In addition to sharing common needs for belonging and respect, most people in our democratic society want to contribute effectively and creatively to the accomplishment of worthwhile objectives.
   B. The majority of workers are capable of exercising far more initiative, responsibility, and creativity than their present jobs either require or allow.
   C. The inert capabilities of workers represent untapped resources which are presently being wasted.
II. Kind and Degree of Participation
   A. A manager's basic task is to create an environment in which his subordinates can contribute their full range of talents to the accomplishment of organizational goals. He must attempt to uncover and tap the creative resources of his subordinates.
   B. The manager should both allow and encourage his subordinates to participate in routine decisions and also, when possible, in

important matters as well. In fact, the more important a decision is to the group, the greater should be his efforts to tap the group's human resources.

   C. The manager should attempt to expand continually the areas over which his subordinates exercise self-direction and self-control as they develop and demonstrate greater insight and ability.

III. Expectations of Participation

   A. The overall quality of decision-making and performance will improve as the supervisor or manager makes use of the full range of experience, insight, and creative ability of his subordinates.

   B. Subordinates will exercise responsible self-direction and self-control in the attainment of worthwhile objectives that they understand and have helped to establish.

   C. Subordinate satisfaction will increase as a by-product of improved performance and the opportunity to contribute creatively to this improvement [10, p. 151].

LIMITATIONS OF GROUP PARTICIPATION

Participation has its limits as well as its advantages. In general, such methods provide employees with a voice in the affairs that directly concern them. But it must be recognized that not all employees wish to participate in decisions, nor should it be assumed that all employees are capable of contributing to solutions of problems that lie outside their immediate operating areas. In years past, many employers were not even concerned about what employees thought about their own jobs, much less what they thought about departmental or organizational operations. Today, with increasing levels of educational attainment among workers and high degrees of awareness resulting from mass media communications, there may be a temptation among supervisors and managers to think that employees know more than they actually do or that they are interested in more than they really are.

To be sure, some employees have much to contribute to the solution of organizational problems, but not all employees. The majority are capable and willing to contribute (more than they are asked) to the solving of immediate problems they encounter in their jobs and in their work group, but few are able to contribute to solutions of top-level organizational problems. The limitations of industrial democracy, as opposed to political democracy, were discussed earlier in this chapter. It should be noted that the philosophy of democracy in an organization often gives way to emphasis on various procedures for employee participation. Suggestion systems are a means of participation, as are employee committees of various kinds; but these are not substitutes for a democratic climate in which employees feel free to discuss problems with their supervisors on an individual face-to-face basis.

One final limitation on employee participation should be mentioned, particularly, in regard to labor unions representing employees. Participation in planning change or resolving operational and human problems carries the implication of responsibility for the implementation of the agreed-upon solution. For some employees, there is a hesitancy to participate in such activities because of the responsibility that is part of participation. This applies to some labor representatives and shop stewards who would prefer not to be a part of the problem-solving process if it would diminish their effectiveness as critics of the solution. In addition to workers who do not wish to seal their own fate by participating in decisions which affect them, some labor leaders look upon participative methods with skepticism. They consider participative management methods a device to weaken the allegiance of workers to the union. The validity of this is dependent upon the relations between the company and the union and the extent to which trust and good faith has accompanied their bargaining.

MOTIVATION

If one accepts the foregoing assumptions regarding human behavior and the value of participation, it might seem unnecessary to discuss the motivation of employees separately. One might easily believe that all an organization has to do is to open its doors and promise that all employee suggestions will be heard, if not acted upon, and that thereafter workers would flock to its personnel office to sign up. They would show up daily filled with enthusiasm and ideas ready to put in a full day's work for the privilege of being a member of the organization. Anyone who has had a modicum of job experience knows that such a picture is pure fantasy. It is a fantasy because people are complex and driven by many motives, all of which cannot be entirely satisfied by participation.

Most supervisors or managers can testify that it is relatively easy to get four or five people to work together, but the problem is compounded when the number is fifty or 100; it becomes very complicated when 1,000 men are involved. That is why in traditional organization, as well as in modern organizational practice, the total number of workers in an organization is divided into smaller, more manageable groups.

As was pointed out in Chapter 4, motivation refers to why people want things and try to get them. When studying motivation, one studies the needs, wants, desires, and impulses *within* the individual and how he goes about satisfying them.

One of the things that behavioral scientists have discovered about motivation is that people often are not very clear about their own needs and desires. Sometimes they do not know what they want; at other times, they think they know what they want, but their actions show that they want something entirely different. In such instances, unconscious motivations are said to exist, and such motives are not conveniently divided into neat little compartments which are easily labeled.

Motivation has different connotations and different meanings to people. From a psychologist's point of view it refers to the set of drives or strivings actually operating in the personality of the individual. Every living, active human being is continuously motivated in this sense. Often supervisors, parents, and teachers commonly think of motivation as a term meaning how to get someone to do just what is wanted of him. Obviously, there is going to be a clash of interests when the employee is motivated to hold down production and his supervisor wants him to increase it. It can be seen clearly how conflict can occur on the job when one person tries to make another person do something he does not want to do. In the job situation this is not uncommon.

How can employees be motivated to perform better on the job? Although feelings of anxiety can motivate some individuals, it must be recognized that employee performance is also determined by the satisfaction the employee obtains. The desire for higher economic rewards, greater recognition, and higher status are all motivating forces which can spur an individual to higher levels of performance. Employees have a variety of needs and when they can get satisfaction for some of these needs from their job, their performance will improve. People differ in their abilities and in their "will to do," or motivation. Therefore, they may not respond to the same organizational rewards. Some employees may not seek advancement or higher salaries; however, it is doubtful if the same employees would want to be demoted or take a cut in pay. Not all employees place high value on social contacts with fellow employees, nor do all group members feel the same level of need to be accepted by coworkers. In short, the elements that motivate one employee may have little appeal to the next; however, nearly all workers have something that they want (or fear losing) which motivates them to work.

While motivation is an internal and sometimes hidden aspect of a person's personality, *incentives* are generally outside the individual and are a form of stimulation. Incentives offered on the job may take a tangible form, such as money, safe working conditions, or plush physical surroundings, or they may be intangible rewards, such as praise, recognition, or approval. Employee behavior results when his motives are brought together with an incentive. A motivating situation is, therefore, a result of something usually outside the individual—an incentive—satisfying something inside the individual—a motive.

The Importance of Motives in Employee Behavior

Motives are mainsprings of action and as such are the reasons for behavior. They arouse, maintain, and determine the general direction of that behavior. When one knows the motives of a worker, it is easier to understand his behavior. The actual degree of achievement is dependent upon both motivation and ability. With low motivation the performance suffers in much the same way it does when ability is low. Surveys show that employees who fail often have the knowledge and skill that is necessary, but, partly due to lack of motivation, lack the necessary habits or attitudes.

To develop the proper motivation, the supervisor must help the employee satisfy his needs. Salary and job security are no longer enough motivation to ensure proper cooperation and loyalty in an employee. This is not to say that salary and job security are not important to the worker—they are—but in recent years a changing emphasis has given more attention to social and personal satisfactions. This is possible because the former needs have been relatively better satisfied in most industrial organizations.

INCENTIVES

It is necessary to recognize individual differences in employee motives. Yet some pattern of motivation should be understood if incentives are to be provided in an organization. Not all employees will react the same way to incentives provided on the job. The incentive program of any particular company must be tailored to the needs of the majority of the people working for it. Incentives can be both financial and nonfinancial and may be positive or negative, depending on the employee's reaction to them. A bonus would be rewarding and positive; a fine would be punishing and negative. Positive incentives usually encourage repetitive behavior and can help build good working habits. Negative incentives may be effective in breaking bad working habits, but may not be effective in developing good ones. Negative incentives which emphasize fear or perceived threats carry the danger that recipients will react in a nonpredictable manner. For example, subordinates may retract their willingness to do more on the job than they are forced to do, thus, human performance may actually be lowered rather than raised when fear is used as an incentive. Also, the use of negative incentives is generally ineffective in the long run because such methods are contrary to the democratic values found in our modern society.

Positive incentives are intended to provide stimulus for behavior which is rewarding to the individual. Generally, it is accepted that people will repeat the patterns of behavior that they perceive as being satisfying or rewarding, while avoiding that behavior which they find unsatisfying or threatening. It should be remembered that both positive and negative incentives can be used simultaneously. The overall combination of positive and negative, financial and nonfinancial incentives to be found in industry is too extensive to be given adequate treatment in this textbook; however, a broad look at such incentives is outlined in the following table. The left-hand column indicates the generalized categories of human needs and motives. The center column gives examples of positive incentives, both financial and nonfinancial, which are commonly found in job environment. The third column indicates some of the negative incentives which might be found on the job or in a work group (see Table 10–1).

Financial Incentives and Their Use. Salary increases, bonuses, and other financial incentives satisfy primary economic needs of employees. These may affect the job very directly by contributing to a positive attitude of the employee. It has already been mentioned that monetary considerations are not the sole motivating force for employees. However, if pay is inadequate or considered unfair by employees, other aspects of the job may come under criticism—superiors, work groups, the job itself. For this reason a sound human relations program cannot be built on a poor salary schedule in any organization.

Aside from a sound wage and salary schedule and the provision of fringe benefits, many companies have attempted to go further by offering financial incentives to encourage increased production or to obtain widespread employee participation. Some companies have installed formal suggestion systems, whereby employee ideas on cutting costs or improving production tools or techniques are financially rewarded when they are used. In some cases, a standard award is given regardless of the amount of the savings to the company. Other firms will pay the employee a percentage of the savings derived as a result of the suggestion. In either case, the employee is provided a formal outlet for his suggestions and encouraged to contribute his ideas to the company. Despite the noble intentions that may be in the minds of the planners of suggestion systems, the program can produce some reverses to the morale of employees. If the financial rewards are considered by the employees to be inadequate for the caliber of ideas that they submit, the system may be regarded as a management instrument for picking the brains of the workers rather than as a channel of upward communications. Another difficulty of suggestion systems can lie in the complex and drawn-out process of evaluating and selecting suggestions that are to be rewarded. Sometimes the committees used in the formal suggestions system are slow to notify employees about the status of their ideas. Under such circumstances employee enthusiasm

TABLE 10–1. Employee Motivation and Incentives Found on the Job

Motives and Human Needs	Examples of Positive Incentives	Examples of Negative Incentives
Economic security	Adequate wages and salaries Fringe benefits, bonuses Retirement benefits and pension funds	Inadequate wages and salaries Threat of job loss
Psychological security	Promotions Stability in working conditions Fair and consistent treatment Knowing place in group and with the superior Feeling of being competent in the job assignment	Demotions Inconsistent treatment on the job Uncertainty of position in the group or with the superior Uncertainty and fear of incompetency in the job assignment Public disciplinary action
Physical security	Safe working conditions Proper equipment to do job Adequate heating and ventilation Adequate rest periods	Dangerous and unsafe working conditions Improper and inadequate equipment Inadequate creature comforts supplied
Recognition and social needs	Sense of belonging Compatible work group and good working relationship with peers Rewards and recognition for performance Status symbols	Ostracization Incompatible work group Withholding or ignoring performance recognition
Self-realization (self-expression and self-respect)	Participation Opportunity to use creative ability on job Being treated as an individual Trusted	Impersonal treatment Stultifying and monotonous job Being deprived of authority or responsibility

can wane. Successful suggestion programs must be properly administered, must provide rapid and adequate recognition for ideas that are submitted, and must have a reward system which employees recognize as being equitable. If any of these key elements is lacking, the organization can lose the benefit of employee ideas on safety, improved methods, or cost-saving techniques; and it can create an object which becomes a source of employee dissatisfaction and ridicule.

Profit sharing is another financial incentive used by companies to encourage employees to take an active interest in the operations of the firm. There are a number of methods used to determine the amount of the profits to be paid to each employee. Regardless of the technicalities of administering a profit-sharing plan adopted by an organization, advocates of such plans usually cite the advantage as a strengthening of the sense of involvement employees feel toward the company as being worth any possible administrative difficulties. Theoretically, the employees share a portion of the profits derived from their efficiency and labor, and this contributes to their motivation to reduce waste, increase production, add to sales volume, and generally improve overall efficiency which will cut operating costs.

Although profit sharing has been successful in many companies, some have abandoned the program because of the problems it can create. The reasons for failure in some plans have been attributed to the fact that profits depend on a great many factors other than individual performance. Workers may not understand the complicated process of computing profits and, therefore, may suspect the amount they receive as being the result of some administrative manipulation. Other problems can arise because of the long periods of time between the actual time that the profit-sharing payments are made (annually or quarterly) and the period in which they were earned. When profits in the organization are high, the program may work well; but when profits are low, the profit-sharing plan can have difficulty. It is easy to see why this can occur. Under profit sharing, a bonus can come about when economic conditions beyond the control of anyone in the organization permit the organization to gain advantageous financial position. As a result, the workers often do not understand why they received a bonus. It is also reasonable to realize that they may not understand why they do not receive a bonus payment when operations do not generate sufficiently high profits to warrant one. For this reason some companies have actually paid a profit-sharing bonus when no profits were made. It should be obvious that such practice cannot be sustained for long by any organization.

Another innovative financial incentive program is known as the Scanlon Plan. The plan consists of two basic parts—(1) a wage incentive and (2) a new form of suggestion system. The wage incentive is based on a formula designed to distribute the gains of increased production proportionally among all employees involved. Each formula is tailored for each individual company, but, typically, wages are based on the sale value of goods produced; for example, for every 1 per cent increase in productivity there is a 1 per cent increase in wages and salaries. Normally, this program pays bonuses to clerical, sales, and support personnel, as well as to production employees. This provides an incentive to all employees to offer suggestions which might not be offered otherwise for improved methods because they share in the financial rewards of higher productivity, regardless of their department or function.

The suggestion system of the Scanlon Plan operates through committees composed of workers from each department who evaluate and screen ideas from fellow employees. These departmental committees, which meet periodically, refer suggestions that affect the plant as a whole to a plant-wide screening committee which includes members of top management, as well as union leaders [11, p. 682].

Financial incentive programs of any variety are an example of how sound human relations practices are an element necessary to the success of any administrative process or system. Financial incentives must be based on a clear set of standards which are comprehensible to workers. Employees should understand why the rewards are being given or why they are not. This requires a systematic communications network which keeps employees informed about important conditions which may affect the amount of the financial reward. Also, any financial incentives must be awarded in a spirit of being earned by the recipients, not in a paternalistic climate in which the company makes employees feel they are being "given" something out of the benevolence of the organization.

UNION POSITION ON FINANCIAL INCENTIVE PROGRAMS.   Union reaction to financial incentive programs depends on a number of factors. In general, the union does not agree to any financial plan which will jeopardize the going wage level of the industry. Furthermore, organized labor does not favor any financial incentive based on the necessity of workers to speed up their production. Union opinion can change regarding the acceptability of financial incentives when the record shows they do not increase the wage disparity between employees. For example, early union resistance to profit sharing has weakened considerably, and, in recent years, profit-sharing programs have even entered into collective bargaining agreements between labor and management.

NONFINANCIAL INCENTIVES AND THEIR USE.   These are the day-to-day incentives that work to satisfy employee needs. Good and safe working conditions would be provided to maintain a positive incentive in the worker. Friendly working surroundings both satisfy the social needs of belonging and encourage the team feeling. This helps keep absenteeism and turnover at a minimum. The supervisor has the responsibility of providing leadership that is conducive to this group feeling. A sense of participation satisfies the need for recognition and self-expression. A knowledge of *what* is being done and *why* increases the significance to the employee, and participation is an excellent way of encouraging this. This often results in an increased feeling of responsibility in meeting group goals, and the employee usually feels his importance as an individual is considered by the company. Recognition is a fundamental need of all employees if job satisfaction is to be achieved. Both criticism and praise are means of recognition. Criticism should be given privately and directed toward the job and not the person. This does not degrade the individual. Public criticism can result in negative incentives and can affect the entire work group, causing unsatisfactory performance in meeting group and organizational goals.

Competition can be employed as an effective incentive on an individual or group basis. It is widely accepted that, ideally, the more tension is reduced, the greater the chance that the group will work together. But a harmonious group is not necessarily a productive or effective one. If everyone agrees, it may mean that either group members do not care enough to differ or that no one is thinking. The objective of a group leader should not be to suppress conflict, but to manage it so that it does not cause animosity between group members and lower group efficiency. The balance is not an easy one to strike, but competition tends to be an effective incentive when equals are competing and when the individual or group members who do not win in the conflict do not suffer personal indignity or humiliation.

The sense of developing skill and acquiring new knowledge and in growing on the job are stimulants toward better performance. An opportunity to grow in a different assignment may give a sense of progress even though no promotion is involved. Planned job rotation provides a flexible work group and can motivate a group of employees by providing the opportunity to try new jobs and break a monotonous or dull routine. A sense of developing competence is enhanced by proper training programs, which are discussed in Chapter 12.

In satisfying the drive for achievement an individual's performance often improves if he can see how his effort relates to the complete product. This sense of achievement helps the individual distinguish between effective action and mere activity. Even in the work group, a knowledge of the group results can provide a sense of individual achievement. Not only do employees want to know how their work fits in with the total production picture, but each worker is interested in how well he is performing in his job in the group. In this regard, an objective evaluation of his performance by his superior is important so that any weaknesses can be corrected through careful coaching or additional training.

Orientation and proper job placement can be a motivating factor because the employee obtains a feeling of personal security and of greater accomplishment. When interests, personality, and aptitudes closely match the requirements of the job, the chance is much greater that better performance will result. The satisfactory induction into a new task increases the sense of security and of belonging to the transferee or the new employee.

A cursory review of the incentives provided on the job will reveal that they can be divided into two broad categories—those provided through the interpersonal relationships with fellow workers on the job (subordinate, superiors, and peers) and those provided through the nature of the work, personnel policies, and practices of the organization. Although human relations is primarily concerned with the effectiveness of the former variety of incentive-motive match, the total personnel program and treatment of workers by the organization cannot be ignored.

Elton Mayo discovered during employee interviews for the Hawthorne Studies (see Chapter 3) that some employees who were full of grievances against supervisors and convinced that they had been unfairly treated did not attribute their ills to the company. On the contrary, they were eager to tell their stories, believing that the company or some sufficiently remote executive would offer them redress once their situation was fully known [9, p. 96].

Such employee faith in an organization must be based on his perception of honest and just treatment of workers. It also sheds light on a fact often overlooked by students of human relations. What the company does in the way of personnel programs is important to workers and can often counter some of the lack of satisfaction derived by the worker in his interpersonal relations with his fellow employees. Furthermore, worker dissatisfaction with organizational policies can reduce the effectiveness of personal relations he has with his supervisor.

Modern concepts of organization and leadership stress group processes, but they do not ignore the other factors necessary to sound human relations. Such factors as organizational personnel practices contribute to the worker's sense of value to the company. For example, when personnel systems and procedures are routinized to the point of being impersonal, little sense of belonging or loyalty is engendered in employees. Company training programs play an integral part in the development of employee skills in human and technical processes. If the content and methodology of training programs does little more than provide workers with a sense of being automatons in the production schemes, there is little hope that organizational members will be concerned about the problems of reaching organizational objectives. Therefore, training programs which fail to balance technical competence with human development can spell the failure of the firm in utilizing the full potential of its human resources.

Leadership styles employed by company officials and supervisors help create a climate which either fosters employee ideas or stifles initiative. The quality of face-to-face communications and the amount of accurate information which is transmitted to employees contribute to the overall effectiveness of organizational members when working together in the attainment of mutual goals. Thus, supervision and leadership, training, and communications are explored in the following chapters in order to determine their part in the practice of sound human relations.

SUMMARY

1. The intent of modern theories of leadership and organization is to raise organizational effectiveness; however, many supervisors resist changing from traditional concepts because they do not recognize the benefits that might be derived from making such a change. Traditional organization creates a pattern of one-to-one relationships between superiors and subordinates, whereas modern concepts emphasize group relations. This shift in emphasis involves greater skills in group processes and communications on the part of the supervisor. Such skills require a different attitude in the leader, which he is not always willing or able to take.

2. Supervisors who employ high-pressure methods may achieve impressive short-term results. Such gains may not be enduring and may actually cause substantial long-run costs to the organization in terms of subtle or overt resistance from subordinates, higher than usual turnover, increased accident rates, or other losses in human efficiency. The hidden danger to the use of high-pressure methods is that supervisors who achieve impressive short-term results may be promoted or transferred before employee discontent makes its presence felt; thus, high-pressure leadership by any particular supervisor can go undetected for some time, and some other supervisor may assume the results of the high-pressure supervisors. This factor, plus the fact that pressure from one's immediate superior often causes a chain reaction in which those beneath the high-pressure superior use the same tactics on their own subordinates, can result in an organizational climate permeated with undue stress.

3. Modern concepts of organization and leadership do not endorse high-pressure methods, but they do not preclude the use of authority. The primary difference between traditional concepts of leadership and modern ones is the degree to which subordinates are permitted to participate in making decisions. The supervisor still retains the same degree of authority he would have in the traditional organizational context; however, the way in which he might exercise that authority is changed considerably. Group influence is utilized as a behavior-setting mechanism rather than the singular force of a supervisor's authority.

4. The use of group participation is limited by the realities of the industrial situation. Production deadlines, budgets, and other factors cannot be ignored when the workers are allowed a voice in how the activities of their department are to be conducted. Participation does not mean that havoc is permitted. The supervisor necessarily must provide the guidance and information essential to the decision-making process. The purpose of participation is to permit the thinking and suggestions of employees to help the group achieve better performance. In the process, group members receive the satisfaction of being able to express themselves and to use their problem-solving ability.

5. The democratic process which is encouraged in industry is often confused with the political concept of democracy. In the industrial situation every employee does not have the right to vote on every major issue in the organization. Only in the broadest sense of the word is an industrial organization democratic. Therefore, when we refer to democratic planning or decision-making within an organization, we are not referring to the right of every employee to vote on every action affecting the organization. More accurately, we are referring to group planning, effective communications, and participation in decision-making which affect the way some, but not all, things are to be done.

6. Employee participation is a vital tool in meeting the rapid social and technological changes which occur in industry. The instigation of change in an organization is not a one-man job. The participation of others is invaluable for pinpointing difficulty, collecting information, and lending cooperation, because persons involved in planning change are in a better position to understand why it is needed. By being a part of the initial stages of planning change, a person is usually more willing to try to make the change work once it is implemented.

7. Changes that occur in an organization need a carefully defined direction. To insure that change occurs rationally and smoothly, any change needs planning if resistance to that change is to be minimized. Such planning should include a statement about why the change is needed, who is to be affected and how the change will benefit the persons involved.

8. Motivation refers to the reasons why people want things and try to get them. It has different connotations to different people. It is important to realize that motivation is a complex internal set of desires, ambitions and goals which often remain hidden in a person's personality. Incentives are external and are offered as a means of stimulating behavior. Positive incentives offered on the job are financial rewards, recognition, or status. Negative incentives are those which impose a threatening situation on the recipient. Fear of losing a job, fines, and the withholding of recognition are examples of negative incentives that can be used in the job situation.

9. Financial incentives are sometimes formalized into programs such as suggestion systems or profit sharing. One financial incentive program which attempts to combine these is called the Scanlon Plan. Nonfinancial incentives involve condition and treatment which motivate individuals in their day-to-day behavior on the job. Many of these day-to-day incentives are provided by the interpersonal relations an employee has with his fellow workers and with his superiors.

DISCUSSION QUESTIONS

1. Why do some supervisors resist changing their traditional concepts of leadership?
2. What are the hazards of using high-pressure methods of leadership in a group?
3. What are the realities of life in an organization which can limit the use of employee participation?
4. How does political democracy differ from concepts of democracy practiced in industry?
5. Why is participation an important element in modern industry for making decisions?
6. What employee motives can be satisfied by incentives provided on the job?
7. How does the Scanlon Plan differ from most profit-sharing plans?

BIBLIOGRAPHY AND SELECTED COLLATERAL READINGS

1. CARTWRIGHT, D., and A. ZANDER, *Group Dynamics: Research and Theory*, 3rd ed. New York: Harper & Row, 1968.
2. COCH, L., and JOHN R. P. FRENCH, JR., "Overcoming Resistance to Change," *Human Relations*, I (1948), 512–32.
3. HERZBERG, FREDERICK, *Work and the Nature of Man*. Cleveland: World Publishing Co., 1966.
4. HERZBERG, FREDERICK, and others, *The Motivation to Work*. New York: John Wiley and Sons, 1959.
5. LAWRENCE, PAUL R., and others, *Organizational Behavior and Administration*, rev. ed. Homewood, Ill.: Richard D. Irwin, Inc., and The Dorsey Press, 1965.
6. LIKERT, RENSIS, *New Patterns of Management*. New York: McGraw-Hill Book Company, 1961.
7. MAIER, NORMAN R. F., *Principles of Human Relations*. New York: John Wiley and Sons, 1952.
8. MARROW, A. J., D. G. BOWERS, and S. SEASHORE, *Management by Participation*. New York: Harper & Row, 1967.

9. MAYO, ELTON, *The Human Problems of an Individual Civilization*. New York: The Viking Press, 1960.
10. MILES, R. E., "Human Relations or Human Resources?" *Harvard Business Review*, 43 (July–August, 1965), 148–51.
11. STRAUSS, GEORGE, and LEONARD SAYLES, *Personnel, The Human Problems of Management*, 2nd ed. Englewood Cliffs, N.J.: Prentice-Hall, 1967.
12. WATSON, GOODWIN, and EDWARD M. GLASER, "What We Have Learned About Planning for Change," *Management Review*, American Management Association (November, 1965).

11

Supervision
and Leadership

In the preceding chapters the discussion has included such topics as characteristics of formal organization, internal and external systems affecting the behavior of the organization, and human needs and employee motivation. (From an organizational standpoint, leadership is a necessity in order to keep the activities of the organization under control and directed toward organizational goals. In a work group, the activities of the members need the direction and support of a leader if the group's efforts are to be effective. Even when the importance of leadership is conceded, the question of how to lead requires an answer.

Not all leaders are effective. Not all leaders are inspiring to their subordinates. How does the leader improve his own performance and, in turn, that of his subordinates? The first step in the solution is to determine what a leader does.

The pyramidal shape of an organization places leaders at different levels in the management hierarchy and in widely varying functions. Each manager or supervisor may be confronted by an entirely different set of circumstances, personnel, and technological environment. With this diversity, is there any commonalty to the activity of the leaders in an organization? In quest for an answer to this it is useful to consider the functions of management.

FUNCTIONS OF MANAGEMENT

The development and establishment of the systems in an organization are often accompanied by policies and procedures and practices and rules. Writers do not all agree about the functions managers perform, and some raise questions about the transferability of management functions from one enterprise to another or even from one department to another. For instance, could a manager of the production line take over the managing of the sales department and use any of the management skills he used in the production department? Generally, it is conceded that he could if he is familiar with certain managerial principles. This transferability of management skills from one department to another or from one enterprise to another is termed the *principle of universality of management.*

A number of writers have been concerned with the functions of management. Taylor and Barnard were two authors who expounded on the role of management; however, a Frenchman named Henri Fayol was one of the first writers to develop a list of functions which were accepted as being basic to the process of management [17]. Although the terminology used to describe such functions is not always the same, generally those designated by Fayol are accepted today. Fayol's list of management functions are planning, organizing, staffing, directing, and controlling.

In order to understand the role of management in the operations of an organization a brief explanation of each of these functions is presented in the following summary.

PLANNING. Planning is a function that determines in advance what should be done. It consists of selecting the objectives of the enterprise and then establishing the policies, procedures, programs, and other means of achieving these objectives. When looking ahead and planning for the future, a manager must also decide which alternative courses of action should be followed. A manager may receive assistance in making plans from subordinates, peers or superiors, but, ultimately, he is the one who prepares various plans. Planning is intellectual in nature and is something which must be constantly pursued by a manager, even while performing his other functions.

ORGANIZING. Organizing is the determination of the necessary activities and resources required to achieve organizational objectives. It means the rationalization and assignment of these to groups and departments. This function requires that, in addition to assigning areas of responsibility to others, a manager must delegate the necessary authority to carry out the assignment. Authority is a necessary element to a management position, and *delegation* of authority is the key to organization.

STAFFING. Staffing refers to management's responsibility to recruit, select, and train the people necessary to fill the positions needed in the organization. This includes the necessity of establishing present and future requirements in the organization. Indirectly, it would include the establishment of programs for the promotion, appraisal, development, and rotation of personnel and the system of compensation and incentives used by the organization.

DIRECTING. Directing is the function in which a manager guides, teaches, coaches, and supervises his subordinates. It includes not only giving orders, but also disseminating information necessary to the execution of organizational objectives. This involves more than telling people what to do, or how to do it; it carries the wider implication of telling why things are to be done.

CONTROLLING. In the controlling function, the manager must see whether activities and events are going according to plans. Here we can see how the functions are related. It would not be possible to check on the progress of the work if there were no plan to check against. Controlling carries a deeper implication than mere checking; it also includes taking corrective actions where activities or events do not meet the specifications established by plans [10, pp. 22–23].

The management process is one which is performed continuously by managers at all levels in the organizational hierarchy. The term *manager* includes all positions of authority in an organization, from the president down to the first-line supervisor on the assembly line. The president may spend considerably more time in planning and organizing than a foreman, but in either office the functions are present even though the time and emphasis is different. It should be understood that these basic management functions are highly related and that their separation is more academic than practical. A manager may not separate them and devote a given amount of time to each one, although he may try to set aside time to plan and organize the activities within his scope of responsibility.

In Fayol's list of management functions no special mention is made of coordination, which some other writers list as a separate function. This was not an oversight. Fayol recognized the importance of coordination; however, he considered it the essence of management rather than a separate function. A manager's task is to achieve orderly group effort and unity of action in the pursuit of a common objective. Such a task implies that coordination is a necessary part of a manager's job.

Fayol's formal classification of a manager's functions leaves room for further interpretation. Many aspects of a manager's activities cannot be categorized simply; but even if their jobs were defined in much more detail, supervisors and managers would differ considerably in the way they carry out their activities. This factor contributes to the difficulty of clearly defining management as a science. The diversity of methods that individual managers use to obtain effective results leads many students of human relations to the conclusion that management is an art. The fact that there may be various methods of managing or leading a group does not mean that all methods are equally effective. Perhaps the arguments between those who believe that efficiency in manpower utilization can only be accomplished through scientific methods and those who believe that intuition, personal charm, and common sense constitute the art of leadership are waging a battle of semantics. Good leadership requires that the leader do his homework; that is, carefully plan the objectives and activities of the group. However, motivating the group actually to perform those activities and reach those objectives requires more than the rationalizing of a course of action. Possibly *management* should not be defined as either a science or an art because, in reality, it requires elements of both to be effective.

THE LEADERSHIP FUNCTION

So far in this text the terms *leadership, supervision,* and *management* have been used interchangeably. The discussion which follows in this chapter will be more concise if, to begin with, *leadership is* defined more carefully. Although these three terms are widely used synonymously, *leadership* is a specialized function or job in a group or organization. Good leadership on the part of an individual acts as both an energizing agent to group members and as a catalyst for their activities. This is accomplished by the leader through opening and maintaining good communications within the group and any necessary outsiders, coordinating the activity of the group, and stimulating and guiding the activity of the group.

When the leadership function is considered in the context just mentioned, it is easier to understand the statement, "I like my supervisor as a person, but as a boss he is lousy." This could be interpreted to mean that the supervisor is a pleasant, friendly individual, but he is ineffectual at providing the motivation and leadership that the group needs. The reverse statement might also be made, "I don't care for my supervisor personally, but I think he's a good boss." This situation could mean that the boss is not personally likable because of some aspect of his personality, but he does provide the guidance and direction the group needs in order to function effectively. However, it is difficult to believe that the group would function well over a long period of time if all members of the group disliked the leader intensely.

Supervisors, managers, or executives are individuals who are placed in positions of authority in the organizational hierarchy, but, unfortunately, not all such persons are necessarily good leaders. In broad terms, managers and supervisors might engage in the functions described by Fayol and still not sufficiently motivate subordinates to perform well, in which case, they are really administering a program, not providing leadership. Assuming that a work group is well trained, provided with necessary equipment and adequate physical facilities, the leadership of the supervisor will help make the difference between excellent or poor group performance. Thus, the most apparent fact is that the problems of leadership are not restricted to any level or to few levels of management within an organization, but they permeate group activities at all levels from the first-line supervisor, foreman, to the president and members of the board of directors.

If one accepts the premise that a supervisor will get work done efficiently and effectively only if he can motivate the behavior of his subordinates to do it this way, then his basic problem becomes one of creating a situation in which his subordinates can satisfy their individual needs while, at the same time, working toward organizational goals. To accomplish this, supervisors must support or help subordinates achieve some degree of satisfaction for their ego needs and their other human needs. The attempt to reduce potential conflict between individual goals or needs and organizational objectives seems to require that the supervisor adopt a pattern of interaction with his subordinates that the workers view as supportive. Likert's principles of modern leadership (Chapter 9) imply that in order to be supportive a supervisor should be sensitive to the needs and feelings of his subordinates, respect and trust them, be receptive to their ideas and suggestions, and have a sincere concern for the welfare of his men [17, p. 74].

M. R. Feinberg indicates that the primary means for a supervisor to motivate his subordinates is to show that he is conscious of their needs, ambitions, fears, and of the fact that each person in the group is an individual. The insensitive supervisor, who is, perhaps unintentionally, aloof, cold, impersonal, and uninterested, usually finds it very difficult to get his people to put out any extra effort [8].

Some management theorists are convinced that such an approach to leadership is unsuited to industrial situations and that a harder approach is necessary. One of the tougher approaches to leadership is typified by Robert N. McMurry, who expresses the view that since so many members of lower, middle, and even top management are dependent, insecure, and ineffective, and produce primarily because they are directed by one or two hard-driving strong autocrats, the outlook for the widespread introduction of a genuinely humanistic, democratic-participative philosophy of leadership in the near future is very dim. He considers the inadequacies and deficiencies of the democratic human relations approach so great that they render that approach unrealistic. McMurry suggests that subordinates be given a reasonably high latitude for freedom of action, but always within a rigidly controlled structure, with a supervisor always having the final say. Under this philosophy of leadership the superior would structure the subordinates' activities for them, make policy decisions which affect them, and keep subordinates in line [13, pp. 82–90].

The assumptions about human nature which support the tougher traditional concepts of leadership generally categorize the majority of workers as indolent, possessing little ambition, having a distaste for responsibility, resistant to change, gullible, and with a nature which prefers to be led. In short, these assumptions generally embody the basic ideas summarized in McGregor's Theory X concept of management (see Chapter 4). In contrast, modern concepts of leadership, which are usually more permissive, are based on an opposite set of propositions about human nature. However, advocates of tougher management control over workers frequently believe that to give way to worker needs leads to the abdication of management. In extreme cases, advocates of this approach to management point out that happiness is not the primary concern of a business enterprise—profits are; therefore, to place the human element before the material objectives of the firm is to undermine the firm's chances for survival.

PROBLEMS OF BEING A LEADER IN THE INDUSTRIAL SITUATION

Based on the opposite views of leadership, ranging from permissive or soft at one end of the spectrum to strong or autocratic at the other, a supervisor may find it difficult to choose the most effective pattern or style of leadership for himself. He is confronted with the problem of weighing the human considerations against "production or profit" considerations. In trying to develop a pattern of leadership, a supervisor faces the problem of determining how much importance he should ascribe to efficiency as opposed to human satisfaction. Where does he draw the line? How does he effectively blend elements of both?

Some managers and social scientists have begun to question the assumption that increasing the specialization of workers inevitably leads to higher productivity and lower costs. There appears to be a point where theoretical increases in efficiency are outweighed by losses in worker motivation and responsibility. Where is the balance between the achievement of maximum production efficiency and maximum human satisfaction? How does the leader obtain the cooperation of subordinates in reaching production goals?

The notion of "employee orientation" versus "production orientation" was strongly emphasized by the research studies conducted by members of the Survey Research Center at the University of Michigan. This group of social scientists followed the lead established by Elton Mayo in conducting the Hawthorne Studies in the investigation of employee-supervisor relationships. One of the earliest and best known studies made by the Michigan group of this relationship took place in the clerical offices of a large life insurance company shortly after World War II. The objective was to identify the styles of leadership used by department heads and to determine the effect, if any, these styles had on the productivity of each department. Based on the predominant style of leadership used by each supervisor, the supervisors were divided into three groups:

1. Supervisors who believed that their principal responsibility was to get work out and that their subordinates should do what they were told so this could be accomplished were placed in the group known as "production-centered." It should be noted that the supervisors placed in this group were not so categorized because of the manner in which they treated their subordinates. Such supervisors may have been very friendly toward their subordinates. The principal factor was the way such supervisors perceived themselves and their role in the group. They felt that they were fully responsible for production and that subordinates were to do only as they were instructed.

2. Another group was composed of supervisors who believed that because their subordinates were actually doing the production job, they should also have a voice in how the work should be done. This group of supervisors were labeled "employee-centered." They acted essentially as coordinators rather than directors of group activity. The members of this group were not selected because of the way they treated their subordinates, but rather on the basis of their intentions to permit employees to have a voice in the activities of the work group.

3. The third group of supervisors was composed of supervisors who displayed a mixed pattern of leadership, not being dominant in either production- or employee-centered techniques.

The results of this investigation indicated that groups headed by supervisors who practiced close supervision did not produce as much as groups headed by supervisors who practiced more general methods of directing their subordinates. It was also concluded that supervisors categorized as "production centered" headed work units which generally did not attain the same high levels of production as the work groups headed by "employee-centered" supervisors [12].

A number of factors are believed to have contributed to these results. One was the belief that supervisors of high-producing units are an important link in the channels of communication; that is, high-producing units were more often kept informed than were low-producing units.

Subsequent studies of the relationship between a supervisor and his subordinates indicate that the effectiveness of a supervisor is not only a problem of the interpersonal relations between himself and his subordinates. It has been pointed out that the influence a supervisor has on his subordinates is very much dependent upon the relationship he has with his own superior. That is, if a superior emphasizes production with the supervisors beneath him, those supervisors are, in turn, more likely to emphasize production in their relationship with subordinates. Simply stated, this means that supervisors tend to treat their subordinates in the same way they are treated by their own superiors. This confirms the belief that the development of sound supervisory methods must be encouraged at all levels in the organization because the behavior of supervisors cannot be divorced from the behavior of their superiors any more than the behavior of employees can be divorced from that of their supervisor [11, p. 175].

Unfortunately, it is not easy to define *employee-oriented* even if it does appear to have certain advantages in meeting both employee satisfaction and higher production levels. There are many ambiguities attached to employee-centered leadership methods which need further investigation and analysis, yet certain patterns and practices that contribute to the effectiveness of employee-centered methods do seem to emerge. Herzberg et al. summarize a few of these major characteristics:

1. Being sympathetic on both work and personal problems of employees.
2. Sharing information with employees.
3. Being less critical of employees.
4. Being willing and able to help employees in their work while maintaining a leadership position.
5. Allowing greater participation in decision-making among employees.
6. Being consistent in giving orders and in maintaining discipline.
7. Letting employees know where they stand in their job progress.
8. Giving general rather than close supervision.
9. Interacting socially with employees [11, p. 183].

When employee-centered practices are analyzed, the distinguishing difference between them and the practices of production-centered supervisors was that subordinates receive satisfaction from the sincere interest the employee-centered supervisors have for them as individuals. Production-centered supervisors, in contrast, may be seen by subordinates as pushing to get the job done with little concern for them or their welfare. There is an important point to be added to this finding. Those employee-centered supervisors who get the best results tend to recognize that high production is also one of their responsibilities.

DUAL RESPONSIBILITIES OF LEADERSHIP

The dual acceptance of supervisory responsibility lends two distinct dimensions to the role of leadership. Some social scientists identify the two leadership roles by the terms *initiating structure* and *consideration*. Aspects of the leader's role in the *initiating structure* are consistent with traditional concepts of management; that is, it includes exercising authority over the activities of subordinates by maintaining discipline, defining standards of performance, and evaluating performance of subordinates. In order to conduct the initiating structure of his role, the supervisor would rely on his competence in each of the management functions mentioned earlier in this chapter.

The second dimension of leadership is called *consideration*. It includes the interpersonal and social relationships that the leader develops with his subordinates. This aspect of leadership has an important impact on the cohesiveness of the group. If the leader is friendly and approachable, finds time to listen to his subordinates, communicates openly, and attempts to treat subordinates fairly, the chances are the group members will respond to him and to each other in a similar way. Although this factor implies that the leader attempts to build supportive relationships with his subordinates, it does not imply that he is lax, nor does it imply that he is not competent in the technical aspects of his job [16].

STYLES OF LEADERSHIP

Often in an attempt to categorize the methods that leaders use to obtain results from the efforts of others, three styles of leadership are cited as the way leaders handle the initiating structure in a group. Before mentioning what these styles of leadership are called, it should be remembered that they are really convenient terms to help identify patterns of leadership behavior. The actual spectrum of leadership styles is very broad, and few leaders use only one method.

Shortly before World War II, psychologists Kurt Lewin, Ronald Lippitt, and Ralph White, working at the University of Iowa, undertook an investigation of the nature of leadership. The results of their study indicated that three different patterns of leadership could be used by leaders of groups. Each separate style created a different attitude, pattern of behavior, and range of accomplishment for group members.

Autocratic Leadership. Autocratic leadership is often identified with dictatorial or unreasonable methods. While this may be the case with some autocratic leaders, it does not constitute the full meaning of autocratic leadership. More accurately, in the industrial setting this style of leadership is consistent with production-centered supervision, which was referred to earlier in this chapter. The leader mainly seeks obedience from his subordinates. He plays the dominant role in making decisions and in determining the activities of all group members.

There are some dangers to this method. If the leader is quarrelsome and aggressive, his subordinates may react negatively to his dominant leadership and may react by restricting output. Also, a pattern of relationships which force group members to be dependent upon the leader for directions may reduce their effectiveness when he is absent. The group may even fail to function. This loss of effectiveness in the absence of the leader is dependent on many factors, but it is largely attributable to the dominant role an authoritarian leader has in group activities.

Democratic Leadership. The methods of democratic leadership are often referred to as participative. The leader attempts to obtain the ideas of the group through discussion or consultation. However, the democratic style of leadership is often misunderstood because of confusion with the term *democratic*. Often, this style of leadership has been oversold as a panacea for all industrial problems. Such is not the case; results have varied from very good to very poor when what passes for democratic methods have been tried. There are degrees of participation, ranging from a situation where the supervisor merely consults with his subordinates before he makes a final decision to a situation where the supervisor hands the problem over to the group and lets them make the decision. In either case, the supervisor retains the ultimate authority and responsibility for the decision, even though a group process was used to arrive at that decision.

Laissez-faire Leadership. A style of leadership which Auren Uris calls free-rein is more widely known as laissez-faire. Leaders employing this method act more or less as information givers to members of the group. The situation is somewhat reversed from the democratic method in that individual group members consult with the leader before making their own decisions. This method is the most permissive of all, and some detractors of this method consider it irresponsible and spineless [18, p. 29]. Much of the criticism against laissez-faire leadership stems from the fear that not to take an active role in leadership is to abdicate the authority and responsibility of management. There are few situations in industry when some form of active leadership, whether autocratic or democratic, does not have to be exercised by superiors to insure that work is not done haphazardly. However, the laissez-faire technique of leadership is quite applicable, in varying degrees, in research laboratories and similar activities where groups of scientists, engineers, or technicians work on projects requiring individual skills, abilities, and knowledge. Other types of jobs where laissez-faire methods are appropriate are sales jobs where salesmen call on customers independently, teaching, and positions where performance depends on individual initiative and knowledge.

In a short summary of the comparison between the three styles of leadership the direction and extent of the communications necessary for making a decision vary in the group in the way they are characterized in Figure 11–1. The impact of each of these communications networks will be discussed further in Chapter 14.

EVALUATION OF LEADERSHIP STYLES

Leadership requires more than administrative ability. It is a process of guiding, directing, and influencing the actions of others toward some objective. The situations in industry that require this activity are myriad, and no single method of leading is necessarily appropriate in all cases. Most supervisors find that they will use a blend of the three styles of leadership discussed here.

The classification of leadership styles is based on an oversimplification of supervisory behavior. The three classifications do allow students to study the principal characteristics of each style even though few supervisors rely on the same pattern of leadership all of the time. There are ample pros and cons to be aired about any style of leadership, and to attempt to make any flat statement regarding the best methods would be misleading.

There has been a tendency in modern industry to confuse our democratic values with the scientific research in the area of leadership. Most persons want to believe that democratic group methods lead to better results than autocratic action, but as has been mentioned earlier, democratic group methods are somewhat vague and varied. These variations, numerous and complex, are probably the primary source of confusion in determining which method is most effective. However, there are several factors which influence the supervisor to follow one style or another as a general pattern of behavior or in a given situation. Four of these major considerations are discussed in the following section of the chapter.

The Personality, Attitude, and Values of the Leader

At one time it was the vogue among social scientists to try to isolate and describe the personality traits of leaders. There was once the belief that some individuals possessed a certain charisma which made them natural leaders. This charismatic quality was supposedly made of charm, wit, and other personal characteristics which would give certain gifted persons the advantage in leading others.

There are certain characteristics that are generally possessed by leaders—higher than average energy, average or above average intelligence, a capacity for abstract thinking, ingenuity, and perseverance. These are personal characteristics which are often displayed by leaders, but these same characteristics may be present in many persons who are not, and who do not want to become, leaders. Therefore, to spend much energy

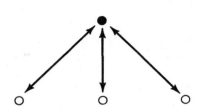

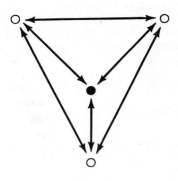

AUTOCRATIC METHOD:
1. Leader makes decisions.
2. Communications are essentially downward.

DEMOCRATIC METHOD:
1. Decision making is a group process. All members are encouraged to participate.
2. Communications are open, both between group members themselves and between the group and the leader. Leader acts as the coordinator of group discussion.

LAISSEZ-FAIRE METHOD:
1. Decisions are made by individuals, but not as a group.
2. Communication takes place between individual members and leader

FIGURE 11–1. Communications Directions in the Three Major Styles of Leadership. (Dark circle denotes leader; light circle denotes subordinate.)

trying to build a personality profile of leadership is somewhat futile until the state of the art of determining these personality factors is perfected considerably.

The question of why a man wants to lead is one that is not easily answered. In each instance, the answer might be different. In most cases the leader leads because by doing so he receives some satisfaction for his own needs. He may seek the prestige of the job and the recognition that accompanies the leadership position.

The motivation of leaders may vary widely, but the attitude and values of the supervisor and the way he perceives his role in the group does not seem to affect the methods he will use to lead his group. A danger of training supervisors in set supervisory methods is that such methods often stress personality factors to be sought in the leader rather than providing an understanding of group behavior. Some individuals who are placed in leadership positions are friendly, secure people who do not feel compelled to assert their authority. Some individuals, because of personality or background, are shirt-sleeve, first-name sort of people; others would feel completely uncomfortable using the same informal manner. Furthermore, if such individuals did feel uncomfortable being informal, they would probably appear quite artificial to their subordinates when trying to use this method. Any pattern of leadership should strive for flexibility, yet be compatible to the individual leader. It might be stated that the type of leadership any given supervisor will use depends on at least four internal forces: his value system and personality, his confidence in his subordinates, his leadership inclinations, and his feelings of security.

Value System and Personality. A supervisor's value system and his personality are influenced by how strongly he feels that individuals should share in decision-making or how convinced he is that the supervisor who is paid to assume responsibility should personally carry the burden of decision-making.

Confidence in His Subordinates. Supervisors differ greatly in the trust and faith they have in other people. If the supervisor does not feel that his subordinates are competent or trustworthy to carry out the assignments of the group, he may feel obliged to oversee the activities of each subordinate personally.

Leadership Inclinations. The leadership inclinations of the individual enter into the type of leader he will be. Some supervisors are highly directive and authoritarian. Issuing orders is easy and natural to them. Other supervisors may operate more comfortably in a group context and encourage the participation of subordinates in determining group action.

Feelings of Security.   Supervisors who release personal control over the decision-making process by allowing others to have a voice in it may thereby reduce the predictability of the outcome. Some supervisors have greater need than others for being sure of the predictability of the results of decisions. As was mentioned earlier, much of the supervisor's security is derived from the relationship he has with his own superior. If he is insecure in that relationship, he may have difficulty in feeling secure with his own subordinates and with their participation in decisions for which he is responsible.

THE ATTITUDES AND COMPETENCE OF THE GROUP MEMBERS

Regardless of the supervisor's personality, on many occasions he must adapt his behavior to the feelings or ability of the group. Some individuals in the group may fear and resent a supervisor, no matter how friendly he attempts to be. He is perceived to be in a position of authority and this creates a barrier between himself and those members of the group. This can occur through no fault of his own. The supervisor may find that occasionally he has a member among his subordinates who is exceptionally brilliant and/or a nonconformist. In some cases, these individuals are unacceptable to the rest of the group and their ideas are rejected or not seriously considered. Additionally, some group members may not be participation oriented. When group participation is imposed on all members, it may create as much resentment as authoritarian methods.

Other problems of choosing a leadership style can occur when the group is comprised of members with special employment problems. These problems can be physical (handicaps), social (minority groups), or educational (language barriers). In each situation the supervisor may find it necessary to deviate from his normal pattern of leadership in order to meet the particular social, physical, educational, or psychological problem of some group member. A supervisor faces the task of showing consideration for each of the individual's problems, especially as they relate to the performance of the job, without showing favoritism to any particular member of the group. Other groups which may require specialized leadership methods are elderly employees, nearing or past retirement age; members of some religious groups; members of a different ethnic group; and women employees.

Women employees may require methods of supervision different from those used with men because of their psychological and physical temperament. Women generally place a high value on friendly relations with peers and superiors. In many cases, women may not be as anxious as men to advance because they are not the sole support of their family and, therefore, may find it more important to work in a pleasant social

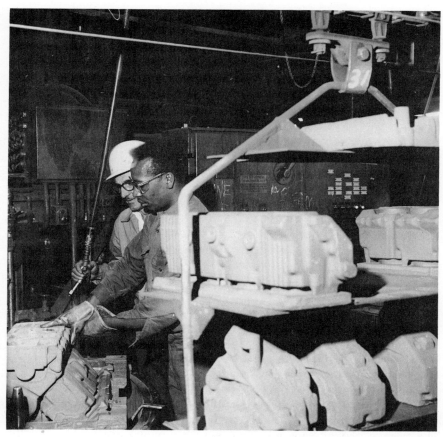

Courtesy of the Educational Affairs Department, Ford Motor Company.

A supervisor faces the task of showing consideration for each of the individual's problems, especially as they relate to the performance of the job.

environment [19, p. 260]. However, with the increase in the number of women in the labor force, it is not uncommon to have women employees who are just as concerned as men about advancement, wages, job security, and other conditions of employment. One must exercise care when making broad generalizations about the motivation of women employees.

Keith Davis does summarize a few items which supervisors can use for guides in handling women employees. These same guides can be applied to all male work groups as well. For example, supervisors probably should not criticize women as thoughtlessly as men, because they are more likely to take criticism personally. Women should be given reassurance by being told in a sincere way when their work is good. While men may resent close supervision, some women seem to want their work reviewed often so that they can know if they are making satisfactory progress.

A supervisor faces the task of choosing a style of leadership that is appropriate for the job situation and the person he directs.

Women generally display more emotion than men; hence, a supervisor should not be seriously concerned with an occasional emotional outburst. The overt display of emotion in women (e.g., crying) which is not usually seen in male behavior may be misleading because men may be just as emotional. Outward signs of emotion in males appear to have been curbed by cultural patterns in the United States.

Surveys indicate that women enjoy a more consistent pattern of work than men; thus, it might be wise for a supervisor to assign small work units to women whenever possible rather than piling up several days' work in a single assignment [4, p. 276]. In the final consensus it would appear that women are no more difficult to supervise than a group of men, although they may be more sensitive to abrupt treatment than men.

The method of leadership that a supervisor finds effective in a group, whether or not it has members who have special employment problems, will depend in a large measure upon the type of subordinate attitudes and characteristics the supervisor has developed. Subordinates learn from their supervisor, and if he has influenced certain attitudes in the group, he may find the members are capable and willing to participate in the decision-making process. Some of the attitudes and characteristics the supervisor might attempt to develop among his subordinates are (1) maturity and independence, (2) readiness to accept responsibility for decision-making, (3) tolerance for ambiguity or general directions rather than specific directions, (4) interest in problems confronted by the group, (5) knowledge and understanding of the relationship between organizational goals and the activity of the group, and (6) willingness to gain experience through dealing with a broad range of problems confronted by the group.

Some of these group attitudes are not easy to develop, and most certainly will not develop at all without the active encouragement of the leader. Certainly it would be folly for a supervisor to encourage the development of these attitudinal qualities if the group did not possess the training, skill, and competence to cope with the technical problems confronted by the work group. Thus, a sound and continuous training program must include both attitude and technical development of employees. The relationship and balance between these two factors will be discussed more completely in the next chapter.

The Organizational Climate

Democratic management cannot flourish in an unfavorable climate. Its principles must be accepted throughout the organization. The character of the climate is most affected by the management philosophies of the executives who hold power near the top of the organizational structure. If they are inclined toward participative methods, it becomes easier for their subordinates to practice such methods at all levels. If top executives are unfavorably disposed, it becomes more difficult for participation to flourish in the organizational levels below them. For example, human relations training will have little impact on supervisors' behavior unless their own superiors practice human relations. The social environment of the organization is greatly affected by the treatment one layer of management receives from above and, in turn, passes on to those beneath it.

Although the human considerations previously mentioned are important, organizational structure itself is a factor in influencing supervisory patterns. The shape of the organization, whether it is tall or flat (see Chapter 9), is based consciously or unconsciously upon theories about the span of control. Essentially, this theory stems from the assumption that subordinates need to be closely supervised in order to perform well. If the conclusions reached by the research of many social scientists is accurate, close supervision may be an encumbrance to high production in many industrial situations. If this is the case, a broader, more decentralized organization would appear to be beneficial in many cases where it does not now exist. But supervisors cannot arbitrarily increase or reduce the number of subordinates reporting to them, regardless of what may be theoretically ideal. They are confronted and often influenced by the environment of a formal organizational structure which they cannot change.

Other impersonal factors accompany formal organization that restrict or influence the style of leadership which supervisors can exercise. Automation may affect rates of production to a greater extent than techniques of leadership on the production line. Assembly-line operations have built-in performance requirements in order to sustain the flow of work. Computer applications, with ultrarapid data scanning and tabulation capacity, can detect inefficient operations quickly enough to have reports available almost simultaneously with performance [3]. Cost accounting and other systems of checking controllable costs, wastes, and production provide checks on the results of operations. Budgets, performance ratings, promotional policies, and various statistical records act as impersonal, but close control systems which influence supervisory behavior. These controls are designed to assure that the organizational objectives which have been planned are met and that the outcome of organizational performance and behavior corresponds to the plan.

A supervisor cannot circumvent all of the pressures these systems and procedures impose on him and his work group. If the controls set by the organization are considered excessive, a tendency may develop among organizational members, including supervisors, to appear to meet standards of performance without really doing so. Examples of this type of behavior were cited by Chris Argyris in one of his studies on the impact of budget controls on those being controlled. He gave repeated examples of short-run compliance with control standards that in reality had either short-term or long-run cost consequences for the organization [1]. Other examples of the outward compliance to standards which in fact were not met are cited by Peter Blau in a study of government employment interviewers. Because of a quota system interviewers were maximizing the number of interviews they conducted, but in the process they neglected the quality of performance in the interviews [2]. The same type of evasion can occur in outside sales activities when salesmen report enough customer contacts to satisfy the record but neglect to take enough time to do a thorough selling job.

In summary, the organizational climate, constituted by the human associations and relationships between organizational members, and the impersonal bureaucratic systems and procedures influence the style of leadership that a supervisor may feel free to exercise.

VARIABLES AFFECTING THE CHOICE OF LEADERSHIP STYLES

The Nature of the Problem. Aside from the three major factors discussed thus far that help determine the style of leadership a supervisor will employ, there are other forces which affect his methods in any given situation. Among the variables that are important is the nature of the problem confronted by the group. Some complex problems are beyond the experience and knowledge of the group. To engage the group in prolonged discussion may confound rather than resolve the situation. This does not mean that complex problems should not be discussed by the group, but that the leader should be sensitive enough to the capabilities of his subordinates to realize when the discussion becomes frustrating rather than constructive.

The Speed with Which a Decision Must Be Made. This is another factor to be considered. A single individual can usually make a decision in a much shorter period of time than a group. The democratic participative process can be time consuming, particularly when the problem is complex. Careful planning may help reduce the necessity for many "crash" decisions, but certain situations require on-the-spot action and do not permit consulting the whole group. There are some decisions which are so routine and simple that to deliberate the issues each time they occur would be a gross waste of the group's time and effort. The danger to any rationale which centralizes decision-making in the hands of the leader is that he will misjudge the importance of even minor decisions in the minds of his subordinates.

The Type of Activity in Which the Group Is Involved. One key variable in the style of leadership which is most effective is the type of activity in which the group is involved. When the nature of the job requires that each member of the group work independently, it becomes most difficult for a supervisor to exercise close personal control over each member's activity. Truck drivers, route salesmen, traveling salesmen are typical examples where close control is impractical. In these situations, impersonal organizational controls, such as quotas or statistical records, have to be relied upon to a great extent.

The physical dispersion of subordinates is not the only situation where the supervisor may find it impractical to attempt close supervision. In many research-oriented organizations the supervisor may have to develop a pattern of leadership which is nearly laissez-faire. Each of the researchers may be far more technically competent in his field than the leader, and any attempt to control the subordinates' activities may cause severe professional resentment. Even when this is not the case, the intrusion of the supervisor may handicap the subordinate. This does not mean that no control is possible. Such factors as time and budget necessarily influence the activities in most private or industrial organizations. The interpersonal relationship between superiors and their subordinates must, however, be maintained in a much more permissive manner, in which exchange of ideas and opinions can flow freely and openly between all members of the group and the leader. In the final analysis, the performance of a highly technical group has to be judged by the results it achieves, rather than by the procedures it uses. The procedures used are more often established by professional standards of competence than by administrative directives.

No doubt there are other variables which influence the style of leadership most appropriate to the situation and personalities of the individuals involved. The uniqueness of each work group makes it difficult to develop any single pattern of leadership that will be appropriate to all situations.

The spectrum of possibilities among leadership methods is illustrated in Figure 11–2. At the left is the autocratic method in which the leader makes all decisions and then tells his subordinates what to do. In this situation he exercises his full authority to get the group to do as he tells them. It should be noted that subordinates do have some latitude to act. This area of freedom may be small, but it cannot be ignored by the autocratic leader. Subordinates can subtly restrict output or openly rebel by concerted action, such as striking. In individual cases the employee can quit if he finds the work situation intolerable.

The center of the spectrum finds a more equitable balance between the authority exercised by the supervisor and the amount of participation the group can exercise. On the opposite extreme of autocratic methods are the more permissive, laissez-faire methods. This end of the spectrum finds much more freedom for subordinate action. The leader does retain some authority.

ADAPTABILITY OF LEADERSHIP PATTERNS

If a supervisor is to be effective, he must be flexible in the methods he uses to direct his subordinates. Most supervisors learn to adopt a mixed style which combines elements of both employee- and production-centered methods. The problem created by the necessity for flexibility is that the leader must become sensitive enough to his subordinates' attitudes and the demands of the situation that he knows which method is most appropriate at any given time. A flexible style is no more effective than any rigid style of leadership if it is not responsive to the demands of the situation. Nor does flexibility imply that a leader should vacillate between permissiveness and being autocratic. The balance between sensitivity to the needs of subordinates and being cognizant of organizational goals is delicate and makes the job of supervision a difficult one. The apparent conflict between flexibility and consistency is not so ponderous when one realizes that it is the consistency with which a leader views his subordinates that helps them to understand his behavior.

In order to function effectively, no single set of rules will suffice a

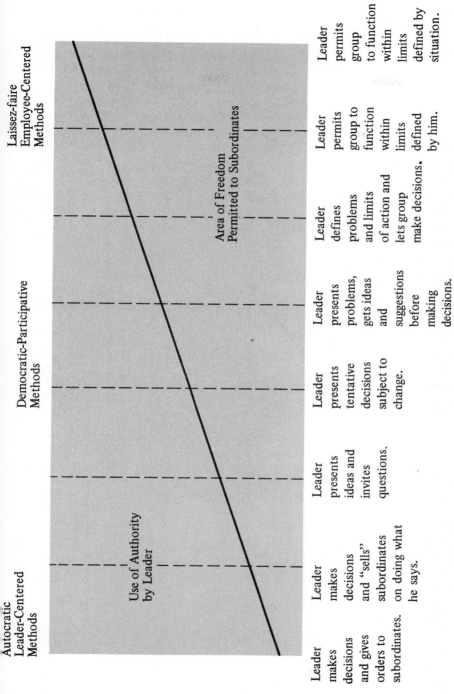

Autocratic
Leader-Centered
Methods

Democratic-Participative
Methods

Laissez-faire
Employee-Centered
Methods

Use of Authority
by Leader

Area of Freedom
Permitted to Subordinates

Leader
makes
decisions
and gives
orders to
subordinates.

Leader
makes
decisions
and "sells"
subordinates
on doing what
he says.

Leader
presents
ideas and
invites
questions.

Leader
presents
tentative
decisions
subject to
change.

Leader
presents
problems,
gets ideas
and
suggestions
before
making
decisions.

Leader
defines
problems
and limits
of action and
lets group
make decisions.

Leader
permits
group to
function
within
limits
defined
by him.

Leader
permits
group
to function
within
limits
defined by
situation.

FIGURE 11–2. Spectrum of Leadership Styles. (Adapted from Tannenbaum and Schmidt, "How to Choose a Leadership Pattern," *Harvard Business Review* [March–April] 1958.)

leader. His ability to appraise accurately the abilities and reliability of his subordinates is the key factor to choosing the most appropriate and consistent methods of leadership. To do this he must know them and must build a sound basis for interpersonal relationships.

Interpersonal Relationships

Face-to-face relations between a supervisor and his subordinates are placed into three broad categories by Carl Rogers. The first he calls employee contacts, which include casual contacts, training on the job, giving assignments, directions, and other face-to-face meetings directly related to the day-to-day operations of the group. These employee contacts provide the opportunity to (1) treat employees as individuals, (2) create rapport and free expression in employees, (3) motivate employees constructively, and (4) become familiar with individual employee attitudes and values.

A second type of face-to-face meeting with employees occurs in a more formal situation which Rogers calls interviews. These are scheduled meetings that are held in connection with employment, job appraisal, transfers, promotions, or resignations. This type of situation may be more formal than the casual employee contacts made daily with subordinates. It is important that any barriers which may arise because of this formality be eliminated as quickly as possible so that the real attitudes of the subordinate can be expressed openly.

The third face-to-face relations occur in a counseling situation. Often this occurs when a subordinate is in need of advice regarding his job or even some aspect of his personal life. Frequently, the circumstances surrounding this type of meeting may be tense or the result of frustration. This may be the case particularly when a discipline problem must be settled. Regardless of the reason for the counseling session, it is probably wise to hold such meetings privately [14].

The supervisor may be surprised at the nature of the questions some of his subordinates will ask. Often the employee will discuss personal problems which are not directly related to his work or the organization. There is no set pattern to follow for the supervisor in such cases, other than not to ridicule the subordinate because his problem may seem trivial. Counseling, whether a formal or casual setting, is an aspect of interpersonal relations which is most delicate, and the supervisor must be wary of becoming involved in some aspects of the subordinate's personal life. The opportunity to build sincere and long-lasting rapport with subordinates is often present in counseling situations.

Leonard Sayles and George Strauss discuss a variety of situations where a subordinate will initiate personal contact with his supervisor

[15]. An employee may seek organizational aid from his supervisor when he has a problem with one of the organizational systems. "Whom should I see to get my typewriter adjusted?" is a type of question belonging to this category. Workers also seek technical aid from their supervisor because of his experience, knowledge, and skill. Personal aid and support are sought by employees from their supervisor. Subordinates may need reassurance regarding their performance or advice on how to improve their chances for advancement. This often calls for counseling by a supervisor. In such cases, the subordinate initiates a personal contact to provide information requested by the supervisor. Other contacts initiated by employees may be at the supervisor's request: "Come and check with me when you are finished typing a draft of that letter."

Certainly the foregoing situations for contacts are not the only reasons why employees seek an opportunity to talk to their boss. However, they do illustrate the potential problem a supervisor may have in distinguishing between the myriad reasons why a subordinate initiates face-to-face contacts. A supervisor must be sensitive to the situations in which his subordinates approach him. Obviously a supervisor cannot devote his entire energy attempting to "psyche-out" every question a subordinate asks, but he can try to be more responsive to his subordinate's needs. He can also try to make enough time available for each employee so that he is sure he understands the nature of the questions the subordinate asks. Too short a discussion or one that is rushed can distort the meaning of an employee's request, thus causing the supervisor's response to be inadequate or inappropriate for the worker.

The total task of leadership is composed of too many facets to be explained simply. No set of rules will be satisfactory; however, understanding the role of the supervisor and the nature of human beings is the first step toward developing a pattern of leadership which is both natural and effective. In the next two chapters, the role that training plays in helping organizational members develop technical and interpersonal competence will be explored.

SUMMARY

1. Organization is accompanied by systems of control over the functions and activities of the organizational members. Organizational activity is determined in a large degree by managers who are responsible for planning, organizing, staffing, directing, and controlling the personnel and functions within the scope of their authority.

2. Leadership is a special function in the organization which provides direction, stimulation, and coordination to organizational activities. Good leadership provides motivation for group members to do what is neces-

sary to achieve organizational goals. The difficulty in determining good leadership is seated in the problem of deciding what methods should be used to motivate employees and how concerned a leader should be about the personal goals of his subordinates as opposed to the organizational objectives which are his responsibility.

3. In trying to develop a pattern of leadership, a manager or supervisor is confronted with weighing human considerations against production goals. The result of this dichotomy has given rise to the notion of "employee-centered" versus "production-centered" leadership methods. The results of research are inconclusive as to which of these methods is consistently the most effective; however, in one major study conducted by the professional staff of the Survey Research Center at the University of Michigan the employee-centered methods used by some supervisors attained higher production records and greater employee job satisfaction.

4. There appear to be two distinct dimensions to the role of leadership. One is the *initiating structure* in which the leader maintains group discipline, sets standards of performance, and sees that such standards are met by the group. The second dimension of leadership is called *consideration*. This aspect of leadership includes the interpersonal relationships which the leader establishes with his subordinates. Although this factor implies that the leader tries to be friendly with his subordinates, it does not mean that he is lax.

5. There are three principal styles of leadership often used by managers and other group leaders. In practice, these styles are seldom found in their pure definition because most leaders blend several styles of leadership to fit both the situation and their own personality. However, the three classifications do provide a definitive framework for observation and analysis of leadership methods so that they can be compared. *Autocratic* leaders often place organizational objectives above the personal needs or ambitions of their subordinates. Frequently such leaders prefer to make decisions affecting the group without anyone else's advice or suggestions. In this style of leadership, group activity is centered around the leader and group members are expected to do only as they are directed.

Democratic leadership methods in industry are often equated with the degree of participation in which group members are encouraged to engage. Leaders using this method may actively solicit opinions and suggestions on matters which affect the group.

Laissez-faire is also known as free-reign leadership. Although this method is not commonly used in most situations found in industry, it is appropriate when group members are highly skilled and capable of carrying out their responsibilities without much direct guidance or interference from a superior.

6. The attitude and values a person has and the way he perceives his role in the group will influence the methods that a leader will employ. These

internal factors will change in the leader as other external factors are considered in the situation. Some of the external factors which affect leadership methods are the attitudes and competence of group members, the organizational climate, and the nature and circumstances of the problem confronting the group.

The total task of leadership is too complex to be explained easily, but if a supervisor is to be effective, he must be flexible in the methods he uses. He must have the ability to perceive accurately the nature of the problems confronting the group and the capabilities and motivation of his subordinates so that he can adapt his leadership style to the most appropriate one prescribed by the situation.

DISCUSSION QUESTIONS

1. What are Fayol's five functions of management?
2. What is meant by the statement, "Leadership is a special function in an organization"? Who provides the leadership in an organization?
3. What problems does a supervisor face in trying to determine the methods he should use in directing his subordinates?
4. What is meant by the *initiating structure* of leadership? What is meant by *consideration?*
5. What are the three principal styles of leadership that a supervisor can use to direct his subordinates? What is the difference in the role that the subordinates play in group affairs in each of these styles of leadership?
6. What factors contribute to the style of leadership that a supervisor will select in any given situation?

BIBLIOGRAPHY AND SELECTED COLLATERAL READINGS

1. ARGYRIS, CHRIS, *Impact of Budgets on People.* New York: Controllership Institute, 1952.
2. BLAU, PETER, *Dynamics of Bureaucracy.* Chicago: University of Chicago Press, 1955.
3. BLAU, PETER, and W. RICHARD SCOTT, *Formal Organizations.* San Francisco: Chandler Publishing Company, 1962.
4. DAVIS, KEITH, *Human Relations at Work,* 3rd ed. New York: McGraw-Hill Book Company, 1967.
5. DRUCKER, PETER, *The Practice of Management.* New York: Harper & Row, 1954.
6. ECKER, PAUL, and others, *Handbook for Supervisors.* Englewood Cliffs, N.J.: Prentice-Hall, Inc., 1963.

7. FAYOL, HENRI, *General and Industrial Management*. Translated by Constance Starrs. London: Sir Isaac Pitman and Sons, Ltd., 1949.
8. FEINBERG, M. R., *Effective Psychology for Managers*. Englewood Cliffs, N.J.: Prentice-Hall, Inc., 1965.
9. FIEDLER, F., *Theory of Leadership Effectiveness*. New York: McGraw-Hill Book Company, 1967.
10. HAIMANN, THEO, *Professional Management*. Boston: Houghton Mifflin, 1962.
11. HERZBERG, FREDERICK, and others, *Job Attitudes: Review of Research and Opinion*. Pittsburgh: Psychological Service of Pittsburgh, 1957.
12. KATZ, DANIEL, and others, *Productivity, Supervision, and Morale in an Office Situation, Part I*. Ann Arbor, Mich.: Institute for Social Research, 1950.
13. McMURRY, ROBERT N., "The Case for Benevolent Autocracy," *Harvard Business Review*, Vol. 36, No. 1 (1958).
14. ROGERS, CARL R., *Counseling and Psycho-Therapy*. Boston: Houghton Mifflin, 1942.
15. SAYLES, LEONARD R., and GEORGE STRAUSS, *Human Behavior in Organizations*. Englewood Cliffs, N.J.: Prentice-Hall, Inc., 1966.
16. STOGDILL, R., and A. COONS (eds.), *Leader Behavior: Its Description and Measurement*. Columbus, Ohio: Bureau of Business Research, Ohio State University, 1957.
17. TANNEBAUM, ARNOLD S., *Social Psychology of the Work Organization*. Belmont, Calif.: Wadsworth Publishing Co., Inc., 1966.
18. URIS, AUREN, *Techniques of Leadership*. New York: McGraw-Hill Book Company, 1953.
19. VOLLMER, HOWARD M., and JACK A. KENNEY, "Supervising Women Is Different," *Personnel Journal* (December, 1955), 260.
20. WICKERT, F. R., and D. McFARLAND, *Measuring Executive Effectiveness*. New York: Appleton-Century-Crofts, 1967.

12

Training Programs

Early concepts of training, which evolved as a result of time and motion studies, emphasized specific skills development in rank-and-file employees. According to the beliefs fostered by the efficiency experts in Frederick Taylor's day, there was "one best way" of doing a job, and once that method was taught to the worker, training could be terminated.

Today, in the broadest sense training encompasses activities ranging from the acquisition of a single motor skill to the development of a complex technical knowledge, inculcation of elaborate administrative skills, and development of attitudes toward intricate and controversial social issues [9, pp. 2–3].

Modern training programs that place emphasis on employee development are considerably more complex than the training proposed by Taylor and his associates. This complexity can be attributed to many prevalent factors, including the rapid development of technology, which has increased the knowledge and skill requirements of all but a few jobs in industry. Perhaps the most significant aspect of technology that complicates modern training programs is described by the word *change*. It is not simply a matter of new sets of social, economic, and technical factors replacing older ones, but of new ones themselves being replaced at a faster and faster rate. The concept of change is not new; what is new is the acceleration in the rate of change. This has come as a result of the tremendous increase in technological and scientific activity; significantly, the rate of that increase is not constant, but exponential [12, p. 3].

The rapidity of change has complicated the educational process in schools, as well as in industry. The fact that the educational level attained by most Americans is higher than ever does not always close the gap between the skills needed in industry and what employees have learned in school.

Another factor that has added to the urgency of industrial training has been the growth of labor unions, accompanied by an emphasis on seniority. General social trends have placed an added weight on job security, meaning that training programs must meet the needs of teaching new employees job skills and attitudes, while retraining older employees displaced by automation and other technological advances. The Manpower Development and Training Act (MDTA) passed by Congress in the early 1960's has helped to alleviate mounting technological unemployment, but the pressure on private industrial firms to retain and retrain employees has added another dimension to industrial training problems which were unknown fifty years ago. For example, one nationwide manpower program being undertaken by industry is designed to provide jobs and training for half a million hard-core unemployed persons. This program, sponsored by the National Alliance of Businessmen (NAB), receives federal funds to help cover the costs of training; however, the resources of private business and labor will be used to provide the training and many of the necessary corollary services to help the trainees adjust to the job environment. An undertaking of such magnitude by business and labor was unheard of as little as a decade ago.

PROBLEMS OF DETERMINING TRAINING NEEDS

The cross currents of social, political, economic, and technological pressures have increased the complexity of establishing training programs in industry. Often the influence of so many forces outside the firm clouds the issue when determining the internal needs of a company. Only a decade or so ago, surprisingly few industrial firms had a systematic method for investigating their internal training needs [8]. Although some progress has been made recently in determining organizational training needs, informal hit-and-miss methods are still relied upon in many firms. The reason for this lies in the enormous difficulty of determining some less obvious training needs. For example, the fact that numerous accidents occur in a plant may not necessarily mean that a safety training program will reduce the number of accidents. The accidents may be caused by faulty equipment or even poor supervision rather than employee negligence. If employees seem dissatisfied with their supervisors, teaching supervisors human relations will not necessarily lead to increased employee satisfaction if company personnel policies or organizational structure influence supervisors to violate the principles they are taught. If a new employee takes too long to learn how to perform his job, intensive training may not improve his performance if he was selected for a job for which he had little aptitude. Many factors complicate the process of identifying some specific training needs in an organization.

Despite certain limitations, there are some signals which are commonly accepted as being indicative of a need for training. Accident rates, employee dissatisfaction, high turnover, excessive absenteeism, high scrap waste, and other such data may be collected from records and may indicate areas in which training would be beneficial; however, statistics by themselves, without further investigation, do not firmly establish needs. Face-to-face meetings with the personnel having difficulty may reveal useful information that pinpoints specific training needs. In some cases, training may not be the answer. A solution to a problem often lies in changed procedures or methods of operation suggested by the people having to cope with the problem.

Even after careful scrutiny of statistics and conferences with the appropriate personnel in the organization there are times when training needs are not determined because the root of the trouble is still hidden. In most cases careful investigation will uncover and identify the training needs. William McGehee and Paul Thayer suggest that the planning of an organizational training program include the following threefold analyses:

1. *Organizational analysis:* determining where within the organization training emphasis can and should be placed.
2. *Operations analysis:* determining what should be the content of training in terms of what an employee must do to perform a task, job, or assignment in an effective way.
3. *Man analysis:* determining what skills, knowledge, or attitudes an individual employee must develop if he is to perform the tasks which constitute his job in the organization [9, p. 25].

The systematic threefold investigation suggested by McGehee and Thayer is helpful in locating general activities that require training and to help identify personnel who can benefit most from training programs.

Most profit-making organizations are concerned with motivating employees, new and old, to maintain high production standards. Even in firms committed to sound human relations practices it would be shortsighted to pay an employee high wages, encourage him to participate in company affairs, and then expect him to perform a job for which he was inadequately trained; therefore, training is an integral part of the human relations practiced in an organization. Not all employees require the same degree of training. In some minimum-skill jobs, adequate training can be provided in either a few hours or a few days on the job. In other, more technical jobs, the training process may take months or even years and require classroom instruction, as well as on-the-job experience. The development of personnel to fill some top administrative positions may take half a working lifetime.

One of the reasons many business firms try to hire men for management positions with as much education and job experience as possible in the fields in which it has positions available is to reduce the time and expense in developing managers. Hiring seasoned managers is not always possible with today's industry-wide demand for capable and experienced managers. A firm usually must provide training for its own management personnel so that as vacancies occur in higher levels of the organization it will have a man within its own ranks ready to move up. A business needs to be concerned with training at all levels in the organization, not just with management; but training programs for rank-and-file workers pose different problems than those posed at the management level. *Training* at lower levels in the organization usually is accomplished by instruction, drill, and discipline on the job and this is in contrast to the *development* of managers which emphasizes a maturing and growth in the individual's capacity to operate and make decisions; thus, different techniques must be employed. Before the methods used in training can be determined, the nature of the skills and knowledge required by the job must be established. Then training can be designed to provide the necessary skill with a minimum waste of effort, time, and money.

CHANGE IN TRAINING NEEDS AT DIFFERENT LEVELS IN THE ORGANIZATION

Organizational structure is often alluded to as a pyramid because of the relatively few people in top-level positions when compared with the larger number of persons filling positions beneath (see Figure 12–1). Top-ranking positions are usually easy to identify because they are few in number and the title of the positions indicate their importance. Members of management who occupy positions in middle echelons of the organization are more difficult to label because of the diversity of titles assigned to the positions in middle management and the wide latitude of responsibility and authority delegated to each position. It must be recognized that the term *middle manager* is often a convenient means of categorizing the management positions which are neither top-ranking nor in the first line of supervision.

First-line supervisors are the lowest-ranking members of the management hierarchy, being the first line of management to have direct authority over the rank-and-file workers. Most commonly, first-line supervisors are called production foremen, office supervisors, or some other term denoting the activity or function that is their primary responsibility.

Rank-and-file workers are also known as *operative employees.* They have no authority over any other personnel in the organization. There are instances when a worker will be appointed by his supervisor to lead other rank-and-file employees on some work project, but this practice of delegation does not technically make that worker part of the management hierarchy.

The use of the organizational pyramid as a model illustrates the varying levels of authority and responsibility to be found in an organization,

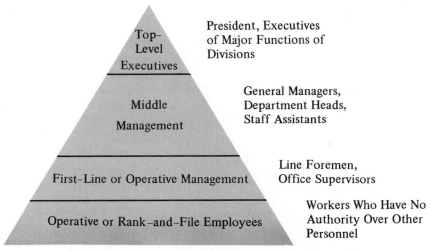

FIGURE 12–1. Traditional Organizational Pyramid.

but it does not identify the differences in the skills and knowledge required at each level. Some generalizations about the differences can be made when the activities of the personnel occupying positions at each level are analyzed.

Emerging Organizational Structure and Changes in Training

The organizational pyramid shown in Figure 12–1 serves to illustrate the traditional organizational hierarchy. There are some trends in industry which appear to be modifying the usual shape of the pyramid. The impact of technology is reducing the number of unskilled or semiskilled jobs at the rank-and-file level. Some organizations have found their middle ranks being expanded by an increased number of technicians, engineers, scientists, and administrative personnel. At the middle and upper echelons, there is a growing tendency toward team and committee decision-making groups. Modern industrial leadership is so complex that chief executives need the combined judgment of several top line and staff managers who share a corporate-wide view of the organization's operations even though they are responsible for specific functions or areas of management.

The result of the trend toward elimination of minimum-skill jobs at the lower ranks of the firm and the growing numbers in middle positions is the reshaping of the organizational pyramid. In Figure 12–2, the emerging organizational pyramid is superimposed on the traditional one so that a comparison can be easily made. The implications of this emerging organizational structure touches the training and development of personnel

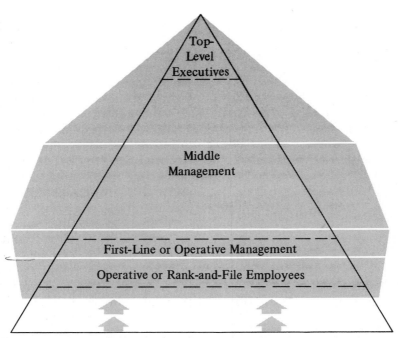

Unskilled Jobs Being Displaced by Automation and Technology
Workers being upgraded through training, retraining, and counseling.

FIGURE 12–2. Emerging Organizational Pyramid Superimposed on Traditional Organizational Pyramid.

at every level in the organization. Workers at lower levels must be upgraded through training, and middle management personnel need to be developed in such a way that their view of organizational problems is not confined to the perspectives of their own specialized function.

Most of the jobs at the rank-and-file level require that greater emphasis be placed on competence both in motor skills and in computational and other technical skills. In addition to training in the foregoing areas, safety training should be included as an integral part of the total training program if the job involves working around mechanical or hazardous apparatus and surroundings.

Despite the fact that rank-and-file training most often emphasizes the development of technical or manual skills, modern trends in industry and management call for an expansion of training programs to include the development of other creative capabilities in workers. If workers are expected to contribute to organizational effectiveness and efficiency through participation in group planning and decision-making, then training must expand the workers' perspective enough to allow their contribution to be more than superficial. To aid in the achievement of meaningful employee participation, training for even rank-and-file employees should include elements that increase their interpersonal competence and information that increases their awareness of the internal systems and external social, economic, and political forces that affect the operations of the firm. Without neglecting the technical training that operative workers need in order to perform their jobs, training should also provide them with the conceptual and interpersonal skills which make them more flexible and intelligible in company affairs.

As a man ascends the organizational hierarchy, jobs usually require more skill. At higher levels jobs are also less repetitious, have less routine, and allow for greater discretion and choice. This change may require more skill, and in most cases it requires different skills. The difference lies in the domain of both interpersonal and conceptual competence. *Conceptual skills* include the ability to think analytically, apply the scientific method in solving problems (Chapter 3), and make decisions objectively. *Interpersonal skills* refer to the effectiveness with which group members can work together as a cohesive work unit. Some authors refer to interpersonal competence as how well a person gets along with others. There is nothing basically incorrect about this statement, but it does oversimplify the situation. Effectiveness in a group involves other attributes besides personal charm. Knowledge and skill in one's field and an understanding of group dynamics are also components of interpersonal effectiveness.

Not all jobs require sophisticated social skills, but within an organizational context, an individual's effectiveness is highly related to his ability to work with others. No matter whether his job requires manipulation of tools and materials, development of ideas and abstract concepts, or primary face-to-face relations with clients, subordinates, or superiors, the full attainment of his potential effectiveness and satisfaction will be inhibited unless his human relations skills permit him to communicate and respond to others.

Figure 12–3 illustrates the change in the relative importance of three major categories of skills and knowledge that affect job performance at various levels in the organization. As one rises in the organizational hierarchy, emphasis on human and conceptual skills and awareness of the international and external forces that exert pressure on the firm's operations increases. There are exceptions to this generalization in certain staff or technical positions, but this characteristic is common enough to act as a guide in the development of training programs in most industrial organizations.

The diversity of skills required in each position and at each level adds to the complexity of rationalizing the training needs of a company so that they can be incorporated into an integrated and continuous program. In order to conceptualize a company's total training program, several factors should be determined. First, what degree of skill is required in each of

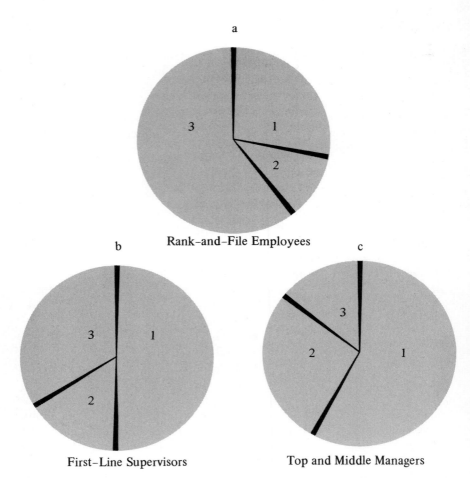

Rank-and-File Employees

First-Line Supervisors   Top and Middle Managers

1. Conceptual and Interpersonal Skills: communications, planning, organizing, decision making, directing, instructing, discipline.

2. Knowledge of Organization and External Systems: company policies, labor relations, political, economic and social conditions.

3. Technical Skills and Knowledge: quality control, cost control, manual skills, safety, equipment operation.

FIGURE 12–3. Relative Importance of Skills and Knowledge Affecting Job Performance.

the three major areas of competence affecting the worker's performance in a particular job? It has already been stated that not all jobs and all or-ganizational levels require the same degree of interpersonal effectiveness, technological skill, or sophistication in understanding the internal and external systems affecting the organization. Therefore, standards of per-formance in each area need to be carefully established so that they are both realistic and meaningfully related to the particular job in question.

252

Second, what degree of competence does the individual possess who is going to fill a particular position? This factor poses the problem of measuring the achievement or knowledge of an applicant so that it can be compared with the job requirements. In some instances this is not difficult, particularly when the attributes in question are observable and measurable, such as manual dexterity or manipulative skills; but in some other activities where the human attributes to be measured are less demonstrable, the problem often has to be resolved by the subjective judgment of a supervisor or by some staff expert.

A third factor in the rationalization of a training program is the determination of the methods that are to be used to provide employees, rank and file or manager, with necessary knowledge and skill in each major area of competence so that they can meet the performance standards of their jobs.

Table 12–1 indicates the relationship between each major area of competence important to job performance and some of the sciences and disciplines which contribute to that competence. In Column III, examples of topics are listed that are typically covered by company training. The list of sciences and disciplines which appear in Column II is not all-inclusive. Many more might be added. The same is true of the examples given of the specific subjects that are commonly found in company training programs.

The sciences and disciplines listed in Column II are categorized in accordance with the major area of competence to which they have the most obvious relationship; however, it should be understood that the groupings are only a convenience and that a high relationship exists between many of the sciences. For example, although political science is useful in understanding the political climate which is external to the organization, it is also useful in explaining the drive for power within the ranks of the organization. Psychology is not only useful in helping to understand the actions of fellow workers, but also in deciphering the motives and behavior of individuals outside of the organization, such as customers and competitors. Therefore, the disciplines listed in Column II have multiple applications and should not be construed to be useful in only one major area of competence.

A few words should be given to clarify the fact that one individual need not master all the sciences and disciplines listed or all the topics listed in order to be proficient in the performance of his job. A general knowledge and understanding of each would be useful, but not mandatory. A person may only need depth in one or two disciplines and a working acquaintance with some of the others. The sciences, disciplines, and subjects that are important to a particular job have to be determined through careful analysis so that training can concentrate on making up deficiencies an employee might have in those areas.

TABLE 12–1. Relationship Between Major Areas of Competence Affecting Job Performance and Company Training Programs

Column I	Column II	Column III
Major Areas of Competence Important to Job Performance	Examples of Sciences and Disciplines Which Contribute to Competence in Job Performance	Examples of Specific Subjects or Topics Which Can Be Given in Company Training Programs
Human relations skill and interpersonal competence	Anthropology Psychology Sociology Other social and behavioral sciences Philosophy Verbal and written communications Human relations	Leadership and supervisory techniques Sensitivity training Conference leadership methods Theory of learning Communications skills (verbal and written)
Technical skills and knowledge	Accounting Engineering Finance Industrial relations Marketing Personnel administration Production management Public relations Statistics Research and development Qualitative analysis	Manual skills Computational skills Safety training Cost control Salesmanship Equipment operation Traffic management Clerical procedures
Operating systems: Internal: social, technical and administrative systems designed and controlled by the organization	Decision theory Labor relations Operations research Organizational theory Probability theory Systems analysis	Orientation training Company history and development Production scheduling Supervisory training in provisions of the company collective bargaining contract
External: environmental factors which are beyond the control of the organization	Economics Money and banking Geography History courses Law classes Political science Foreign languages Literature courses	Classes in basic economics and other subjects which add to the worker's understanding of the company's role in the community, industry, and society

TRAINING METHODS

The determination of the most appropriate training methods to be used in a particular training program is influenced by many factors. Before a final decision can be made regarding the actual method of instruction, several questions should be answered. What has to be taught? Who is to be trained? How many people are to be included in training? How much time should be allowed for training? What equipment, facilities, and resources are available for these purposes? Who is going to conduct the actual training sessions? In each company the answers to these questions will be different and the choice of methods might vary; however, the ultimate choice of methods will usually fall into one of four categories: (1) on-the-job training, (2) classroom instruction, (3) some combination of the two, and (4) supplemental or individual study. Each of these methods has its advantages and limitations and the effectiveness of each will vary depending on what is to be taught, the aptitude, interest and ability of the trainees, and the competence of the instructor.

On-the-Job Training.   The most common method of training used in industry is on-the-job training (OJT). This method offers several advantages, from a cost standpoint, to the company, and from a human relations viewpoint much is to be gained from it. This method of training is one in which the employee's immediate superior, or some person who is designated by him, actually instructs the new worker in the skills, procedures, and tasks related to the job. The worker is placed in an environment that is a real one; that is, he is actually producing and using the same equipment, materials, and techniques that the job requires. He is involved in the productive process from the very beginning. On-the-job training has the advantage of allowing the worker's superior to have direct personal contact with him from the early stages of instruction. This period provides an opportunity for rapport to develop between them, and allows the supervisor to evaluate and correct the course of the learning process as it occurs. This coaching by the superior provides the trainee with both face-to-face contact with his boss and an opportunity to learn the standards of performance and behavior expected of him. This method allows the trainee to practice in precisely the same conditions, both social and physical, that will prevail when his formal training period is completed. In other words, the trainee learns by doing, which most learning experts agree is the best way to learn certain motor tasks. The trainee follows the day-to-day operating plans of the work unit and is given a chance to associate with his fellow workers from the start of his employment.

There are drawbacks to this approach. Because the trainee may lack experience, production errors or mistakes in judgment may occur and hinder the quality or quantity of production. Although on-the-job training does not require additional capital investment in special equipment, there are other costs which can accrue. Scrap wastes, worker injuries, underuse of machinery, overtime or delays in production schedules caused by inexperienced operators can add to increased costs of production. At first glance these considerations seem to be primarily allied to accounting rather than to human relations. They are cost factors to be sure; however, new or inexperienced trainees who are aware of their own inefficiencies that contribute to higher costs and delays may feel anxious about their contribution to these factors. The trainee anxiety may interfere rather than enhance the learning process and add to training time unless the supervisor explains that such deficiencies are normal in the early stages of training. Such assurance may not be forthcoming from a supervisor who is pressured by a tight production schedule and, therefore, is too harried to pay proper attention to training. When this occurs, one of the major limitations of on-the-job training is that production is placed before learning.

Another drawback to on-the-job training lies in the fact that often supervisors are not acquainted with methods of instruction or how the learning process takes place in the worker. This lack of sophistication on the part of supervisors compounds the difficulty of training, and potentially good workers are labeled by the supervisor as lazy, slow, or disinterested. When this occurs, chances are that good rapport will not develop and that this will affect their relationship long after the training period is over.

Classroom Training. Classroom training has certain advantages when instructing workers on theories, concepts, and policies of the company. Classroom training may involve regular group meetings in which instruction is given by a special instructor or short "stand-up" meetings of the work group conducted by their immediate supervisor. The primary characteristic of classroom instruction is that employees are not expected to produce, at least in a monetary sense, while training is being given.

Some types of training may best be handled in a classroom situation if there are enough new employees to warrant holding such training in groups. During *induction* or *orientation* training, new groups of employees can be given the history and background of the company, tours of the facilities, and other instruction that help familiarize them with the organization and their place in it. Sales training, management development, supervisor work shops, safety training, and other aspects of the training program are often handled best in a classroom or conference setting where audiovisual aids, group discussions, or lectures can be employed in the process.

One variation of classroom training for rank-and-file workers is called *vestibule training*. In this method the trainee uses the same or similar equipment, materials, and procedures that are used on the regular production line, but the training area is removed from the immediate production area so as not to hinder the work of the production department. The main advantage of this type of training is that emphasis can be placed on learning rather than on production. This helps eliminate the anxiety that some new workers would feel when placed immediately on the production line. Yet the trainee still has a chance to learn by doing the tasks associated with his job. The worker also has an opportunity to adapt to the job and work environment before having to take his place in the production department. This is particularly advantageous when the work environment is unusually noisy or the operation of machinery may be dangerous for inexperienced workers.

Vestibule training has its shortcomings. The trainee will have to adjust to a new supervisor, work group, and physical environment when he has completed training. Frequently the machines used in instruction are outdated and not used in the production line; thus the trainee finds that he is unfamiliar with the equipment he is assigned to in the production department. Unless care is taken to insure that the same standards of performance that are required on the job have to be met during vestibule training, the worker may find himself frustrated by the pace and standards he encounters on the job. The same principle applies to any simulation training device or method where the trainee is placed in a situation which is intended to prepare him for actual conditions found on the job.

Classroom training for managers has certain benefits which cannot be duplicated on the job. Because classroom training occurs when the manager trainee is not on the job, the trainee may find that he can take a more objective look at what he does in his job and exchange ideas with men in other departments who face similar problems. This exchange of ideas may result in the trainee developing solutions of a different nature than he would have thought of by himself to the day-to-day problems he encounters. Management development can be facilitated by training workshops that are held by the company, on or off the company premises, or by actually sending managers and supervisors to seminars or classes conducted by colleges or other professional institutions and associations. The primary benefit of this method is that it exposes the trainee to new ideas which broaden his perspective or add to his appreciation of the problems of management faced by men in other positions or other companies.

While classroom training for rank-and-file and management personnel has advantages, there are certain disadvantages. Many skills cannot be

Photo by Hugh Rogers. Reproduced by permission of the Monkmeyer Press Photo Service.

Photo by Zimbel. Reproduced by permission of the Monkmeyer Press Photo Service.

The method of training must be geared to the subject and the capabilities of the student.

learned in the classroom situation. The classroom situation may be artificial and, in effect, distort the realities that must be accommodated on the job. The noise, distractions, and interruptions that occur in the actual job environment may be factors the trainee must learn to tolerate, just as he must master specific body or hand motions and intellectual responses.

Another drawback of classroom instruction has to do with the nature of human mental processes; that is, retention of most learned material is very short-lived unless the material is used or otherwise reinforced periodically. Unless classroom material is closely related to the actual physical and mental activity performed on the job, much of it will be forgotten by the trainee.

Combination of Methods.   Classroom training takes the man away from his job, and on-the-job methods do not provide the freedom of time or objectivity because of job pressures; therefore, many firms utilize a means of combining the two methods so that the experience gained on the job is supplemented by periodic classroom instruction. The primary example of this combination for operative employees occurs in *apprenticeship* training. While the provisions for classroom training differ in various trades and crafts, usually the apprentice works full time on the job and is required to take classes in night school about four hours a week. The period of apprenticeship may last from two to six years, at which time those who satisfactorily complete the training program are issued a certificate of completion. Provisions for apprenticeship training in which standards of performance on the job are determined are usually worked out by the labor union with employers.

Other combination methods of training may be inaugurated by the company to provide supplemental instruction to employees and prepare them for advancement. This method is useful in breaking the day-to-day routine of many jobs for employees and provides an opportunity for the individual worker to obtain an insight to his own job which he might not otherwise have a chance to develop.

Independent or Supplemental Study.   The methods of providing employees a chance to develop their own potential are many. Some companies encourage workers to attend classes in adult school or college by reimbursing employees who satisfactorily complete approved classes. The reimbursement may pay for the entire cost of the class, including tuition, textbooks, and other materials, or some portion of the cost.

Many companies encourage employees to take correspondence courses. Courses in technical fields, humanities, and social sciences are available in large numbers and provide the individual a chance to work on them at their own pace at home without facing the possible embarrassment of reciting before others in a classroom situation.

Teaching machines and programmed texts have broadened the opportunity for many employees to learn at their own pace, with no set time limit or student competition. Some companies have developed short programmed instructional materials to help supplement other methods of training in basic industrial skills. Programmed instruction texts use a method of presenting short bits of information to the reader. Questions are asked about the written material and as quickly as the reader can answer them he can move on to more written material. The questions which follow each section of written material are not designed to test the reader's knowledge so much as they are to reinforce the information presented in the written text. The students can progress as rapidly as they wish or repeat sections in the text as often as they like until they have mastered the material.

Mechanical visual devices being developed and perfected by major electronics companies utilize video-tape and closed-circuit television for instruction. As these electronic devices become economically feasible for more firms, it will be possible for large numbers of employees to participate in educational and technical programs in their own home or at learning statious located in various places throughout the company plant.

Some companies have suggested reading lists of books or articles which are believed helpful to managers or technical personnel. The reading lists usually include both topics which are relevant to the employee's own field and some which are more general in nature. Employees can, at their own discretion, read the suggested books with no obligation to make book reports. In some instances, informal group meetings are held in which interested persons can discuss the books they have read.

Safety Training. Safety training may begin with employee orientation and be incorporated in classroom or on-the-job training procedures. Such training is particularly important to employees involved in a hazardous working environment in which high-speed machines are used during the work process or in which they are exposed to high-voltage electrical equipment. Even in situations where the job itself may not be dangerous—traveling salesmen, truck drivers, rolling equipment operators, and so on—the supervisor must insure that safety procedures are followed. He can do this by stimulating employees toward attitudes of safety consciousness for themselves and also for others.

Many large companies have staff specialists or consultants who are responsible for safety training and maintenance of safe working conditions. The job of maintaining safe working conditions must go beyond the engineering of machines and safety equipment. Safety training designed to accomplish a safe job environment requires making safe working habits a part of each employee's job training. The supervisor must involve each employee in a continuous safety training program. To do this a supervisor may find the following suggestions useful not only in training, but in stimulating employees toward voluntary adherence to safety regulations and procedures:

1. Help employees see the need for safe working habits by explaining consequences, such as accidents, when safe working procedures are violated.

2. Involve all employees in solving safety problems and establishing safe working standards.

3. Give recognition to workers who follow safe working procedures.

4. Stimulate safety consciousness in employees by making safe work a part of each group member's job goals.

5. Share responsibility for safety with all members of the work group.

THEORIES ON TEACHING

All of the methods used in both the formal and informal company training programs are intended to provide information and to develop employee skills in the quickest and most productive way. In the majority of cases training involves having someone do the instructing. Whether instruction is provided on the job by a supervisor or by a teacher in a classroom situation, the person should possess some understanding of the learning process if he is to employ the most effective means of instruction. The implication of this fact is that anyone in the organization who is going to have the responsibility of training others should be provided with training in learning theory and methods of instruction. To overlook this point is to relegate the success of the total training program to the effectiveness of supervisors and managers who may have little understanding of one of their fundamental responsibilities.

Although there is a plethora of research and literature on theories of learning, there is a surprisingly limited amount of proved evidence to substantiate them as they apply to industrial training. Most theories are based on a premise that important features of human learning are found in animals. Although this may be basically true, some education theorists point out that human beings transcend, in many ways, animal learning patterns [3, p. 40].

The problem in attempting to define a neat theory of learning lies in the many aspects of motivation which are involved in learning, and research has not yet been able to relate them all into a single cause-effect relationship in the learning process. Although there are theoretical questions about the importance of motivation in learning, there is general agreement that a motivated learner learns better than an unmotivated one [11, p. 277].

Rather than attempt a discussion of all the pros and cons of various learning theories which describe what has happened to the student's behavior *after* he has learned, this section of the chapter will concentrate on a few points concerned with how material or skills that are to be taught can best be learned by the trainee with the idea of improving rather than describing the learning process. Jerome Bruner has developed a list of features which are concerned with the process of instruction rather than learning. His theory of instruction is congruent with other theories of learning and development, only the emphasis is prescriptive rather than descriptive in the sense that it sets forth rules concerning the most effective ways of achieving knowledge or skill.

Bruner states that a theory of instruction has four major features. Essentially, they relate to an understanding by the instructor of (1) the student's predisposition to learning, (2) the structure of information to be taught, (3) the most appropriate sequence of information to be taught, and (4) the nature and pace of the rewards given to the student [2, pp. 40–41].

Predisposition Toward Learning. The experiences which most effectively implant in the student a predisposition toward learning should be specified. For example, what sorts of relationships with peers, superiors, and the company will tend to make the new employee willing and able to learn when training begins. There are a large number of variables which affect the predisposition to learn in an individual. Age, sex, intelligence, aptitudes, interests, personal goals, and initiative are all factors which affect not only what a person will learn, but also how long he or she will take to learn. This feature of instruction is known as taking into consideration the individual differences of the students. It might be added that the supervisor or instructor can do little to change many of the individual differences found in the learner, but if these differences are known, they can be used as guides in selecting the methods of instruction which will be most effective.

Structure of Information to Be Taught. A body of knowledge should be structured so that it can most readily be grasped by the learner. How should information be broken down and simplified for convenience of learning? Here it is important to remember that the optimal structure or simplification of a body of knowledge is not absolute, but relative, and that it should always be structured to the status and ability of the learner. The major implication of this feature of a theory of instruction is that the individualization of instructional materials should be based on what is to be taught and to whom. Not all materials are of the same magnitude of difficulty, nor do all students possess the same degree of aptitude and ability; thus, instruction has to be geared to accommodate both the materials covered and the ability of the student.

Appropriateness of Sequence of Information to Be Taught. The most effective sequences in the presentation of materials should be specified. Normally, it is wise to present material in a sequence which goes from the simple to the complex or from what the student already knows to the unknown; however, the realities of many jobs do not present tasks in this sequence. Because the tasks involved in a job to be taught to a trainee do not necessarily fall into a simple-to-complex sequence of events, how should such tasks be taught? Suppose a particular job to be taught to a trainee is comprised of six separate operations, each with a different degree of difficulty to perform; furthermore, the sequence of the tasks does not run from simple to complex. What would be the most ideal means of teaching the whole job to a trainee? The ideal arrangement of the operations is shown in line 1 of Figure 12–4, and the normal arrangement found on the job is given on line 2. The degree of difficulty is indicated by the size of the circle, and the sequence of the way they should be presented is indicated by the number within the circle. The instructor can still teach the job in the normal sequence and, at the same time, teach the easier parts first by setting up a teaching plan in which the first time through the series he does the most difficult tasks and allows the learner to do the simpler ones. Each succeeding time through the series the instructor permits the trainee to do a more difficult task, until finally he has performed all of the operations in the proper sequence that they are performed on the job; yet he began by learning the easiest tasks first and then proceeded through each operation of increased difficulty.

Nature and Pace of Rewards Given to Student. The nature and pacing of rewards and punishment used in the learning process should be determined. No doubt there is a point in the learning process when it is better to shift away from such extrinsic rewards as praise from the instructor towards the intrinsic rewards which are inherent in the achievement of some difficult task or comprehension of a complex concept. The timing of this shift is important, but unfortunately, it is not well understood.

There are more uncertainties about how to shift from extrinsic rewards to intrinsic ones, and the problems connected with transferring immediate rewards to longer-range need satisfaction ought to be resolved in each individual situation, but the use of rewards seems to be relatively simple: Behavior which seems to lead to reward tends to be repeated, whereas

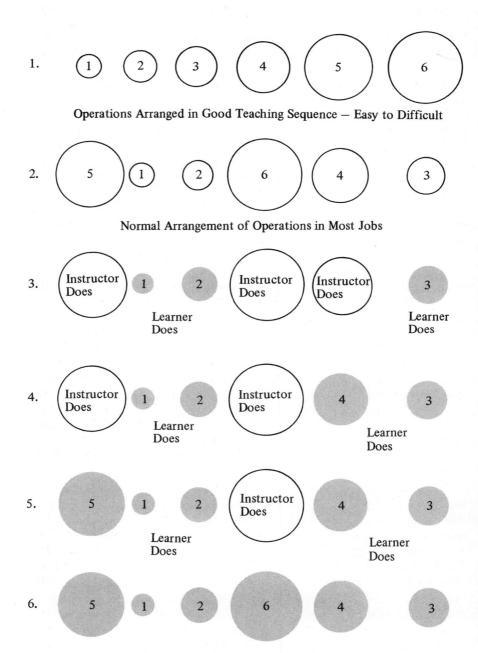

1. Operations Arranged in Good Teaching Sequence — Easy to Difficult

2. Normal Arrangement of Operations in Most Jobs

Learner Does All Operations — Supervisor Checks Closely

FIGURE 12–4. How to Teach a Difficult Operation.

behavior which seems not to lead to rewards or seems to lead to punishment tends not to be repeated. Psychologists often refer to this principle
as the "law of effect."

Because the job of training is directed toward changing behavior—
that is, getting workers to perform in certain ways—the concept of reward
and punishment is an important factor in the role that supervisors or
instructors play in the learning process. The role and place of supervisors
in the organizational hierarchy usually gives them control of the means
for need satisfaction for many workers. The supervisor, whether he is
conscious of it or not, is in a position to be constantly shaping the
behavior of his subordinates by the way in which he utilizes the rewards
at his disposal. This impact on the worker's behavior is far longer lasting
than just the duration of a formal training period; it influences the relationship which develops between the superior and his subordinates for as
long as they belong to the same work unit or organization. Therefore, it
is beneficial to the effectiveness of supervisors and instructors to understand more clearly what impact rewards have on group behavior patterns so that changes can be planned in advance, rather than merely
accepted after they have occurred.

Although learning is a process most individuals enjoy under the proper
circumstances and motivation, there are instances where training will be
resisted by employees. New employees may have difficulty learning
because of their unfamiliarity with the processes, concepts, or mechanical
skills being taught. However, this is not the same brand of resistance that
may occur among older workers who feel that training or retraining for
them implies that they were performing poorly before. In part, resistance
to training can be overcome by a careful explanation of the need for
training, and by careful planning of the methods of instruction that
are used.

The four factors outlined in the theory of instruction may help a
supervisor plan his methods of instruction more effectively, but there are
other ingredients in the teacher-student relationship which are not easily
outlined or qualified. The personal attributes which make up the
personality of a good instructor are no more clearly defined than the
"personality profile" of good leadership; however, a systematized method
of instruction is a useful device of new or inexperienced instructors until
they can get the feel of the teaching process and develop techniques
comfortable to them and their students. The following procedures, suggested for supervisors when instructing new subordinates in the operation
of their departments, are not intended to be inflexible or all-inclusive.
There are other methods which might be as effective in some situations,
but generally the following steps will help an instructor do a more
effective job of teaching if he has not developed a unique method of
presentation more appropriate in his situation.

Useful Steps for a Supervisor in the Process of Instruction

I. *Prepare* the worker for instruction.

A. Put him at ease. He cannot think straight if he is embarrassed or scared.

B. Find out what he already knows about the job. Start where his knowledge ends by relating what is to be learned to what he already knows.

C. Get him interested. Relate his job or operation to the final product so he knows his work is important. The desire to learn comes only after interest is stimulated.

D. Put him in the right position. Make certain he can see the job from an angle from which he will work; do not have him see the job backwards.

II. *Present* the operation.

A. Explain, demonstrate, illustrate, and ask questions of the why, when, where, what, and who variety.

B. Put it in small doses. Few people learn six or seven new ideas at one time and understand them.

C. Make the key points clear. Understanding the key points will add to his understanding of the flow and sequence of the operations he is performing.

D. Be patient and go slowly. Get accuracy at first, then develop speed.

E. Point out danger points of the job and show how to do it safely.

F. Repeat job and any explanation necessary.

III. *Let him try out* the job.

A. Have him do the job under observation.

B. Have him do it again, explaining to you what he is doing and why. It is easy to observe motions and not really understand what you are doing. Teach him to understand what he is doing and why.

C. Have him explain the key points.

D. Correct errors. Do not be hypercritical of small mistakes, but be sure he does the job safely. If he develops methods of doing the job which are as effective as the ones you were going to teach him, allow him to use them, but be sure such methods will not cause the trainee to form sloppy habits or do poor work.

E. Continue I and II until he knows the whole operation. He may have to do the job several times before he masters each separate operation.

IV. *Follow up* and evaluate.

A. Put him on his own. Let him get the feel of the job by doing it himself.

B. Tell him to whom to go when he needs help. Make this definite; designate someone. The wrong person may not give him correct answers or advice and the trainee may learn to do the job incorrectly.

C. Check his progress frequently, from every few minutes at the beginning to every few hours and then every few days. Be on the watch for incorrect and unnecessary actions; repress any urge to take over and do the job yourself. If you must, do it only when it is necessary to show a point.

D. Get him to look for key points as he progresses. Be sure he knows them.

E. Taper off the extra coaching as he is able to work under normal supervision.

The foregoing steps are generally accepted as appropriate when instructing trainees in operations or skills which are demonstrable and observable. The instructional procedures in this case follow, in a large measure, the features of a sound theory of instruction; but there are areas of training and development in which such procedures would not be appropriate. Many modes of behavior expected in the employee are not easily broken into tangible and separate steps. Conceptual and human relations skills are examples of instances where the preceding method in instruction would not be applicable.

In the next chapter some methods and problems associated with human relations training will be explored. Even though the techniques of instruction may differ from those described in teaching operative skills, the principles of instruction which were explained earlier in this chapter still apply to human relations training.

SUMMARY

1. Training concepts in modern industry have changed from those envisioned by the efficiency experts of Taylor's day. Today, industrial training programs encompass activities ranging from the acquisition of a single motor skill to the development of complex technical knowledge and administrative skills. Many factors have contributed to the need for expanding the scope of training programs. The rapid growth and change of technology require the constant updating of knowledge and skills in employees. The general need for the development of specialized skills by organizational members requires training not ordinarily provided in schools and, thus, it must be provided in company training programs.

2. In order to determine the training needs of a particular firm, McGehee and Thayer suggest a threefold analysis which includes an organizational analysis, an operational analysis, and a man analysis. Information obtained from such an overview of the firm will help in the planning of a company training program.

3. The training needs found at each level in the organizational hierarchy may differ in the degree to which emphasis will be placed on conceptual skills, interpersonal skills, technical skills, or knowledge of the internal and external operating systems affecting the organization. Usually the skill requirements in each of these areas changes as one ascends the organizational ladder, and training programs must accommodate the change if men are to be adequately prepared to handle increased responsibility and authority.

4. The diversity of skills required in each position and at each echelon in the organization requires that several factors be determined so that they can be integrated into the company's training program. (1) What degree of skill is required in each of the following areas: conceptual skills, interpersonal skills, technical skills, internal and external operational systems? (2) What degree of skill in each of these areas does the individual possess? (3) What methods will increase the skill of trainees in each of these areas to the necessary level in the shortest time and in the least expensive way?

5. A variety of training methods are used in industry. The majority of industrial training programs utilize on-the-job methods in which the trainee learns as he produces. Other training methods are classroom instruction, some combination of on-the-job training and classroom training, and, in certain circumstances, individual study. Each of these methods has both advantages and drawbacks and must be selected on the basis of how well they meet the needs of the individual and the organization.

6. Whether training is to be given on the job or in a classroom situation, a large part of its success will depend upon the ability of the instructor. Therefore, training on teaching methods and learning theory is often necessary for supervisors and other organizational members who are responsible for the training and development of subordinates. Many aspects of learning theory are in need of further research because the cause and effect relationships in the learning process are not entirely understood. Despite the limitations of present understanding about the learning process, a theory of instruction is useful to both classroom instructors and on-the-job trainers. One theory of instruction has been developed by Bruner which considers the following four features: (1) the student predisposition toward learning, (2) the structure of the information to be taught, (3) the sequence of the information to be taught, and (4) the nature and pace of the rewards.

7. Based on the information known regarding each of the four features contained in Bruner's theory of instruction, the following steps in the process of instruction are useful to the trainer: (1) prepare the worker for instruction, (2) present the operation or subject matter, (3) let the worker try out his performance, and (4) follow up and evaluate the learner's progress. When the subject to be taught is either demonstrable or one which requires motor skills in manipulation, the four steps in the process of instruction will probably be a valuable aid; however, when the skills or knowledge to be taught are more conceptual or abstract in nature, other methods may be more appropriate and effective.

DISCUSSION QUESTIONS

1. What outside social, economic, and political influences affect the training programs of large industrial firms? Do the same outside influences affect the training programs of small (fifty or less employees) firms? If so, in what way? If not, why not?

2. What impact has technology had on industrial training? What implications for human relations training has the increase in technology had?

3. In what ways do training requirements differ between the rank-and-file and supervisory positions?

4. How should training in conceptual skills be handled in a company training program?

5. What advantages are there to sending managers to a two-month professional management training seminar conducted in a large university? What disadvantages?

6. What aspects of supervisory training might be different from the training given to middle management?

7. Why is it important for supervisors to receive training in methods of instruction?

8. What should be done by an instructor to prepare a student for training?

BIBLIOGRAPHY AND SELECTED COLLATERAL READINGS

1. BASS, B. M., and J. A. VAUGHAN, Training in Industry: The Management of Learning. Belmont, Calif.: Wadsworth Publishing, 1966.
2. BRUNER, JEROME S., Toward a Theory of Instruction. Cambridge, Mass.: The Belknap Press of Harvard University Press, 1966.

3. DE GRAZIA, ALFRED, and DAVID A. SOHN (eds.), *Programs, Teachers, and Machines*. New York: Bantam Books, 1964.

4. GOMERSALL, EARL R., and M. SCOTT MYERS, "Breakthrough in On-the-Job Training," *Harvard Business Review*, Vol. 44, No. 4 (July–August, 1966), 62–72.

5. HAIRE, MASON, *Psychology in Management*, 2nd ed. New York: McGraw-Hill Book Company, 1964.

6. HALSEY, GEORGE D., *Selecting and Developing First-Line Supervisors*. New York: Harper & Row, 1955.

7. MAGER, ROBERT F., *Preparing Objectives for Programmed Instruction*. San Francisco: Fearon Publishers, 1962.

8. MAHLER, W. R., and W. H. MONROE, *How Industry Determines the Need for an Effectiveness of Training*. New York: The Psychological Corporation, 1952.

9. MCGEHEE, WILLIAM, and PAUL W. THAYER, *Training in Business and Industry*. New York: John Wiley and Sons, 1964.

10. STRAUSS, GEORGE, and LEONARD R. SAYLES, *Personnel: The Human Problems of Management*, 2nd ed. Englewood Cliffs, N.J.: Prentice-Hall, Inc., 1967.

11. TIFFIN, JOSEPH, and ERNEST J. MCCORMICK, *Industrial Psychology*, 5th ed. Englewood Cliffs, N.J.: Prentice-Hall, Inc., 1965.

12. VENN, GRANT, *Man, Education, and Work*. Washington, D.C.: American Council on Education, 1964.

13

Methods of Training in Human Relations

HOW SHOULD HUMAN RELATIONS BE TAUGHT? TO WHOM? WHEN?

If one accepts any or all of the objectives of human relations mentioned in the first chapter, an important question arises. How can the perspective, skills, and abilities to use this tool effectively be developed? A question with serious overtones of skepticism is: Can human relations be taught? Isn't human relations, after all, just common sense?

Let us consider this last question before investigating some of the problems, ramifications, and solutions to the others. It is true that common sense plays a vital part in the practice of human relations just as it does in the exercise of any discipline or in resolving problem situations in our daily lives. To assume, however, that common sense alone is all that is necessary would be a gross oversimplification for several reasons. First, it assumes that everyone has the same commodity, known as common sense, and in the same proportion, which is not true. True, some people appear to have an intuitive sense of tact, diplomacy, and consideration; however, these traits are not universally distributed—at least not in equal proportions among mankind. If they were, perhaps the need for human relations courses would be substantially reduced. Also, common sense is, in part, developed as an outgrowth of our own experiences, and all people have not been exposed to the same set of circumstances or treatment. For example, how many supervisors utilize autocratic methods primarily because that is the type of supervisory treatment they were exposed to before becoming supervisors?

Now to the question, "Who should be taught human relations?" Earlier in this text it was mentioned that human relations was the responsibility of all members in an organization: top-ranking executive, first-line supervisor, and rank-and-file employee. It is true that the impact of certain members in a group is greater than others; however, this does not mean that the others have no impact by their behavior and actions. It follows, then, that in an organization the use and teaching of human relations cannot be confined solely to any particular level, but rather it should be universal. However, it is probably most essential to give human relations training to those organizational members who are directly responsible for the results of working groups, namely, at the supervisory level and at other levels where close interpersonal relations are essential to the effectiveness of group action. This automatically gives rise to the difficult question of how and when human relations should be taught.

The chairman of a large chain of restaurants who was reported as having made a large donation to Columbia University for a medical research building turned down a request for a small contribution to the same university's graduate school of business, of which he was an alumnus. The reason for his refusal was that, in his opinion, unlike engineering or medicine, the subject of business and of making decisions cannot be taught.

This businessman does not stand alone in his sentiments. Criticism of business education in general, not to mention criticism of the teaching of human relations, has caused concern about the content as well as the relevancy of business courses taught in our colleges and universities. The inquiries directed at the education of business executives in which criticisms and recommendations are made are the Gordon-Howell Report and the Pierson Report [5, pp. 173–209; 14, p. 227]. Both reports suggest courses dealing in some aspect of human relations for undergraduate business students.

Malcolm McNair does not fully agree with the recommendations sighted by the Gordon-Howell or Pierson Reports. In fact, he points out that there are dangers inherent in overemphasizing human relations. He states:

> Good human relations do not lend themselves to anatomical dissection with a scalpel. How do people normally acquire good human relations? Some of course never do. In the case of those who do enjoy success in human relations and at the same time retain their sincerity, the result, I am convinced, is a composite product of breeding, home, church, education, and experience generally, not of formal Human Relations courses.
>
> Hence, in my view it is a mistake in formal education to seek to do more than develop an awareness of human relations, preferably as an integral part of other problems [7, p. 706].

Despite the stormy problems involved, human relations courses are being taught in our junior colleges, colleges, and universities at both the undergraduate and graduate levels. In addition to our academic institutions, human relations training courses are conducted by business and industry at supervisory through executive levels. The curriculum, objectives, methods, and results vary widely when such factors as level of supervision, type of industry, particular firm, and instructor are taken into consideration. The diversity in content and methodology should not necessarily be construed as bad because, particularly in regard to training courses conducted in industry, each firm is generally in the best position to assess its own needs, time, and economic resources for such training.

Regardless of whether human relations training occurs in school or on the job, the ultimate goal has a lot to do with a change in the attitude on the part of the student. There are also several conditions we know are attendant to effective learning. One is that learning is built on previous experience. Another is that learning is most effective when closely related to the experience of the individual. This poses something of a problem in regard to students who have limited job experience; but few students attain college status without some job experience, and the rest certainly have had social contact with some form of group action wherein the findings of the behavioral sciences will be helpful in explaining the interactions they have seen and experienced.

TRAINING METHODS

The very nature of human relations, involving the interactions between people, has lent itself to some particularly useful methods of teaching. Most of the methods depend to some extent upon the participation of the students involved in the training session. Some of the methods commonly employed in human relations training are described below.

Case-Study Method. This technique was developed by law and business schools and most notably popularized by Harvard Business School. Case studies are now widely used in training courses in both schools and industry. Usually a realistic situation with pertinent facts is presented to the group. Because the members of the group are not personally involved in the problem, they can assume an objective viewpoint in deriving a solution.

Several objectives and benefits can be obtained through the use of the case-study method. The student's powers of observation, logic, and reasoning ability can be heightened through skillful instruction. He can also become aware of another person's viewpoint when a fellow student provides a different solution to the problem when given the same set of facts.

There are several pitfalls in the use of case studies. First, if the case is discussed verbally by the group rather than being written, the discussion can ramble off into nonessential topics. This can be minimized to a large extent by a skillful group leader. Another danger is that the students will try to solve the problem of the case in terms of black and white answers, trying to identify good and bad characters, rather than delve into the deeper, more important causes of the problem. Another potential weakness of the case method is that the case study used may be poor, unrealistic, or unrelated to what the students know or understand. Poor cases are not necessarily a weakness of the case method, but they can influence the results derived by using such a method; hence, if the best results are to be obtained, careful selection of case studies should be made to insure that they are pertinent and well written.

Incident Process Method.   The incident method is a variation of the case method developed by Paul and Faith Pigors. In the usual case method the entire problem is presented to the students, whereas in the incident method only a brief incident is presented. This particular method requires that the student seek additional information from the group leader, who is the only person who has the whole slate of pertinent facts before him. Normally, the students must ask for additional information which can be answered by a short factual statement. There are five phases or steps to the incident method.

1. *Presentation of the incident:* For example, a secretary says to her boss:

Here's the suggestion Mr. White said would be in the box.
MR. FRANKLIN: What does it say?
SECRETARY: (*After reading the suggestion aloud.*) This looks like a clear case of insubordination.
MR. FRANKLIN: It's more than that. Wilson has made a pest of himself by asking over and over again for next Friday off. He must think I'll give it to him if he keeps asking.
SECRETARY: What are you going to do with him now?
MR. FRANKLIN: I don't know yet, but I'll let you know. Right now I'm going over to discuss it with Mr. White.

This incident obviously needs further explanation, but it is the starting point from which the students seek the *facts* necessary to resolve the problem.

2. *Fact finding* through questions and discussion with the instructor: The students need to keep their questions directed toward the finding out of the facts pertaining to the case, not opinions. For example, in relation to the incident above, "Who is Mr. White?" or, "What did Wilson say on his suggestion?" Not, "Did Mr. Franklin like Wilson?" After questions and discussion one student summarizes the findings for the group.

3. *Defining the central issues:* The students decide what the main

problem of the case is, if possible. If not, they may have to backtrack and question the instructor for more facts so that the central issue can be defined.

4. *Arriving at a solution individually:* After the problem has been defined in step 3, each individual is asked to write out his decision briefly. This is then discussed by the group.

5. *Evaluation and generalizations:* The final step is to discuss the broader meaning of the case and the underlying causes for the problem so that suggestions for preventing a recurrence can be outlined.

The incident method when used for training purposes in human relations has the added feature usually not present in the case-study method of drawing the participants into the discussion with greater emotional involvement, especially in steps 3, 4, and 5 [15].

Role-Playing Method. Role playing, although developed through psychodrama, is a technique that has branched out broadly in adult education and supervisory and executive training. When carried out conscientiously as a device for creating changed attitudes and behavior, role playing is successful to the extent that it can be moved from the highly structured toward the unstructured and spontaneous. It is successful when it frees people from patterns of rigid thinking and acting and enables them to look at themselves and others in a new way—to see themselves as others see them. The development of empathy and sensitivity is one of the primary objectives of role playing.

The technique of role playing is one of creating a life situation, usually one involving conflicts between people, and then having members of the group play the parts or roles of specific personalities. Only the situation is given and the dialogue must spontaneously grow out of the situation created. Because no script is provided for the actors, the end result is open to the way the persons involved play their role. There is no rigid procedure to follow, even though problems may be set up so that conflicts can be resolved and thus end in some type of agreement.

One of the difficulties of role playing is overcoming the reluctance of fear of displaying inner feelings. This can be overcome to a large extent by the atmosphere that the instructor sets for the group and by explaining what the outcomes of role playing should be.

A number of the advantages of role playing are (1) it helps participants to appreciate other points of view, as when a student plays the part of a teacher; (2) the participants become involved emotionally, thus broaden their experience beyond the "logic and rationale" used in the solution of case studies; (3) because the participants usually are somewhat tense, they become more self-conscious and analytical of their own behavior than they normally would be in real life; and (4) it permits participants to use their imagination because there are no lines to memorize and they can improvise, and as they are not playing "for keeps," no harm is done if they make a mistake [20, p. 579].

Although a number of persons may participate in each role-playing situation, seldom can the whole group get involved without the result being chaos and loss of the effect of the process. However, Maier discusses a method known as *Multiple Role Playing* wherein the class is divided into smaller groups and each is given the same problem to play out. Thus, everyone can get firsthand experience in role playing and group decisions. A corollary benefit is that no particular group is embarrassed by being in the spotlight [9, p. 147]. Even the observers can benefit through a role-playing session from the discussion of the outcome and the mistakes that might have been made.

Group Discussion Methods.   The group discussion method is also referred to as *conference training*. Usually the size of the training group is kept small, below twenty, so that all members can participate in the discussion. This technique was developed and applied in industry during World War I. Recently it has been used frequently for human relations training of foremen and middle managers. The benefit of this method is that it escapes the limitation of straight lecturing by the instructor and allows the participants to discuss the problems and situations they actually face on the job, as opposed to hypothetical situations.

The conference leader or instructor must be flexible and informal, acting more as a moderator than as an expert. He must encourage group participation and guide the discussion rather than cram answers down the throats of the trainees. Lectures, films, and other audiovisual aids may be used, but it is important to keep in mind that these aids are secondary in importance and that the needs of the training group are primary. For this reason the conference leader needs to be tactful and patient when the group wishes to expand on a topic of discussion. The group must not feel that the schedule is more important than the topics discussed by them.

Group discussion methods induce genuine learning when the leader (1) concentrates on asking questions rather than on providing answers and (2) is sure that his questions are relevant to the problems actually faced by the group [20, p. 560].

Sensitivity Training.   Sometimes sensitivity training is called *laboratory training*. It is a method of group training where the emphasis is on what goes on within the group and each individual member of the group, rather than on the content of the class. It is a controversial method because the members of the training group, called *T-groups*, often feel frustrated by the unstructured situation in which they find themselves. T-groups usually need to be small in number because the interaction between the members calls for a high degree of individual participation. Members of the group are not given any topic or schedule to follow or to guide their discussions, although the leader does usually outline what is expected from the training session. The sessions are designed to help human beings (1) explore their values and their impact on others, (2) determine if they wish to modify their old values and develop new ones, and (3) develop awareness of how groups can inhibit as well as facilitate human growth and decision-making [3, pp. 64–65].

At the outset, the leader tends to provide that assistance which is designed to help the members to (1) become aware of their present potential for establishing authentic relationships, (2) become more skillful in providing and receiving nonevaluative descriptive feedback, (3) minimize their own and others' defensiveness, and (4) become increasingly able to experience and own up to their feelings. Once this has been done, the leader withdraws as the functional leader and the T-group is on its own. The emotional response of each individual is going to be different just as it would be in other life situations, and the resulting confusion, tension, and frustration is what makes this type of training so dynamic and challenging. It is not an oversimplification to state that some participants feel that sensitivity training is one of the most beneficial educational processes they have ever experienced, while others feel it is a total waste of time. In either case, during a well-conducted T-group session the participants, in effect, train one another. The results, therefore, are largely dependent upon the voluntary contribution and participation of each member.

A great deal of research and pioneer work has been done in sensitivity or laboratory training by the National Training Laboratory for Group Development and the Human Relations Research Group, University of California at Los Angeles. The evidence available thus far indicates that changes in behavior do result from participation in T-groups. However, more time and research needs to be completed before the effectiveness of T-groups can truly be measured and evaluated. The critics of T-groups charge that the technique artificially stimulates people emotionally, which can lead to bad feeling rather than to insight and sensitivity.

Organizational Training Laboratory (OTL). OTL is a relatively new concept in management training which is similar in nature to T-group training. While OTL is identified with sensitivity training, there are some striking differences. First, OTL is planned to avoid the highly emotional personalized problems which often spike T-group sessions. The role of the instructor or trainer in the OTL is that of research behavioral scientist rather than that of psychotherapist. The OTL trainer creates behavioral dilemmas and a climate wherein the participants experiment with alternative patterns of behavior, gather data on their behavior, test the validity of their perceptions and generalizations from their experiments, and learn how to apply the methodologies of learning to future dilemmas. The trainer also serves as a consultant to the group and, on rare occasions, to individual members of the group.

Another primary difference in emphasis between OTL and other forms of sensitivity training is that, whenever possible, the OTL training groups, ranging in size from five to eight persons, are made up of individuals who work together in the same department or division of a given company. This means that groups are made up of supervisors and subordinates who actually work together. The basic assumption upon which this practice was built is that if the people who are in training together are the people who work together, then the transfer of learning from the training to the work situation will be greater. The training sessions usually last about two weeks, though the training period may be extended over a longer period of time. During this time a series of problems are posed to the group under such conditions that the individual manager and his work team have an opportunity to test the old habits of decision-making and the assumptions which underlie them. To the extent that old methods of problem-solving are ineffective, new alternatives are created. The new alternatives are tested for their feasibility in solving problems by comparing them with old alternatives. This is accomplished under precise conditions where the participants themselves develop methods of studying both their own behavior and that of the group as a whole. Each member learns how to measure and evaluate the consequences of the forces operating upon him and his group in their work.

In this method of training the greatest single impact on learning is expected to come from the feedback of data derived from the individuals' experiences in the daily behavioral exercises. Each successive day is a new experience or series of experiences designed to exploit the problems developed by the supervisor or manager and his work group. Training is planned so that each day's experiments depend on the learning of the previous day, and it is effective in directing the group toward involvement in the more complex problems of managing and organizing.

The sequence of the laboratory begins with individuals testing some of their unclear assumptions which influence their decisions regarding working relations, their power in the organization and their effectiveness in dealing with others in decision-making. The training then moves to areas of influence in the group, both strengths and weaknesses, in order to identify resources and resolve difficulties. As skills improve, the group moves into problems of group goals, relationships, and experiments with personal modes of behavior of influencing and being influenced while trying to achieve significant organizational and personal goals. Finally, there are problems of group competition, collaboration, and organizational analysis. These phases of training are separated here for description, but in reality is part of a recurring cycle necessary for continued growth and development [13, pp. 58–67].

The organizational training laboratory has not yet been used extensively enough to determine its long-range effectiveness, but early experience indicates that OTL creates a marked increase in the dissatisfaction participants feel with their own lack of attention to superiors, subordinates, peers, and individuals outside of the organization. There is even evidence that OTL participants begin to pay more attention to such matters as organizational rules after training than they did before. There is a contrasting reduction in the attention they pay to themselves. This heightened sensitivity to others and to the problem-solving process appears to be reflected in the concern OTL participants give to accomplishing work-group objectives once they return to their jobs.

THE PURPOSE OF HUMAN RELATIONS TRAINING

The training methods described are not the only ones used to teach human relations, nor are some of them confined only to human relations training; but they are important enough to warrant special attention. Obviously, many of the techniques can be combined or modified to suit the needs of the group being trained. It is difficult, if not impossible, to say which technique is best, because the results of the training depend upon numerous factors. First, the willingness of the student to learn and to change must be considered. Second, the personality and skill of the instructor is a factor. Third, the past experience of the student with human relations training will influence him. Finally, the real test for the effectiveness of human relations training is the application of the human relations skills on the job that the student has learned. This ultimately depends upon the attitude of the student rather than the techniques used to teach him.

Though a number of evaluation attempts have been made, the results of human relations training are difficult to evaluate in objective or concrete terms. The impact of human relations training touches so many aspects of the organization that many of the changes in the organizational climate are almost imperceptible. Most supervisors are sincere and hardworking and try to do the job assigned to them. Many of them find it difficult to change their methods of supervision and, indeed, may not see any good reason why they should change. But as democratic concepts become more widespread and rooted in industrial organizations, the need for many supervisors to modify traditional attitudes and methods becomes more imperative. Human relations training must prepare supervisors for making change by incorporating the same group processes and participative methods that they are expected to practice with their subordinates. Simply stated, the training process in human relations must exemplify the principles that are to be put into practice.

Explanations should be stated as clearly and briefly as possible without oversimplifying the complexities of group dynamics. Experienced supervisors, even those with little formal education often can understand theoretical concepts developed by the behavioral scientists as well or better than many younger men or inexperienced college students. They may not always agree with every theory that they hear, but this resistance is healthy as long as it does not stem from an unreceptive and inflexible perspective.

Most of the approaches discussed in this chapter provide the trainee with the opportunity to play an active part in the learning process. Role playing, sensitivity training, and discussion groups are particularly designed to involve training participants, and even case studies, incident process, and lectures can be effectively adapted to the ideas, opinions, and comments of the trainees. In this way, human relations training not only provides a set of principles to guide the behavior of supervisors, but it also gives them a chance to develop interpersonal skills. These skills are the ability to listen to what others have to say, the ability to evaluate what is heard so that the facts in a situation can be separated from emotional interpretations, and the ability to communicate what is on one's mind without insulting the sense of dignity of the listener.

The purpose of human relations training, then, is to increase the trainee's ability to work with others more effectively, to understand the internal and external social and psychological factors which impair the full use of one's ability, and to improve his sensitivity to the needs of other group members, whether they are subordinates, peers, or superiors.

SUMMARY

1. The question of how human relations should be taught poses some problems in training. Questions related to when it should be taught and to whom need to be resolved so that the most effective methods to be used in a training program are to be selected. Some critics of human relations training believe that common sense is the basis of human relations and that formal training is unnecessary.

2. Despite the criticism of some experts about an overemphasis being placed on human relations, training is being given in academic institutions and in company training programs. The nature of human relations, that is, the interactions between people, lends itself to some methods which involve the students who participate in the training.

3. The case-study method is widely used both in industry and in school. In this method a realistic situation is presented to the trainees, who then seek solutions to the problems described in the case. This

method permits the trainees to analyze the circumstances of the case objectively since they are not personally involved in the situation described in the case. As each student's solutions are discussed by the group the students can see how their own solutions differ from those put forth by other students. The differences in each student's perspective is dramatized, and the exchange of ideas can help the students to recognize that problems involving the opinions and behavior of human beings seldom have a single solution, but have rather a number of alternatives from which acceptable solutions must be chosen.

4. Incident process methods are similar to case studies, except the entire circumstances surrounding a problem are not revealed at one time to the students. Information is given piecemeal so that students must analyze the information that they have received in order to determine what else they need to know before deciding the best solutions to the problem. There are five phases in the incident process method: (1) presentation of the incident, (2) fact finding, through questions and discussion with the instructor, (3) defining central issues, (4) arriving at a solution individually, and (5) evaluation and generalizations.

5. Role playing is a method in which the students are presented with a problem situation, and then students act out the roles of the characters who were involved in the problem. The participants in this method are not given any script to follow and are expected to react spontaneously; thus, the end result is dependent upon the way the students act out their roles. Such a method is intended to help the participants develop empathy and sensitivity to the point of view of others and to broaden their experience beyond the logic and rationale used in solving case studies.

6. Group discussion methods are one of the most common means of training foremen and middle managers. This method escapes the limitation of straight lecturing by an instructor and allows the participants to discuss the problems and situations they actually face on the job. This method will induce learning when the discussion leader concentrates on asking rather than answering questions in order to extract the thinking and opinions of the group members.

7. Sensitivity training is one of the most controversial methods of human relations training recently developed. This method concentrates on the development of self-awareness of each participant. Emphasis is placed on what interactions occur between group members rather than the content of the class. The group sessions are intended to help participants explore their values and their impact on others, to determine what, if any, modification in values they wish to make, and to develop awareness of how groups can inhibit as well as facilitate human growth and the discussion-making process.

8. Human relations training is not intended to change a person's total

personality. It is concerned, however, with helping organizational members become more adaptive and receptive to the opinions and behavior of others. A change in attitudes on the part of some supervisors and managers is often necessary in the wake of modern concepts of industrial democracy. Human relations training can provide an opportunity for such individuals to evaluate their own attitudes and to explore other modes of behavior which may be more effective in motivating their subordinates. Most training methods employed in human relations training provide the trainee with an opportunity to participate in group discussions so that training sessions not only provide information to the trainee, but also give him a chance to develop the interpersonal skills of listening, evaluating objectively what is seen or heard, and communicating what is on his mind without affronting others.

DISCUSSION QUESTIONS

1. Why is common sense not enough to insure good human relations practices?
2. In what ways does the incident process method differ from the case-study method?
3. Why do most methods of training in human relations usually involve groups of people rather than individual study?
4. What are the major criticisms of the methods used in human relations training?
5. What are the possible disadvantages to role playing? What are the advantages?
6. How does sensitivity training (T-groups) differ from the other methods of human relations training?

BIBLIOGRAPHY AND
SELECTED COLLATERAL READINGS

1. ANDERSON, WAYNE, "How Effective Is Human Relations Training for the First-Line Supervisor?" *Personnel,* Vol. 40, No. 3 (May–June, 1963), 62–66.
2. ANDREWS, KENNETH R., *The Case Method of Teaching Human Relations and Administration.* Cambridge: Harvard University Press, 1953.
3. ARGYRIS, CHRIS, "T-Groups for Organizational Effectiveness," *Harvard Business Review,* Vol. 42, No. 2 (March–April, 1964).
4. BRADFORD, LELAND P., and others, *T-Group Theory and Laboratory Method: Innovation in Re-education.* New York: John Wiley and Sons, 1964.
5. GORDON, R. A., and J. E. HOWELL, *Higher Education for Business.* New York: Columbia University Press, 1959.
6. HARRELL, THOMAS W., and JAY THEODORE RUSHMORE, *A Casebook in*

Industrial and Personnel Psychology. New York: Reinhart and Co., Inc., 1958.

7. HECKMANN, I. L., JR., and S. G. HUNERYAGER, *Human Relations in Management.* Cincinnati: South-Western Publishing Co., 1960.

8. LYNTON, R. P. and U. PAREEK, *Training for Development.* Homewood, Ill.: Richard D. Irwin, 1967.

9. MAIER, NORMAN R. F., *Principles of Human Relations.* New York: John Wiley and Sons, 1952.

10. MAIER, NORMAN R. F., and others, *Supervision and Executive Development.* New York: John Wiley and Sons, 1964.

11. MASLOW, ABRAHAM H., "Notes on Unstructured Groups," *Human Relations Training News,* Vol. 7, No. 3 (Fall, 1963), 1–6.

12. MINER, J. B., *Studies in Management Education.* New York: Springer publishing, 1965.

13. MORTON, ROBERT B., "The Organizational Training Laboratory—Some Individual and Organization Effects," *Advanced Management Journal,* Vol. 30, No. 4 (1965).

14. PIERSON, FRANK, and others, *The Education of American Businessmen.* New York: McGraw-Hill Book Company, 1959.

15. PIGORS, PAUL, and FAITH PIGORS, *Case Method in Human Relations: The Incident Process.* New York: McGraw-Hill Book Company, 1961.

16. ROETHLISBERGER, F. J., "Training Supervisors in Human Relations," *Harvard Business Review* (September, 1951), p. 52.

17. SAYLES, LEONARD R., and GEORGE STRAUSS, *Human Behavior in Organizations.* Englewood Cliffs, N.J.: Prentice-Hall, Inc., 1967.

18. SCHEIN, EDGAR H., and WARREN G. BENNIS, *Personal and Organizational Change Through Group Methods.* New York: John Wiley and Sons, 1965.

19. SMITH, H. C., *Sensitivity to People.* New York: McGraw-Hill Book Company, 1966.

20. STRAUSS, GEORGE, and LEONARD R. SAYLES, *Personnel: The Human Problems of Management,* 2nd ed. Englewood Cliffs, N.J.: Prentice-Hall, Inc., 1967.

21. TANNENBAUM, ROBERT, and others, *Leadership and Organization: A Behavioral Science Approach.* New York: McGraw-Hill Book Company, 1961.

22. WHYTE, WILLIAM F., *Leadership and Group Participation.* Ithaca, New York: New York State School of Industrial and Labor Relations, Bulletin No. 24 (1953), 9–15, 17–26.

14

Communications

Many of the topics included in the study of human relations are related to the quality of communications between organizational members. Gaining the cooperation of group members, coordinating organizational functions, motivation, leadership methods, and improving interpersonal competence involve problems related to communications. Effective communications are dependent upon the degree of understanding that occurs between the sender and the receiver of written, verbal, or symbolic messages. Without understanding, communication has not really taken place. In this regard, the problem and barriers to sound communications in a large organization usually are not caused by a lack of formal channels, but rather because of the differences in perspective and preconceptions of the human beings involved. Normally workers want to know information relative to their job, which includes knowing about a broad spectrum of company plans and activities. Workers resist efforts to propagandize them with superficial speels telling them what a good company they work for. Employees can and do determine whether or not a particular firm is a good outfit; whether or not management is sound, honest, and just. Their experience and observation of management's actions as well as its words lead them to know what is believable and what is not.

Most enlightened management practices today are not intentionally designed to dupe employees; more often, they tend to commit the sin of omission when it comes to giving information which will directly affect the employee's working environment. Because many formal methods and media of communications have been established in large organizations, management may assume that workers "get the word." Company plans to enlarge operations, modernize, automate, close plants, cut back production, and so on, are vital bits of information to workers who see this information as having an effect on their jobs. Often such information is made public through press releases before it reaches employees through internal communications. Even more important than telling employees what plans are in store is the notification of what impact such plans will have on the workers and their jobs.

Communication is a two-way process in which information is accurately received and understood so that action can be taken. Organizational communications easily can fall into the category of a monologue simply because of the number of people to be reached and the urgency of time. When accurate information is not adequately provided for and by management, worker's informal communications, in the form of rumors, usually fill the need to "know what is going on." The nature of informal communications under more detailed investigation of the communications process will appear later in this chapter. For now, the communication problems created in a large-scale organization should serve to indicate the constant and careful effort that is necessary to establish two-way channels of communication between management and rank-and-file workers. On the more personal level occurring in small work groups, the solution of many human relations problems is dependent upon the success of face-to-face communication between the individuals involved. When differences of opinion arise between individuals on the job, such differences cannot be resolved unless they are understood, and they cannot be understood unless the parties involved are prepared to listen to each other's viewpoint. The attitude of employees can be hostile to management and the organization when they sense that their voices fall upon closed ears or minds. Needless to say, the more people involved, the more difficult it becomes to establish a dialogue. In firms employing half a dozen people, the task is not an easy one; in companies employing over half a million persons, the problem becomes almost insurmountable. Yet if successful operations are to be set in motion, sound communications must first be established.

HUMAN RELATIONS AND COMMUNICATIONS

Because of the significant influence interpersonal relationships have on the quality of communications between organizational members and the effect that good communications skills can have on interpersonal relationships, the practice of human relations is an inseparable aspect of the communications process.

When observing, writing, speaking, and listening are included as components of the communications process, it is estimated that many supervisors and managers spend as much as 90 per cent of their time communicating. The importance of communications to management and organizational effectiveness should not be underestimated; yet the communications process is little understood by many individuals whose primary responsibility is to send and receive organizational communications.

Communications is an extremely broad topic and needs to be separated into component parts in order to be studied effectively. Often the media used in organizational communications are quite evident: letters, inter-office memos, house organs, company manuals, intercom systems, and telephones. What is not always evident is the real substance of communications, that is, the content and meaning of the messages. Because of the growth of our technological ability to build and refine mechanical means of communication—television satellites, transistorized transmitters and receivers, long-distance dialing systems—the industrial use of the term *communications* tends to refer to the means of conveying messages rather than to what is conveyed. No doubt the mechanical devices used in organizational communications networks are indispensable to modern industry, but what is just as important to organizational effectiveness is an improvement in the degree of understanding reached between organizational members.

Though understanding is the essence of communications, it should be noted that understanding is not synonymous with agreement. Many subordinates may *not* agree with what their supervisors have to say, but understanding may have taken place. Similar disagreements occur between company and labor officials, salesmen and customers, staff advisers and line managers. Even differences in opinion must be clarified by understanding so that the evidence and attitudes which support different viewpoints can be analyzed and evaluated.

In addition to disagreements which can develop as a result from differences in viewpoint, many misunderstandings occur because organizational members who occupy positions in different functions and echelons tend to have differing perspectives which do not allow them to see organizational problems in the same way. Although differences in perspective between organizational members are an important deterrent of the lock-step, "think alike" syndrome, when such differences impair effective internal communications, the viability of the organization is threatened.

Peter Drucker believes that groups found in various levels of the organization's hierarchy can develop differences in perspective which limit their ability to communicate with others. Three of these groups are comprised of *top management,* who are primarily interested in the financial and economic problems of the business; *middle managers and supervisors,* whose main concern is essentially directed either toward problems of supervision, production, and the technical operations of the company or toward those of their own department; and the *operative employees,* whose interests are centered around their own jobs and work groups.

Drucker comments on these differences:

Each of the groups sees the same thing, the enterprise, from a different viewpoint and within a different angle of vision. What one group sees as obvious and plain fact, the other simply cannot see at all. Each group, though seeing only a part of the picture, fancies that it sees the whole. And each group, convinced that it sees the whole, is convinced that its viewpoint is fair and logical. Present management efforts (to communicate) are, by and large, like the attempt to establish "communication" between a Chinese and a Spaniard by putting them both on the telephone; unless one of them knows the language of the other, the most perfect telephone system will not enable them to talk to each other [3, p. 191].

It would be an overstatement to say that these differences of perspective deprive organizational members of a common language, but to overlook the differences in attitude, interest, and day-to-day responsibilities fostered in the different echelons of the organization would be a gross mistake.

COMMUNICATIONS PROCESS

Perhaps the first step in improving communications is a clear understanding of what actually happens in the communications process. Surprisingly, little study was devoted to the mechanics of the communications process until man was confronted with the problem of developing input and output control systems for electronic computers and other automated equipment. The science developed to control the input and output processes of machines is called *cybernetics*. The term was coined by Norbert Wiener from a Greek word meaning steersman. One of the fundamental principles of cybernetics is *feedback*. This means that a continuous flow of information must flow back and forth between the originator and the intended receiver of communications so that adjustments can occur during the operations of the machine. Translated into human terms, *cybernetics* is the process by which a person who is speaking watches the reactions and listens to the effect of what he says on his audience. What he hears and observes is the feedback he needs in order to adjust his conversation to fit the needs of the situation. If the audience looks puzzled, the speaker may repeat what he said or say it in another way. This process continues until some action or response from the audience indicates that the message of the speaker is understood (or at least until the speaker thinks it is).

The communications process between one man and another and man and machines pose the same fundamental problem: that is, accurately reproducing the message for the receiver (listener or reader) which was transmitted from the sender (speaker or writer). In order to accomplish this task, Claude Shannon and Warren Weaver, pioneers in the field of cybernetics, have developed five essential steps in the man–machine communications process:

1. There must be an information source to produce the original message.

2. A transmitter is necessary to send a signal over a suitable channel.

3. A channel or medium must be present to transmit the signal from the sender to the receiver.

4. A receiver is necessary to perform the inverse operation of the transmitter and reconstruct the message from a signal.

5. A destination is necessary. This is the mechanism or thing for which the message is intended [11, p. 101].

In a situation where both the originator and destination of the communication are human beings, the steps in the process are similar. In Figure 14–1, a model of the communications process illustrates how verbal messages are sent and received by two persons.

Human communications must also include feedback in which the speaker receives an indication of whether or not his audience has understood his message. Thus, the communications process between human beings is more complicated than the basic engineering model (see Figure 14–1) might imply because there are many variables to be met and controlled besides signs, codes, noise, redundancy, and feedback. These additional variables are caused by psychological influences, which are dis-

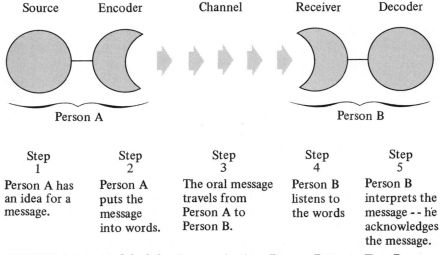

Source	Encoder	Channel	Receiver	Decoder

| Person A | | | Person B | |

Step 1	Step 2	Step 3	Step 4	Step 5
Person A has an idea for a message.	Person A puts the message into words.	The oral message travels from Person A to Person B.	Person B listens to the words	Person B interprets the message - - he acknowledges the message.

FIGURE 14–1. Model of the Communications Process Between Two Persons.

cussed shortly. They can affect the outcome of human communications to a greater extent than physical determinants. However, once the five steps in the communications process are understood, one can begin to comprehend the type of breakdowns that can occur. Examples of some of the problems and breakdowns that can occur at each step of the communications process are outlined briefly as follows.

Step 1: The Origination of the Message. Not all messages are easy to verbalize. Some abstract ideas are very complex and seem to defy being placed into words. Not only are some ideas complex, but they are emotional in nature. Love, grief, and elation are emotions which are difficult to articulate meaningfully, and no words seem to describe the feeling that the originator wishes to express. Other messages are difficult to articulate because they are unpleasant to the sender. Having to tell a worker that he is going to be laid off because of a production cutback may be very difficult to say—not because words do not clearly express the message, but because the message itself may be unpleasant. Many supervisors find it difficult to express themselves in matters that relate to discipline because the subject is distasteful to them.

Often a message will not be understood by anyone because the sender is unclear in his own thinking about the subject. He cannot find the words to express himself because he does not fully understand the topic. This is often the case when a new trainee is asked to explain some aspect of a job he has just learned. He cannot explain it because he does not understand it thoroughly enough to do so.

The first step in the communications process is an important one since the tendency in communications is for messages to become more garbled, rather than clearer, as they go through each of the steps in the communications process. Thus, a message which is not clearly understood by the originator stands little chance of being understood by the receiver.

Step 2: The Message Encoded, or Put into Words. Closely related to the problems associated with step 1 are the problems the originator of the message has in actually saying what he has on his mind. Although the sender may know what he wants to say, he is limited in his capacity to say it. This limitation may stem from a limited vocabulary, in which case the sender simply cannot use the precise words necessary to express himself because he does not know them. The problem of selecting the correct word to convey the intended meaning of a thought is also related to *semantics.* The same word often can have different meaning to different people because of each individual's perspective and because of the dynamics of language. Technical jargon can be misleading to an outsider unfamiliar with the meaning of the terminology associated with a particular field. Thus, limitations in vocabulary and semantics barriers can impair the sender from making clear what he means.

In addition to the hindrance of vocabulary and semantics, the emotional state of the sender can impair the communications process at step 2. If the sender is excited, he may speak too rapidly to be understood. If he is afraid or angry, the quality of his speech may be distorted so that he cannot be heard clearly. These and other emotional factors can contribute to the distortion of communications before the words leave the speaker's mouth and affect the quality of the communications process in each of the remaining steps.

Step 3: The Channel or Actual Transmission of the Message.   In steps 1 and 2 of the communications process, the sender had complete control over communications. The sender had the idea, information, or message in his head; he selected the words or symbols he believed expressed the message; and he controlled the quality of voice he used. Once the words leave his mouth, he begins losing control over the process. Distractions, noise, or interruptions can interfere with the transmission of his message. The sender can combat these elements by repeating his message or by speaking in a louder voice. The communications process having reached the third step, the sender finds that if he is to insure his message gets through to the receiver, he must adapt his methods to suit the needs of the situation.

Step 4: The Audience Receives the Message.   Once the communications process reaches this step, the communication is out of the sender's control. Now the audience, one or more, plays a dominant role in what occurs. This fact underlies the importance of listening in the communications process. Surprisingly few people realize that in order to understand, listening cannot be a passive activity. A person can speak at a normal rate of 100 to 200 words per minute. But a person's brain can process information at a much faster rate. For example, some individuals have learned to read at rates exceeding several thousand words per minute, but to do so requires concentration.

The concept of feedback in human discourse is related to listening. Certain barriers stand in the way of good listening. The reason for these barriers lies in the tendency of the listener to prejudge or evaluate what is said rather than to sense what is said from the point of view of the speaker. Good listening requires that a person reverse his role and forego whatever authority and initiative he may possess until he has heard what has been said. Remember, he may not agree with what he hears, but in order to disagree he must have *understood* what was said.

When listening is not present, one-way communication may have occurred, but not understanding. Without the mutual element of listening in communication, there are just two ideas, two feelings, two judgments missing each other in psychological space [9, p. 47].

All listening is not at the same level. Neither does all listening require the same skill. The first level of listening is to make sense out of sound. This means be able to distinguish the sender's words. This is done every day when people read a book while a radio is playing, or when an employee is concentrating at his work station while other persons converse nearby. This level of listening is really closer to awareness than understanding.

The second level of listening is when understanding begins. This is where the listener concentrates on what is being said. This is also when semantic difficulties can begin.

The third level is to distinguish fact from fancy. This requires evaluation on the part of the listener and depends on his knowledge, intelligence, and past experience.

The fourth level of listening is the highest level and requires the greatest skill and concentration. The highest level of listening involves not only hearing, but the added dimension of *empathy* on the part of the listener so that he can understand what is said from the speaker's point of view. This is the rarest type of listening, but it is the most important one if understanding is to occur and is to overcome the differences in the organizational perspectives mentioned earlier.

Step 5: Interpretation and Evaluation of the Message. This stage of the communications process is when understanding actually takes place. The degree of understanding is related to how well the person listened and also to the same vocabulary limitations, semantic limitations, and limitations of perspective mentioned in steps 1 and 2. The same emotional barriers are present. If the listener is angry, afraid, or disinterested in what the speaker has to say, distortions of the message are likely to occur. Thus, the effectiveness of communication depends to some degree on the willingness of the receiver to try and understand what is said, as well as the sender's adroitness in expressing himself.

BARRIERS TO COMMUNICATION

Some of the inherent problems of communication were discussed in each of the steps of the communication process. The principal barriers to communication between human beings can be placed into three broad categories: physical, psychological, and semantic. In most circumstances, these barriers are not absolute blocks to communication; rather, they contribute to the difficulty of making oneself understood by distorting the messages that are sent and received.

Physical Barriers. Physical barriers are environmental factors which actually prohibit or limit the extent of communications. Factors of distance, lack of time, and noise and such external disruptions as failure of mechanical communications equipment can physically interfere with the communications process. Even when mechanical devices are used, not all physical barriers are due to equipment failures. For example, in one business-machine-repair company, each serviceman was provided a small transmitter-receiver that could be attached to his belt. This electronic device was used to contact repairmen so they could respond to emergency repair jobs. On numerous occasions one particular repairman could not be reached over his receiver. Each time he was questioned about the matter the repairman claimed he never got the message because his receiver was broken. After a careful check, it turned out that the repairman was in the habit of putting the receiver into the glove compartment of his vehicle before going into a customer's office to make a service call. When asked why, he explained that the exposure of the set on his person embarrassed him. He felt that such a device made him appear to be on the end of a string held by his boss—it deprived him of making independent judgments, and, therefore, lowered his status in the eyes of the secretaries and office personnel whose office machines he repaired.

In this case the solution to the problem was the attachment of the receiver to the serviceman's repair kit rather than his person. In this manner the device merely became a piece of equipment the repairman used on his job rather than a symbol of servitude.

Psychological Barriers. Psychological barriers arise from personal differences in perspective between persons communicating. Emotions, social values, and differences in position in the organizational hierarchy can contribute to psychological distances between people that are as great as physical distances. In upward communications a subordinate may hesitate to tell his supervisor unfavorable news because he fears it may affect his own relationship with the boss. For this reason as well as other differences in perspective, upward communications may be considerably slower than those flowing downward. If upward communications are to be improved in terms of accuracy, supervisors and members of management must continuously encourage their subordinates to convey information to them, including that which is not highly favorable.

Semantic Barriers. Semantic barriers arise because much of what people say is subjective. Words and symbols, except in technical languages, seldom have a single meaning, nor is everything that is said based exclusively on fact. Yet, neither the supervisor nor his subordinates can wait until everything they say to each other can be proved. Words such as *great, small, good,* and *bad* are open to interpretation by the listener or reader. Thus, the intended meaning of a comment by a supervisor using words with relative meaning may be easily misinterpreted by a subordinate unless they are both using the same frame of reference— *good* performance to a supervisor may not be the same to a subordinate; *high* levels of production to a supervisor may mean *unrealistic* levels to his subordinates.

Because of these and other barriers to communication the supervisor must initiate the improvement in the quality of his communications with subordinates. To do this he must cultivate an open and attentive attitude toward listening to what his subordinates say. He must also make an effort to say what he means in terms that can be understood easily by those who make the attempt to understand. By showing that he is willing to try to improve what may be his own imperfect communications skills, he encourages his subordinates to respond in a like manner.

The remainder of this chapter discusses some of the elements of communications that can lead to better understanding between a supervisor and his subordinates.

PRINCIPLES OF GOOD COMMUNICATION

The diagram illustrating the five major steps in the communication process does not indicate many of the variables which are part of the human process of communications. For example, it does not include the effect that a person's facial expressions or posture and gestures have on the effectiveness of communications. These nonverbal variables are an integral part of the process and can enhance or inhibit the rapport between the sender and the receiver, which in turn improves or blocks understanding. Familiarity with the communications model and each step in the communications process is a valuable tool when analyzing the breakdown that may occur in understanding between two or more people. Such knowledge is useful to persons who want to improve their ability to communicate by carefully planning the purpose of a particular message they have to send, choosing the words to be used and selecting the method of communicating most appropriate to the subject and the intended audience. In this way the sender can reduce the distortion of his message and increase the amount and accuracy of the information his audience receives. But the speaker needs to be aware of his own built-in biases, idiosyncrasies, and attitudes which he imparts as he speaks. Simply stated, do the actions of the speaker reinforce what he says or do they contradict it?

The role of sender and the role of receiver are constantly being reversed in the process of most day-to-day communications, so improving one's skill in speaking or writing only tackles part of the problem; one also must develop his listening ability. Without listening, the feedback process in human communications cannot be fully effective.

In most situations in industry the communications process is a continuous one; that is, communications between organizational members occur over a long period of time, and any given message is only part of a much longer dialogue. The importance of this fact is that each message is evaluated by the listener within the context of other things that the speaker has said in the past. Any contradictions, overstatements, or abrupt changes in viewpoint on the part of the speaker may contribute to the listener's confusion or lack of understanding.

There are some precautions the sender can take to minimize extremely poor communications. In addition to defining in his own mind the purpose of a particular communication, he can be sure that each message is well planned by following the suggestions outlined below.

Make Sure Messages Are Accurate. Incorrect information can undermine the confidence a listener has in what the speaker says. If a supervisor is speaking, an inaccurate statement can give official status to an error which may be difficult to rectify at a later time. Inaccuracies may occur when conveying facts or figures and by the choice of words which make up a message. Errors in facts and figures may be less difficult for the speaker to detect than errors in his choice of words because of semantic differences. The same word may not have the same meaning or connotation to two people from different educational backgrounds, social upbringing, or geographic sections of the country; however, such differences in meaning may not be readily apparent.

Words are labels or symbols attached to ideas or things, and people relate the two within a framework of their knowledge and experience. If words are to communicate ideas effectively between a sender and a receiver, words must have the same meaning to both persons. It is this lack of common agreement about the meaning of words that gives rise to vagueness, misunderstanding, and conflict between individuals. Because of semantic differences, the meaning of words to the speaker is only relative in importance in conveying a message. It is the interpretation of the listener that determines how well a message is understood.

Consider the Characteristics of the Audience or Receiver. Because of the gap in the understanding of words, the sender, in order to be effective, must consider the characteristics of his audience or receiver. First, he must consider the receiver's familiarity with the language. In addition to considering the listener's position and function in the organization and its possible effect on his viewpoint, his background, experience, intelligence, education, character, and interests must be considered. In many cases, a study of each of these characteristics in a listener may take more time and effort than the speaker deems necessary. When this is the case, the speaker's success in communicating will depend on his ability to perceive and be sensitive to these elements in the listener. This ability requires empathy, a quality which can be developed in a sender, but requires that he make a conscious effort to give up his own isolation and bias.

Make an Effort to Communicate Honestly. No matter how carefully one plans his communication, mistakes may be made in reporting facts and figures. Generally, such mistakes are accepted by the audience as being unintentional unless they have reason to suspect that the speaker is trying to put something over on them. The basis for a listener's judgment regarding the truth of a speaker's statement is often dependent on the past experience the listener has had with the credibility and integrity of the speaker. Since most organizational communications are part of a continuing relationship, if the motives of the speaker are suspect, whatever such a person attempts to communicate will also become suspect. Not only is this true in communications within the organization, it is true in communications between organizational members and persons who are not members of the organization.

A customer who does not trust the word of a salesman is not likely to place an order with him. Union officials who have no confidence in what a company official says are not likely to negotiate in a spirit of mutual trust, and vice versa. The point is that the sender must make an effort to be as accurate as possible in what he says and also to convey the honest intentions of what he says. To do this means that words must be followed by action consistent with what has been said.

Avoid the Use of Gobbledygook. Often a simple message is distorted beyond recognition because it is couched in officious-sounding, meaningless phrases. Aside from speaking in abstract terms, many speakers believe they impress the listener by using long words when simpler words would convey the same message. To be sure, the terminology of many specialized areas of business is technical and precise meanings cannot be conveyed to the listener without resorting to technical terminology. But it does no harm to define esoteric terminology for listeners who may be unfamiliar with it.

Messages which are simple and direct do not have to be childish. What is called for is that the message be clear and to the point. This does not infer that the speaker should talk down to the listener. Such action tends to create resentment in the listener, which only serves to block communication.

Try to Make Communications Timely. People will invest time and effort in understanding only in proportion to the importance of the message conveyed to them. A worker may spend several hours computing the number of vacation days he has accumulated, but not spend five minutes trying to understand a management directive concerning reduced production costs. Interest must be created in what is to be communicated *before* it is communicated.

It is usually advantageous to communicate with employees when the topic is already important to them. Some communications have an adverse effect on the group if given at the wrong time. For example, to attempt to discuss an operational change with employees at a time when they are concerned about labor contract negotiations may defeat the necessary acceptance of the change because the attention of the group is elsewhere.

These five suggestions will help reduce poor communications and would apply to either oral or to written communications which are formal in nature. Although such guides might help make informal or social conversation more meaningful, they are not as necessary there as they are in written communications.

FORMAL COMMUNICATIONS

Formal communications are those which have a direct relationship to the operations of the work group or organization as a whole. Not all on-the-job communications are formal. Often social conversation between workers, supervisors, and managers is more an expression of friendship, common interest, or social politeness than a means of communicating vital company information.

The purpose and intended audience of formal communications will have an effect on the methods and channels of communication used. If the contents of the messages are factual in nature, the choice between spoken or written communications depends on the complexity of the material and the reading ability of the intended audience. The more brief and simple the message, the better it lends itself to the spoken word.

Communications intended to be persuasive, rather than factual, are usually more effectively presented by word of mouth in face-to-face conversations. This is particularly true when the issues involve strong emotional feelings. Face-to-face communications provide the advantage of rapid feedback. Questions can be asked as the message is being conveyed, and the message can be clarified as it is delivered. While there are some messages which can most effectively be communicated in writing, the lapse of time that occurs between the time the writer sends a message and the time he receives a response from his audience can be a disadvantage if time is short and immediate feedback is required by the sender.

Formal Channels of Communications

Communications necessary to coordinate various organizational functions and personnel may follow any one of many patterns. Usually, each organization attempts to devise a formal pattern of communications to insure that all necessary information reaches all concerned organizational units. It is important that information from each organizational unit reach some centralized point in the organization so that any action necessary to maintain the continuous flow of production can be taken. For instance, it is necessary that orders sent in from traveling salesmen be processed by someone in the organization to insure that the correct quantity and quality of the order is shipped to the customer. Once the order has been received by the order department, the shipping department must be notified to send the order, the credit department must be informed so it can bill the customer, the shipping department may have to notify the production department so that it can replenish the stock that has been sold. The process of communications is endless within an organization. Some communications flow between personnel in different departments—sales and credit—others flow between different echelons in the organization—plant manager and department heads, employees and their supervisors.

Generally, formal communications follow the same lines and patterns that would be found on the organization chart. The lines and route that formal communications follow in an organization are called channels of communication. The three channels of communication which are prevalent are *downward, upward,* and *horizontal* (those which cut across the organizational structure). Actually, the flow of communications upward and downward follow the same channels, but the nature, content, and barriers of communications flowing downward may differ considerably from those flowing upward. The direction of formal communications are significant to the types of problems encountered which impair *two-way* communications.

Downward Communications. Traditionally, downward communication is the top-to-bottom communications channel. Orders, information, and questions which originate at the top of the company are passed downward through lower levels of the organization until they reach the intended receiver somewhere below the level of the originator. Downward communications occur when the president calls a meeting to reveal his plans for the coming year to his department heads or vice presidents or when a supervisor calls a group meeting of his subordinates to discuss the weekly work schedule in the department. In both cases someone in a higher organizational position communicates to persons in lower positions than himself.

Some students of downward communications believe that rank-and-file employees receive only about 20 per cent of a message originated by a company president after it has been passed down a chain of command involving five levels of management [8, p. 8]. While the extent of loss in downward communications may not be nearly 80 per cent in all organizations, problems related to reducing distortion and increasing the amount of accurate information that reaches rank-and-file workers are widespread throughout industry. Company meetings, bulletin boards, and news items in company papers and magazines help to facilitate downward communications, but these are essentially printed media and are not necessarily read by all employees.

Because it is necessary that some downward communications reach everyone, oral communications are often the most effective means of insuring this; but oral communications seem to suffer the greatest loss of efficiency in conveying a large amount of accurate information to employees. As many aspects of human relations are involved in oral communications, the following discussion will concentrate on the problems of oral, rather than written, communications.

What are the barriers to downward oral communications? The answers to this question are many, but a few reasons may contribute more than others to the deficiency of downward communications. First, people do not hear all the things that are said to them; therefore, they cannot repeat what they do not hear. Second, a person forgets a large part of what he hears in a very short period of time unless the message is reinforced periodically in some way. Unless a person who is given a message passes it on almost immediately, there is bound to be some loss in the content of the message. After it has passed through the hands or minds and mouths of four or five people, the rate of loss will be significant. This rate of loss will increase as the period of time increases between the time that each person hears the message and the time he repeats it. Thus, a large portion of the president's message would be lost before it reached the rank and file, even if every member in the organizational hierarchy was willing to communicate downward, fully and accurately.

In addition to the inherent inefficiencies in listening and remembering, there are other factors which contribute to the loss in communications. These factors are related to the overall organizational climate and to the psychological and social make-up of organizational members. Often, a man who occupies a position in the chain of command (communications channel) is adverse to passing on all the information he has; thus, he censors or "filters" the communications he passes downward, based on what he thinks his subordinates should be told. Sometimes this attitude is called *obscurantism*. This refers to the opposition some people have toward free inquiry and enlightenment. Sometimes this attitude stems from a sense of insecurity or defensiveness a manager or supervisor may have in holding a leadership position in the organization. Sometimes an individual supervisor does not understand the need for downward communication. To some supervisors downward communications may denote idle conversation, meetings that are a waste of time, or listening to ideas or questions from people whom he does not believe are qualified to question what he says.

Another factor which contributes to the depletion of downward communications is the lack of knowledge on the part of managers regarding what should be communicated downward. No single list of what should be communicated downward would fit the needs of every company. What management considers important might be one thing, and what workers want to hear another. Although what is important to the management and workers is a matter to be settled in each organization, there are some subjects which are generally important to workers in any organization. One survey conducted by the National Association of Manufacturers revealed that workers want to know:

1. About the company—its background and present organization.
2. About the company's products—how they are made and where they are sold.
3. What the company policies are—especially new policies; as they affect themselves and their fellow workers.
4. The reasons for changes in methods and information about new products—this information is wanted in advance.
5. What is expected of them and how they are measuring up to performance standards.
6. How their jobs fit into the scheme of company operations and what chances for advancement are.
7. What the outlook is for business—what the prospects are for steady work.
8. About the company's sales and income—its profits and losses.
9. Should circumstances make layoffs necessary, they want to know as far in advance as possible the reasons and how they as individuals will be affected [5, p. 11].

The items included on the list may not be all-inclusive, but they do provide a guide for determining what communications are important to workers. The list also indicates the broad range of subjects that workers are likely to be interested in hearing about from management.

Upward Communications. The channel which carries information and ideas upward from the rank-and-file level to the president's desk is known as *upward communications.* This is the reverse process of downward communications and the communication loss is just as great. Part of the reason for the loss in upward communications is due to the inefficiencies of listening and remembering described earlier; however, the quality of upward communication is related to the timing, tone, and amount of communication that comes downward. If members who hold lower positions in the organizational hierarchy do not believe that they receive adequate information from higher up, then there is little chance that they are going to pass upward all they know.

A major barrier to free and open upward communications stems from the fear that subordinates have of the real and potential authority their superiors hold. Few subordinates are anxious to convey bad news to their boss for fear that such news will reflect on their own performance. Conversely, success and good news may be exaggerated out of proportion by subordinates when reporting to supervisors in the desire to receive credit for their own accomplishment. In either case, the superior does not receive an accurate picture from the reports he gets from his subordinates. News of a major breakdown of a mechanical nature in a production department may be mollified to the point of being a minor temporary delay by the time an upward communication carries it to the plant manager or president. Likewise, a small gain in sales may be construed to be a sweeping sales increase when news is carried to the top.

Most exaggerations which can be checked by facts and figures are detected ultimately, but many bits of information which should flow upward are withheld and never reach top management. There are few ways of determining this type of communications loss. For example, a rank-and-file employee may have an idea which cuts costs or improves efficiency but is discouraged by his supervisor from mentioning it to anyone else because the supervisor feels that such a suggestion from anyone but himself might reflect on his own efficiency. When subordinate ideas are suppressed by superiors, soon many ideas stop being passed upward.

Supervisors should be in a good position to sense the attitudes of workers in their work groups. When workers display dissatisfaction with some aspect of company policy or working conditions, the supervisor should be the first one to be able to report such dissatisfaction to higher management so that something can be done about it. Yet, it is not uncommon for top management to be surprised when employee morale sinks to a point where some collective action, such as a walkout, is threatened by employees.

It is true there are some conditions workers might want changed that management can do little about. Many requests of workers are not necessarily expensive and would add immeasurably to their satisfaction, but top management never hears about such requests because they are filtered out along the channel of upward communications.

Horizontal Communications. Another channel of formal communications is one that reaches across the organizational structure, that is, one worker with another, one supervisor with another, or one department head with another. Automation, technology, and specialized fields of management have added to the importance of horizontal communications. The result of rapid technological change has made it necessary for managers and supervisors, who may be generalists, to consult with staff experts, scientists, and engineers, thus forming horizontal lines of communication.

The method of horizontal communications may be through staff meetings, individual face-to-face conferences, or written reports, which are distributed to managers, regarding the research or advice of staff specialists or other line department personnel. Problems associated with horizontal communications seldom stem from a lack of such communications but stem from the large number of various horizontal communications. Many supervisory personnel have difficulty keeping up on their report reading and their staff conferences. Both activities are time-consuming, and unless the topic of such reports and meetings is relevant to the immediate problems faced by a supervisor, he may resent the time he has to spend away from his other job responsibilities.

Although status is not usually an overt barrier to horizontal communications, because theoretically neither party in the process is subordinate to the other, there are some problems which emerge from differences in perspective. These often result from separate fields of interest. Staff experts, technicians, scientists, and other specialized personnel may have difficulty communicating with line managers because they differ in background and training (see Chapter 9, Line and Staff Relationships). The competitive climate of an organization may be another barrier to open horizontal communications. A sales manager may view the credit manager as a hindrance to his own department's objectives. One foreman may be unwilling to share information he has which could help other foremen cut operating costs because he knows that the others are being considered also for a promotion that he wants. Thus, barriers born of semantic differences, personal bias, and competition can impair the effectiveness of communications across organizational lines.

The channels of communications which link the president with the rank-and-file employees and each member of the organization in their functions are as necessary to the efficiency of an organization as the need for food is for a man. Two-way communication serves to allow for immediate response and verification of information and ideas of organizational members, regardless of the direction of the communication. Only when two-way communications exist within the organization at every level, as well as with agents external to the firm, can there be the full participation of all who are in a position to contribute to organizational efficiency and receive personal satisfaction from their contribution. Only when the barriers to communication are known can steps be taken to reduce them so that two-way communications can exist. Barriers to free and open communications usually stem from individual differences in organizational members; however, there are also barriers that arise because of the formal networks or patterns of communications a firm uses to disseminate and retrieve information within its organization.

FORMAL PATTERNS OF COMMUNICATIONS

Considerable research has been conducted on the problem of designing communications networks which link organizational members. The complexity of the relationships increases rapidly as the number of persons in the group increases. Chester Barnard points out that if the simplest possible relationship between two persons is merely knowing each other, then complexity of the relationships within a group would follow the pattern following:

Column I Members in the Group	Column II Number of Possible Relationships	Column III Increase in Relationships with Each Addition to the Group
2	1	—
3	3	2
4	6	3
5	10	4
6	15	5
7	21	6
8	28	7
9	36	8
10	45	9

Adapted from Chester I. Barnard, *The Functions of the Executive*. Cambridge, Mass.: Harvard University Press, 1938, p. 108. Copyright 1938, President and Fellows of Harvard College.

When there are only two members in a group the number of relationships is one, when there are ten persons in a group the number of possible relationships has increased to forty-five. Imagine the complexity of the communications problems when an organization has several hundred employees. The complexity of the relationships within a group is important to the communications process because as the number in the group increases, so does the difficulty of the leader's job to coordinate group activities which involve sending and receiving information.

Alex Bavelas and Harold Leavitt, two of the leading authorities on the psychological problems of communications in the United States, have experimented with the effectiveness of various group communications patterns. The purpose of their experiments was to gauge the effect various communications networks had on the speed and accuracy of performance, the extent to which leadership emerged in a group, and the impact that communications patterns had on the flexibility and adaptability of the group when faced by unusual problems. Another aspect of the research was to discover what effect various communications networks had on the morale and satisfaction of group members [2, p. 27].

Without going into the lengthy details of the experiments themselves, the various communications patterns were tested in groups comprised of five members. The two principal networks are shown in Figure 14–2a. One pattern was labeled as a *circle* pattern, in which no group member played a central role in the communications process. The other pattern was labeled as a *star* pattern, in which one group member was assigned a central role in the communications network; that is, all members of the group had to communicate through him when they wanted to send or receive information with any other member of the group. The star communications pattern is similar to the network most often found in industrial organizations. Variations of the star pattern are found in Figure 14–2b.

The common characteristic of the star communications pattern and any of its variations is the centralized role that one member has in the network within the group. In the examples shown in Figure 14–2b, "C" was always that central person. In a work group, a supervisor would have the same role. However, in an industrial situation varieties of communications networks are used which utilize aspects of both the circle and star patterns. Examples of various networks which might be found in industrial organizations are shown in Figure 14–2c.

When the three examples of networks in Figure 14–2c are compared, one can see that in the centralized star pattern all lines of communications lead to C, but no lines of communications exist between A, B, D, or E. In the modified star pattern, two lines of communications lead to C from A and E. In addition to the upward and downward lines of communications, lines of horizontal communications link A and E, B and D. In the decentralized circle pattern, all members of the group have lines of communication linking them together, so every member in the group is in touch with all other members. Few formal organization communications patterns used in industry link every organizational member with every other employee in the company. However, informal group communications may follow a pattern similar to the one shown as the

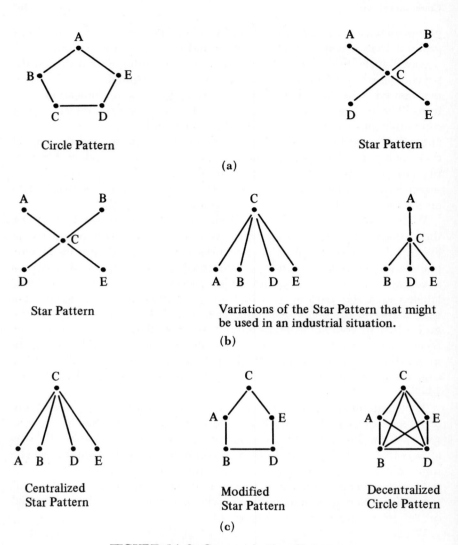

Circle Pattern

Star Pattern

(a)

Star Pattern

Variations of the Star Pattern that might be used in an industrial situation.

(b)

Centralized
Star Pattern

Modified
Star Pattern

Decentralized
Circle Pattern

(c)

FIGURE 14–2. Communications Patterns.

decentralized circle pattern. More will be said about informal communications later in this chapter.

The question posed by these variations of networks is which one is most effective? The answer to this question depends on the definition one uses for the word *effective*. Each pattern has its advantages and its liabilities. For example, when the results of the laboratory experiments testing various communications networks are compiled and analyzed, the relative benefits and shortcomings to each pattern begin to emerge and can be summarized in the following way.

Factor in the Group	Centralized Star Pattern	Modified Star Pattern	Decentralized Circle Pattern
Speed of performance in group	very fast	fast	slow
Accuracy of performance by group	good	good	poor
Degree to which leadership emerges in group	very strong	strong	none
Extent of group satisfaction	very poor	poor	very high
Degree of group flexibility in adapting to change	slow	moderate	very fast

The generalizations which can be drawn from the foregoing comparisons are limited because the results were obtained in a laboratory situation rather than in an industrial setting, but some conclusions which have been drawn from laboratory experiments may be useful in solving communications problems faced in actual work groups. It appears that highly centralized communications systems, typified by the star pattern, foster a higher degree of speed and accuracy in group performance. Such gains are obtained at a cost in group satisfaction and flexibility. If the working environment in an organization presents conditions which are static, routine, and seldom involve change or unexpected events, a star network may operate quite efficiently, unless group morale drops to a point where some other pattern has to be inaugurated. If the conditions of the work group are dynamic, where unexpected changes occur without any means of predicting them, the star network may limit the efficiency of the group, and a system of communications which is less centralized will have to be adopted by the organization.

Harold Leavitt's observations on communications patterns seem to corroborate these conclusions. He believes that the structure of the communications network in a group, independent of the persons in the group, seems to set limits on the group's performance. He goes on to state:

> Groups whose problems require the collation of information from all members work faster when one position is highly centralized and the others relatively peripheral. But the morale, the self-correctiveness, and perhaps the creativity of such groups may be better when the communication network is more equalitarian and when each member has more than one source of information.

Highly centralized groups may often be used for their consistency with general organizational designs, their speed, and their controllability; but they are also used as psychological defense devices to protect superiors' "weaknesses" from being exposed to subordinates, and vice versa [6, p. 241].

INFORMAL COMMUNICATIONS

Though few organizations utilize a formal communications pattern which is completely open and decentralized, informal communications that exist within an organization often follow a pattern which is open and decentralized. But even informal communications systems seldom include every member of the organization.

Informal communications are often referred to as the *grapevine*. Actually, there is no single grapevine but rather a series of informal communications lines that run up, down, and across the formal organization. The effectiveness of the grapevine is probably greater than most managers would like to believe since effective communications depend on the interpersonal relationships between the persons communicating, and in the grapevine the persons involved usually have face-to-face personal relationships. The social relationship of many participants in the grapevine means that nonwork-centered information is carried in the system, as well as work-centered data.

Some managers are often concerned by the company rumors circulated by the grapevine. The content of rumors is seldom checked for accuracy and no one seems to assume responsibility for the gossip that passes through the informal channels of communications. Despite this, the same managers often fail to recognize that they themselves use one of the "grapevines" that exist in the ranks of management since most, if not all, members of the organization are a part of some informal communications system.

Informal channels of communication cannot be diagrammed the way formal networks can because the lines of informal communications change as rapidly as the personal relationships between organization members do. Job-oriented communications are not confined exclusively to the work place because many on-the-job friendships are carried over into the social lives of the employees.

Informal communications patterns are an integral part of informal group structure and, therefore, cannot be controlled by the formal organizational structure, company policies, or management desires. Informal communications seem to serve many functions for employees; among them is the need to have friendly relationships with others. This desire cannot be suppressed in any acceptable fashion in an organization that operates within the framework of a democratic society. Another function served by the grapevine is providing organizational members with information which helps them make sense out of their environment. If the firm neglects to provide ample information about its operations, future plans, and anticipated changes, organizational members will "speculate" about the answers.

Since the organization cannot control the operation or content of informal communications, the alternative to having false work-oriented rumors pass through the grapevine is to constantly keep employees informed about its operations, most particularly those of worker interest outlined earlier in the chapter. This action will not necessarily diminish the activity of the grapevine, but it will help insure that the content of the rumor or gossip is more closely associated with fact.

THE INFLUENCE OF
COMMUNICATIONS ON EMPLOYEES

The process of communications is complex and involves many dimensions, both formal and informal. The conveyance of a message or many messages from a sender to a target audience is only one such dimension. Often transmission of material, along with its reception, is considered the totality of communications. In most organizations this limited concept of communications is not enough. The purpose of many communications in an organization is beyond dissemination and collection of information; action on the part of the intended audience is also expected. This means that the motivational aspect of communications must be considered. Cognitive material, which relates facts, problems, and suggestions, is a necessary part and content of organizational communications, formal and informal. Communications expected to be more than "understood" by an audience must also consider the emotional aspects of the message which facilitates either acceptance or rejection. Unless the organizational climate is one in which members feel free to discuss, question, and explore the content of communications, the result may lead to hostility, distrust and other negative attitudes among employees which tend to reduce the flow and acceptance of relevant communications and to stimulate motives which distort communications, up, down, and across the organization. Consequently, every individual, most particularly those occupying supervisory positions, responsible for any part of the communications system in an organization should plan carefully what he communicates and the way it is communicated.

Most of what is communicated by a supervisor goes beyond what he says. Some supervisors may never say the wrong thing, yet may fail to influence their subordinates to act beyond the minimum requirements of the job. Other supervisors who may not necessarily be as articulate and who may violate many rules of good leadership may gain the respect of their subordinates and be able to influence them so that they obtain high levels of production. The difference may lie in the desire of these supervisors to *know and communicate* with their subordinates and their receptivity to the subordinates' desires to know and communicate with them.

SUGGESTIONS FOR IMPROVING COMMUNICATIONS SKILLS

Although a knowledge of organizational communications channels and the communications process is valuable in helping individuals improve their communications skills, such knowledge will not necessarily aid a person to be more effective in face-to-face communications and relationships. A genuine effort must be made by the individual to level with others in daily job contacts. In this case, "to level" does not mean to say just anything that one feels like saying or to let others have "a piece of one's mind." Such communications are liable to breed resentment and hostility in others. Leveling does not mean confining remarks to polite and noncontroversial comments, since this often leaves important and pertinent things unsaid and may lead to gaps in information necessary to resolve issues and problems confronting the group. The kind of *leveling* referred to in face-to-face communications involves saying the things one believes are most significant about current problems in the work or in personal relationships with the intention of helping others to learn or to resolve problem situations.

Four factors determine the effectiveness of leveling in the communications process. They are (1) the conditions under which leveling occurs, (2) the speaker's behavior, (3) the listener's behavior, and (4) the expectations of the listener. One proponent of improving the quality of face-to-face communications, Robert Morton, explains how each one of these factors affect communications, and he suggests the following ten points as guides to improve leveling:

> 1. *Focus on behavior rather than the person.* It is important to refer to what a person does, rather than to comment on what you imagine he *is.* Use adverbs (which relate to actions) rather than adjectives (which relate to qualities) when referring to a person. Thus, it is better to say that a person "talked a good deal in the meeting" than to call him a "loud-mouthed person."
>
> 2. *Focus on observations rather than inferences.* Observations refer to what you can see or hear of the behavior of another person, or its effect on you. Inferences are interpretations of the behavior ("You were defensive" or "You are a driver"). The sharing of inferences may be valuable, but it is important that they be so identified.
>
> 3. *Focus on description rather than judgment.* Describing is reporting what has occurred. Judging is evaluating in terms of good or bad, right or

wrong, pleasant or unpleasant. Judgments come out of a personal frame of reference or value, whereas description is more neutral.

4. *Focus on descriptions of behavior in terms of "more" or "less," rather than either-or.* The more-or-less terminology stresses quantity, which is objective and measurable, rather than quality, which is subjective and judgmental. Thus, a person's participation may be anywhere from low to high, rather than good or bad. To think in terms of categories—for instance, authoritarian or permissive—rather than in terms of more or less easily leads to the conversation of a description into a casual interpretation: "He behaves this way because he is authoritarian."

5. *Focus on behavior related to a specific situation—preferably to the here and now—rather than on behavior in the abstract.* What people do is always tied in some way to time and place. Information is most meaningful when given as soon as appropriate after the observation or reactions occur.

6. *Focus on the sharing of ideas and information rather than on giving advice.* When ideas and information are shared, the receiver is freer to decide for himself, in the light of his own goals, in a particular situation and at a particular time, how to use the ideas and information. When you give advice you tell him what to do with the information, and thus restrict his freedom to determine for himself the most appropriate course of action. You also reduce his personal responsibility for his own behavior, since he is doing what someone else told him to do.

7. *Focus on exploration of alternatives.* The more attention given to the possible alternatives for the attainment of a particular goal, the greater the probability that the best solution to any problem will be found. It is all too easy to carry around a collection of set answers and courses of action, which we automatically apply to every problem that arises.

8. *Focus on the "contract" that exists between persons in any significant relationship.* The information provided should serve the needs of the recipient rather than the needs of the giver. Help and feedback should be given and perceived as an offer, not an imposition. (*Note:* The establishment of an open and supportive atmosphere in which decisions can be made and ideas can be exchanged freely is nearly impossible when a person in a position of leadership, whether first line supervisor or top executive, does not curb his own ambition to dominate others. When this occurs, the leader usually becomes more concerned with letting subordinates know who is boss than he is with encouraging others to express their ideas.)

9. *Focus on the amount of information that the person receiving it can use, rather than on the amount that you have and might like to give.* To overload a person with information is to reduce the possibility that he may use what he receives effectively. When we give more than can be profitably used, we are actually satisfying some need of our own, instead of helping the other person.

10. *Focus on what is said rather than why it is said.* The aspects of information that relate to the *what, how, when,* and *where* are observable

characteristics. The *why* of what is said, however, goes from the observable to the inferred, and brings up questions of motive. To make assumptions about the motives of the person may prevent him from hearing or lead him to distort what you are saying [7].

The guides for improving interpersonal communications suggested by Morton are particularly relevant when the exchange of ideas, opinions, or attitudes is essential to understanding between group members. Such situations often arise when managers, supervisors, or workers are collaborating when making plans, arriving at decisions, or exploring problems confronting the group. Usually, such occasions call for each person's best contribution. Yet often ideas new to the speaker, as well as his colleagues, are poorly phrased. The merit of an individual's idea may not be brought to the surface and clarified if he feels threatened or intimidated by the rest of the group's impatience with his momentary inability to clearly articulate his views.

The problem of leveling is compounded if group members have personal differences that interfere with their capacity to remain objective. The barriers to leveling may stem from personality differences or because of varying perspectives regarding the topic of conversation. It is not uncommon for labor negotiations to break down because the dialogue between negotiators turns into personal assaults. The same lack of understanding can occur in discussions between members of two different departments in the same company. The conflict that arises between line and staff managers is frequently the result of lack of effort to level with each other. Constructive dialogue that helps to resolve problems and/or differences of opinion seldom can take place when the principals feel defensive about the positions they hold.

In the chapter that follows, face-to-face interviewing situations will be discussed, in which the application of the techniques of leveling described in the foregoing section have particular relevance in fostering effective communications.

SUMMARY

1. Communications are an inseparable part of human relations. When observing, writing, speaking, and listening are considered as a part of the communications process, many organizational members spend up to 90 per cent of their time communicating. Because of the technological achievements which help improve the mechanical *means* of communications, the content of communications are frequently overlooked.

2. The purpose of communications is to reach an understanding of messages transmitted from a speaker or writer to a target audience. Understanding does not necessarily mean agreement. But before honest

disagreements can occur, an understanding of the issues in the discussion must be reached. This can only be achieved if one listens carefully to what is being communicated.

3. The science of machine language is called *cybernetics*. The process of communications between man and machines involves five steps which provide for feedback; these five steps are paralleled in the communications between human beings. They are the origination of a message, the encoding of it, the transmission of the message, the receiving of it by the intended audience and, finally, the interpretation of it. Each of these steps presents its own problems and barriers to communications.

4. In order to overcome some of the barriers to two-way communications and to reduce extremely poor communications, a person might use the following suggestions: make sure the message is accurate, consider the characteristics of the audience, communicate honestly, avoid gobble-dygook, and make communications timely. These suggestions apply to either written or oral communications.

5. Formal communications that have relevance to organizational matters usually are passed along channels patterned after the formal organizational structure, or chain of command. Three channels of communication exist in most firms. They convey information downward, upward, and across organizational lines. Much of the inefficiency of downward oral communications is attributed to poor listening and remembering by organizational members. Other factors are the filtering, withholding, and distortion of communications as they pass from top-ranking company officials to rank-and-file employees.

Upward communications may be even more inefficient than downward ones because of the tendency of subordinates both to withhold information they do not believe their superiors want to hear and to exaggerate the information they think their superiors like.

Horizontal communications are necessitated by the increased technology and specialization that has occurred in industry. However, such communications are often inhibited by barriers which arise from differences in perspective and by organizational competition.

6. Considerable research has been conducted to determine the most effective patterns of communications within an organization. Experiments conducted in laboratory situations have attempted to measure the differences in group performance, speed, and accuracy when various communications patterns are used. Two patterns or networks tested are, first, the *star* pattern, in which one group member plays a key role in the transmission of information between the other group members, and, second, the *circle* pattern, which is open and decentralized and no single group member plays a dominant role in controlling the communications. A preliminary summary of the results of these experiments seems to indicate that in a centralized communications system group members

solve problems more rapidly and accurately, but they do not receive much personal satisfaction and are not flexible to changing conditions. In decentralized communications, group members appear to have more satisfaction and be more flexible, but they were not as fast or accurate in solving problems.

7. Informal communications are often called the grapevine. Actually, many grapevines exist within an organization. Information in these informal channels can be social gossip, as well as job-oriented conversation. No formal pattern can be diagrammed for informal communications systems because the pattern is highly dependent upon the interpersonal social relationships of organizational members which are constantly changing.

8. Supervisors influence their subordinates by more than the spoken or written messages that they communicate. Their attitudes and their willingness to accept subordinates as individuals are important elements in the influence they exercise over the group's willingness and attitude toward communicating upward and toward performing efficiently.

9. Important to the effectiveness of organizational and face-to-face communications is the degree to which leveling occurs in the daily interpersonal relationships between organizational workers. Leveling, in this instance, refers to one's ability to say what is necessary in order to help others learn and resolve current problems. Four factors affect the degree to which individuals are able to level with each other. The conditions under which communications occur, the behavior of the speaker, the behavior of the listener, and the expectations of the listener are the principal elements which determine the quality and meaningfulness of communications and interpersonal relations between organizational members.

DISCUSSION QUESTIONS

1. How does the means of communication affect the degree of understanding that occurs?
2. In what ways can differences in perspective between a superior and a subordinate affect communications?
3. What is the relationship between cybernetics in man-machine communications and person-to-person communications?
4. Why are semantic differences a problem in communications?
5. What is the function of listening in communications?
6. What is the difference between formal and informal communications?
7. How does the structure of a communications network affect group performance?

8. What are the barriers to downward communications? Are they the same in upward and horizontal communications? In what ways do they differ?

9. What influence does nonverbal communications have on the process of communications? Give some examples of the way nonverbal communications affect understanding.

BIBLIOGRAPHY AND SELECTED COLLATERAL READINGS

1. BARNARD, CHESTER I., *The Functions of the Executive.* Cambridge, Mass.: Harvard University Press, 1964.
2. BAVELAS, ALEX, "Research on Communications," *Social Science for Industry: Motivation.* Proceedings of a third seminar arranged by Stanford Research Institute, March 23, 1955.
3. DRUCKER, PETER, *The New Society.* New York: Harper & Row, 1950.
4. EISENSON, JON, and others, *The Psychology of Communications.* New York: Appleton-Century-Crofts, 1963.
5. "Employee Communications for Better Understanding." The National Association of Manufacturers. Industrial Relations Division. New York: National Association of Manufacturers, 1951, p. 11.
6. LEAVITT, HAROLD J., *Managerial Psychology,* rev. ed. Chicago: University of Chicago Press, 1964.
7. MORTON, ROBERT B., "Leveling with Others on the Job," *Personnel* (November–December, 1966).
8. NICHOLS, RALPH G., *Listening Is Good Business.* Washington: Industrial College of the Armed Forces, 1964.
9. ROGERS, CARL R., "Barriers and Gateways to Communication," *Harvard Business Review* (July–August, 1952), pp. 46–52.
10. RUBENSTEIN, A. H. and C. J. HABERSTROH, *Some Theories of Organization,* rev. ed. Homewood, Ill.: Richard D. Irwin, 1966.
11. SHANNON, CLAUDE E. and WARREN WEAVER, *Mathematical Theory of Communication.* Urbana, Ill.: University of Illinois Press, 1949.
12. THAYER, L., *Communication and Communication Systems.* Homewood, Ill.: Richard D. Irwin, 1968.
13. TIFFIN, JOSEPH, and ERNEST J. McCORMICK, *Industrial Psychology,* 5th ed. Englewood Cliffs, N.J.: Prentice-Hall, 1965.
14. WIENER, NORBERT, *Cybernetics,* 2nd ed. Cambridge, Mass.: Massachusetts Institute of Technology Press, 1961.

15

Interviewing

Obtaining effective results through the efforts of other people requires an expansion of human skills beyond technical competence; namely, the ability to communicate with others. When a subordinate says, "My boss and I do not speak the same language," what he is really saying is that he and his boss have not found a way to reach each other's minds. Their failure to communicate usually is not a matter of differences in vocabulary, but a matter of emotion, perception, or willingness to listen to each other's viewpoint. Suspicion, hostility, or fear may distort the sense of the words they use with each other.

A minimum of noise, maximum of immediate and continuous feedback, and as much redundancy as required by a specific situation must be provided in an ideal system of communication. One system of communication that provides an optimum potential for these three factors is the interview. When a person earnestly desires communication with another and when he really wants to make certain he is understood and understands, he will meet and converse with that other person face-to-face in private. This setting is characteristic of an interview and makes it one of the most effective and efficient of interpersonal communication media [9, p. 19].

It should be obvious that a supervisor's effectiveness diminishes in proportion to the number of subordinates with whom he is unable to communicate; yet, a supervisor must be alert to the danger of two-way communications with his subordinates that lack the leveling element discussed in the previous chapter. If leveling is not a part of the working relationship between a supervisor and his workers, he must remember that his subordinates will tend to relate information and ideas to him they believe he wants to hear. Conversely, they will withhold or diminish information they think he does not want to hear. Thus, over the long-run, a supervisor must develop relations with his subordinates in which they will convey both good and bad news.

314

Even when a supervisor is successful in establishing rapport with his work group, he should also develop the communications skill necessary to obtain both sufficient and accurate information from others in order to make decisions, take action, or direct others to take action. One of the common communications tools used in business and industry to do this is the personal interview.

PERSONAL INTERVIEWS

Broadly speaking, nearly any communicative contact between two people can be defined as an interview. However, most interviews in business have a specific objective and a limited amount of available time for any single interview.

The objective of the personal interview will vary depending on the situation. Employment interviews have one objective; an interview in which a supervisor is reviewing the job performance of a worker has a distinctly different objective. The primary objective of the interview determines what information is exchanged and, in some degree, the way the interview is to be conducted.

Good interviewing requires more than a facility with words. It involves patience, self-confidence, the ability to phrase questions well, sensitivity to facial expressions or other overt signs of emotion, and a wide range of general interests and knowledge. Experience in meeting and dealing with people is a valuable asset and can be developed over time, but a firm grasp of the objective of the interview is essential for the experienced as well as the novice interviewer. Therefore, regardless of the purpose of the interview, the interviewer would improve his effectiveness by preparing for it.

Some of the questions the interviewer might ask himself in preparation for an interview are

1. What is the primary objective of this interview?

2. What information do I wish to obtain or convey?

3. Will there be any written records or documents I should have on hand?

4. How much time will this interview take?

5. If the other person involved in the interview is known to me, is there any special or particular method of interviewing that should be used during the interview in order to facilitate better communications?

Once answers to these questions are determined, steps can be taken to help insure the success of the interview. If the nature of the interview is one that requires privacy, such as an employee counseling or disciplinary situation, a place should be chosen where there will be no interruptions so that the conversation will not be overheard. In other cases, privacy may not be essential and brief meetings can be held in a mutually agreeable and convenient place.

The nature of the interview and the experience of the interviewer will influence how much preparation should be given to the interview. In some cases, only short notice will be given and long preparation will not be possible. Often interviews are casual and appear to be combined with social purposes. In such cases, discussions may be held while having a cup of coffee or while having lunch. If appropriate, an interview could be held during a golf game. While many jokes have been made about combining business conferences and golf, the point is that the location of an interview is often less important than the content and quality of the communication.

INTERVIEWING METHODS

The techniques that can be used to obtain information during an interview range from a straightforward exchange of questions and answers to a very informal and unstructured conversation. The most effective method of interviewing will depend on a number of factors: the objective of the interview, the amount of time available, and the personality of both the interviewer and the interviewee.

DIRECTIVE TECHNIQUES

Directive interviewing techniques are also called *patterned* or *structured* interviews. In such situations the interviewer usually plays the dominant role during the course of the interview; that is, he determines what questions are asked and how much latitude the other person or persons have in giving answers. In its strictest form, directive interviewing resembles interrogation, which evolved from the military method of questioning prisoners. Obviously, in industry such techniques are not generally applicable, but there are instances when the primary objective of an interview is to convey quickly and concisely information with only a minimum of necessity for elaboration or exchange of ideas.

NONDIRECTIVE TECHNIQUES

Quite apart from directive interviewing methods are *permissive* or *nondirective* techniques which were developed as an early tool used by psychologists. This technique permits the interviewee to talk at random until he hits upon an issue of importance. Then his attention is directed toward an exploration of the topic along with his feelings and attitudes toward it. This method is also known as *client-centered interviewing* and represents one of the nondirective techniques of interviewing developed for use by counselors who were not necessarily trained psychologists. The loose structure of this interviewing technique does not mean that the client is permitted to explore useless blind alleys with meaningless prattle. In most cases, client-centered interviews involve subtle direction. The objective is not just to talk, but to examine systematically certain important experiences in the client's past which may underlie his mental difficulties [1, p. 17].

The use of this method may afford an opportunity to the employee to "sound off" about a particular problem. This "sounding off" may have therapeutic value. Such a technique requires the listener to be nonevaluative. This means that regardless what the interviewee says, the listener does not indicate either his disapproval or his approval. Depersonalizing oneself enough to master this technique of nonevaluative listening is a vigorous discipline which needs to be developed if success is to be obtained.

Supervisors often find it difficult not to show signs of disapproval or approval during interviewing sessions with subordinates because such behavior runs contrary to the role they play during most other aspects of their job. They are usually called upon to give approval or disapproval to the actions and behavior of employees during normal work routines and decision-making situations. Their usual role is, of necessity, directive, and it requires maintaining a strong set of managerial values. Thus, for a supervisor to transpose himself into the blank personality required during a client-centered interview is usually both unfamiliar and uncomfortable.

In the majority of interviewing situations in business and industry, a combination of both directive and nondirective methods is used. A supervisor or manager is required to participate in a wide variety of interviewing situations, and the interviewing methods that he will need to employ in one case may not be appropriate in another. He seldom can rely on one interviewing technique to the exclusion of others.

There are some interviews which are particularly important from the standpoint of human relations because they deal directly with actions that affect the lives of other persons, rather than with the collection or exchange of technical information. These situations deal with:

1. The selection of personnel for employment or promotion.
2. The disciplining or criticising of an employee's performance or job behavior.
3. Employee counseling.

EMPLOYMENT INTERVIEWS

The employment interview is complex because in a matter of from twenty minutes to an hour the interviewer is trying to obtain an accurate understanding of the experiences of many years. The lifetime of a job applicant contains thousands of experiences producing attitudes, motivations, and behavior that are, in many cases, unknown to the applicant himself. Furthermore, when such information is known to the applicant he can and does modify it, either slightly or substantially. In light of this probability, the interviewer must avoid making hasty judgments and carefully attempt to substantiate his appraisal of the applicant through an effective line of questioning which avoids offending the applicant; at the same time, the interviewer must obtain the information he needs to reach a decision.

In addition to interviews, other selection and screening devices may be used, such as application forms or employment tests. The supervisor should also avail himself of the information from these tools when possible.

EMPLOYMENT INTERVIEWS FROM THE VIEWPOINT OF THE INTERVIEWER

Employment interviews, as most other formal interviews, can be divided into three phases or parts: the opening, the main body, the close.

The Opening of an Interview. The opening phase of an employment interview is critical. The interviewer is apt to make his preliminary judgment of the applicant during this first impression stage of the meeting. The applicant's appearance, his bearing, his handshake, his facial expressions, and his voice may contribute to an impression which unduly influences the interviewer's judgment. If the overall impression of the applicant is favorable, the *halo effect* may affect the critical judgment of the interviewer; if the first impression is unfavorable, the interviewer may prejudge the applicant's qualifications before they have been adequately examined and discussed. Because of the danger of obtaining a fixed impression before the interview is really under way, the interviewer should make a conscious effort during the first few minutes to forget that he is an interviewer and act as if he were greeting a friend or work associate.

The applicant has no reason for delaying his evaluation of the interviewer in these first few minutes. The appearance, voice, manner, and speech of the interviewer are important during this period in establishing

a desirable effect, a feeling in the applicant that the interviewer is someone he likes and respects and that he is interested in him as an individual,
not as a machine. The reason that a positive impression is important is
that it will encourage the applicant to talk more freely and frankly. Getting an applicant to talk is one of the basic skills of an interviewer.

Some additional factors relating to this early phase of the interview
should be considered. Privacy is strongly recommended. If the interviewer wants a frank discussion, he should be free of interruptions or
telephone calls; these may happen just as the applicant is beginning
to be frank and may cause the applicant to withdraw or withhold
information he was about to relate. It may be a good time for the interviewer to tell the applicant about the company because while the interviewer is talking it will give the applicant a chance to relax and develop
confidence in the interviewer. Telling the applicant about actual job requirements at this time should be avoided because it may cause him to
slant his answers to fit the requirements.

The Main Body of the Interview.   Up to this point, the interviewer may
have done most of the talking. During the main body of the interview, his
effort should be directed toward having the applicant do most of the
talking. The interviewer should remain friendly and attentive and talk
only enough to get the applicant to answer questions or avoid rambling
from the topic. Some recommendations used by interviewers to get an
applicant to talk and still get the information wanted are

1. Don't ask questions that can be answered yes or no. Questions should
be worded so that the applicant has to talk. The interviewer will often
ask for an elaboration by saying, "How did you come to be interested?"
and "How do you feel about that?"

2. Pauses for a few seconds after the applicant is seemingly finished
with his answer before the next question is asked give the applicant a
chance to add further information and are sometimes quite helpful. The
interviewer who feels he must fill every silence should be aware that
his eagerness to talk is often a concern for his own comfort rather than
the applicant's.

3. Several different subjects may be introduced to see which is most
provocative in encouraging the applicant to talk. The interviewer should
return to important topics on which the applicant was hesitant to determine if the lack of response was significant.

4. Repeating part of key sentences of the applicant in a questioning
tone will indicate that elaboration is wanted.

5. Questions should be asked one at a time, giving the applicant an
opportunity to answer before the next one is asked.

6. The questions should be clear, but no indication should be given as to the expected answer.

7. The interviewer should be interested; he should offer uninterrupted attention and be neither critical nor impatient.

8. Highly personal questions should not be asked until rapport has been established.

9. The applicant should not be brought abruptly back to the point when he has digressed. He should be directed, however.

10. Language appropriate for the applicant should be used.

The preceding methods are directed primarily at getting the applicant to speak freely, but there is also a need for the interviewer to be careful in the phrasing of his comments and questions. If an interviewer is not careful about the way he frames his questions, the applicant may be led to give what he believes is the desired answer because the wording seems to imply a preferred answer. Care must be taken not to phrase a question in such a way as to encourage the applicant to stretch the truth. One method for obtaining truthful answers from applicants is to employ non-directive methods of interviewing in which the interviewer listens non-evaluatively. In this way, the applicant is given a chance to express his feelings without being censured or criticized. It should be emphasized that the manner of the interviewer is as important as his words in establishing such an attitude. A warm, relaxed manner is basic to achieving this goal. The interviewer must not lose sight of the fact that the applicant's behavior during the interview is strongly influenced by that of the interviewer. A cold and humorless interviewer may cause those he interviews to appear shy, retiring, and too serious, while the same applicants may give quite different impressions with a different interviewer. The interviewer must be constantly conscious that the actions he observes in the applicant are partly the product of his own actions.

The Close of the Interview.   The close of the interview is as important as the opening. This is the time for the interviewer to be sure he has not overlooked anything important, a time for him to encourage the applicant to present anything the previous discussion has omitted, and the time for the interviewer to be especially watchful as the applicant may have dropped his guard and some actions may be more nearly representative of his true behavior than anything he has done or said thus far. He may express hostility toward others; he may volunteer unrealistic ambitions and goals; or he may become firm, mature, and positive when he may have been previously responding to a pattern created by the interviewer. The interview is not over until the applicant has left. The interviewer's manner may be more relaxed at the end, but his observation cannot be.

INTERVIEWING AND SUPERVISOR-EMPLOYEE RELATIONS

The degree to which a supervisor will be involved in employment interviewing depends on the size of the company, the particular type of job for which the applicant is applying, and the personnel policies of the particular firm regarding the employment process. Whether the company is large or small or whether the job opening is in a production department or in a sales department, the principles of employment interviewing provide a useful guideline for the supervisor during the initial contact between himself and a job applicant. Such interviewing principles also have broad application to the first meeting between a supervisor and a new employee. This is true even if the supervisor did not play a major role in the selection process.

Once a new worker has been placed on the job, the process of developing sound personal relations between him and his supervisor begin. The quality of this relationship will be affected by many factors, including the personalities of the individuals involved. There are several elements in the relationship between a supervisor and his subordinates which are of particular importance because they involve human relations skills rather than technical competence. Two such elements are the use of criticism and discipline; another is employee counseling.

CRITICISM OF EMPLOYEES

One of the supervisor's responsibilities is to develop his subordinates into effective and productive group members. This is true regardless of the department in which the supervisor is in charge. The development of an employee takes time and involves many processes requiring personal contact between the worker and his supervisor. Orientation and job training are two initial processes used to develop employees. Over a longer period of time, performance evaluation and on-the-job coaching by the supervisor grow in importance and involve a deepening personal relationship between supervisor and subordinate. The use of criticism can be a critical element in the long-run relationship between a supervisor and the individual employees for which he is responsible. Criticism occurs from the beginning of the training process of a new employee and continues throughout his job career with a company. The value of criticism in helping to improve an employee's performance will depend on the circumstances and the manner in which it is given. Criticism can be a constructive process when it points out what has been done correctly as well as what needs to be improved. However, criticism is often viewed by both supervisors and subordinates as a destructive element because "what is wrong" is often emphasized while "what is right" is disregarded. For this reason, supervisors and employees alike frequently feel uncomfortable when criticism is being leveled. The discussion here is directed toward the function of criticism used to help improve a worker's performance.

A supervisor who attempts to be a colleague of his subordinates rather than a boss may believe that the use of criticism will jeopardize his relationship with the work group. Therefore, he may be tempted to "let things slide" when an employee's performance actually warrants criticism. In so doing, a supervisor may allow the unsatisfactory performance of an employee to persist until some incident absolutely requires criticism, causing the supervisor to criticize the past as well as the present unsatisfactory performance of the employee. In such cases, the employee may be shocked to find that his past performance was not satisfactory, particularly when no comments had been made.

The opposite problem in the use of criticism occurs when a supervisor constantly finds fault with the performance of his subordinates. A supervisor who is hypercritical may find that employees develop the attitude that they cannot do anything right—so they stop trying. The problems created by the overuse of criticism can be just as detrimental to group morale and performance as those created by not criticizing an employee's performance when such criticism is needed.

In an attempt to circumvent the problem of criticizing employees, some supervisors employ the technique of praising an employee for something before the use of criticism. The danger to this technique is that the worker learns to beware of the supervisor when he hears praise. Furthermore, the use of praise in this manner tends to decrease its meaningfulness. Praise should be given when it is due, not as a constant prelude to criticism.

If praise should not be used before criticism, how should criticism be mixed with praise? One answer to this question is the technique of sandwiching criticism between doses of praise; that is, praise the worker, level with him in the criticism of his performance, and finally lift him up again with praise. This method may work in some cases, but if it is used consistently, it can become as ineffectual as the method of preceding criticism with praise.

A method which is useful and often more honest than any praise-criticism combination is for the supervisor (1) to explain what the problem is, that is, what the deficiency in the worker's performance has been; (2) to offer alternative ways of correcting the situation; and (3) to offer encouragement which starts the employee off on a change in job behavior. In this way, as the employee's behavior changes toward improved job performance, the supervisor has legitimate grounds for giving praise and further encouragement.

Often the process of giving criticism is part of the daily contact the supervisor has with his employees. He may discuss problems of performance with each worker as part of the training and coaching he gives during the regular work routine without the necessity of having a private interview to discuss such problems. Regardless of whether criticism is made during an interview or as part of the job routine, the following guides will help to improve the effectiveness of criticism.

(1) *Criticize in private.* The reason for criticism is to direct performance toward higher levels, not to belittle or humiliate the worker. If an interview is used, it should be held in some place where other group members will not overhear the discussion. This does not mean that an employee should be summoned to the supervisor's office only when something is wrong. The phrase referring to this practice is "being called on the carpet." Under such circumstances, criticism may be leveled in private, but the work group soon learns that being summoned to the supervisor's office probably means receiving adverse criticism from the supervisor. If it is necessary to criticize a worker's performance right at the job station, the remarks should be leveled in a constructive manner in which the supervisor does not deliberately humiliate the worker by raising his voice or making a display of the criticism he is giving a worker.

(2) *Direct criticism toward the action or performance of the worker, not toward the individual worker himself.* An attack on the individual worker usually leads to defensiveness on his part which inevitably reduces the chance that he will learn constructively from the criticism. Demeaning an employee for poor performance raises hostility and resentment without getting at the reason for substandard performance.

One difficulty in confining criticism to the action of the employee rather than directing it toward the individual is in how to control one's temper. The supervisor should not allow himself a temper tantrum each time he criticizes a worker's performance, but if the action of an employee has been serious enough to anger the supervisor, he is probably wiser to let the employee know it. On no occasion should the supervisor take the extreme liberty of permitting himself to find an emotional outlet for his anger at the expense of employee dignity.

(3) *Attempt to learn the reason for the employee's actions.* If a worker's performance is inadequate, what was the cause: lack of training, misunderstanding of instructions, malfunctioning equipment? Perhaps poor employee performance in the future can only be curtailed by taking some action not involving the employee himself. More careful maintenance of equipment or more detailed or clearer instructions from the supervisor may be called for. If the reason for substandard performance was that the employee's training or ability was insufficient, other steps

would have to be taken to prevent reoccurrence of the problem; criticism won't correct it.

(4) *Explain the importance of the need of a change in employee performance or behavior.* Often employees do not understand how their performance relates to a larger scheme of events. Only when such relationships are explained can they be expected to understand their contribution to the organization's activities.

An explanation of the importance of each individual's contribution to the whole can provide a basis in which an employee can develop a sense of pride in his own performance. Without a sense of pride in what he does, it seems unlikely that an employee will take a genuine interest in improving his job performance.

(5) *Provide a plan of action to improve performance.* After a discussion has been held in which the actual behavior or performance of the worker has been reviewed and the reasons for such behavior have been examined, the final step is to develop some alternative plan of action so that the employee's performance can be improved. This may possibly involve training that is additional to what he has already received or, possibly, retraining or closer supervision for a period of time. Whatever action is necessary to help the employee improve his performance should be outlined to the employee so that he knows what is expected of him. The employee should be left with a constructive course of action to follow and a definite means of obtaining assistance if he has further difficulty in meeting performance standards.

EMPLOYEE DISCIPLINE

The general guides that have been outlined for using criticism of an employee's job performance also have application to situations where behavior on the job calls for discipline. The breaking of work rules or company regulations by work-group members creates disciplinary problems for the supervisor which may be quite different from substandard job performance. A supervisor may find that employees who perform their jobs quite satisfactorily are the same ones who violate company rules; that is, workers whose production levels rank high in the work group may also break company rules by consistently arriving late for work or by taking longer coffee breaks than other work-group members. A supervisor may find that by ignoring such behavior he invites similar behavior from other employees who cannot maintain the same levels of production if they reduce the time spent on the job. It is necessary for the supervisor to take some action.

For purposes of discussion, in the context of modern management it is important to define discipline as an educational process rather than as punishment, which was the concept of traditional management. This means that the objective of discipline is to teach the employee a mode of behavior acceptable to the requirements of the job, rather than to punish him for breaking a rule. This ideal is not recognized by all supervisors and definitely does not conform to the concept of discipline held by those who favor the traditional view of management (Theory X of McGregor). It must be recognized that all company rules are not of equal importance, but all rules should have a valid reason for their existence. The first step in maintaining *discipline*, in the modern meaning of the word, is to inform employees of the company rules that apply to all and, more specifically, to inform employees of particular rules which apply to the department in which they work. Thus, discipline begins with the orientation of new employees and is a continuing process throughout all phases of job training.

Rather than attempt to provide a supervisor with a list of specific methods for coping with employees who violate company rules, a few general principles may prove more valuable in helping him determine the appropriate disciplinary action he should take in any particular situation.

(1) *Employees should be informed about possible disciplinary action.* This means that all new employees should be told *what* company rules apply to them, *why* such rules exist, and, finally, the *action* that will be taken if the rules are broken. Depending upon the nature of the rule that has been broken, the action taken by the supervisor may range from little more than a verbal warning to dismissal from the job. Usually, dismissal is the ultimate disciplinary action taken for violation of a major company rule. Examples of when this ultimate action might be necessary occur when one employee intentionally injures another while on the job or when a worker deliberately damages company equipment or property.

(2) *Disciplinary action should take place as soon as the infraction is discovered.* It is important that the supervisor take whatever disciplinary steps he intends to take as soon as possible after he finds out the rule has been broken by an employee. Prolonged delays between the infraction and the discipline may imply that the supervisor doesn't care about a certain rule. It may also lead others to believe that they can break rules and get away with it if they can keep out of the supervisor's way for a long enough period.

(3) *Discipline should apply to all workers.* If a sense of justice is to be conveyed by a supervisor regarding discipline, all known infractions by employees should be disciplined and all known violators should be disciplined. This means that discipline should be impartial insofar that it is accorded to anyone who is known to have broken a rule. The supervisor can do much to undermine the group's morale if he knowingly allows some members to break the rules and get away with breaking it while

other members are disciplined. To play favorites with some by looking the other way when they break rules will rapidly lead the work group to believe that the supervisor is unjust. If this occurs, it is likely that the suspicion with which workers regard the supervisor will extend to matters regarding all aspects of his responsibility.

(4) *Discipline should be consistent.* In addition to making sure that all subordinates who break rules are disciplined, the supervisor must be sure that whatever disciplinary action is taken is commensurate to the infraction. To discipline severely one individual for an infraction of a rule and to let another off with a verbal warning for the same violation will certainly cause suspicion among employees. If disciplinary treatment of two employees is to be different for seemingly the same infraction, the supervisor had better be sure that he has a justifiable explanation. When this situation occurs, it is probably advisable that he state his reasons to the work group even if questions are not asked by either the offender or the group.

The foregoing discussion of discipline has not included the participation of labor unions. In cases where a union represents the workers in a company or a particular department, it is imperative that the supervisor be well versed in both the company rules and the limitations of the disciplinary action that can be taken for each type of violation. These are well defined in the contract that has been negotiated between company management and the labor union representing the workers. A supervisor should be aware that if the employees in his department are unionized, practically all formal disciplinary action by him will result in a union grievance. Therefore, the supervisor must be sure that the disciplinary action he takes with any employee is within the prescribed limits of that labor contract. The following discussion is made under the assumption that the company can dismiss an employee whose performance or job behavior is not satisfactory. In many companies labor contracts prohibit or severely limit the possibility of firing an employee that is a union member. Whether or not the company has a free hand in dismissing workers, the human relations problems are much the same. Once a person has been hired, he deserves an opportunity to prove that he is capable of the work he has been hired to perform and is deserving of remaining a permanent employee as long as the economic condition of the company permits.

EMPLOYEE DISMISSAL

Dismissal of an employee is the ultimate action to be taken only after all other avenues of resolving the employee's problem have been pursued to practical limits. Even when all possible courses of action to avoid employee dismissal have been exhausted, the decision to dismiss an employee is likely to be an emotional situation when the supervisor actually conveys the news. The supervisor may tend to believe that the action was long overdue; the employee may consider the dismissal unjust and caused by unsympathetic temperament from his boss.

Because the act of firing an employee creates, by its very nature, a highly volatile situation, the supervisor should consider several elements in the separation process when such action is necessary. Unless an employee's action—malicious destruction of company property, or the like—warrants immediate dismissal, the supervisor should give the employee ample warning of the possible ultimate action and the reasons that such a dismissal action might be taken. The supervisor should not devote his energy only to building a case to justify a dismissal action; he must be certain to inform the worker of the inadequacy of his job performance or his unsatisfactory job behavior. The supervisor should have enough evidence about the unsatisfactory employee behavior and what attempts have been made to improve it to be able to demonstrate to the employee that he is being justly treated. The employee should be given a precise reason(s) for the dismissal. If adequate forewarning has been given, the employee should not be surprised.

Despite precautions and the forewarning given by the supervisor, the employee may make a dramatic display when the dismissal announcement is made. In such instances, the supervisor will do little to improve the situation if he is tactless or hostile during the private dismissal interview. In most cases, the supervisor will do well to allow the employee to vent nonviolent feelings before attempting to help the severed employee gain a perspective of the situation in order to determine the best course for future action.

By remaining calm, the supervisor may be able to point out how the employee may benefit by a change in jobs. Of course, this may be unrealistic when unemployment is high and economic conditions make finding another job difficult. Thus, when dismissing an employee it is a good practice to have made a consideration of the alternatives available to him after the dismissal. Usually, the supervisor should be willing to provide references for future employers. This can be done, in most cases, regardless of the cause for dismissal. The supervisor should not conceal the reason for dismissal from inquiries by future employers, but the events or reasons causing dismissal of the worker need not be stated in such a way to preclude hiring the former employee without fair consideration of his capabilities. In other words, supervisors should state as objectively as possible the reasons why an employee was dismissed without attacking his personality or inferring that he would not work well in a job requiring skills or aptitudes different from those of the job from which he was dismissed. This may be difficult if the cause of dismissal was dishonesty or some other breach of personal integrity.

In some cases, an employee is released through no fault of his own, but rather because of organizational or production changes. An element which can help the severed worker make the transition between jobs in such cases is a severance allowance that will help sustain him during a short period while he is seeking other employment. Not all companies have such programs, but where they do the supervisor should explain the operation of the company policy so that the severed employee understands the economic limitations he will encounter. In some instances, a company will actually try to place a former employee in another job. Placing an employee with another company is not a widespread practice and usually occurs when company operations are being curtailed.

Although firing an employee may be a disturbing experience to the supervisor, as well as to the dismissed employee, reactions of other members of the work group should be considered. They may be curious, if not apprehensive, about the dismissal of one of their fellow workers. Few employees would object to the dismissal of a worker for obviously *fair* and *sufficient* reasons, but often the severance of an employee is shrouded in an aura of secrecy. The problem created by secrecy is that employees may develop a different perception of fair and sufficient cause for dismissal. If the supervisor does not state his reasons for his action, the work group may believe the supervisor acted from personal motives at the expense of an innocent member of their group. It is incumbent upon the supervisor to state his reasons without disclosing any confidential information that might damage the personal reputation of the particular employee involved. There may be no practical way to avoid some secrecy if the reason for dismissal would be damaging to the severed individual. Saul W. Gellerman suggests that management's best strategy is not to get into this type of situation in the first place by cultivating a sound human relations climate and giving the inadequate employee every reasonable assistance and consideration before taking the last irrevocable step of firing him [5, p. 121].

EMPLOYEE COUNSELING

One of the more controversial activities in which a supervisor is sometimes involved is that of employee counseling. The concept of such counseling was originally proposed as a result of the Hawthorne Studies when it was discovered that having workers talk about their job problems seemed to help the human relations climate in the work group. The objective of employee counseling by a supervisor is to improve group morale and to help individual workers adjust to the social, psychological, and physical job environment. Such a well-meaning objective can hardly be refuted; however, the practice of employee counseling may fall short of its purpose unless the supervisor is well prepared and unless the counseling is done conscientiously.

A company program in employee counseling may result in the formalization of employee communications which should be a routine part of the supervisor's daily contact with his work group; that is, employee job-related problems should be openly and continuously discussed with employees during the process of on-the-job training, coaching, and performance evaluation rather than as a separate task to be accomplished during a counseling session.

An element which complicates the process of employee counseling is that many employee problems appear to be job related but actually originate in some other aspect of the employee's life. Family problems or a sudden economic crisis may affect an employee's job outlook and performance. In such cases, employee counseling may become an immensely complex process which requires extraordinary perception on the part of the supervisor. Two elements arise regarding a supervisor's involvement in employee counseling: (1) ethical problems, (2) practical considerations of employee counseling.

The ethical consideration is precisely how far should the supervisor delve into the private life of a subordinate when that supervisor suspects that the employee on-the-job behavior and performance is being affected by the off-the-job problems. In matters regarding excessive drinking or moral issues, should the supervisor advise an employee to change his behavior? If the supervisor does advise him and the employee refuses to change, what course of action is open to the supervisor? Answers to these questions are too complex to be answered easily and depend on the degree to which the employee's private life actually affects his job performance. While no absolute answers are available, if job performance is measurably affected and the supervisor is unable to provide necessary counseling and help, he should be prepared to direct the employee to a qualified professional such as a clergyman, doctor, family counselor, and so on.

The practical problems related to employee counseling deal not only with the competence of the supervisor to advise employees on personal matters, but also with the amount of time and effort the supervisor can afford to devote to such matters without neglecting his other job responsibilities. Many supervisors are astutely aware of the ethical and practical considerations; thus, they become reluctant to be deeply involved in employee counseling as they do not want to get into a situation with which they are unprepared to cope. The majority of supervisors recognize that they are not trained psychologists and they hesitate to advise an employee regarding his private life, even when that life affects his job performance.

Maladjusted workers can result from a multitude of causes found in the work environment. Mismatches can occur between one's abilities and the mental and physical requirements of the job. Employees may lack the opportunity for creative thinking on the job because work is routinized. An individual may feel that he is lost in an impersonal system of a company that is designed to handle large numbers of people rather than to recognize individual abilities and needs. The point is that the problems most employees have on the job are usually symptomatic of larger or more deep-rooted problems. Employees seldom become suddenly dissatisfied with their job, the company, or their boss without reason. A worker may harbor his feelings for a long period until something provokes him. Once the feelings are released, the employee may find he has gone too far or said too much. If the employee's pent-up feelings have been emotionally released in the presence of the work group, the result may be embarrassment and/or resentment on the part of others. These can be forces disruptive to the work group and until hostilities subside, group cohesiveness and productivity can be affected.

Employee counseling, properly conducted, can be used to help avoid the accumulation of minor employee problems to a point where they become major ones disruptive to group effort. Following the modern concept of human relations, employee counseling becomes an instrument for preventing problems as well as one to be used for resolving them. A supervisor must recognize that employee counseling is not a substitute for regular and continuous contact between himself and each of his subordinates.

Even when a supervisor accepts his own limitation in employee counseling, he will find that his position as leader of a work group will probably mean that workers will call upon him for advice and guidance (not only on job-related matters but even on personal matters). Thus, he will find that whether or not his company has a formal employee counseling program he will, at times, be required to counsel his subordinates.

The mechanics of counseling interviews are varied, but the primary purpose is to discover from what the employee says the real reasons for the problems he is having on the job. Once the problem is brought into the open and its real cause(s) uncovered, a mutual search for acceptable solutions can begin.

In order to conduct a counseling interview, the supervisor will find it necessary to alter the usual role he plays in the work group. If the situation is one in which there is conflict between himself and a subordinate, it is particularly important that the supervisor be able to emphasize the necessity of finding an acceptable solution to the conflict for all involved and not use his authority for reaching a solution that is possibly acceptable only to him. In broad terms, conflict between supervisors and subordinates can be resolved in three ways.

1. Because of his position, the supervisor can exercise his authority and provide the solution to the conflict himself without regard for the subordinate's point of view. When this occurs, the supervisor may win the point, but if it is not fully accepted by the subordinate, that subordinate may resist in ways difficult to detect but which may affect the productivity of the group. Thus, the supervisor may have his way on one point, but, ultimately, the subordinate retaliates in a way which creates more problems for the supervisor. Another danger inherent to this method of conflict resolution—that of the supervisor always providing the answer— is that, over the long run, the work group may come to depend upon the supervisor to resolve all conflict problems arising within it. The net result is that creativity in the group diminishes, little initiative is exercised by individuals, and little may be accomplished by the group when the supervisor is not present to resolve problems for them.

2. Another method of conflict resolution between a supervisor and a subordinate is for the subordinate to provide the answer to the problem. There is nothing unsatisfactory with this method when the resolution of the conflict is acceptable to the supervisor as well as to the subordinate; but when it is not, the supervisor's position of leadership and influence may be jeopardized if he permits the attempted implementation of an unworkable solution.

Implicit in either of the two methods of conflict resolution described thus far is the concept of win or lose. If the supervisor dominates, the subordinate loses, and vice versa.

3. The last method of dealing with conflict-resolution situations underlies the real purpose of employee counseling and the spirit of human relations. In this method, a mutual search is made for acceptable solutions to conflict and problems. This method calls for honest two-way communication in which both the facts and the feelings of the individuals are brought to the surface. The critical point in this method is that the *satisfactory solution* to conflict is the factor emphasized, not who wins. In order to make this system work, the supervisor will have to learn to *listen actively* to what the subordinate has to say. This means that in addition to being nonevaluative, the supervisor must permit and encourage the subordinate to express his feelings concerning the problem. This approach is contrary to the "I want no excuses" used by some supervisors when confronting a subordinate whose job behavior or performance does not meet expectations.

One aspect of the third method of conflict resolution is that *both* the supervisor and the subordinate may be required to alter their behavior. This compromise means that once the effect of each other's behavior is mutually known, each individual may then adjust his behavior to the extent necessary to reduce or eliminate the conflict.

Conflicts are bound to emerge between organizational members, so employee counseling, or for that matter the practice of human relations, should not be equated with an absence of conflict. On the contrary, the purpose is not to eliminate difference of opinion between organizational members, it is to help them resolve such differences in a constructive manner which will not discourage individuals from offering their viewpoints on the myriad of open-ended questions which must be faced every day in the dynamic environment of the work place.

SUMMARY

1. One of the supervisor's vital face-to-face communications skills is his ability to conduct personal interviews. To do this, he must prepare himself by knowing the objective of each interviewing situation so that he can determine the information he needs to gather or convey. This will help him establish the framework of the interview within which he can plan the time, length, place, and interviewing method to be used.

2. A range of interviewing techniques can be used by the supervisor. A directive or patterned interview is one in which the topic, tone, and direction of the interview is primarily controlled by the interviewer. The nondirective or permissive interview is one in which the person being interviewed is permitted to elaborate on the topics he finds most interesting or pertinent. Although nondirective interviews are usually informal and unstructured, the objective is to systematically examine the problem at hand so that solutions can be found. This can be a valuable communications method when the problem involves conflict between individuals because the method allows the interviewee to expound his personal feelings and enables him to relate the problem from his point of view.

3. Employment interviews are complex because in a relatively short time the interviewer must obtain enough information about an applicant's life-long experiences, attitudes, and ambitions to make the decision whether to give him further consideration for employment or to reject him. The interviewer must attempt to remain objective during the interview so that he will not be overly swayed by the "halo effect" or a favorable first impression; he should not be unduly critical if the applicant does not favorably impress him at the beginning of the interview. During the employment interview, the interviewer needs to know how to get and to keep the applicant talking so that as much information as possible can be obtained with which to evaluate the applicant's qualifications.

4. Supervisors find that certain interviews and face-to-face communications are particularly difficult to handle because the situation is potentially threatening emotionally both to themselves and to their subordinates. These circumstances usually involve human rather than technical topics, such as criticism, discipline, and employee counseling. During regular daily contacts and in special interviews in which the supervisor appraises the job performance and behavior of employees, he needs to know how to give constructive criticism and direction. To motivate employees to improve job performance, a supervisor should never use tactless criticism because it can create resentment and hostility in the work group which can cause job performance to deteriorate instead of improve. When criticizing an employee's performance, the supervisor should follow some basic guides: criticize in private; direct the criticism toward the action, not the person; learn the reason for the action; explain the need for a change in performance; and provide a plan of action.

5. The purpose of discipline is to educate the employee toward improved job behavior rather than to punish him for breaking rules. Within this modern meaning of *discipline*, the supervisor must inform employees of the standards of performance and job behavior expected of them. He must provide the training, motivation, and direction which permit employees to behave within the expected limits of the job.

6. Dismissing an employee from his job is the ultimate action that the supervisor can take. This action carries psychological as well as economic penalties; therefore, it must be handled with great care. The supervisor must fully inform the worker of the causes and deficiencies in his behavior which led to dismissal and must help the dismissed employee determine his future courses of action. The supervisor must also consider the reactions of the work group when it becomes necessary to dismiss one of the group.

7. Employee counseling is complicated by the complexity of reasons which contribute to employee dissatisfactions. The supervisor must learn to be perceptive enough to detect whether the reason for an employee's problem originates on the job or in some aspect of the employee's private life. This gives rise to two important considerations in employee counseling—the ethical elements and the practical elements of a supervisor getting involved in the private life of his subordinate. Even when employee problems are job related, supervisors often question the amount of time they can devote to such an activity during an already busy schedule. The benefits of employee counseling, when properly conducted, seem to outweigh the liabilities because such communications allow employees to discuss many small problems before they grow into major ones and, thus, become disruptive forces in the work group. To achieve this communication the supervisor must learn to listen actively to employee complaints and not to attempt to force his own solution to the problem

without working with the individual employee to find a mutually acceptable solution. The latter course of action means that the supervisor
must sometimes be prepared to change his own behavior as well as expecting the employee to change. Thus, employee counseling is not intended
to eliminate conflict between members of a work group, but to help
resolve such conflicts.

DISCUSSION QUESTIONS

1. Under what circumstances is it practical for a supervisor to use nondirective interviewing techniques with subordinates? Directive techniques?
2. How might a supervisor prepare for an interview with a job applicant?
3. Why should a supervisor hesitate to criticize an employee's performance or job behavior when it does not meet his expectations?
4. How would you respond to a supervisor who says, "I don't fool around
   when I discipline an employee. I let him have it. When I'm through,
   he knows he had better not repeat his mistake or he's going to get it"?
   What suggestions might you give him regarding the purpose of
   discipline?
5. What major human factors should a supervisor consider when trying
   to decide whether or not to fire an employee whose job performance is
   unsatisfactory?
6. In what ways can employee counseling be beneficial to group morale?
   When might employee counseling be detrimental to an employee?

BIBLIOGRAPHY AND
SELECTED COLLATERAL READINGS

1. BASSETT, GLENN A., *Practical Interviewing: A Handbook for Managers*. New
   York: American Management Association, 1965.
2. "College Graduates in Industry," National Industrial Conference Board
   Report. Studies in Personnel Policy No. 89. New York: National Industrial
   Conference Board, Inc.
3. DUNNETTE, M. D., and W. K. KIRCHNER, *Psychology Applied to Industry*.
   New York: Appleton-Century-Crofts, 1965.
4. ENDICOTT, FRANK, *Survey of Well-Known Business and Industrial Concerns*. An unpublished report of the placement department of Northwestern
   University.
5. GELLERMAN, SAUL W., *The Management of Human Relations*. New York:
   Holt, Rinehart and Winston, 1966.
6. GROSS, MARTIN L., *The Brain Watchers*. New York: The New American
   Library of World Literature, Inc., 1962.
7. *Leadership on the Job: Guides to Good Supervision*. Edited by the staff of

Supervisory Management. New York: American Management Association, 1957.

8. LEVIN, RICHARD I., and C. A. KIRKPATRICK, *Quantitative Approaches to Management.* New York: McGraw-Hill Book Company, 1965.

9. LOPEZ, F. M., *Personnel Interviewing—Theory and Practice.* New York: McGraw-Hill Book Company, 1965.

10. PAUL, GRACE, *A Short Course in Skilled Supervision.* Chicago: The Dartnell Corporation, 1966.

11. PITT, GAVIN A., *The Twenty-Minute Lifetime.* Englewood Cliffs, N.J.: Prentice-Hall, 1959.

12. ROGERS, CARL, and F. J. ROETHLISBERGER, "Barriers and Gateways to Communication," *Harvard Business Review,* Vol. 30, No. 4 (July–August, 1952).

13. WHYTE, WILLIAM H., JR., *The Organization Man.* New York: Simon and Schuster, 1956.

16

Human Relations
in Perspective

Most of the discussion in this text has attempted to point out the known benefits of human relations. At the same time, it is important to recognize that human relations, as with any singular approach to management, has limitations. These limitations grow out of the organizational climate within which the supervisor must operate, the nature of the human beings with whom the supervisor must interact, and the values and perspective the supervisor himself holds. For example, there are real limits on how far a supervisor can go to satisfy a subordinate's ambition for advancement because seniority rights may impose restrictions on advancement.

LIMITATIONS TO THE APPLICATION
OF HUMAN RELATIONS

A supervisor may find that his own approach to participation is ineffective because he suddenly tries to involve everyone in every decision. Of course, participation has little meaning for employees if the decisions they are asked to make have no real relationship to them or to their jobs. Furthermore, a supervisor must cope with his own limitations in interviewing and counseling skills. If he becomes preoccupied with methods, he may overlook the content of the communications, and good communications techniques are not a substitute for good ideas. There is a need for forthright, clear expression that leaves no doubt about what the supervisor wants and means [3, p. 162]. These are examples of operating limitations and they stem from either personal or organizational modes of dealing with people. Such limitations are real, but should not preclude a person from investigating human relations as a valid approach to management.

MANIPULATION

There are ethical considerations beyond the realm of the operating limitations of human relations. Some critics fear that human relations will be used to dupe employees into doing things they do not really want to do and that participation is allowed at only a superficial level in order to give employees a feeling of involvement while decisions are really being made by management. In a broad sense of the word, the whole process of management is manipulation; that is, if one considers manipulation to be getting other people to do what you want them to do. The problem is that in a negative sense manipulation implies hidden motives and trickery. The proponents of human relations do not imply that these tactics are or should be the basis for human relations. Workers resent being tricked regardless of the style of leadership that is used. Inevitably, employees learn when they have been tricked, and when they do learn, the mutual trust between supervisor and subordinate essential for co-operative effort is lost. The man who uses manipulation in the guise of human relations or in any other mode of leadership is the potential loser over the long run.

Many supervisors fail to recognize that their leadership roles place them in positions where their actions dominate the words they speak. Their integrity is on display. A lack of integrity will impair a supervisor's chances to implement human relations, and it will also affect the quality of his leadership regardless of the methods he uses, resulting in a failure that even human relations cannot repair.

PRODUCTION VERSUS HUMAN RELATIONS

Some critics claim that human relations is emphasized too much and that production, not good will, is the legitimate goal of an organization. Therefore, the critics continue, the supervisor's prime responsibility is production. This argument may be valid, as far as it goes, but often it leads to the conclusion that there is an inherent and irresolvable dichotomy between the practice of human relations and high levels of production. The answer to this challenge is in the recognition that production and profits are necessary for the survival of the organization, but that these objectives are attained through *human endeavor* as well as through mechanical processes. If a manager's responsibility is to obtain results through other people, he must know as much about people as he knows about the technical aspects of the job to be done.

The objective of human relations, as conceived by a majority of those considered authorities, is not to restrict production but to create a work environment where human beings can use a greater portion of their latent potential to achieve organizational goals. This is not to say that there are not conflicts between the achievement of organizational goals and the attainment of individual satisfactions. Human relations practice will not eliminate these conflicts. Instead, human relations is intended to allow the intelligent and creative resources of human beings to be applied to the resolution of the many conflicts that do occur in the organization. The management values used to resolve organizational problems affect the methods that will be used to obtain the solutions.

MANAGEMENT VALUES AND HUMAN RELATIONS

Thus far, the value system used in industry to achieve objectives has usually centered on the use of some ultimate power. That is, it has relied on the power of a manager to tell his subordinates what to do and very often how to do it. As a result, solutions to human and organizational problems have been traditionally passed down from the top. Part of the reason for the reliance on autocratic methods grew out of the form of ownership of early industrial organizations. The ownership of most firms was concentrated in the hands of a few individuals who were also intimately involved in the management of the firm.

Over time, the corporate form of ownership grew in prominence. This spread ownership of the firm among large numbers of persons. In the process, the owner-manager of most large companies rapidly gave way to hired professional managers. Although the form of ownership changed, methods of making decisions remained essentially the same as they had been during the early era of the industrial revolution; that is, all orders continued to be passed down from the top.

REASONS FOR THE DOMINANCE OF THE TRADITIONAL APPROACH TO MANAGEMENT

Until recently, the majority of workers in the United States were not well educated. Modes of travel were crude and slow, mass communications were inadequate, and most of the population in the United States, as well as in all but a few countries, was predominantly oriented to rural modes of living. As long as these social factors remained in force, the traditional assumptions held by most business leaders (as in Mc-Gregor's Theory X) seemed to work fairly well. Since the beginning of the twentieth century, the social, educational, and economic status of the majority of the population in the United States has improved. Today science and technology, mass higher education, and mass-media communications have changed the perspective and attitudes of lower-ranking employees as well as managers. A worker's behavior is no longer based largely on impressions gained within a small circle of people, places, and local events. Certainly, there are sizeable segments of the general population, most notably Negroes and other minority groups, who have not reaped the same social and economic benefits as the rest of the population. But the existence of disadvantaged groups does not appear to be the primary reason why some managers cling to the overgeneralizations expressed in Theory X. National employment statistics indicate that, up to this point in history, Negroes and certain other disadvantaged groups have been largely excluded from many segments of industrial employment. In general, the exposure of most modern managers to large numbers of employees from the ranks of the educationally and socially disadvantaged has been limited. Therefore, it seems that the widespread negative view of the potential capabilities of employees applies to the general work force rather than to certain disadvantaged segments of it. The assertion that most workers are by nature either indifferent or antagonistic toward the organization appears to be based on management perceptions to the prevailing social conditions of the early twentieth century, rather than the realities that exist today. At least, management's interpretation of the reasons for employee indifference may be incorrect.

Misinterpreting Employee Behavior. Those managers who have observed employee resistance to organizational goals may be confusing cause and effect. Douglas McGregor pointed out that employee indifference and hostility are often observable, but they may be the *result* of managerial methods that have over a long period provided rewards for only the lower level of human needs while ignoring or even preventing the achievement of intrinsic rewards associated with higher-level needs. Because the lower needs have been reasonably well met for most employees, these needs have become less of a motivational factor in work than they once were. Today the higher needs (recognition, self-realization, and so on) are inadequately satisfied on the job for the majority of workers. Because of this frustration, much human energy appears to be spent seeking personal satisfaction and expression outside of the organization and, perhaps, also in the exercise of ingenuity to beat the internal systems of the organization [7, p. 15].

Excessive reliance on the traditional assumptions about human nature places the manager in the position of explaining employee resistance to his authority as obstinacy. The only counterreaction that appears to be open to him is to increase the threat of punishment, i.e., disciplinary action, diminished opportunity for advancement, loss of job, or other threats against the employee's security in the organization. This negative course of action by a manager or supervisor usually tends to aggravate the symptoms he is trying to eliminate.

HUMAN RELATIONS NOT A SUBSTITUTE FOR MANAGEMENT CONTROLS

While the case for changing the traditional approach to organizational and subsequent management controls is now fairly well established among modern theorists, it should not be presumed that the desire to eliminate the traditional approach is valid. The Hawthorne Studies were the basis for the assumption that social relationships made by workers were determinants of their satisfaction. To the extent that social intercourse does make work more enjoyable and perhaps more productive, allowing social dialogue may be a sound practice. Yet, this is not always possible in some jobs. Some work requires a high degree of concentration and social conversation would be a disruptive element.

The results of the Hawthorne Studies should not be interpreted to mean that the supervisor's responsibility is to permit unfettered freedom in the work group. His primary objective should be to create a social environment conducive to both human satisfactions and production. If the nature of the work confronting the group is incompatible with simultaneous social satisfaction, then it is up to the supervisor to encourage other means for meeting social needs: rest periods, lunch periods, nonworking hours, and so on.

As is now recognized, man's social needs are not his only need, nor is human relations directed toward the satisfaction of only one need to the exclusion of all others. Social science research has helped to identify and explain a host of human needs that are met or frustrated in the work environment. This has contributed to a more realistic set of expectations regarding human behavior on the job. In general, McGregor expressed these assumptions as his Theory X. The intention of McGregor in developing Theory Y was to counter the long-standing overgeneralizations underlying the traditional concepts of management. Unfortunately, some managers, disregarding the fact that they were no more of a complete or all-encompassing set of assumptions than the traditional assumptions of human behavior had been, quickly adopted the modern concepts of Theory Y.

There are some individuals, perhaps a much larger number than most managers and supervisors realize, who wish to participate more fully in organizational affairs. For such individuals, more democratic management methods can mean that they can participate in many decisions that affect them and the organization. This would appear to serve to integrate more closely organizational and individual goals through the lessening of stringent controls. There probably always will be some individuals who do not seek greater participation in the organization. Such individuals may have become accustomed to the extrinsic controls of the organization (rules, regulations, wages, and so on) and are not able to operate well without them. Other employees may resist and overtly undermine the organizational systems and objectives no matter how humane or reasonable such constraints may be. Thus, the supervisor finds that in the reality of the work place he encounters individuals who desire varying degrees of participation. An attempt to behave in a singular fashion, only autocratically or only democratically, may miss the mark for a large part of the work group.

IMPACT OF SOCIAL CHANGE ON HUMAN RELATIONS

The supervisor is caught in more than the throes of a transitional period. Every era is, in some way, a transitional period; but the second half of the twentieth century is one in which changes occur more rapidly. The realities found in the modern industrial scene place the supervisor in the position of having to operate within a dynamic organizational environment, an environment that he cannot entirely control. His work group may be one of hundreds in an organization. He cannot realistically make dull and laborious work stimulating and creative for his subordinates. Labor unions may have a stronger influence than he has in making employee promotions, wage increases, and in enlarging fringe benefits. He has little voice in organizational structure or management systems of control that affect the organizational climate within which he must operate.

There are even larger and more dramatic social forces at work which will affect the role of managers and supervisors. The direction and implication of many social changes are not yet fully understood, but several known elements of change that affect the industrial community will probably make the human and technical responsibilities of the supervisor even more demanding than they are today.

Increase in Organizational Size. Organizations are likely to grow increasingly in size and will continue to grow in influence socially, politically, and economically. Thus, the confrontation between individual freedom and organizational limits will grow accordingly. The problem of relieving the tension between individuals and the organization with its concomitant systems of control will continue to pose a challenge to the supervisor's human relations skills.

For the supervisor, the growth in organizational size has far-reaching implications. While the number of workers that report directly to him may not change, the number of organizational contacts that he will be required to maintain may increase. New staff departments, technical assistants, and organizational functions mean that communications will become an increasingly difficult task. Keeping informed so that he can answer subordinates' questions regarding company policies and objectives will become a larger and more complex responsibility of the supervisor.

The importance of the supervisor as a communications link between his own subordinates and higher echelons of management will place increasing demands upon the communications skills of the supervisor. This will involve the need to improve both verbal and written skills, but, more importantly, the perceptions and listening ability of most supervisors will have to be expanded and sharpened.

Minority Group Relations.   Since the enactment of the Civil Rights Act of 1964, more jobs are being filled by members of minority groups, most notably Negroes, Latin Americans, and Orientals. Many occupations in a wide variety of industries are increasingly opening their doors to minority groups. This poses several problems that must be considered by the supervisor. The first problem has to do with the degree of preferential treatment he should give to minority members in hiring, training, and counseling. Frequently, the top-level managers who formulate hiring policies are not faced by the problems of implementation confronting lower-level managers, especially first-line supervisors. Since every supervisor's time and energy is limited, he will have to decide which of his responsibilities he can afford to forego or let slide while giving extra attention to workers unaccustomed to the work environment into which they have been placed. It seems inevitable that some portion of the additional impact of on-the-job training and counseling for disadvantaged employees will fall upon the supervisor.

Another problem related to the increase of minority-group workers has to do with race relations. The supervisor himself may be receptive to Negroes or other minority groups entering the work group, but what does he do about the possible subtle and overt prejudice in other members of the group? How does he maintain the group cohesiveness necessary to maintain production when he must cope with more than the intergroup disagreements that may grow from differences in psychological and social values that exist between employees eminating from different social and ethnic backgrounds? Prejudice is usually a deep-rooted element in a person's personality and the supervisor is not usually in a position to bring about immediate changes in a subordinate's attitude. Yet, if he is to remain in his position of leadership, a supervisor cannot allow either overt or even subtle behavior of a biased nature to jeopardize the group's performance. Because the supervisor's own attitude and behavior toward minority members is a strong influence on the modes of the group, he must constantly work toward setting the example of positive behavior he expects from others.

Automation and the Changing Nature of Work.   Cultural changes in this century, created by the dual processes of urbanization and industrialization, have changed the nature of many jobs. For most employees, work is no longer a private affair in which they can obtain personal satisfaction from seeing the results of their individual contribution to the total work process. There is no easy way for a supervisor to conceal either the lack of status or the personal attractiveness of some jobs.

Changes in technology affecting work processes will mean that supervisors will have to maintain a constant outlook for ways and means of implementing changes in work assignments and job procedures. Changes in work procedures are often accompanied by changes in social relationships among the workers. This underscores the increasing importance of establishing an open environment in which group members are receptive to social change as well as to technical change. To the extent that technology and automation increase the rapidity of change, the supervisor will find that his responsibility for training and retraining will occupy a larger portion of his time and energy.

Labor Relations.   As organizations grow in size and as technology continues to change required job skills, the union's role in implementing change will probably increase. The pace and manner in which change occurs will continue to be a major concern of unions. This means that the supervisor may have to contend to an increasing degree with shop stewards and other union officials on more issues than he may have had to in the past. To do this effectively, the supervisor will have to be extraordinarily well versed on the provisions and implications of collective bargaining agreements and will have to possess a more complete knowledge of tactics used in the process of negotiation.

The elements of change mentioned here are by no means exhaustive, nor are they the only forces that will have an impact on the supervisor's responsibilities. The fact is, each of the foregoing elements raises additional questions and problems that are going to require answers. One factor that emerges from any discussion of the social forces that will affect the supervisor's role is that traditional methods of supervision will grow increasingly inadequate to meet the increased number and complexity of problems confronting the work group. Few individual supervisors will possess either the knowledge or the time to cope adequately with all of the human and technical problems that are created in a dynamic organization.

The evidence gathered thus far indicates the importance of allowing group members to participate in planning for change as well as in implementing it. This means that the supervisor must be prepared to consult with his subordinates on matters related to changes in methods and processes used in work and on matters related to human conflict and motivation. If he has hesitated or refrained from doing so in the past, he has little alternative but to learn how to do so in the future.

ORGANIZATIONAL CLIMATE AND HUMAN RELATIONS

A variety of managerial systems influence the organizational climate. Such systems can range from one which assumes that labor is largely a commodity to be sold freely and purchased, to one which considers employees essential parts of an organizational structure. In the former system, the manager's job (including the supervisor's) is conceived as consisting of decision-making, direction, and surveillance, relying primarily upon coercion as a motivating force, with little provision for the effects of human emotion and interdependence. In the latter system, decision-making is considered a process rather than a prerogative exclusively held by management. As such, the manager's responsibility consists not of deciding himself, but of making certain that the best possible decisions are reached [6, p. 216].

It is improbable that a supervisor who works in a company where the management systems closely resemble those that consider labor a commodity can or will use participative methods of supervision with his subordinates, particularly if his own direct superior is autocratic. Thus, the practice of human relations is curtailed by more than the supervisor's own resistance to participative methods.

A supervisor may not control many social and technological changes nor may he influence many aspects of organizational climate, yet he does affect the attitudes of his own work group. A great deal of evidence indicates that many employees consider their boss, his actions and treatment of them, to be the most irritating factor in their work situation [5, p. 212]. The supervisor with his concomitant influence over the lives of his subordinates can also be the prime factor in making work more satisfying for them.

Most persons who are made supervisors are approved for such responsibility because they possess the necessary technical capability. Seldom are the human relations skills of the individual given more than a cursory review. Again, the point is not that technical competence should be sacrificed for human relations, but rather that human relations is such an integral part of the supervisor's job that it should not be ignored in preparatory and on-going training. Ideally, human relations should be one of the considerations for evaluation of a supervisor's performance.

Yet, when so little attention is paid to human relations by the organization, it is not unusual for supervisors to pay little attention to it until some problem makes attention necessary. This can be a tragedy in industrial life, particularly in lower-level jobs where the intrinsic satisfactions in work may already be minimal. It is also tragic in terms of the human dissatisfaction manifested in the needless waste of energy spent on resentment, hostility, and interpersonal conflict which contributes to a loss of organizational effectiveness.

BARRIERS TO IMPLEMENTING HUMAN RELATIONS

Looking back, managers find the typical model of management behavior in the autocratic industrial leaders of earlier industrial history and looking ahead they see the problems of an automated society and increasing pressures of the community at large affecting their methods and styles of leadership. Presently, they look around and find more and more demands being made on their time, energy, intelligence, and patience. They are caught in this era of transition for which their education and experience may not have prepared them [1, p. 12].

A supervisor must deal with people who desire strong, decisive leadership and he must also cope with subordinates who resent and overtly resist any display of authority. How then does a supervisor manage the disparate roles he must play? Must he be a man of many faces? In a sense, yes. He must be flexible and he must comprehend the forces around him. But the requirement of being flexible cannot be met by following an overgeneralized list of do's and don't's. It is more important that a supervisor learn to be receptive to the participative concept of management and be prepared to examine his own attitudes in dealing with other organizational members.

When it comes to implementing human relations practices, knowing what to do at the verbal level and actually being able to carry through at the behavioral level is one of the major problems of supervision. Many supervisors simply do not put into effect the human relations practices of which they are aware.

The reasons for not wanting to adopt a participative approach to management stem from more than habit. Some supervisors fear a loss of prestige in the group if they ask for help in making decisions. Others may try to protect their leadership position by preventing subordinates from learning what they know. By protecting their inside information rather than sharing it some supervisors feel that they maintain the importance of their position and, therefore, make themselves indispensable to the work group [4, p. 66].

HUMAN RELATIONS AS A POINT OF VIEW

Most business practitioners and tough-minded theorists reject any management concept if its only basis for acceptance is that it would make for a pleasant change. Any concept must be justified on the basis of results. Human relations should not avoid the same scrutiny as any other approach to management; however, it has often been rejected on the basis that such an approach complicates simple problems by bringing into consideration the human element.\Human relations is not a simple approach, nor is it an easy one. Human relationships are not always simple, and treating them simplistically does not make the human equation any easier. Yet, one must avoid playing amateur psychologist by reading hidden or artificial meanings into every human act or saying. Compared to human relations, an autocratic approach is much easier and simpler, because one can deal with his subordinates impersonally, with little concern for them as separate and unique human beings. It is easier for a supervisor to give orders, particularly difficult or unpleasant ones, to a subordinate who he does not consider personally. From this, one can conclude that human relations becomes a point of view as well as a style or method of management. To achieve such a point of view requires self-examination. Self-examination may be painful because it often involves the recognition that one's approach to supervision needs to be changed. A supervisor can seldom contain his examination to a single aspect of his supervisory behavior. A broader examination is in order; one that questions the whole set of human values he believes in and tries to live by.

It appears relatively easy to practice human relations artificially in the hope that each employee's productivity will somehow increase. This viewpoint is often adopted because the supervisor can tangibly gauge the results of his efforts; that is, he can observe or measure the performance of his subordinates before and after he has "practiced" human relations. If a supervisor is unsatisfied with the results, he can revert to his old style of leadership and chalk off human relations as a poor approach. Obviously, such a superficial attempt is of little value and does not involve a change in the point of view of the supervisor.

A philosophical commitment to human relations is one based on the conviction that most employees can and will achieve fuller and more meaningful lives if they are given the opportunity to utilize their potential on the job. As employees are encouraged to develop a problem-solving approach to their work through open and honest participation in devising solutions to the complex problems confronting the work group, they grow as human beings and become more valuable employees. Not all employees know how to do this and some may not wish to; but few employees below the ranks of mid-management are given the opportunity to grow as individuals on the job. Yet, personal development is a well-received concept for managers. Many management development programs are designed for this very purpose. This same approach is seldom incorporated in training programs for rank-and-file employees.

Supervisors may resist the attempt to develop subordinates beyond the skill level necessary to perform a perfunctory service in the work group because they consider such a task beyond the realm of their responsibility. Such a limited view of the supervisor's role neglects the fundamental responsibility of the supervisor to develop members of his work group. The task of providing subordinates with the opportunity to learn and to grow as independent and thinking individuals adds new dimension and challenge to the job of the supervisor.‖A supervisor who places priority on developing rather than dominating subordinates will find that many aspects of his own job take on a different context. The way he handles discipline, employee grievances, production problems, and interpersonal conflicts will change so that emphasis is placed on the issues rather than on the politics of the situation.

Human growth and learning take place in the work place when individuals are encouraged to use their talents, skills, and intelligence. This means that there is a likelihood that some individuals will make mistakes; therefore, the supervisor must be prepared to help each worker learn from his mistakes. This requires human contact at the most sensitive level. If care is not taken, criticism can easily be directed toward the individual employee instead of toward the error as it should be.

Most persons can function satisfactorily in positions of leadership when everything is going well, when production is high, morale is good, and working relationships run smoothly. The real test of a supervisor's ability to manage is how well he copes with others when things go wrong, when mistakes have been made, or when a crisis faces the group. The supervisor's success in meeting such situations, particularly those involving human interactions, depends on his subordinates' attitudes toward him as a person. These attitudes are developed over time as a result of his actions and his character as observed by his subordinates. If his behavior reflects immaturity, irresponsibility, distrust, and frustration, it is unlikely that he can motivate his subordinates toward positive aspects of maturity, responsibility, trust, independence—or high levels of production.

Finally, the practice of human relations may not only provide a means of raising the standards of performance of a work group, but it may also allow each member of the group to grow as a person capable of contributing to the process of group effort. Each employee can gain personal satisfaction from his association with the group through greater use of his capacities. The supervisor can grow from the exercise of new dimensions of leadership and personal contact with his subordinates. The rewards in production and personal satisfaction appear to be great enough to warrant the risks to be encountered in the participative approach. In an age of dynamic change, the human relations approach to management makes sense because it permits a larger base of knowledge to be applied to tangled and complex human and organizational problems and because, in an age of impersonalization in many of the aspects of industrial life, it helps add significance to work which, unfortunately, many men and women now find unchallenging and laborious.

BIBLIOGRAPHY AND SELECTED COLLATERAL READINGS

1. BASSETT, GLENN A., *Management Styles in Transition*. New York: American Management Association, 1966.
2. BOROW, HENRY, *Man in a World at Work*. Boston: Houghton Mifflin, 1964.
3. CASEY, JOHN, "Human Relations: Putting Theories into Practice," *Leadership on the Job: Guides to Good Supervision*. New York: American Management Association, 1966, pp. 161–65.
4. CHAMBERLAIN, NEIL W., *Enterprise and Environment: The Firm in Time and Place*. New York: McGraw-Hill Book Company, 1968.
5. GILMER, B. VON HALLER, *Industrial Psychology*, 2nd ed. New York: McGraw-Hill Book Company, 1966.
6. MARROW, ALFRED J., and others, *Management by Participation*. New York: Harper & Row, 1967.
7. McGREGOR, DOUGLAS, *The Professional Managers*, Caroline McGregor and Warren G. Bennis, eds. New York: McGraw-Hill Book Company, 1967.

Subject Index

Name Index